CROATIA

Marcus Tanner is a London-based writer, journalist, editor and commentator specialising in Eastern and Central Europe, the Balkans and Celtic countries. He is the author of *Ireland's Holy Wars* (Yale, 2003), *The Last of the Celts* (Yale, 2006) and *Albania's Mountain Queen* (2014).

T0349965

MARCUS TANNER

CROATIA

A History from the Middle Ages
to the Present Day

FOURTH EDITION

YALE UNIVERSITY PRESS
NEW HAVEN AND LONDON

For information about this and other Yale University Press publications, please contact:
U.S. Office: sales.press@yale.edu   yalebooks.com
Europe Office: sales@yaleup.co.uk   yalebooks.co.uk

Printed and bound by CPI Group (UK) Ltd, Croydon, CR0 4YY

Library of Congress Control Number: 2019930216

ISBN 978–0–300–24657–5 (pbk)

A catalogue record for this book is available from the British Library.

10 9 8 7 6 5 4 3 2 1

MIX
Paper | Supporting
responsible forestry
FSC
www.fsc.org
FSC® C013604

Contents

Illustrations

Maps

Note on Spelling

In any book about a country that has been ruled by several other countries there are bound to be problems over spelling. In the interests of simplicity I have used the modern Croatian version for all towns and places that lie inside, or partly inside, the present borders of the Republic of Croatia. Thus at all times I have used Rijeka, rather than the Italian word Fiume, Zadar, rather than Zara, Dubrovnik, not Ragusa, Zagreb, not the German word Agram, and Srijem rather than the Serbian word Srem, except where the word is used in a purely Serbian context, that is the Autonomous Region of Slavonia, Baranja and Western Srem. For places and people outside Croatia I have opted for whatever form seemed to be most appropriate or most familiar to an English-speaking reader. For the joint kings of Hungary-Croatia I have used English versions of the names wherever possible, for example Charles Robert, and the Hungarian name elsewhere, e.g. Kalman. Maria is perfectly well known, however, so I have not used Mary when referring to the Hungarian queen. On the same principle I have kept Charles V and Prince Paul in English, but used Franz-Jozef and Karl for the last two Habsburg emperors. I have generally referred to the Habsburgs as emperors, even though the Habsburgs were the kings of Hungary and Croatia.

Preface

In the summer of 2017, the people of Dubrovnik began to protest about the huge numbers of visitors, saying they were overwhelming the town. About 540 cruise ships disgorged three-quarters of a million day-trippers to the so-called 'Pearl of the Adriatic' in 2017. The total number of tourists that year, however, was far larger, reaching well over a million – vastly outnumbering the estimated 44,000 locals and completely clogging the famous marble-tiled main street, the Stradun. The UN's cultural arm, UNESCO, warned that if numbers were not cut, the town's World Heritage status would be at risk.

For most Croats over the age of about forty, complaints about the number of tourists in Dubrovnik – and many of the islands of the Adriatic – were justified but ironic: they could remember a time when Dubrovnik, and the rest of Croatia, cried out for foreign guests.

In the autumn of 1991, as the war for independence from the Serb-dominated Yugoslav state spread over Croatia, the Yugoslav army surrounded and bombarded Dubrovnik in an attempt to dislodge a small Croatian garrison. Clouds of smoke from the shells rose over the Old Town's red-ochre roofs. By the following spring, the siege was over. But that summer, foreign visitors stayed away. A British reporter described a 'silent city where bullet-riddled cars litter the streets and boats lie moored under tarpaulin in the harbour. Heaps of rubble, glass and planks of wood are piled against the stone walls of the historic Old Town, and newspaper kiosks and ice-cream stalls are gutted shells.'

Though few people appreciated it, that year Croatia's fortunes were about to turn. The former Yugoslav republic was admitted into the club of sovereign states. It was, said President Franjo Tudjman, the fulfilment of a 'thousand-year-old dream of independence'. But few dreams had been fulfilled in such unpromising circumstances. Recognition had been enmeshed in controversy. Germany had strongly supported recognising the republic's declaration of independence, but Britain and France had opposed doing so. And while Europe's statesmen had quarrelled over whether Croatia should be recognised, the country had remained in the throes of a bloody war of independence against the Yugoslav army, the militia of the Croatian Serbs and a variety of other Serbian paramilitary groups.

Fighting had devastated the country and left it effectively partitioned. From Karlovac in the north to the outskirts of Zadar on the Adriatic Sea, a long swathe of hilly territory had fallen under Serbian control. Alongside two smaller chunks of land that they held in eastern and central Croatia, the Serbs had seized almost a third of the republic's territory.

The economy of what had been the richest of Yugoslavia's six republics was ruined. The main railway lines running east and south of Zagreb were cut; likewise the Autoput Bratstvo i Jedinstvo, the Motorway of Brotherhood and Unity, which ran in a straight line across the flat plains of Slavonia from Zagreb towards Belgrade. Oil pipelines, refineries, power stations and water supplies had been blown up or put out of action because they lay partly in Serb-held territory. The once prosperous resorts on the Dalmatian coast had been abandoned by holidaymakers, the hotel rooms now crammed with refugees. Most towns suffered from a chronic shortage of electricity. Many people had been driven from their homes. About 300,000 Croats had fled westwards from the Serbs to take refuge on the Adriatic islands, in deserted coastal hotels or improvised camps. A smaller number of Serbs had gone east, either to Serb-held territory in Croatia or to Serbia proper. Hundreds of villages had been bombed and burned beyond repair or recognition. On the banks of the Danube, the eastern town of Vukovar resembled a smaller version of post-war Dresden or Warsaw. The town had been pounded almost to the ground in a punishing three-month siege by the Yugoslav army and Serb paramilitaries, which ended only with the town's surrender in mid-November 1991.

The war had shocked the Croats, who were unprepared for it. Most of them had grown up in the enforced peace and stability of President Tito's Yugoslavia and knew nothing else. But warfare had, in fact, often been the lot of the Croats, ever since they migrated south across the Carpathians and settled along the shores of the Adriatic in the seventh century. In the tenth and eleventh centuries, the cities along the Dalmatian coast were ransacked and torched by the Venetians, while the wooden fortress-towns of Slavonia felt the pressure of the territorial ambitions of the Magyars. Union between Croatia and Hungary was compacted in 1102, but provided no defence against the Mongols who swept in from the east in the thirteenth century and devastated Zagreb, or against the Ottomans who reached Croatia in the fifteenth century and annihilated the country's nobility in 1493. In the 1520s, as Ottoman armies overwhelmed more territory, the Pope sent a message to the Croatian parliament, urging the Croats to continue to resist the armies of Islam and referring to Croatia as 'the ramparts of Christendom'. This generous title availed the country nothing. The Ottomans swept on, almost to the gates of Zagreb, destroying nearly all traces of the seven-century-old civilisation that they encountered.

The Habsburg conquests of the 1680s and 1690s freed the Croatian lands from Ottoman rule, inaugurating a prolonged period of relative peace that would last until the collapse of the Austro-Hungarian Empire at the end of the First World War. Even under the Habsburgs, however, Croatia was only partly at peace. Much of it was placed under direct military jurisdiction. In this zone, known as the Vojna Krajina, or Military Frontier, the entire adult male population was obliged to maintain itself in a permanent state of armed readiness for battle. Ottoman raids remained a feature of life in the Vojna Krajina well into the nineteenth century.

The twentieth century, meanwhile, spelled a return to the political turbulence and hugely destructive wars of the more distant past. The carnage of the First World War was followed by even worse destruction in the Second World War, when Croatia – by now part of Yugoslavia – became a battleground between competing Yugoslav Communist, Croatian Fascist, German and Italian forces. The victory of Josip Tito's Partisans in 1945 brought an iron peace that lasted for forty-five years. But a third war in the twentieth century followed in 1991, as the Yugoslav state collapsed, and as Croatia demanded its independence. What most of the former Soviet republics achieved through a simple proclamation in parliament, the Croats had to pay for in blood, in a four-year war with the Serb-led Yugoslav army and its Croatian Serb auxiliaries.

Croatia is a border land. It lies on the geographical border between Central Europe and the Balkans, and between the Mediterranean world and continental Europe. It lies also on a cultural and religious border. To the east is Orthodox Christian Serbia, to the north and west, Catholic Italy, Austria and Slovenia, and to the south, half-Muslim Bosnia. The very shape of the country reinforces the impression of a frontier. Nothing is compact, square or secure. Instead, the country curves round Bosnia in a narrow arc, in the shape of a crescent moon, or a boomerang. At few points is Croatia more than a hundred miles wide; at many, it is far less. In the far south, around Dubrovnik, Croatia is only a few miles wide, hemmed in between the Adriatic Sea on one side and the mountains of Bosnia on the other.

The fate of a border land is always to be precarious, and frequently to move; medieval and modern Croatia overlap only in parts. It is to be buffeted in one direction or another, to be trampled on, crossed over, colonised, defended and abandoned in turn by stronger neighbouring powers. The search over the centuries for a benevolent, strong patron took the Croats into the orbit of Hungary, Venice, Austria and Yugoslavia. In 2009, this same search took Croatia into NATO and, in July 2013, into the European Union. One reason why Croats remain generally positive about membership of both supranational organisations is precisely because they promise to provide the kind of lasting peace and security that in the past was either missing or compromised by a complete loss of independence.

The Croats have, of course, derived benefits from multiple invasions, mass migrations and colonisation, and are far from unappreciative of them. They consider themselves part of the Slavic family of nations, but well know that they also bear the genetic imprint of countless migrants, invaders and settlers, and of those shadowy inhabitants of the land before the Croats themselves arrived. The blood of ancient Illyrians, Greeks, Romans, Serbs, Vlachs, Germans, Hungarians, Italians, Czechs, Slovaks, Jews and others flows in the veins of contemporary Croats.

The Croats are not homogenous. They themselves are fond of pointing to the marked differences in appearance and culture between the peoples of different regions. The people of Dalmatia are taller, leaner and darker-haired than the people of the north, where many have blond hair. The Dalmatians are thoroughly Mediterranean in their cuisine, habits and lifestyle. The northerners are far less demonstrative, and tend to see the southerners as flashy.

Before the Second World War, the gulf between these two regions was very wide. In nineteenth-century Austria-Hungary, when Dalmatians went to Slavonia it was usually to work as seasonal labourers for the wealthier farmers of the plains – who treated them as virtual strangers, and mocked their land as a barren place whose unlucky inhabitants 'only harvested stones'. These differences have narrowed as people migrate from one side of the country to another; moreover, the Dalmatians harvest tourists these days, not stones. But the differences have not disappeared entirely.

There are stark contrasts also in the look of the land. Northern Croatia and Slavonia are green and only gently hilly. This is a land of woods, orchards, farms and tidy villages. Imposing castles and baroque churches are just part of the legacy of the centuries of Habsburg rule, which lasted from 1527 to 1918. The capital, Zagreb, which is in the north, has the cut and air of a grand, provincial Austrian city. Along these cobbled streets, in the formal parks and imposing squares decked with solemn monuments, the air is heavy with the memory of the ordered, if stifling, world of the Habsburg monarchy. South of the Gvozd mountains and across the wild moors of Lika one descends into a very different world. In Dalmatia the sunlight is strong and harsh, the hills barren and studded with olive groves. The cities are wholly Mediterranean in appearance, dotted with the remains of ancient Rome and of Dalmatia's later rulers, the Venetians. A few miles inland, beside the eerie and silent mudflats at Nin, rise the humble, squat turrets of the churches of the first Croat settlers.

Because they inhabit the rim, or the ramparts, rather than the middle, the people of this border land are not relaxed about their culture, heritage or identity. There is always the lurking danger that the rest of Europe may forget about them or – worse – confuse them with the people to the east or the south. Since Croatia joined the European Union, one of only two former Yugoslav republics to do so, nervousness on this account has declined. Now that EU and NATO membership have confirmed Croatia's 'Western' identity, Croats feel less need to do so themselves. But a marked resistance to being included in 'the Balkans', still a term of odium, remains.

The people of this border land are still aware that beyond their narrow boomerang of territory, beyond that river, on the other side of that mountain, their own world stops and another different one begins. Similarities with the rest of former Yugoslavia are acknowledged and even embraced – but the differences are also insisted on. Inevitably, memories of a common life in Yugoslavia, for good or ill, are fading. It will soon be forty years since Croatia became an independent state. By then, only pensioners will have real memories of what life in the joint southern Slav state was actually like.

While the Croatian resorts have become increasingly familiar to English-speaking holidaymakers, some of whom have bought property there, the history of the people and country remains less well known. A great deal of literature was published on the former Yugoslavia in the 1990s, as the world gazed on in baffled horror at the spectacle of wars blazing only a few hours' drive south of Vienna – first in Croatia and Bosnia and then later in Kosovo. Inevitably, however, most of those books dwelled on Yugoslavia as a whole, or on the war in Bosnia, which followed quickly on the conflict in Croatia and soon eclipsed it in terms of material devastation, the scale of atrocity and the forced movement of people. The war in Bosnia haunted Europe's conscience in a way that the war in Croatia never did. The tourists who flock to Croatia today are barely aware of it. The hugely popular Adriatic islands were barely touched by the conflict, while the damage done to Dubrovnik, Sibenik and Zadar has been repaired. Few foreigners make the long detour to the eastern town of Vukovar, which was practically levelled in 1991 and remains, in part, a ruin.

It was out of a desire to remedy a certain gap in people's understanding of Croatia, and out of a conviction that it warranted study on its own, and not as a bit-player in a wider drama, that I began to compile a brief account of the war in Croatia in the early 1990s. But it was impossible to write about the war of the 1990s without referring back to the war of the 1940s, and impossible to write about that without referring to the first Yugoslavia and the political climate of the 1920s and 1930s, which then threw me back to the national awakening of the 1840s. In the end, I decided to start with the first Croat principalities of the Dark Ages.

Any attempt to cover such a broad canvas with the equivalent of a few brushstrokes lays the writer open to the charge of missing out an enormous amount. It must also be made clear that this is not a book about the Croats but about the lands that make up contemporary Croatia.

A complaint could justifiably be raised that to talk about 'Croatia' in this sense is anachronistic – an attempt to read back into the past a country whose existence was notional for centuries and whose borders were only fixed finally by Tito in 1945. Of course, this is true in part. Croatia has shifted like ectoplasm across the board of south-eastern Europe over the ages. And while the term 'Croatia' stretches far back into history, it is open to question whether it meant much, if anything, to the mass of the people who inhabited these lands before the national movement of the nineteenth century. At the same time, the school of thought that holds that the modern Croatian identity was simply manufactured, and is somehow false and counterfeit, ought also to be rejected. By Croatia, I mean the Triune Kingdom of Croatia, Slavonia and Dalmatia, which formed the core of the early Croat kingdom from the ninth to the eleventh centuries, to which virtually every *sabor* (parliament) and *ban* (viceroy) laid claim from the Middle Ages to 1918, which were briefly united in an autonomous Croat *banovina* before the Second World War – which were then incorporated (with various additions and subtractions) to the Yugoslav Republic of Croatia, and which now form the borders of the contemporary republic.

Of all the countries that have emerged since the collapse of Communism and the second 'springtime of nations', Croatia has perhaps the richest, most tangled and most turbulent past. It is a controversial and compelling history.

1

'The Unfaithful Croats'

He cursed the unfaithful Croats and their descendants before God and all the saints for his violent death, saying the Croats should never again have a ruler of their own tongue but should always be under foreign rule.

Legend of King Zvonimir's death[1]

In the village of Nin, where the dry rocky Karst of the Dalmatian hinterland meets the Adriatic Sea, stands a small, cruciform church. Squat and of simple dimensions it looks ancient and indeed is so, dating from the ninth century at the earliest and the eleventh century at the latest. It is said that the Church of the Holy Cross of Nin was built in such a way that the rays of the setting sun would fall on the baptismal font on the feast day of St Ambrose, the patron saint of the Benedictines of Nin. The font, known as Višeslav's font after the ninth-century Croatian ruler who was baptised in it, and inscribed in Latin 'Here the weak man is brought to light', has been removed to a museum. But the dedicatory inscription to a local ruler or *župan* by the name of Godečaj, or Godežav, remains by the entrance.

If a nation can be said to have a centre, then the Church of the Holy Cross of Nin has a good claim to fulfil that function for the Croats. In this region the Croats settled in the seventh century. Here its first rulers built their homes and fashioned houses of worship. Here the Croat leaders accepted the Christian religion from Rome that has been a continuous thread running through the vicissitudes of their history. The Holy Cross of Nin, the much larger church of St Donat in Zadar, the Church of St Nicholas on the island of Brač and perhaps a hundred chapels or funeral monuments are practically all that remain to bear witness to the life and vitality of the old kingdom of Croatia which came to an end at the close of the eleventh century and whose architectural legacy was largely destroyed in the Mongol invasion of the thirteenth century.[2] Those early dukes and kings we glimpse through a glass darkly, in fragments of sculpture on church walls, on fonts and on tombs. They are shadowy figures moving in and out of focus, occasionally falling under the spotlight at a moment of brilliant clarity, only to recede back into the darkness of which we know nothing. They have left few traces of their turbulent reigns. To our eye they would appear colourful indeed. This we know from opened funeral caskets of early Croatian women-folk. Byzantine-looking in heavy gold earrings and jewellery. Among their relics are the grave of Queen Jelena in the Church of Our Lady of the Islands near Split and the font of Duke Višeslav. In the Church of St Michael of Ston is a rare surviving portrait of one of these early Croatian rulers – a depiction of the church's royal patron with his donation in the palm of his hand. But Croatian history did not begin with the baptism of Višeslav in about 800. By that time Croats had been settled in the Balkan peninsula and on the shores of the Adriatic for almost a century and a half.

The Croats are a Slav people in spite of their name, which points to a separate Iranian source. At the beginning of the fourth century, when the Roman Empire was falling into decay, the Croats lived alongside other Slavic tribes in the marshy, flat lands north of the Carpathian mountains, between the Dnieper, the Dniester, the Pripet and the Vistula, an area covered today approximately by the Ukraine, Poland and Belarus. In this swampy domain, later called White Croatia, they had little contact with Roman civilisation, for they were several hundred miles north of the nearest Roman provinces of Dacia, Moesia, Scythia and Pannonia. As far as is known the Slavs of that region were a settled, pastoral people who hoed fields with ploughs, raised livestock, kept bees and lived in clans – *plemena*. Some may have lived com-munally in extended families, for the southern Slavs for centuries clung to the system of extended families and property held in common, known as the *zadruga*. The Slavs appear to have had their own princely rulers and to have respected the principle of primogeniture, as the notion of hereditary succession was established among the Croats by the time they settled in Pannonia and Dalmatia. The Croats also divided their new country rapidly into *župe* (counties), which suggests they brought these administrative divisions with them from White Croatia.

Little is known about their religion, as the pre-Christian Croats did not write and therefore left no written evidence. Nor did they leave behind religious monuments. Speculation about early Slav belief sys-tems is based on fragmentary evidence from Byzantine and Arab sources. But this relates to Bulgars or Russians, and there is no certainty that pagan Russians and Bulgars held the same beliefs, or practised the same rites, as did the Croats. No one is even sure which was the chief deity in their pantheon. Perhaps it was not much more than an affair of rituals carried out in groves and on hilltops with the odd sacrifice.

The Croats may have lived under the lordship of nomadic Hunnic. Germanic or Asiatic rulers in their old homeland, from whom they got their name, for the word *Horvat* or *Hrvat* is not of Slavic origin – a source

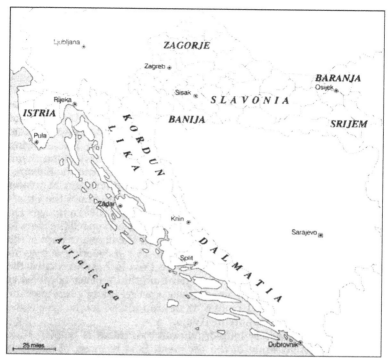

The regions of Croatia

of frequent scholastic controversy. Some Croat scholars have opted for the Iranian theory, pointing to Greek accounts of the Horvatos, or Horoatos, a community of Iranians who lived at the mouth of the Don around 200 BC. Partisans of this theory refer also to a region of Iran that the ancient Persians called Harahvatis. Others believe the Croats are an amalgam of Slavs and Ostrogoths, as the Ostrogoths certainly were present in Dalmatia before the Slavs arrived. All agree, more or less, that the Croats were a Slavic, or mostly Slavic, tribe by the time they left their old homeland, moved south across the Danube and the Sava in the seventh century and settled in the Balkan peninsula.

The Croats migrated into the Roman province of Illyricum, which was later divided into the provinces of Dalmatia and Pannonia, during the decay of the Roman Empire, when Avars and other barbarian tribes were laying waste the cities of the empire. By 396 St Jerome, whose home in Stridon may have been the town of Zrenj, in Istria, was complaining of Goths rampaging in the vicinity, saying, 'bishops have been captured, priests killed, horses tied to Christ's altars and martyrs' relics cast around. Everywhere there is sorrow, horror and the image of death.'[3]

After the division of the empire into two halves in 395, the province of Dalmatia (which extended north beyond the modern borders of Dalmatia to the River Sava and eastwards to the Drina) was assigned first to the western portion of the empire. But from 480 it belonged to the eastern Byzantine Empire. Byzantine lordship over Dalmatia did little to protect the coastal cities of Dalmatia from attacks by nomadic Avars, who had made their base in the Pannonian plain. It was during the time of these Avar invasions that the Slavs, Croats among them, made their first tentative moves south of the Danube into the Balkans. At first they came for the purpose of raiding. Later they came in greater numbers with a view to permanent settlement. Sometimes the Croats and other Slav tribes joined the Avars in their destructive rampages. On other occasions Byzantium's hard-pressed rulers persuaded the Slavs to attack the Avars. There is no agreement over the date and pace of the Croats' 1,000-mile migration to the south. The uncovering of convincing evidence for the existe ce of White Croatia has discredited the ninteenth-century theory that this great migration never occurred at all, but there are still disagreements over whether it took place after the fall of Salona, between 614 and 630, or around 795, at the time of the war between the Franks and the Avars.

It was probably a very long-drawn-out movement of peoples. Huw Evans' exhaustive study of the archaeological remains of the early Croats notes that:

> the Slavic migration, or invasion, has the quality of seeping treacle, a slow, steady and unordered advance, a movement that had no specific objective, but nonetheless continuously moved forward .... The rate of arrival of the Slavs may have been such that the first-comers, although facing a largely collapsed civilisation, were strongly affected by the contact [with it, whereas] groups of Slavs who arrived later would have been less subject to the influence of late antique culture. ...[4]

The Croats migrated into a deteriorating landscape. Until then, the Roman cities on the Dalmatian coast had been largely bypassed by barbarian raiders, thanks to the high mountains of the Dalmatian interior. In the long period of peace that followed Rome's piecemeal subjugation of the Illyrian inhabitants of Dalmatia, between 240 BC and the failed Illyrian revolt in the first decade AD, some of these cities grew large. Chief among them was Salona, near Split, which the Byzantine Emperor Constantine Porphyrogenitus (905–59)[5] described as being half the size of Constantinople.

By the time the Croats moved into the Balkans, Salona had evolved into the principal Christian bishopric in the region, becoming an arch-bishopric in about 527. Jadera, or Diadora (Zadar), certainly had become a bishopric by the fourth century, when Felix represented the see at the Council of Milan. The other towns, Epidaurum, near Dubrovnik, Trogir, Aenona (Nin) and Julia Parentium (Poreč), were also towns of substance, enriched with amphitheatres, forums, basili-cas and triumphal arches. The countryside around these towns was not Romanised, however. The inhabitants of the interior were either Illyrians or members of other tribes who were settled in the region by the Roman government.

The attacks of the Avars and the Slavs dealt a severe blow to these besieged outposts of a dying civilisation. In 600 Pope Gregory wrote an anguished letter to Maximus, the Bishop of Salona, near Split, express-ing his sorrow and impotence over the continual raids, and saying that he 'shared his grief about the Slavs'. But the Pope's commiserations availed Salona nothing. Between 614 and 630 the Avars descended on the city and sacked it before moving down the Adriatic coast to destroy Epidaurum, Narona (Metković) and other towns.

The Latin inhabitants of these ruined cities fled for sanctuary to the Adriatic islands off the coast. As a peace of sorts returned, many of them made their way back to the mainland, where they laid the foundations of two new cities. In central Dalmatia, the refugees from Salona moved into the vast, ruined palace of the Emperor Diocletian,[6] located a few miles away from Salona at Spalato.

In this giant hulk with its vast walls, sixteen towers, huge mau-soleum, reception halls, libraries, cavernous underground cellars and hundreds of other rooms, the survivors of the barbarian onslaught created the city of Split. They converted the mausoleum of this notor-ious persecutor of Christians into a cathedral and dedicated it to St Duje, after Bishop Domnius of Salona, one of the victims of Diocletian's purges. The watchtower over the main entrance was converted into small churches, two of which, St Martin's and Our Lady of the Belfry, survive. The refugees from Epidaurum moved a short distance down the coast and founded another new city, which was to become known as Ragusa, or Dubrovnik.

It was during this time of upheavals that the Croats settled in Pannonia and Dalmatia. It seems certain they had settled in Dalmatia by the middle of the seventh century, as Pope John IV despatched an abbot named Martin to Dalmatia with money to ransom the Latin Christian refugees and instructions to engage the region's new Slav set-tlers in dialogue. Martin returned to Rome after visiting several areas of Dalmatia, which suggests that the region was already safe enough to travel around in. Abbot Martin's journey tallies with the tenth-century account of the Emperor Porphyrogenitus, *De Administrando Imperio*, which was intended as a briefing on the empire for the attention of his son and heir. Porphyrogenitus said that the Croats had not come as invaders, but had been invited, indeed ordered, into the Balkans by his predecessor, the Emperor Heraclius, following the sacking of Salona, and with the purpose of relieving the empire of the murderous assaults of the Avars.

The Emperor claimed that the Croats had been led by seven siblings. He also said the Croats had been heretics or Arians until their reception into mainstream Christianity later in the seventh century. Porphyrogenitus' claim that the Croats were invited into Dalmatia is contradicted by the fact that the Byzantine-controlled cities of the coast were forced to pay tribute to them. The story of the 'invitation' was most probably an attempt to rationalise an invasion that the empire had been unable to prevent.

The Croats fanned out over a wide area when they crossed the Danube. Some remained on the Pannonian plain and mingled with other, earlier Slav settlers, from which the terms Slovinska Zemlja (Slovenia) and Slavonija (Slavonia) eventually developed.[7] The majority, grouped in seven or eight clans, journeyed south towards the Adriatic, into Dalmatia and Istria. There, on the coast, they encountered the wrecked remains of Salona and Epidaurum and the newer Latin communities which were rising out of the marshes at Ragusa and the old imperial palace at Spalato, or Split. The other Dalmatian towns, Jadera (Zadar), Aenona (Nin) and Tragurium (Trogir), appear not to have been destroyed by barbarian invaders. In the anarchic conditions of the seventh century these towns had been left to fend for themselves. They would still have appeared highly civilised to the Slav immigrants settling outside their walls.

The new Slav settlers were not simple barbarians in the way the Avars appear to have been. They did not attack these enfeebled outposts of imperial civilisations, even though they probably could have done. Instead, they imitated and tried to absorb them. They took up the Roman names for towns and modified them. Thus Senia became Senj, and Salona – what was left of it – Solin. In the interior of Dalmatia the Slavs would have come across the remnants of the Illyrians and the tribes who had been settled there by the Romans. These natives were pushed out of the coastal areas and forced into the hills. They may have been the ancestors of the Vlachs, nomadic pastoral communities which reappeared in the Middle Ages and were not related to the Croats.

As the Byzantine Empire recovered its strength from the sixth century under Justinian, its influence revived over the Dalmatian cities of Dubrovnik, Split, Zadar and the Adriatic islands, which formed a Byzantine unit of administration known as the *archonate*. The growing influence of Byzantium was also felt among the Croatian clans which had settled in the interior of Dalmatia, for they accepted the lordship of the Emperor Constantine II Pogonatus in 678.

The seven or eight Croat clans in Dalmatia each occupied a certain region, which they subdivided into *župe* (counties) ruled by a *župan* (ruler or sheriff). The overall ruler of several *župe* was the *knez* (prince). The southernmost area of Croat settlement, which became known as Red Croatia, comprised three such dukedoms or principalities. One of these, Dioclea, evolved into Montenegro, while a second, Zahumlya, or just Hum, was later called Herzegovina. According to the great Croat historian, Vjekoslav Klaić,[8] it was the clan that occupied the heartland of Dalmatia, between the River Cetina in the north, the Velebit mountains in the west and the plain of Duvno in the south, which carried the clan name Hrvat (Croat), on account of which the region was known as White Croatia – Bijela Hrvatska. The names of the other Slav clans were lost.[9] Not every local prince was known as a *knez*. Klaić maintained that the ruler of the region surrounding Bihać appears to have held the title of *ban*[10] and that, after the victory of the Croat *knez* over the *ban*, the term was absorbed into Croat political culture, the *ban* henceforth occupying a position second only to the prince. 'When in subsequent centuries the Croat princes and kings spread their authority into other regions, throughout the conquered regions they introduced bans as their deputies,' he wrote.[11]

In 800 the Frankish armies of Charlemagne added Dalmatia to their domains. Byzantium recognised this change of lordship in the Treaty of Aachen in 812, retaining the cities of Zadar, Trogir and Split and the islands of Krk, Rab and Osor, which were governed as a *theme* (province) by a Byzantine representative in Zadar. In Dalmatia the principal result of Frankish rule was the evangelisation of the Croat rulers; some may have become Christian before the ninth century, but if they did so they left no trace in the form of stone churches, although it is possible they built wooden structures which have completely perished. Some Croats must have been Christian already, for the worlds of the Croats and the Latin cities were not hermetically sealed off from each other. But the rulers were either not Christian or of no fixed religion until the mass baptisms of the Frankish era, which are commemorated in Višeslav's baptismal font.

The Croat princes did not resist Charlemagne's rule. But when he died in 814, and was succeeded by his son, Louis the Pious, northern, Pannonian Croatia revolted unsuccessfully between 819 and 822 under the local ruler, Ljudevit. The Dalmatian ruler, Borna, opposed the rebellion, which suggests that the local Croat rulers were politically divided at the time. And it was Dalmatia, with its adjacent seaboard network of civilised Latin towns, which led the way towards the creation of a more modern state. One sign of the development of Croat society in

Dalmatia was the adoption of more sophisticated titles. Vladislav, who ruled from 821 to 830, styled himself Duke of the Croatians and Dalmatians,[12] and it was during his rule that we hear for the first time of a new bishopric being founded at Nin.

The Nin bishopric was a crucial development for the Croats. Later, it took centre-stage in a struggle between champions of an autonomous Croat national Church and those who favoured subordination in all matters to Rome. In the early days, Nin was a small, Latin town and the first bishop, Theodosius, was from Syria. But it developed quickly into a centre of Slav resistance to the centralising tendencies of Rome. The remarkable Bishop Grgur, or Gregory, promoted Nin as an ecclesiastical capital for the embryonic Croatian state, contesting the claims of the Latin bishoprics on the coast, and especially those of the archbishopric of Split.

Under Vladislav's successors, Mislav (835–45) and Trpimir (845–64), the Dalmatian–Croatian dukedom expanded, although it remained under the ultimate sovereignty of the Franks. A Bulgarian army was defeated at Zvornik, in eastern Bosnia, which secured the wildernesses and forests of the interior of Dalmatia (what we would now call central Bosnia), for the Croat state. Another sign of the developing civilisation of the Croat rulers, and of their desire to strengthen ties with the West, was the decision by Trpimir to invite the Benedictine order into his domains. A Saxon Benedictine, Gottschalk, spent two years at Trpimir's court between about 846 and 848 before being summoned to Mainz on charges of heresy, and it was probably thanks to Gottschalk's influence that in 850–2 the first Benedictine monastery in the Croat lands was built at Rižinice, near Klis.

The Croats in Dalmatia were building their own churches by this stage and the few structures that survived the Mongol invasion of the fourteenth century, such as St Donat in Zadar, illustrate the vigour of the new culture. These were not only crude imitations of the structures they saw in the Latin cities but displayed considerable originality of design. A characteristic feature of early Croat art was the decorative use of winding and interwoven patterns carved on to stone, above doorways, on fonts and on other precious objects. This art form, which is known as plaitwork, bears a strong resemblance to early Celtic art. The Croats may have brought it with them from White Croatia, or learned it from the old Illyrian inhabitants of Dalmatia.

Little is known of life at the courts of the Croatian dukes, though the charters they handed to various bishops and monasteries cast light on Croatia's progress towards a feudal society.

Duke Trpimir's presentation of the Church of the Blessed George to the Archbishop of Split refers very precisely to the amount of land that was being presented along with the church, and to gifts of slaves, for example. Other documents, concerning a dispute over the ownership of that church between the Bishop of Nin and the Archbishop of Split, refer to Mutimir's (892–910) retinue of cup-bearers, chamberlains and chaplains. It is clear from these documents that Croat society had already developed a class structure and that the Croats now had a strong sense of land ownership.

Trpimir's son, Zdeslav (878–9), succeeded to the throne with the support of the Byzantine Emperor Basil I. Zdeslav launched the first and last attempt by a Croat ruler to detach the Croat Church from Western Christendom and accept Byzantine jurisdiction. The move was not popular. Although the Croat dukes and the Dalmatian cities acknowledged the political sovereignty of the Byzantine emperors, their ecclesiastical loyalty was to Rome. Zdeslav was murdered within a year. His successor, Branimir (879–92), reversed the decision and returned Croatia to the Roman obedience.

Under Mutimir's successor, Tomislav (910–c.929), the early Croatian state reached its zenith. Tomislav united Dalmatia with Pannonia and upgraded his title from that of duke to king with the permission of the Pope. As a result he became lord of a substantial state, roughly covered by modern Croatia, Bosnia and the coast of Montenegro. After allying with Byzantium and defeating Bulgaria, Byzantium then ceded Tomislav sovereignty over the *theme* of Dalmatian cities and islands.

The rise of Croatia under Tomislav excited the admiration of his contemporaries; Porphyrogenitus described Croatia as a great military power, which was capable of fielding more than 100,000 footsoldiers and a fleet little smaller than that of Venice. The reference to 100,000 soldiers must have been a great exaggeration, but it suggests that Croatia was seen as a substantial military power.[13] Considering the scale of his alleged achievements, Tomislav is a curiously opaque figure. It is not known when, where or how he died. And another curious matter is that although Porphyrogenitus lauded the Croats' military strength, *De Administrando Imperio* does not refer to Tomislav by name. According to legend he was crowned on the Field of Duvno (Tomislavgrad) in 925. But no one knows precisely when, or whether this event really took place. Like many early Croat rulers, Tomislav fades in and out of the picture. He was certainly present at the height of the power struggle between Grgur of Nin and the archbishopric of Split, which was to have such important consequences for the future of the Croatian Church. Yet, in this crucial dispute, Tomislav's role is unknown and no one knows whether he influenced the outcome.

The conflict between the bishops of Nin and Split was no mere turf battle. It involved vital ethnic, cultural and geo-political issues, pitting Slavs against Latins, and the primitive semi-democratic traditions of the

Slavs against the rigid feudal system of Western Europe. At the core of the dispute was the use of the Glagolitic script and the Slav tongue in the Mass. According to popular legend, the Glagolitic script was invented by St Jerome. It is more probable that Glagolitic, like its more successful rival, Cyrillic, originated in the south-east Balkans, most probably from the region of Thessaloniki. The route by which the script reached Croatia was tortuous and is a subject of scholastic controversy. One theory is that it was introduced to Western Europe by the Byzantine missionaries, Constantine (St Cyril) and Methodius, who arrived in Moravia in 863 at the invitation of the local ruler, Rastislav, bringing with them liturgical books written in the Glagolitic script. Three years later they escorted the first batch of prospective clergy from Moravia to Rome for ordination. Their activities aroused furious opposition from the Latin party, supported by the Germans, who resented any support being given to Slav culture and insisted that the only languages permissible for divine service were Latin, Greek or Hebrew. Nevertheless, Pope Hadrian received them cordially and ordained the Slav clergy. Cyril remained in Rome, where he died in 869. As the German clergy gained the upper hand in Moravia it became impossible for Methodius to return to Moravia, but the Pope appointed him to the revived Roman see of Sirmium (Srijem). Methodius' troubles at the hands of the Germans were no concern of the Croats. Yet it appears that his script somehow reached Croatia and gained a foothold in Dalmatia, especially in the Slav bishopric of Nin.

In Dalmatia the use of the Glagolitic script and the Mass in the vernacular became very popular among the expanding number of Croat priests, championed by Grgur of Nin. As with King Tomislav, there are disappointingly few personal details about Bishop Grgur. We know that he defended the use of Glagolitic script and the Mass in the vernacular, and that his ambition was for Nin to become the leading see in a Croatian Church which included the cities of Dalmatia. But the Latin bishops on the coast cherished their direct ties to the see of Rome, and reinforced their claim to ecclesiastical independence from the Croats by putting forward a variety of new spiritual claims. The archbishops of Split began to insist on the 'apostolic' status of their see on the strength of a claim that St Peter had sent St Domnius, known as St Duje, to Salona. The political agenda of the archbishops of Split was ambitious. Their goal was to revive the metropolitical jurisdiction of the old Roman bishops of Salona on behalf of the new city of Split, and so dominate what they considered were the upstart, inferior Slav bishops of the interior.

Pope John X, naturally, sided with the Latin bishops and the principle of uniformity. Everything that Grgur stood for – the Mass in the vernacular, married clergy, beards and local scripts – contradicted the centralising tendencies at work in early medieval Christendom. But rather than alienate the Slavs by banning the practices of the Croat Bishop on his own authority, the Pope called a synod in Split in 925 to decide the issue. Given that there were several Latin bishops, that Grgur was on his own and that Tomislav had no vote in the debate, the result was a foregone conclusion. The synod endorsed Split's claim to become the metropolitan see. Nin was humiliated. The bishopric was simply abolished, on the ground that it was a modern, Slav creation, which did not correspond to a former Roman see. Services in the vernacular were prohibited except in areas where there were no clergy who knew Latin. The rather extreme nature of the conclusions may have perturbed even the Pope, as he then invited both parties to hold another meeting.

At a second synod in 928, held again in Split, the result was exactly the same. This time Bishop Grgur was offered the revived Roman see of Skradin or that of Siscia (Sisak) in exchange for Nin. It was just an insult, as the old Roman town of Siscia had been a wilderness for centuries. Frustratingly, no more is heard of the defeated Grgur.

After the rupture between Rome and Constantinople in 1054 the papacy became ever more hostile towards the kinds of ideas represented by Grgur of Nin. The imposition of Latin services was divisive in Dalmatia, for in 1057, according to the *Historia Salonitana,* written by Thomas, Archdeacon of Split (1200–68), the Slav clergy revolted on the island of Krk, expelled the Latin Bishop and installed one of their own. The rising was put down with the help of the Croat King Petar Krešimir IV (1058–74), who had clearly decided to throw in his lot with the great civilisational force of Rome rather than back the Slav clergy. The rebel cleric leader, named Vulf, probably not a Croat, was brought to Dalmatia for the special entertainment of the Latin bishops, who had him tortured and killed. In 1060 a third synod, again held in Split, ordered yet more draconian measures against clergy who wore beards, who said the Mass in the vernacular or who used the 'gothic' (Glagolitic) script, in line with the decrees of the Lateran Council of 1059.

In spite of persecution, Glagolitic continued to survive in opposition to the Romanising Latin culture of the coastal cities. Rome relented a little. In 1248 Innocent IV permitted the bishops of Senj to use Croatian in the liturgy, and the Glagolitic script. As late as the sixteenth century Glagolitic enjoyed a final burst of activity as the preferred script of a school of exiled Croat Protestants, who produced, among other things, a Glagolitic New Testament in the German city of Tübingen in 1562.[14] But Glagolitic had lost the battle to become the national script of the Croats, and in the seventeenth century this hardy Dalmatian survivor withered in the face of the cultural onslaught of Venice.

The *Kulturkampf* in Croatia over Glagolitic weakened the cause of the embryonic Croatian state. If Grgur of Nin had won his battle, the whole of Croatia would have come under a single ecclesiastical jurisdiction, a development that would have greatly boosted royal authority. As it was, the most powerful ecclesiastics in Dalmatia remained outside the Croat King's control.

The other shadow that cast a pall over Tomislav's reign was the rise of Hungary in the north. The Magyars had ensconced themselves in the sixth century on the Pannonian plain, which earlier had been held by the Avars. They soon made their influence felt. Like the Avars they started out as a roaming, destructive force, conquering Basel in 917, burning Bremen a year later and criss-crossing the Alps, the Rhone, Bavaria and Burgundy, leaving a trail of havoc behind them. Once they settled down in their stronghold on the Danube and the Tisza it was inevitable that they would cast a covetous eye on the Croatian lands to the south. Tomislav beat off a Hungarian attack on northern Croatia in the 920s. But the Hungarians were only deterred, not permanently repulsed.

The cracks that appeared under Tomislav widened after his death, exposing fundamental weaknesses at the heart of this large and impressive-looking state. One problem was the quarrel between the Latin and Slav clergy. Another was that the crown lacked a strong territorial power-base. Unlike more advanced kingdoms in Western Europe, the Croat kings did not own vast tracts of land which they could lease, or bestow on courtiers. They had no great cities. There was no equivalent to London or Paris – centres of ecclesiastical and secular authority as well as commercial activity. The kings moved peripatetically around their domains, shuttling between the small towns of Nin, Biograd and Knin. The large cities, such as Split and Zadar, were virtually independent states, electing their own bishops and governors and jealously guarding their liberty.

The first major crisis followed soon after the death in 945 of Tomislav's son. Krešimir. His successor, Miroslav, was murdered by Pribina, the Ban of Dalmatia. This unleashed a period of anarchic warfare during which Red Croatia, a substantial territory in the south, was lost to the Croats.

The signs of Croatia's weakness were not lost on Hungary, or on Venice. In the ninth and tenth centuries, Byzantium granted Venice administration by proxy over the *theme* of Dalmatian cities and islands. In the 1000s the Doge of Venice, Peter II Orseolo, ominously assumed the title Duke of Dalmatia, and backed his claim with a seaborne invasion. Venice's territorial gains were not permanent. Nevertheless, the ease with which it occupied Zadar, Biograd, Split and Korčula did not bode well for Croatia's future integrity.

Under Petar Krešimir IV (1058–74) the Croatian crown recovered much of the authority it had enjoyed under Tomislav. The King regained control over the Dalmatian cities, partly thanks to the close alliance he forged with the papacy, which was cemented by the help Krešimir lent to suppressing the revolt of Glagolitic clergy on the island of Krk. Under Krešimir the capital was moved from Knin to the coastal town of Biograd and the country divided into three regions – Pannonia in the north, Dalmatia in the west and Bosnia in the east – each of which was placed under the regional authority of a *ban*. Krešimir also founded Šibenik, a new city on the Dalmatian coast which was established as a Slav rival to the older and more independent Latin cities.

From the period just after the death of Petar Krešimir there survives an informative account of life in the medieval Croat kingdom from the deeds of donation of Petar Crni of Split in 1080. Crni was a rich nobleman who, following the custom of the time, was investing some of his money in the foundation of a new church in the nearby village of Jesenice, dedicated to St Peter. 'We invited the the Archbishop [of Split] to consecrate the church on 11 October. Many people from Split and many Croats attended the celebration,' he wrote. 'I bought a slave called Dragača from a priest in Orihovo for five *solidi* … we gave him 100 sheep, two cows and a pair of oxen, which he will keep to satisfy the needs of the church. Besides, we bought a small boy named Zloba from his father and sent him to be educated and to become a priest and serve permanently in this church.'[15]

The fact that Crni placed 'people from Split' and 'Croats' in separate categories suggests there was still a sharp difference between the inhabitants of the old Dalmatian cities and the 'Croatians', even though Slavs had long been migrating into the cities and diluting the ethnic Latin element. Indeed, Crni himself was a Slav who lived in the city.

The death of Krešimir IV exposed all the weaknesses that resulted from the lack of a strong, royal administrative base. Again the kingdom was plunged into anarchic warfare between the faction leaders, the winner being the Dmitar, the governor, or Ban, of northern. Pannonian Croatia. As king he took the name of Zvonimir. Like his predecessor Krešimir, Zvonimir (1075–89) was determined to strengthen Croatia through an alliance with the papacy. He was crowned by a papal legate and repaid Pope Gregory VII's support with a declaration at his coronation, placing Croatia under papal sovereignty. In his coronation oath he said he was 'King of Croatia by the Grace of God and the will of the Apostolic see' and he promised the Pope a symbolic tribute of 200 gold coins each Easter. Zvonimir was criticised strongly by historians in the Communist era for this supposed 'betrayal' of Croat independence. In fact it was a purely pragmatic move that posed no threat to Croatia's independence and bolstered his hold on the throne. Zvonimir died in 1089, most probably of natural causes. It was not until long after his death that chroniclers sought to explain the end of the independent

Croat kingdom by claiming that he had been murdered and had cursed his fellow countrymen, condemning them to rule by foreigners. Thus, according to the thirteenth-century *Chronicle of the Priest of Dioclea*, Zvonimir died at the hands of his own nobles at an assembly at Petih Crkava (Five Churches), near Knin, after failing to persuade them to support him on a papal crusade.

After Zvonimir's death, King Laszlo of Hungary invaded northern Croatia, claiming his right to succeed to the Croatian crown on the grounds that he was the brother of Queen Jelena, while Zvonimir's only son Radovan had predeceased him. Jelena naturally supported her brother's claim, as did many of the nobles in northern Croatia. So Laszlo was able to advance across the flat plains of northern Croatia in 1091 without meeting any resistance. However, he could not cross the Gvozd mountains and advance south into Dalmatia. In the Dalmatian heartland of the Croat kingdom the nobles were strongly opposed to a foreign king, and elected one of their own number, Petar Svačić, as the next king. Laszlo did not live long enough to pursue his claim south of the Gvozd mountains. Nevertheless, he reinforced his claim to the lands of the north by founding a bishopric in the small settlement of Zagreb.[16] This he attached to the see of Ostrogon in Hungary, and not to the archbishopric of Split as tradition dictated.

After Laszlo's death, the crown of Hungary passed to his younger brother Kalman (1095–1116). The new King was a resourceful statesman who was determined to gain through diplomacy what could not be obtained by brute force. In 1097 he assembled a large army in northern Croatia and moved south across the Gvozd mountains. There he met the army of Petar Svačić.

His victory was total and Petar died in battle, lending his name to the mountain called Petrova Gora – Peter's mountain. But, although the threat to his title was now extinguished, Kalman felt that the task of crushing all resistance to his rule in the mountainous interior of Dalmatia might be beyond him. Wisely, he invited the leaders of the twelve largest clans of the south, the Kačić, Kuka, Šubić, Čudomerić, Svačić, Mogorović, Gušić, Karinjan, Polečić, Lisničić, Jamometić and Tugometić, to treat with him. The result was a historic agreement in 1102 signed in the northern town of Križevci and called the *Pacta Conventa*.[17] Under the terms of the pact, the great Croat families recognised Kalman as king. In return, he granted Croatia virtual self-government under a *ban*. He pledged not to settle Croatia with Hungarians, to be crowned separately in Croatia and to visit his new kingdom regularly in order to convoke the Sabor (parliament).

After the *Pacta Conventa* had been signed, Kalman moved south into Dalmatia to Biograd, where he was crowned. Although he had solved the dispute over the crown with the great Croat clans, his problems

were not over. Several Dalmatian cities had fallen under the control of
Venice during the brief rule of Petar Svačić. At Split he was angered to
find the gates of the city were closed to him and he had to camp outside
with his army for several days before the city could be persuaded to let
him enter. This frosty welcome did not dissuade Kalman from his pacific
course, and the charters he issued to Split and Trogir were very conciliatory in tone. The Charter given to Trogir stated: 'I shall allow the
ancient laws to continue ... and I shall not allow any Hungarian or for-
eigner to live in the city unless your gracious love accepts him.'[18] Zadar
put up much more resistance and it was not until 1105 that Kalman
persuaded the city to open its gates and recognise him as king. The independent kingdom of Croatia had come to an end. For the next eight
centuries Croatia was to be ruled as a part of the kingdom of Hungary,
albeit under the Habsburgs from 1527. As the centuries wore on, the
Hungarians began to take a less generous view of the provisions of the
Pacta Conventa than had King Kalman.

2

Croatia Under the Hungarians

Let it be known to Your Majesty that no ruler has ever subjugated Croatia by force. Rather, after the death of our last king, Zvonimir, we of our free will attached ourselves to the crown of the Hungarian kingdom, as we at this time join ourselves to Your Majesty.[1]

The union of the kingdoms of Croatia and Hungary, like the union of Poland and Lithuania, or of England and Scotland, was an unequal affair. The Croats insisted they had entered into the arrangement of their own volition and that the terms of the *Pacta Conventa* made them an associated kingdom, and not a part of Hungary. The Hungarians had a less exalted view of this dynastic arrangement. The kings of the house of Arpad, who ruled until 1301, acknowledged Croatia's separate identity, continued to be crowned separately in Croatia at Biograd, or Zadar, and left Croatia's internal administration to the *ban* and the Sabor. However, they drew a distinction between the lands of northern Croatia, which had accepted King Laszlo's rule in the 1090s, and the lands south of the Gvozd mountains, which had accepted Kalman's rule on the basis of the *Pacta Conventa*. The liberties of Croatia the Hungarians took as referring only to the lands of the south, and when the Hungarians referred to Croatia or, as it was sometimes called, Croatia–Dalmatia, they meant only the lands of the south. Northern Pannonian Croatia was treated as a separate entity, which was neither quite Croat nor part of Hungary. The Hungarians began to call this area the Kingdom of Slavonia – simply, the land of the Slavs – and they placed it under the jurisdiction of a separate *ban* and *sabor*.

The division between Slavonia and Croatia–Dalmatia was not merely administrative. Although Hungary did not absorb Slavonia, it treated the entire territory as a royal demesne and settled it with Hungarian or Hungarianised Croat landlords. The new regime introduced Slavonia to the full rigours of the feudal system as it had developed in Hungary. The primitive democracy of the Croat clans, under which land belonged to *plemena* who elected their local *župans*, disappeared from the region.

There are no records of the proceedings of the parliaments of the old

Croat kingdom. It appears that they consisted of leaders of the big clans and bishops and were summoned mainly for coronations, declarations of war and the dedication of great churches. There was no fixed name for these assemblies or a fixed meeting place. Under the Arpad kings of Hungary, the power to call assemblies devolved from the king to the two *bans*. The first assembly in Slavonia whose records survive, the Congregatio Regni Totius Sclavoniae Generalis (General Assembly of the Whole Kingdom of Slavonia), met in 1273 in Zagreb and drew up thirty-three articles for the approval of the Ban, concerning property, judicial procedures and the payment of taxes.[2] The statutes of the Slavonian assembly became law after confirmation by the *ban*. Parliaments in medieval Slavonia were peripatetic and met usually in large churches and abbeys, at Zagreb, Križevci and, later, at Varaždin. They were unicameral, comprising bishops, magnates and representatives of royal boroughs. In time the work of the assembly increasingly involved the fine-tuning and defence of the prerogatives and obligations of the noble estates with regard to their serfs and the king.

In the southern kingdom, Croatia–Dalmatia, the feudal system was much slower to take root, because the Hungarians made no attempt to displace the traditional Croat clan leaders. Serfdom was not widely established. Kalman's interference south of the Gvozd mountains went no further than inserting a Hungarian as the archbishop of Split and insisting on his two-thirds share of the customs duties from the Dalmatian ports. There are few records of the parliaments being summoned in Croatia–Dalmatia in the thirteenth and early fourteenth centuries, except for the purpose of coronations. Such parliaments as there were met mostly in Knin, Zadar or Nin, usually under the presidency of the bishop of Knin.

The Hungarians counted Bosnia – or Rama, as it was known in the early medieval period – among their possessions under the terms of the *Pacta Conventa*. But the Hungarians were only intermittently concerned with enforcing their claim to this far-off land and the *ban* of Bosnia behaved as an independent ruler. In the 1160s both Bosnia and Croatia returned briefly to Byzantine sovereignty under the forceful Emperor Manuel I Comnenus. But while Croatia–Dalmatia returned to Hungary after the Emperor's death in 1180, Bosnia continued to pursue an independent course under its own *bans*, of whom Kulin (1180–1204) was the most celebrated.[3]

The Hungarians were not indifferent to Bosnia's *de facto* independence and in 1238 they launched an invasion. But that ground to a halt in 1240, when the Mongols invaded eastern Europe. The Hungarians also attempted to assert their jurisdiction over Bosnia through the Church. Bosnia contained only one bishopric, which had previously been under the jurisdiction of the archbishops of Split and later those of

Dubrovnik. But in 1252 Hungary had spiritual jurisdiction over Bosnia transferred to Djakovo, in Slavonia. The Bosnian rulers countered this attempt to penetrate the country by fostering an independent and allegedly heretical Bosnian Church. Bosnia had enjoyed great notoriety as a nest of heretics, certainly since the time of Ban Kulin. Bosnia's rulers were in a state of schism from Rome in the thirteenth century, but it is questionable whether they were truly heretics, or ever embraced the dualist heresy known as Bogomilism. Most scholars now believe that the Bosnian Church was simply independent, and that it died out in the fourteenth century after the *bans* of Bosnia returned to the Roman allegiance and the Francisians began to evangelise the country through monasteries established in central Bosnia from the 1340s onwards. As Bosnia became richer through the development of silver and lead mines, the Bosnian *bans* began to give themselves grander titles. In 1377 Ban Stephen Tvrtko made use of the extinction of Serbia's native Nemanja dynasty to have himself crowned king of both Bosnia and Serbia at the monastery of Mileševo, in the Podrinje region, which alternated between Bosnian and Serbian control. The King of Bosnia also seized large parts of southern Dalmatia in 1380, after which Tvrtko styled himself King of Dalmatia as well.

The loss of Bosnia had important, negative consequences for Croatia. What had formed a geographically solid land mass in Tomislav's reign, bordered by the Adriatic in the west and the River Drina in the east, became a narrower, less defensible entity, arching around Bosnia in the shape of a boomerang. Economically and culturally it was less of a loss, as there were very few settlements of any importance east of Knin.

One of the main reasons why the Croats entered into union with Hungary was the hope that the Hungarians would defend Dalmatia against the assaults of Venice. For a while this held true, but soon after the death of King Kalman in 1116 Venice launched a new campaign, capturing Šibenik. The Venetians then moved north to attack Zadar, much the largest city on the Dalmatian coast and the real object of Venice's ambitions. The attack failed and the Doge died in the assault. But nine years later there was a second, bigger invasion. This time Venice razed to the foundations the town of Biograd, the Croats' former capital and coronation site. A Hungarian–Croatian force under King Bela II (1131–44) expelled the Venetians from Biograd, but the ruined town never recovered from the onslaught. The bishopric died out and Biograd remained what it is to this day, a mere village. During the brief period of Byzantine rule over Dalmatia from 1163 to 1180 Venice held off. But, as soon as Dalmatia reverted to Hungary under Bela III (1173–96), Venice renewed its assaults, concentrating on Zadar and the islands of Lošinj, Pag and Krk. A siege of Zadar that lasted almost ten years brought Venice little benefit, but the island of Rab was lost to the Croats.

The Croat nobles who acquitted themselves well in the struggle against Venice were rewarded with large estates from the Hungarian crown. Two families which were to dominate Croatia for centuries, the Šubićs (later called Zrinski) and the Frankopans, owed their rise to Bela III's patronage. The royal grants to the Frankopans were on the island of Krk. The Šubićs were given land around the Dalmatian district of Bribir.

The death of Bela III in 1196 was followed by another Venetian attempt to subdue Zadar, and, if all else failed, to mete out the same vicious punishment that had befallen Biograd in 1126. On its own, Venice lacked the resources to crush Zadar, which was a wealthy and well-fortified city, backing on to flat and fertile hinterland. But the longed-for opportunity appeared during the Fourth Crusade in 1202, approved by Pope Innocent III. The crusade suffered from poor organisation and a lack of manpower. Of an expected 35,000 knightly volunteers, only about 11,000 had turned up at the assembly point in Venice in the summer of 1202, where delays and a lack of money led to Venice threatening to turf them out or cut off their victuals. Enrico Dandolo, the elderly Doge of Venice, then made use of the crusaders' plight to further the city's territorial ambitions at Dalmatia's expense, and offered to waive the payment of 34,000 silver marks for supplies and refurbishments to the crusaders' impressive armada if they would attack and capture the city of Zadar for Venice. According to a French account, the Doge slyly claimed that the Hungarian kings had 'stolen' Zadar from Venice, presenting the operation as a restitution of the *status quo ante*. It was a description of affairs that would have been indignantly rejected by the city's inhabitants.

The expedition to Zadar was a grand affair, attended by ringing of bells and chanting of prayers by the Venetians, who set off with 50 vessels of their own to accompany the 200 or so ships of the crusaders. The Abbot of Vaux, one of the crusaders, was appalled by this turn of events. 'In the name of the Pope of Rome, I forbid you to attack this city, for the people in it are Christians and you wear the sign of the cross,' he reportedly said. The Doge turned to the knights and reminded them of the bargain. 'You have given me your promise, now I summon you to keep your word,' he said.[4]

The assault began. Against this terrific armada, which included the most up-to-date war machines such as catapults and drills, the city of Zadar, in spite of its defences, had no chance. The King of Hungary provided no aid. For five days the city held out as the crusaders manoeuvred around the wall, using vast catapults to bombard the defences. On the fifth day, as the crusaders began to drill under the towers, Zadar gave up the fight and hung crosses on the walls – a sign of surrender by a Christian community which ought to have entitled the citizens to remain alive. Urged on by the Venetians, the crusaders took no notice. On entering the city they massacred the inhabitants and pillaged everything in sight. Churches were vandalised and torn apart in the search for gold. These enormities carried on until the crusaders departed from the empty husk to Corfu the following spring, from where they intended to proceed to the biggest looting expedition of all, in Constantinople itself. Before they left, they demolished Zadar's seaward-facing wall.

The sack of Zadar was a monstrous act of malice and the Pope was distressed at this desecration of a Christian city and the perversion of the crusade. He complained that the crusaders had commited a grave sin by violating the sign of the cross displayed on Zadar's walls and excommunicated the entire expedition. He also called on Venice to compensate the city for the damage. But the Pope's regrets were not much good to the ruined city and the bishops accompanying the crusade soon persuaded him to lift the excommunication of the crusaders. He did not, however, rescind the excommunication of the Venetians, not that they appeared to care. Needless to say, Venice did not pay any compensation to Zadar either. Unlike Biograd, which virtually disappeared after Venice's murderous assault, Zadar eventually recovered. But the city did not regain its old vitality or its former Slav Croatian character. After the fall to Venice, the peace terms stipulated that Venice had the right to appoint the mayor, the *comes*, as well as the Council. Hungary–Croatia recovered Zadar in 1358. But it proved to be no more than an interlude, as Venice gained control of most of Dalmatia between 1409 and 1420 and was not expelled from these lands until the Napoleonic wars. Zadar reverted again to rule by Italians in 1920 under the Treaty of Rapallo, which lasted until Tito's Partisans drove them out of the city at the end of the Second World War.

With the exception of the city-state of Dubrovnik, which was not an integral part of Dalmatia, the period following the union with Hungary, especially after the sackings of Biograd and Zadar, was one of a decline in Dalmatia's fortunes in comparison to those of Slavonia. The archbishops of Split, for example, were progressively weakened. This had started with the creation of a see in Zagreb in 1094 under Hungarian jurisdiction. It got worse after the see of Zadar was hived off from Split in 1154, and placed under the control of the patriarchs of Venice, as a result of which Split lost control of the Dalmatian islands of Krk, Rab and Cres as well. Shorn of so much of its territory, the archbishopric's income fell sharply and by the late thirteenth century it was much poorer than either Zadar or Zagreb.[5]

For the new bishopric of Zagreb, the eleventh and twelfth centuries were years of growth and prosperity, marked by the foundation of new chapters in the Slavonian countryside at Čazma and Požega. The rise of

Zagreb was checked, however, in 1241 when a vast invading army of Mongols swept in from the east. The terror that this invasion provoked in the flat farmlands and marshes of Slavonia and southern Hungary can easily be imagined, for the Croats had experienced nothing like it in their history. According to the Archdeacon Thomas of Split, who lived through the invasion, the invaders were short in stature, bow-legged from lives spent on horseback, wore armour made of cattle hides, iron helmets, ate no bread and lived on a diet of meat and sour milk that was mixed with the blood of horses. Natural borders did not stop them, he wrote, as they crossed rivers in boats made of branches and animal hides.[6]

The invasion overwhelmed King Bela IV (1235–70) and halted his campaign to subdue Bosnia. After the Mongols crushed a Hungarian army at Miskolc, the King fled with his court to Zagreb. But he left the town when it became clear that the Mongols were still in hot pursuit, leaving the wretched inhabitants to cope with the onslaught as best they could. The result was that the Mongols demolished the town. The new cathedral, which had been consecrated in 1217 in the presence of a great company of Hungarian nobles and bishops, was flattened. Bela IV hurried on to the Dalmatian coast, fleeing from one city to another in an increasingly desperate attempt to evade capture by the Mongols. Finally he took refuge in Trogir, as the Mongol army under its commander Kadan camped outside the city walls. The Mongols demanded the surrender of the King's person. The proud rulers of Trogir rejected the suggestion with contempt. The stage was set for a dramatic contest of wills with potentially disastrous results. However, the outcome was an anti-climax. As the news of the death of the Great Khan, Ogadai, reached Trogir, the besieging horde simply vanished, galloping back towards the steppes of the east as mysteriously and quickly as they had arrived.

Thomas the Archdeacon recalled the arrival of the Hungarian King and Queen in Trogir in his *History of Solin*:

And so the Lord Kadan, having inspected all the surrounding positions, tried several times to see if he could possibly pass on horseback under the town walls. But when he saw that the water, by which the town was divided from the mainland, was impassable because of the deep mud, he withdrew from there.

Returning to his men, he sent a nuncio to the town, instructing him in what to say. Having reached the bridge, the man cried out in a loud voice, saying in Slavonic: 'This tells you the Lord Kadan, leader of the invincible army. Do not take upon yourselves the crime of alien blood but deliver the enemy into our hands so that his punishment should not fall on your heads and you should not perish in vain.

But the defenders dared not answer these words, since the king had commanded them not to respond a single word to the enemy. After this, the whole multitude of them rose up from there and returned along the path by which they had come.[7]

A legend grew up that a Croat army commanded by Fran Frankopan, the lord of Krk, inflicted a defeat on the departing Mongols at Grobničko Polje, near Rijeka, although there is no archaeological evidence that a battle took place there.

The Mongol invasion weakened the authority of the crown throughout Croatia. This in turn inspired more internal conflict between powerful nobles and the cities of the Dalmatian coast. Venice was able to consolidate its hold over Zadar, and the King was at last forced to recognise its title to the city. In Dalmatia, Split and Trogir went to war with each other in a territorial struggle for control of the village of Ostrog. Great feudal lords, such as the Frankopans and Šubićs, became far more independent. After the Mongol invasion, they increased the size of their estates and assumed the right to maintain fortified castles and private armies.

The King tried to check these unfortunate developments. One solution was to give the larger towns the status of royal free cities, in the hope that this might help revive their local economies and counterbalance the overmighty nobles. The first beneficiaries in Croatia were Zagreb, Samobor, Križevci and Jastrebarsko. The royal bull confirming Zagreb's status as a free city was confirmed in 1266, as were the obligations of the citizens, which included presenting the *ban* with an ox, 1,000 loaves and a barrel of wine. But it was also left to the citizens of Zagreb to pay for the cost of rebuilding the city's wrecked fortifications and a new cathedral.

In spite of the devastation wrought by the Mongols, Zagreb was rebuilt quickly. The area under the bishops' jurisdiction, known as the Kaptol, was divided from the town, called Gradec, by the narrow stream of the Medveščak. The proximity of the two settlements, one clerical, the other lay, caused continual disputes over territory, which often ended in blows. The street in Zagreb's Upper Town called 'Bloody Bridge' was given its name in memory of these disputes. On occasion mobs from Gradec invaded the Kaptol, burning whatever documents and papal bulls they could find and even showering the cathedral with arrows. One very precise cause of friction between Gradec and the Kaptol was a quarrel over the use of the mills in the narow stream of the Medveščak, all of which belonged to the Kaptol. But a more general factor was simply the widening of class divisions in late medieval Slavonia. The bishops became increasingly removed from contact with the population, and entrenched at the head of the landowning, serf-owning classes.

The cathedral canons were also turning into feudal gentlemen of leisure, as is illustrated by a fourteenth-century charter concerning the obligations of serfs in the Zagreb archdiocese towards the canons of the Kaptol. The list of duties was onerous, and included ploughing and sowing the Church estates in spring, tending and harvesting the Church vineyards in autumn, building fences, scything pastures and delivering plenty of wood in winter. The canons' stomachs were not forgotten. 'First, for Christmas, each [serf] should bring us a capon, five eggs and two flat cakes,' the charter read. 'For Easter, they should bring a piece of cheese, two flat cakes and ten eggs and each village should give a lamb. ... And all the above tributes are exclusive of any punitive work that may be sometimes demanded of wrongdoers.'[8]

In the interior of Dalmatia, where the old Croat clans held sway, serfdom scarcely existed. But, in the cities on the coast, class distinctions were naturally much stronger. The bishops of the Dalmatian cities were not feudal magnates drawing vast wealth from great estates and their serfs, like the bishop of Zagreb. Instead they sat at the apex of an urban hierarchy, were members of the city council and ranked in status above the prior (mayor). Anti-clericalism in Dalmatia dovetailed with the ethnic struggle between the Slav Croats of the countryside and the coastal Latins, which had been expressed so vividly in the conflict surrounding Grgur of Nin. There were a number of physical assaults on leading clerics, of which the most spectacular was the murder in 1180 of Archbishop Raineri, killed by the men of the powerful Kačić clan when he made the mistake of venturing into the village of Poljice to enforce an archiepiscopal claim to a slice of land. (The murdered prelate was then proclaimed a saint.)

Another manifestation of medieval Dalmatian anti-clericalism was heresy. In the thirteenth and fourteenth centuries the popes feared that the Dalmatians were scarcely less infected by heresy than the benighted Bosnians, which was not surprising as Split was Bosnia's principal trading outlet to the Mediterranean.

Split appears to have enjoyed an international fame – or infamy – as a centre of unorthodox opinions, because an English heretic, one Walter de Anglia, figures in the Split archdiocesan records as having arrived in 1383. Walter may well have been a disciple of the English heretic Wyclif, though the ecclesiastical authorities in Split are unhelpful on this point, describing him only in the vaguest terms as 'a son of hell' who opposed the clergy and the system of tithes, and whose inflammatory preaching had helped to stir up a popular revolt against the authorities which it took four years to quell. It is most unlikely Walter arrived in Split by accident, and more probable that he was drawn by the city's reputation for free thinking.[9]

The death of King Bela IV in 1270, after more than three decades on the Hungarian throne, opened up another debilitating crisis over the succession. The struggle for the Hungarian crown enabled the great Croatian clans, the Šubićs of Bribir and the Frankopans of Krk, to rule Croatia without interference. In 1272 they refused to recognise Laszlo IV (1272–90) as king Bela IV's successor, and Pavao Šubić had himself proclaimed hereditary *ban*. In effect, it was an attempt to re-establish an independent Croatian monarchy. After the extinction of the Arpads and the accession of the first Angevin king of Hungary, Charles Robert (1308–41), Šubić remained the undisputed master of Croat affairs. In his own words, he was 'by the Grace of God and the approval of the Sabor [parliament], Ban of Croatia and Dalmatia, and master of Bosnia'.[10]

Ban Pavao's reign over Croatia came to an end when he overreached himself. In Rome, Pope Clement V encouraged him to attack Venetian-held Zadar, and he died in 1312 during an unsuccessful assault on the city. His death ended the Šubić family's supremacy in southern Croatia: Šibenik and Trogir joined Venice in a coalition against Pavao's son and heir, Ban Mladen, and the worsening fighting gave Charles Robert an opportunity to re-establish the control of the Hungarian crown over Croatia. The King moved into Dalmatia at the head of a large army and after summoning a *sabor* in Knin, forced the Ban to return with him to Hungary. But the King's initiative in Croatia brought only short-term results. The Croat nobles banded together against royal authority and, as the crown and the nobles struggled for control, Venice took advantage of the situation to add Šibenik and Trogir to its Dalmatian possessions in 1322. It then seized Split in 1327 and Nin in 1329.

The next attempt to assert royal control over Dalmatia was left to Charles Robert's son, Louis I (1342–82), who led an army to the seat of noble resistance in Knin and enforced the surrender of the castle. Louis missed an opportunity to recapture Zadar as well in 1342, when the city revolted against Venetian rule, but fifteen years later the King's power was such as to persuade Venice to relinquish its possessions in Dalmatia voluntarily. Dubrovnik, a nominal possession of Venice, also switched allegiances, although it retained its self-government.

In contrast to ruined Biograd or ravaged Zadar, Dubrovnik enjoyed a steady growth in prosperity, thanks to the diplomatic dexterity of its merchant rulers as well as their trading skills. Since its foundation in the seventh century, the city had been attacked seriously only once, by the Normans in 1071. Occasionally it was besieged by Bosnian or Serbian warlords who descended from the hinterland, but for the most part Dubrovnik successfully played Bosnians, Croats, Venetians and – later – the Ottomans off each other, periodically ceding sovereignty to one or other of the powers that encircled it without ever surrendering self-government or the right to conduct its own foreign policy.

Dubrovnik was never large. At its highpoint in the late Middle Ages the population is thought not to have exceeded about 7,000. Nominally Byzantine for the first half-millennium of its existence, from 1205 to 1358 the city accepted the sovereignty of Venice, and a Venetian count was the local head of state. Although the city was never a Venetian colony, the government of Dubrovnik was modelled on the Venetian pattern. Power was vested in two councils, the Grand Council and the Minor Council, which elected the Senate; the equivalent of the doge, the rector (*knez*) had pomp but little power. Until the thirteenth century the people had some role in government, granting popular assent to laws at open-air assemblies. After that the popular element was excluded and it became increasingly difficult to become ennobled – the prerequisite for membership of the Grand Council.

The population of Dubrovnik was predominantly though not exclusively Slav by the tenth or eleventh century, though a local Latin-based dialect survived until the sixteenth century – one of two Latin dialects in Dalmatia that survived the coming of the Slavs.[11] There were also Greeks, Albanians, Catalans and Jews in Dubrovnik, though not many Italians. The inhabitants of medieval Dubrovnik had no political ties with Hungary–Croatia before 1358 and are unlikely in the Middle Ages to have felt attracted to an ethnic connection with Croatia. In fact they made every effort to keep their relationship with Hungary–Croatia on a tenuous basis. This is highlighted by the oaths of allegiance which the city enforced on new citizens. Until 1358, would-be citizens of Dubrovnik made an oath of allegiance not only to the city but to Venice as well. However, after the connection with Venice was severed and references to that republic were deleted from the oaths, no reference to the kingdom of Hungary–Croatia was put in its place. In other words, Dubrovnik used its change of allegiance to maximise its independence, and not to forge closer links with the Croats.

While the other cities of Dalmatia suffered from the almost constant tug-of-war between Venice and Hungary–Croatia, Dubrovnik grew rich undisturbed, exploiting its position on the crossroads between the West and the half-barbarous but mineral-rich kingdoms of Bosnia and Serbia, as well as its position between Europe and the Levant. In the fourteenth century the mining industry expanded in Serbia, and much of Serbia's copper, iron, lead and silver was exported to Italy through Dubrovnik. Bosnia joined in this lucrative trade. The Venetians also had an eye on this growth industry but were reluctant to set foot in the wilderness of Bosnia or Serbia, as the few travellers who ventured in usually brought back horrible accounts of violence and robbery. Instead the Venetian merchants turned to their colleagues in Dubrovnik, who had more experience of this virtually uncharted territory.

Croatia at the end of the fifteenth century

Those few Venetians who journeyed into Bosnia and Serbia themselves used Dubrovnik as a staging post. One surviving account concerns Giacomo Grimani, a Venetian merchant of some substance with business contacts in the Levant, who stopped in Dubrovnik on his way to sell King Tvrtko of Bosnia a precious diamond in 1390. After demanding several thousand ducats for his jewel, Grimani was forced to settle for 400. The affair ended in acrimony, after Grimani demanded payment in cash and King Tvrtko offered only a consignment of lead which the merchant had no use for. His honour impugned, the King angrily returned the diamond to Dubrovnik and no more is heard.[12] The rustic monarchs of the Balkan hinterland were clearly fascinated by Dubrovnik and its sophisticated citizenry. In 1350 Stefan Dušan, the ruler of Serbia who had proclaimed himself tsar after expanding his realm, visited the city.

While Dubrovnik prospered, the fortunes of the Dalmatian cities to the north declined. The death of Louis I in 1382 ended the revival of royal authority. The King had no male heir and the attempt of his daughter Maria to share the crown with Charles of Durazzo triggered revolts. After Charles was murdered in Buda, a long struggle developed for the crown. The election of Sigismund of Luxembourg (1395–1447) failed to unite the factions; in 1396 a group of Croat nobles rebelled against him and declared instead for the son of the murdered Charles, Ladislas of Naples. Sigismund retaliated by inviting the Croat rebels to a parliament in northern Croatia. It became known as the 'bloody assembly of Križevci' after he then had the Ban and his nephews murdered.[13] The bloodshed failed to quell the Croat revolt. Instead, Hrvoje Vukčić Hrvatinić, a supporter of Ladislas, seized most of southern Croatia, enabling Ladislas to have himself crowned at Zadar in 1403. Sigismund, however, remained in control of Hungary, Slavonia and Bosnia, following a successful military campaign in 1408.

In his desperation for funds, Ladislas then sold his rights to Zadar and its surroundings to Venice for 100,000 ducats. That which Venice had fought for so often, it now received on a plate for a paltry fee. This time the gain was more permanent, for a quarter of a century of anarchy had reduced the Dalmatians' will, or ability, to resist the Venetians. The *bans* and assemblies of Croatia–Dalmatia continued to count the Dalmatian cities as part of their jurisdiction, but it was an empty claim. Between 1409 and 1420 Venice consolidated control over Zadar and then over the entire coastline from Zadar to Dubrovnik, and remained in control of the region until 1797. For the Croats it was a disaster. The sale of Dalmatia opened a breach that was to last for centuries. Even when Dalmatia and Slavonia were reunited under the Habsburgs in the nineteenth century, they were not permitted to unite into one administrative territory. Reunion had to wait until 1939, and the formation of the autonomous Croatian *banovina* in royal Yugoslavia.

3

The Ramparts of Christendom

*Today, before lunch and not having had any breakfast, seated at our
assembly, all of us ... did elect, accept, determine and proclaim and send
word to the streets, that the aforementioned most illustrious Lord
Ferdinand should be true, lawful, unchallenged and natural king and master
of this whole glorious kingdom of Croatia.*

Diet of Cetingrad, New Year's Day, 1527[1]

A more determined foe than the Mongols appeared in the form of the
Ottoman Turks. In the 1280s Osman I, a minor Turkic ruler, established a state in north-west Anatolia around the city of Bursa. From this
stronghold, his descendants carried on a campaign of territorial expansion that was to consume the Byzantine Empire within a century and a
half, give the Ottomans control over the entire Balkan peninsula and
bring their armies to the gates of Vienna. By the mid-fourteenth
century, the Ottomans already had a toe-hold in Europe, around
Gallipoli. From there they subdued the Bulgarians and encircled
Constantinople from the west, as well as the east. The strategic city of
Adrianople, west of Constantinople, fell in 1361 and was soon proclaimed the Ottoman capital, illustrating the importance that they
attached to their conquests in Europe.

From Adrianople, Sultan Murat I began the conquest of Serbia.
Under the Nemanja dynasty, which had united the Serbian lands in the
1160s, Serbia had expanded to the point where King Dušan (1331–56)
controlled most of the Balkan peninsula between the Danube and the
Aegean. Dušan gave himself the title of tsar and in 1345 elevated the
head of the Serbian Church, the Archbishop of Peć, to the status of
patriarch, as it took a patriarch to crown an emperor. The Serbian
Empire was short-lived, however, and scarcely outlasted Dušan's
death. Under his son, Uroš V, the tsardom dissolved into a patchwork of
petty lordships. Uroš was driven from the throne in 1366 and, after his
death in 1371, the royal house of Nemanja died out. Serbia by then was
so divided that the most important Serbian princely ruler, Lazar, did not
even claim the title of tsar but remained a mere *knez*. As in Croatia in the

1090s, the extinction of the native dynasty gave powerful neighbours the chance to invade. From the west, King Tvrtko of Bosnia claimed the throne of Serbia for himself. But the most serious threat came from the east. By 1386 Ottoman armies had overrun southern Macedonia and reached the city of Niš, north of Kosovo. Lazar attempted, too late, to reunite the Serbian factions against a common enemy. On 28 June 1389, Vidov Dan – St Vitus' Day – Lazar's army encountered Murat's invaders on the undulating plain of Kosovo Polje. The Serbs were not alone, and counted a substantial number of Bosnians, Bulgars, Croats, Wallachians and Albanians in their ranks. In the battle that followed, Murat was killed along with Lazar. But the result was an Ottoman victory, which sounded the death knell of the Serbian state.

A much reduced Serbian principality survived the Battle of Kosovo by several decades by paying tribute to the Ottomans, and was extinguished only by the fall of the fortress at Smederevo, near Belgrade, in 1459. But after 1389 it was clear it would only be a matter of time before Serbia eventually succumbed.

The defeat of the Serbs at Kosovo Polje opened the way to the rest of the Balkans and allowed the Ottomans to transfer their attention to Serbia's western neighbour, Bosnia. This was an easier challenge. Remote and sparsely inhabited, Bosnia was a kingdom divided against itself owing to the unresolved tripartite struggle for supremacy between Catholics, followers of the Bosnian Church and Serb Orthodox. The partial return of many Bosnians to Catholicism through the efforts of Franciscan missionaries in the mid-fourteenth century, and the annexation of Catholic land in Dalmatia in the late fourteenth century, boosted the Catholic element in Bosnia. But Bosnia remained a country weakened by religious incoherence. In the south-east and east, along the River Drina, much of the population was Serb Orthodox. In the north and north-west and in the valleys of central Bosnia, where the Franciscans had concentrated their efforts, Catholicism was the dominant faith. In parts of the centre, at the core of the old Bosnian state, were the depleted remnants of the Bosnian Church. It used to be believed that disappointed followers of the Bosnian Church who resented forced conversion to Catholicism opened the gates of Bosnia's fortresses to the invading Muslims. It is more likely that Bosnia collapsed in the 1450s and 1460s because it was poor, underpopulated and divided into virtually independent fiefdoms.

The Bosnians did not long outlast the fall of Constantinople in 1453. The capture of the Byzantine capital released more troops for the Ottomans' Balkan campaigns. Vrhbosna, later renamed Sarajevo, fell in 1451. The rest succumbed almost without a fight in 1462–3. *Saptom pade Bosna*, it was said (Bosnia fell in a whisper). One by one the towns opened their gates to the advancing Turks, forcing the wretched King,

Stjepan Tomašević (1461–3), to flee from one redoubt to another. After Jajce surrendered, the King took refuge in Ključ; from there he was dragged back to Jajce, on a promise he would not be harmed. Notwithstanding his pledge, Sultan Muhammed II had the King beheaded in his tent, outside Jajce. It was not quite the end of Christian Bosnia. In the 1460s the energetic King of Hungary–Croatia, Mathias I Corvinus (1458–90), turned back the tide and reoccupied large parts of northern and central Bosnia, including Jajce. In spite of this, the Ottomans continued to stream into Bosnia and Croatia as well, provoking desperate appeals from the Croat nobles for foreign support. Mathias Corvinus resented the Frankopan Lord of Krk's request for Venetian support against the Turks and confiscated the Frankopans' prize possession – the town of Senj. Fearing that the King planned to confiscate the island of Krk as well, the Frankopans surrendered it to Venice in 1480.

Many Christians in Bosnia converted to Islam over the course of several generations. But many others refused, and emigrated from Bosnia to Croatia. Among the refugees were hundreds of minor nobles, who brought to Croatia little but their titles. Many settled in the Turopolje district, south of Zagreb, where they formed a highly distinct community with their own political privileges until the mid-nineteenth century. The most enterprising Catholic refugees fled further afield, to Italy and beyond. Take the career of the humanist Juraj Dragišić. Born in Srebrenica in eastern Bosnia in 1445, his family fled when he was a small child and took refuge in a Franciscan monastery in Dubrovnik. Dragišić entered the order, studying in Rome, Padua, Paris and Oxford. He spent most of his life in Florence, where he was close to the Medici family, acting as tutor to Piero, son of Lorenzo the Magnificent. Returning to Dubrovnik in the 1490s, he was later appointed Bishop of Cagli in Umbria in 1507. His literary output was considerable, and included works in defence of Savonarola and of humanism in opposition to the German Dominicans. In one of the last controversies of his life (he died in 1520) he strongly opposed moves to suppress Jewish books that refuted the claims of Christianity.

After the fall of Bulgaria, Serbia and Bosnia, it was the turn of Hungary and Croatia. As in Serbia and Bosnia, the final, decisive onslaught was preceded by tentative raids, designed to soften up the enemy. The crucial encounter for the Croats took place in 1493 at the Krbavsko Polje, in the hilly moorland of Lika, south-west of Zagreb. The result, as in the Battle of Kosovo, was a rout. The leaders of several hundred of Croatia's noble families were killed, wiping out the country's leadership at a stroke. The way was now open for the Turks to penetrate the rest. A year after Krbavsko Polje, the Turks captured Ilok, a strategic fortress in eastern Slavonia. By 1500 they had taken the Dalmatian port of Makarska. From 1503 to 1512 an uneasy peace held between the Turks on one side and the Hungarians and Croats on the other. But it was only a breathing space while the Ottomans regrouped. After the accession of Sultan Selim in 1512, they launched new offensives. In 1513 the Ottomans overran the town of Modruš, an episcopal see in Lika. By this time the lines of defence of the Hungarians and Croats were shot to pieces, and towns fell in rapid succession. Modruš was followed by Doboj, Tuzla and Bijeljina, the three principal Croat and Hungarian outposts in the north of Bosnia. The Bishop of Modruš, Šimon Kozičić, described the atmosphere of despair in contemporary Croatia to the bishops of the Lateran Council, recalling how he had been 'often forced, while celebrating divine offices, to discard ecclesiastical garments, take weapons, run to the city gates and ... incite the scared population to heroically resist the bloody enemy'.[2]

The ecclesiastical and civil authorities in Zagreb were acutely aware that their city was also threatened and set to work surrounding the cathedral with high walls and towers. Work began under Bishop Osvald Thuz (1466–99), who was given a new home in the Kaptol by King Mathias after his old residence in Čazma, in western Slavonia, became too close to the Ottoman frontline. Osvald's work was followed up by his successor, Luka Baratin, who used the legacy of 10,000 florins left by Osvald to continue work on the new fortifications. In 1510 the Bishop had to apply to Pope Julian II for permission to demolish the Church of St Emerika, which lay in the path of the proposed west-facing defences, in front of the cathedral. The Bishop told Rome of the urgent need to put up the fortifications, as the cathedral lay 'near the land of the Turks who attack these regions with frequent incursions. It is to be feared that the church, if not secured by the erection of good defences, could in a short time be destroyed by the attacks of the said Turks.'[3] The work of building a ring of towers was extremely dangerous, as the nearest Ottoman forces were only a few miles south of Zagreb on the southern bank of the River Sava. While the building was in progress the canons paid a scout, Šimun Horvat, to spy on the Ottoman positions south of the river. However, the Turks held off during the vital period of construction and the work was virtually finished by 1520. The battlements gave Zagreb cathedral the appearance of a fortified castle as much as a church of God, an appearance it retained until the disastrous modernisation of the cathedral district at the end of the nineteenth century; the towers were equipped with guns and cannons that remained ready for use until the early eighteenth century, when they were removed finally to a museum.

The Croats did not accept the conquest of the country with resignation. Several notable nobles and ecclesiastics held up the Turkish advance for a while and earned the admiration of Christendom for their valour. In 1519 Pope Leo X described Croatia as *Antemurale Christianitatis* – the ramparts, or bulwark, of Christendom. Petar Berislavić, who was both bishop of Zagreb and *ban*, stemmed the tide of the Turkish advance with particular effect by uniting Croatia's quarrelsome noble families in defence of the realm. Although the Turks were checked by such charismatic figures as Berislavić, they were never pushed back. Each hard-earned victory left the Croats exhausted and more vulnerable to the next assault.

Ban Berislavić's death in 1520 in battle with the Turks at Vražja mountain, near Korenica, coincided with the accession of the greatest of the Ottoman sultans. Suleyman the Magnificent, and from the first year of Suleyman's reign the Croats endured one defeat after another. In 1521 the crucial Hungarian fortress on the Danube at Belgrade fell. One year later the Ottomans took another highly strategic town, the old royal seat of Knin, which held the pass from northern Croatia to Dalmatia. Although still subjects of the King of Hungary, most Croats had given up hope of receiving military aid from Hungarians after the death of Mathias Corvinus in 1490. He had proved an able defender of Hungary's frontiers against the Turks, but the Hungarian nobles resented his attempts to build up the crown and on his death elected the pliant Ladislas of Bohemia as king. Under Ladislas, who died in 1516, and his son, Louis II Jagellion (1516–26), the powers of the crown evaporated and the aristocracy gained almost total control over the affairs of state. One consequence was a marked deterioration in the status of the peasants. Lacking royal protection, the system of *robota* (forced labour) on noble estates became more burdensome and the peasants were reduced to the status of chattels of the nobles, a development that diminished their interest in defending the country from the Turks.

As Hungary crumbled from within, the Croat nobles pondered transferring their loyalty to the Habsburg emperors. After the fall of Knin, delegations of Croat and Hungarian nobles attended the Imperial Diets at Worms and Nuremberg in 1521 and 1522 in search of men. At the Diet of Nuremberg, Bernardin Frankopan, the leader of the Croat delegation, made a personal appeal to the Emperor Charles V, reminding him that the Pope had only recently referred to Croatia as the bulwark of Christendom. 'Think how much evil will happen to the Christian world if Croatia should fall,' he urged. The Diet offered to raise and fund troops to defend Croatia's exposed southern flank, partly because the Estates of Inner Austria were becoming increasingly worried about their own defences if Croatia should fall. But the Croats were not the only item, or even the main one, on the Imperial Diet's agenda. Charles V was preoccupied with dividing his empire between the Spanish and Austrian branches of the Habsburg family and with the storm stirred up by Martin Luther. At Worms in 1521 Luther was placed under an imperial ban and the Emperor was more interested in suppressing heresy in his dominions than in bolstering the King of Hungary's neglected Croatian subjects.

The Ottoman invasion of Croatia was no ordinary war of conquest. It was not like the *Pacta Conventa* of 1102, when the country had exchanged one dynasty for another. It entailed the almost complete destruction of civilised life, the burning of towns, villages and their churches and monasteries, the murder of the leading citizens, the mass flight of the peasants, the laying waste of the countryside and the enslavement of thousands of those who failed to flee in time. The terror aroused by the Turks induced many petty Balkan princes to sue for peace, in the hope of salvaging something by accepting Turkish over-lordship. The Croat and Hungarian nobles were not immune to the temptation of dealing with the Turks. Some acted out of plain fear, others out of suspicions about the Habsburgs' motives.

But the Hungarian crown did not sue for peace and so the Ottoman juggernaut rolled on. The consequences were frightful for ordinary people. In 1501, officials in Venetian-ruled Zadar reported that about 10,000 people in the countryside around the city had simply disap-peared, presumably dragged off into slavery, during the course of three big Turkish raids. In 1522 the Renaissance poet and scholar of Split, Marko Marulić (1450–1524), author of the first epic on a secular theme in Croatian, *Judith*, gave this graphic account of the miserable air of uncertainty in the Dalmatian cities. In a letter to Pope Hadrian VI he wrote: 'They harass us incessantly, killing some and leading others into slavery. Our goods are pillaged, our cattle led off, our villages and set-tlements are burned. Our Dalmatian cities are not yet besieged or attacked due to some, I know not what, alleged peace treaty. But only the cities are spared and all else is open to rapine and pillage.'[4]

Dubrovnik escaped this fate by conceding nominal sovereignty, though not real independence, to the Sultan, paying an annual tribute. Lying on the southern tip of Dalmatia, the city's merchant princes had sensed the danger that the Ottomans presented early on. They had tried without much success to rouse the rest of Europe to throw back the Turks before they advanced too far. In 1441 the city sent an appeal to the Pope and the King of Hungary urging them to combine to stop the Turks in their tracks. The appeal did not go unanswered and in 1442 Pope Eugene IV urged all the Christian powers to collect ships for an expedition to the Straits of Constantinople to save the city from collapse and prevent the free flow of Turkish armies across the Bosphorus into Europe.

Surviving records throw light on the way that the crusade was organised in Dubrovnik. A committee consisting of three procurators was appointed by the Senate to meet with a papal representative twice daily for the purpose of collecting money at a point near the Rector's palace. There were two keys to the cash box, one in the control of the city's representatives and the other in the hands of the Pope's representative. In October 1443, the authorities gave out alms to the poor with instructions that they should pray for victory over the Turks, and in December of that year the city organised three days of religious processions to give thanks for the victories of the Hungarian King over the Turks at battles near Niš and Sofia. In 1444 the money collected in Dubrovnik for the expedition was handed over to a papal legate, and the ships supplied by Venice and the Duke of Burgundy arrived in the harbour. Unfortunately it was all wasted effort. At Varna, on 10 November, the Turks gained a crushing victory over the Hungarians and the hope of stopping the Turkish advance into Europe was dashed. The expeditionary fleet trailed back to Dubrovnik, its mission unaccomplished. It was the failure of the last papal crusade that made Dubrovnik rethink its allegiance to Hungary–Croatia. Hitherto, the city had banked on the Christian powers co-ordinating their efforts to halt the Turkish advance. From then on Dubrovnik pragmatically accepted Ottoman domination over south-east Europe and marshalled its efforts towards preserving its independence under Ottoman protection.

The Croats had made their stand at Krbavsko Polje in 1493. The turn of the Hungarians came in August 1526 when the news reached Buda of a large Turkish army moving northwards towards Hungary. The reports triggered fresh appeals to the Habsburgs and the papacy for aid, but there was no answer. Although Queen Maria of Hungary was the sister of Charles V's younger bother, Archduke Ferdinand of Austria, Ferdinand himself seems not to have been unduly concerned about the fate of his brother-in-law. The Pope's treasury was empty.

The Ottomans had waited longer than they needed. After the capture of Belgrade in 1521, they could have marched north immediately, as there was little to stop them on the flat plains north of the Danube. Instead they turned back. After the fall of Belgrade, the Hungarians did nothing to shore up their tottering defences. Conventional wisdom is that Louis II would have done best to fall back with his small army on Buda. Instead he raced south to meet the Ottomans on an exposed plain at Mohacs, in southern Hungary. Suleyman crossed the River Drava on 21 August with a force of at least 50,000 men. The result was annihilation. Louis II had mustered only about 20,000 Hungarians. A small supporting army of 6,000 Croats on horseback – among them the bishops of Zagreb, Senj and Djakovo – and 3,000 infantry failed to arrive. The fighting was over within one hour. The King perished: it was believed by drowning in a stream.

The outcome of Mohacs held great significance for the future of Central Europe. The Battle of Kosovo had opened up the Balkans to the

Ottomans; Mohacs opened the road to the heart of the continent. Within a week the Sultan was in Buda.

Hungary was then torn by civil war. On one side was an anti-Habsburg faction, led by Janos Zapolya, an ambitious Transylvanian nobleman who was prepared to become the Sultan's vassal in order to prevent foreigners from taking the throne. On the other side were the supporters of the Archduke Ferdinand, backed by the Queen Maria.

Ferdinand had no problem in confirming his rights to Louis' Bohemian kingdom, where he was elected king by an assembly in Prague in October 1526. But the feud in Hungary was not so easily solved, even after he was elected king of Hungary in Pressburg on 17 December. In the east, Zapolya held a rival coronation. The struggle between the Habsburg and Zapolya factions enabled the Ottomans to consolidate their hold over most of Hungary. The Habsburgs were left in control of a sliver of land in the west and in the north, in the territory that comprises modern Slovakia.

The rout at Mohacs was a momentous event for the Croats. The joint kingdom established in 1102 was ended. The Croats were without a ruler. A few days after Ferdinand's coronation in Pressburg the Sabor assembled at Cetingrad, near Bihać, to elect him as king of Croatia. Most Croats backed the Habsburg candidate, although they were determined to make use of the choice to reaffirm Croatia's privileges and its status as a kingdom.

On New Year's Day 1527 the Sabor met at the Church of the Visitation of St Mary in the Monastery of the Transfiguration under the presidency of the Bishop of Knin and the heads of the Zrinski and Frankopan families.

Following final negotiations with three Habsburg plenipotentiaries, they elected Ferdinand as king of Croatia. The Sabor made it clear to Ferdinand that they had elected him in the hope of gaining more military aid against the Ottomans – 'taking into account the many favours, the support and comfort which, among the many Christian rulers, only his devoted royal majesty graciously bestowed upon us, and the kingdom of Croatia, defending us from the savage Turks ...'. The ceremony closed with a Te Deum and 'a tumultuous ringing of bells'.[5] The document of allegiance was sealed with the red-and-white coat of arms of Croatia, which marks the first known occasion on which the chequerboard symbol was used as Croatia's emblem.

The Sabor of Slavonia, which was dominated by Hungarian magnates, did not share the Croats' enthusiasm for the Habsburgs. In 1505 it had pledged never to accept another foreign (non-Hungarian) prince, and supported Zapolya.

Krsto Frankopan, the brother of Bernardin, emerged as a powerful supporter of Zapolya in Slavonia and joined him in flirting with the

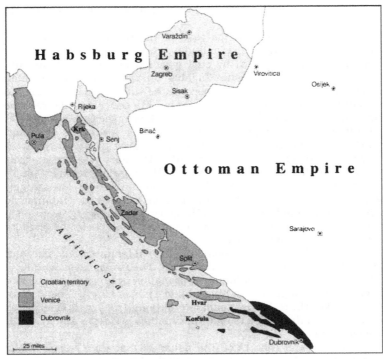

Croatia at the end of the sixteenth century

Turks, although he was killed in the early days of the civil war. Simon Erdody, the Bishop of Zagreb, was another pillar of the pro-Zapolya faction, laying siege to his own diocesan capital in 1529 and burning the outlying hamlets. A force loyal to Ferdinand raised the siege of Zagreb, destroyed the Kaptol, and extinguished this threat to the Habsburg claim. In 1533 a joint session of the Sabors of Slavonia and Croatia–Dalmatia confirmed Ferdinand's title to all the Croat lands.

Croat hopes of recovering large tracts of the country with the aid of the Habsburgs were disappointed. As an election sweetener, before the assembly in Cetingrad, Ferdinand had promised to pay for 1,000 cavalry and 1,200 infantry to defend the Croatian border, while the Estates of Inner Austria, Carinthia, Carniola and Styria voted money to supply garrisons in the frontline cities of Bihać, Senj, Krupa and Jajce in Bosnia. But this investment was insufficient to keep the Ottomans at bay. The Habsburgs' pockets were not deep enough, and the complicated arrangement of their possessions, in which there were many estates with overlapping jurisdictions, made it difficult to harness their resources. Instead, there were stop-gap measures and half-built castles, manned by soldiers who often were not paid for years on end.

The results on the ground were depressing. From 1527 to the 1590s the Croats continued to lose territory. In 1527 the Ottomans overran Udbina, in Lika. In the same year the last Christian-held fortress in central Bosnia, at Jajce, also collapsed. By the end of the 1530s, the Turks had mopped up the last spots of resistance on the southern bank of the River Sava in northern Bosnia, and had advanced through Slavonia as far west as Našice and Požega. In Dalmatia, the Turks conquered most of the land that was not occupied already by Venice. Obrovac fell in 1527 and in 1537 the fortress of Klis, the last Croat stronghold south of the Velebit mountains, succumbed. In the 1540s the pace of the Ottomans' advance in Slavonia was equally relentless, as they pushed westwards as far as the line between Virovitica, Čazma and Sisak.

During the next three decades they continued their advance through the north-west of Bosnia in the direction of the Habsburg garrison town of Karlovac, south-west of Zagreb. The biggest disaster of the period was the loss of the royal free city of Bihać in 1592. The town was razed and the inhabitants – those who were not killed – fled. The loss of Bihać to Croatia was permanent. The city was rebuilt and revived as a Muslim city surrounded by Serb Orthodox peasants. The fall of Bihać was almost followed by the loss of Sisak, which was attacked in 1593 by an Ottoman force under Hasan Predojević, the Pasha of Bosnia. Had Sisak crumbled, the way would have been open to Zagreb. The threat threw the Sabor into panic and a hastily recruited force of about 5,000 professional soldiers under the Ban, Thomas Erdody, was despatched to the town. The Ottomans were too confident. The Croats, made fearless by terror of the consequences of failure, took the initiative and fell on the Turks with ferocity. This rare and surprising victory was not followed up. An attempt to recapture neighbouring Petrinja, where the Ottomans had erected a fortress, was not successful. Nevertheless, the Ottomans had reached their high-water mark in Croatia by the end of the 1590s, leaving a strip of territory around Zagreb, Karlovac and Varaždin under the control of the Sabor and the Habsburgs.

The Habsburgs called the string of garrisoned castles they maintained in Croatia the Military Frontier – Vojna Krajina in Croatian. It was not a piece of territory but simply a series of forts manned by German mercenaries who were backed up by local troops. At first, most of these local soldiers were Croat refugees who had fled north from Dalmatia or trekked out of the interior of Bosnia, ahead of the Ottoman advance. The soldiers manning these garrisoned forts became known as frontiersmen – *graničari* in Croatian.

A decade after Ferdinand established his rule in Croatia the first changes in the Military Frontier's organisation were made, with the appointment of the first captain general of the Krajina, Nicholas Jurišić. In 1553 there were other important changes. The Krajina was placed under a single military commander who was made virtually independent of the *ban* and Sabor, with whom he had only to co-operate, not defer to. In 1578, the finances of the Frontier were remodelled with the establishment in Graz of the Hofkriegsrat, or Court War Chancellery. For Croatia's future, one of the most important decisions of the era was the decision to found a new garrison town south-west of Zagreb, called Karlstadt or, in Croatian, Karlovac. The new town was built on marshy land and appears to have had difficulty in recruiting anyone to come and live in it. The royal charter of the city in 1581 made clear that all settlers were welcome, offering citizenship to all comers, 'whether of German, Hungarian, Croatian or any other nationality'.[6]

The first military commander of the Krajina, Hans Ungnad, an Austrian from Carniola, was not a great success. An assault on Varaždin was held off in 1553, thanks to the efforts of Ban Nicholas Zrinski, who died in heroic circumstances in battle in 1566 while defending the fortress of Szeged in southern Hungary against the aged Sultan Suleyman, who also died there. But in 1556 the town of Kostajnica, an important border town on the banks of the River Una, was lost to the Ottomans. After this loss Ungnad was dismissed. There may have been other reasons for his removal, as he was a Lutheran and he left afterwards for the Lutheran bastion of Wittenberg. Ungnad had complained that the problem was not his ability as a commander but the shortage of resources. The complaint recurred with depressing regularity. A myth grew up about the Krajina of garrison towns manned by fearless, seasoned fighters. The reality was a series of dilapidated fortresses that held off the Ottomans mainly because the Ottomans themselves had become inert. In the 1570s there were only about 3,000 soldiers in the whole of the Krajina, which goes some way towards explaining why towns continued to fall with such alarming frequency. The situation on the Frontier, which was always ramshackle, got worse after the death of the Emperor Maximilian in 1576, for his successor, Rudolf, was uninterested in government and let matters slide while he pursued his own interests in the mysteries of magic in Prague. A report in 1577 recorded a lamentable state of affairs in the garrisons of Senj, Bihać, Varaždin and Koprivnica. But that was nothing compared to the appalling state of affairs in 1615, when a horrified visitor to Karlovac described the guns as having rusted away, the powder wet and the soldiers half-starved scavengers wandering around the tatty fortress half naked.

Changes in the administration of the Krajina in the last half of the sixteenth century caused profound disquiet in the Sabor. The Croats had elected the Habsburgs as their king in the hope of military aid against the Ottomans. What they got was almost a separate state within their shrunken borders, which was run with little reference to Croat institutions. But there was little the Sabor could do about these royal intrusions except protest with growing frequency their right to control Croatia's internal affairs. Their protests counted for little. The Habsburgs were keen to continue the development of the Krajina from a string of forts into a territory, which really acted as a kind of laboratory for absolutism. The only weapon in the hands of an assembly like the Croatian Sabor was money, or rather the ability to withhold it. But here the Sabor was on shaky ground, for Croatia's revenues were too small to count for much and the defence of the Krajina was paid for by the Estates of Inner Austria, not by the Sabor.

What began as a political dispute between the Sabor and the Habsburgs over the Krajina then assumed additional ethnic and religious overtones, as the Krajina was settled on the invitation of the Habsburgs with Vlachs, or Morlachs as they were also known, most of whom belonged to the Serbian Orthodox Church although a minority were Catholic.

The debate over the origin of the Orthodox settlers in the Krajina is highly contentious. Serb scholars have usually insisted that the Orthodox Vlachs were ethnic Serbs, in order to boost the claim that the Krajina should be attached to a Serbian state. Croat scholars have insisted with equal vehemence that the Orthodox Vlachs began to identify themselves as Serbs in the nineteenth century under the pressure of the Serbian Orthodox Church. The debate is somewhat anachronistic as these national categories had little relevance in the feudal or early modern era to peasants and shepherds. It would probably be fair to say that, whether or not the Vlachs originally migrated from Serbia, they did not identify as Serbs until the last century.

The precise route by which the Vlachs reached Croatia is obscure. It would appear that they were pastoral, nomadic people who lived in the mountains of the Dalmatian interior and in Bosnia. They were darker skinned than the Croats, hence the name Morlach, from Maurus, Latin for black. One Croat theory is that they were the inhabitants of Dalmatia before the arrival of the Slavs, having been settled there as legionaries by the Romans. According to this idea, they were pushed out of the lowlands by the Slavs, and forced to retreat to inaccessible mountainous territory, from where they returned after the Croats fled their villages ahead of the Ottoman invasion.

The arrival of the Orthodox settlers in the Krajina in the sixteenth century added a new note of religious conflict to Croatia's internal affairs, though the question of religion was only a part of the Sabor's grievances. In order to attract settlers into Croatia's war-wasted borderlands the Habsburgs exempted the incomers from the feudal system.

There were no serfs, merely soldiers who were expected to spend their lives in military service in exchange for their liberty. This greatly disturbed the Sabor, which was an assembly of estates, representing nobles, bishops and deputies from the royal boroughs. Many of them, like the Bishop of Zagreb, held great estates and owned thousands of serfs. In the tiny patch of Croatia that had remained free of Ottoman rule, the Croat noble class consolidated the harsh feudal system that had spread in from Hungary. What the Sabor found objectionable in the administration of the Krajina was not just the intrusion of the Orthodox Church but the free status of the peasants who lived there. The mere fact that they existed was a temptation to the down-trodden serfs on their estates. The nobles' concern about the existence of the free peasants of the Krajina dovetailed with the advance of the Counter-Reformation, whose great champion in Croatia was Juraj Drašković, Bishop of Zagreb and Ban of Croatia. Drašković believed sincerely in the revival of Catholicism in Croatia and founded the country's first seminary in Zagreb. But he also believed with equal sincerity in maintaining the full rigours of the feudal system and took a leading part in crushing a desperate rebellion by the serfs in 1573 led by Matija Gubec, which the Bishop terminated by arresting Gubec and crowning him with molten iron for his impertinence.

4

'The Remains of the Remains'

*We live in the shadow of the Turkish sword and can survive only if we buy
our lives with lots of money.*

Jeronim Lukić, Catholic Bishop of Bosnia, in 1640[1]

There are no monuments to the Ottoman presence in Croatia today.
The mosques of Slavonia were demolished after the Austrians drove the
Turks from Croatia in the 1690s. Yet the Ottoman impact on Croatia
was immense, scarcely less than the impact of the Turks on the other
southern Balkan nations, the Serbs, Albanians, Greeks and Bulgars. For
the best part of two centuries, most of Slavonia and Dalmatia was under
Turkish rule. For the Croats, Ottoman rule was an unmitigated disaster
with no redeeming characteristics. To the east, the Serbs lost their state
and their independence. But the Orthodox Church, to which they
belonged, enjoyed the erratic and occasionally enthusiastic patronage
of the sultans, enabling the Orthodox hierarchy to remain an active
force within the Ottoman Empire under the *millet* system.[2] The Serbs
were fortunate in the sixteenth century, owing to the rise to power of
Mehmed Sokollu, born Sokolović. Born to an Orthodox Serb family in
the town of Višegrad, he was rounded up in a levy by the Turks, like
many Christian children of the period, and taken to Istanbul for conversion and education and placed inside the Ottoman administration.
At the end of his ascent up the ladder he became grand vizier to the
Sultan, in effect the prime minister of the Ottoman Empire. Although he
embraced Islam, Sokollu remembered his home town and his Serb
Orthodox roots. He endowed Višegrad with the bridge immortalised by
Ivo Andrić's book *Bridge over the River Drina*[3] and brought about the
restoration of the Serb Orthodox Church. The Orthodox bishoprics had
survived the Ottoman invasion, but in reduced circumstances. Peć, the
seat of the patriarchs of the Serbian Church, in Kosovo, had been made
subordinate to the archbishops of Ohrid. In 1557 Sokollu used his
immense powers as grand vizier to restore the patriarchate and ensure
the election of his relative Makarije as the first new patriarch. Other
relatives got first pickings of the sees. The Church took advantage of its

new and improved position to build a great many churches and monasteries, not just in the old Serb heartland, but in the more recent Ottoman acquisitions in Bosnia and Slavonia. One famous surviving example is the so-called Old Serbian church in Sarajevo, which was built around 1530.

The Croats and their Church were not so lucky. The sultans remembered the failed papal crusade of 1443 and looked on the Pope as a dangerous temporal foe. The Catholic clergy, in consequence, suffered from the fact that they were regarded as emissaries of a foreign, hostile power. The oldest and most prestigious Franciscan monasteries in central Bosnia gained a written charter of toleration from the Sultan. But this applied only to a few individual buildings. Outside central Bosnia the Catholic Church was virtually a catacomb Church, especially in the 1520s and again in the 1590s, when persecution of Catholics raged most intensely.

The inability of Catholic bishops to function publicly in Ottoman-ruled Bosnia put them at a great disadvantage to the Orthodox. The Catholics were not allowed to build new churches and had great difficulty in gaining permission to repair the structures they had already. When there were legal disputes over the possession of Church property between Catholics and Orthodox, the Ottoman authorities usually favoured the Orthodox.[4] Many more Catholics than Orthodox emigrated from Bosnia for religious reasons, reducing the proportion of Catholics in the country. Large areas of Bosnia lost their entire Catholic population through a combination of war and emigration. In eastern Bosnia, where Catholicism had always been weak, Catholicism virtually died out. Two examples were the towns of Olovo and Srebrenica, in eastern Bosnia. Olovo had once boasted a popular Marian shrine, while Srebrenica had harboured a substantial Catholic monastery. Yet by the nineteenth century the population of both towns was Muslim or Serb. In north-west Bosnia the change was just as startling. Towns such as Glamoč had certainly been Catholic in the Middle Ages, and in the Ottoman era north-west Bosnia was still known as Turkish Croatia. But the Catholic population almost vanished between the sixteenth and the nineteenth century, by which time the towns were overwhelmingly Muslim and the surrounding villages Serb Orthodox. The consensus of the reports of the few Western travellers who journeyed through Bosnia in the Ottoman era is that the Catholics were still the most numerous religious group in Bosnia in the sixteenth century but that they were less numerous than either the Orthodox or the Muslims by the eighteenth.

This change in religious affiliation, away from Catholicism and towards Islam and Serb Orthodoxy, was most marked in Bosnia. But it affected the parts of Dalmatia and Slavonia that were ruled by the

Ottomans as well. In Slavonia the towns of Ilok, Vukovar and Osijek, for example, became Muslim market towns, while many Serb Orthodox settled in central Slavonia. Often these Serb immigrants built their churches and monasteries on the sites of ruined Catholic buildings.[5]

The Orthodox settlers in Slavonia lived the same kind of village-based farming existence as the few Croats who remained after the Turkish invasion. They were, in fact, very similar people divided only by their religious affiliation. In Slavonia, the Catholic remnant complained that entire villages were converting to Orthodoxy in the hope of better treatment, especially in Srijem region, where, along with central Slavonia, the Serbs had settled in large numbers.[6]

The Orthodox settlers in Dalmatia – the Vlachs – were more primitive, and their nomadic lifestyle inspired a fair amount of revulsion among the sophisticated inhabitants of the Dalmatian cities. A Venetian official in Dalmatia in 1553 wrote in horrified tones that the Vlachs were 'more feral than human. They live near the roads and rob and kill travellers, and despoil them and they think it praiseworthy to live by robbery'. He added: 'They are people of the Serbian and heretical faith and are subjects of the Turk. They are coarse and dirty and live together with their animals, constantly.'[7]

So much for the Venetians. Some of the local Croats were also hostile to the Vlachs, especially Catholic refugees from Dalmatia and Bosnia who fled west and north into Habsburg territory from the 1520s onwards. Many of these refugees settled in the town of Senj, a sheltered port on the Adriatic lying just to the north of Dalmatia, and took up a life of piracy. They became known as Uskoks. The pirates of Senj regularly raided Vlach settlements in Turkish-held Lika, and as the purpose cannot have been plunder, because these villages were very poor, it seems clear that the aim was to drive out the new settlers, or take them captive to sell as slaves. There are reports of Vlachs being sold off in the market place of Split in this period by Croat pirates, and the practice appears to have been widespread.

The refugees' real hatred, however, was reserved for the Turks who had driven them from their land. Some Vlachs even joined the pirates of Senj, undergoing a pretty perfunctory rebaptism into the Catholic religion.[8] So did a number of Muslim Slavs, drawn no doubt by the prospect of a life of adventure at sea rather than by the prospect of allegiance to the Church of Rome. Throughout the last three-quarters of the sixteenth century the Uskoks roamed the Adriatic, raiding Ottoman vessels. The Turks could do little about it. Senj was a well-protected town hugging a sheltered cove and shielded from the rear by the steep Velebit mountains. The Habsburgs did not at first stop the Uskoks plundering the Turks, and appreciated their fervent support for the dynasty.

But from the mid-sixteenth century Uskok affairs became entangled with Venice, and this was the cause of their eventual downfall. The Venetians were increasingly interested in pursuing a policy of detente with the Ottomans and came to look on the Uskoks as pests who were ruining their new policy of peace and trade with the Turks.

The Venetians took to inflicting ferocious punishments on any Uskoks who fell into their hands. The Uskoks in turn began to attack Venetian ships as well as those of the Turks, which they justified on the ground that Venice's friendship with the Turks rendered them a legitimate target. In spite of Venice's protests, the Habsburgs continued to turn a blind eye, even when the Uskoks excelled themselves in 1597 by landing in the Turkish-held fortress of Klis – from which many of their ancestors had fled – and hoisting the Habsburg standard over the town. The Uskoks' courageous, if foolhardy, assault on Klis aroused fury in Venice, which encouraged the Turks to smash the revolt. This the Turks proceeded to do, killing the Bishop of Senj in the battle to retake the town.

The Venetians blockaded Senj in order to starve the town into capitulation. The Uskoks continued to taunt the Venetians with their escapades. Shortly after the battle in Klis several hundred Uskoks sailed into the Venetian-held port of Rovinj, in Istria, where they raided the ships in the harbour and took hostages. The expedition then carried on to the nearby port of Pula, where the Uskoks danced in the main square. But, as Venice tightened the blockade of Senj in the 1590s, the Uksoks were left with less room for manoeuvre. The Habsburgs ceased to take an interest in their welfare as the threat from the Ottoman Empire appeared to decline, and in 1615, after a short war between Venice and the Habsburg Empire over the Uskoks, the Habsburgs agreed to disperse the famous pirates' nest for good. As a result, most of them were deported from Senj and forced to resettle in villages around Karlovac and Otočac, in the Krajina.

The Uskoks were poor people, peasant refugees who lashed out against their tormentors in the only way they knew. On the Venetian-ruled islands of the Adriatic, however, educated noblemen and clergy were pondering a different strategy. They were only too aware of the fact that Croatia had once stretched from the Adriatic to the Drina, and that their Slav kingdom had been reduced and divided between the Habsburgs, Venice and the Ottoman Empire. The common conclusion they drew was that Croatia had been too small to defy its powerful neighbours and that the way ahead was for Croats to ally with their Slav brothers, most of whom were no better off than they were.

The clergy played a vital role in disseminating this new and all-embracing Slav consciousness. As members of an international Church, they had more opportunities to travel abroad, study and compare situations than most laymen, and it is significant that although they were Catholic priests they were remarkably unprejudiced in their dealings with their supposedly 'schismatic' brethren, be they Serbs or Russians.

A landmark was the public lecture delivered in 1525 by Vinko Pribojević, a Dominican friar who had spent three years in Poland. His lecture in the main square of his native town of Hvar dwelt on the origins of the Slavs. Taking issue with the diminished status of the Croats in his own time, Pribojević insisted that most of the famous personalities of classical and more recent history were in fact Slavs, including Aristotle, Alexander the Great, Diocletian and a phalanx of Roman emperors and popes.

Pribojević's lecture caused a stir well beyond the confines of the island of Hvar, and other Dalmatian writers in the sixteenth and seventeenth centuries echoed the theme, including the Benedictine abbot, Mavro Orbini. His book, *The Kingdom of the Slavs (Il Regno degli Slavi)*, in 1601, was the first attempt to provide a comprehensive written survey of all the Slav nations. Designed to demonstrate the essential unity of the Slav peoples and their collective greatness, it had a lasting effect on the Balkan Slavs' historic consciousness. Another leading clerical visionary was Bartol Kašić, a Jesuit from the island of Pag, who was encouraged by his superiors in Rome to compile a Croatian grammar. As a Dalmatian, Kašić might have been expected to employ the local *čakavian* dialect of the Dalmatian coast. Instead he chose the *štokavian* dialect of Bosnia out of a conviction that it was more comprehensible to a far greater number of Balkan Slavs than his own tongue.[9]

The message of these writers and propagandists was that although Croatia's heritage had been annihilated in the lands ruled by the Ottomans, and suppressed in the portion of Dalmatia ruled by Venice, Croatians remained part of an enormous Slavic brotherhood which had the potential to dwarf their oppressors. The great baroque poet of Dubrovnik, Ivan Gundulić (1589–1638), drew courage from the knowledge that the Slav nation stretched from Dubrovnik to the Baltic Sea. Gundulić took immense pride in the fact that his home city of Dubrovnik had remained free from both Venice and the Sultan (for all its annual tributary). In his epic poem *Osman* he wrote:

> A greater part of the Hungarian kingdom
> And the whole kingdom of Bosnia
> And the land that Herceg ruled over
> Have been subjugated by Ottoman power
> And thus it really happened
> Dubrovnik still stands free
> With its old crown its promise kept
> Between the lion and the dragon ...

But Dubrovnik, though 'the crown of all Croatian cities', as Ivan Vidali, the poet from the island of Korčula, wrote in 1564, was very small. The chief object of Gundulić's veneration in *Osman* was Poland, which was then a vast state at the height of its powers, and *Osman* takes the form of a celebration of the Polish victory over the Turks at Chocim in 1621, which the author heralded as the beginning of the end for the Ottoman Empire. The authorities in Dubrovnik were not so sure. Wary of offending the Ottomans – their nominal overlords – they ensured that *Osman* remained unpublished until the nineteenth century, although copies were made by hand and circulated.

These apostles of pan-Slav consciousness on Hvar, Korčula and in Dubrovnik were all very much children of the Renaissance culture which entered Dalmatia through the Venetian occupation and as a result of the Croatian gentry on the islands sending their sons to universities in Italy. The results were seen at the end of the fifteenth century with the first secular plays and comedies in the Slav language. They were for the most part members of the caste of Slav patrician noble families, which felt displaced from power in the Dalmatian cities by the imported Venetian aristocracy. Some were strongly influenced by the Jesuits, who took a keen interest in schemes to unify the various Slav languages to render them more easily penetrable by Catholicism. And although they were highly conscious of being Slavs, they hankered for a more specific identity. They found it in the Renaissance term for the land of the southern Slavs – Illyria. At the same time they began to term the vernacular tongue in which they penned their poems and plays 'Illyrian'. They did not call themselves Croats very often, although there *was* much nostalgia for the old Hungaro-Croat kingdom, largely because Croatia by the sixteenth and seventeenth centuries had really come to be seen purely in terms of the shrunken Habsburg territory around Zagreb, which was called the kingdom of Croatia.

In Gundulić's lifetime the great hope of the Slav dreamers was Poland. But, as Poland's powers ebbed, Russia stood out in greater contrast as the only powerful and independent Slav state. That it was far away made it all the more attractive. The Illyrian intellectuals were not put off by the fact that Russia was Orthodox. The most remarkable of these Croatian Russophile pioneers was Juraj Križanić (1618–83), a Catholic priest from the region of Karlova. Križanić began his research into the Orthodox faith in Rome. But his interest in Orthodoxy soon took him to Moscow, which he regarded as the promised land, even though the xenophobic Tsar Alexis exiled him to Siberia for fifteen years. This bizarre and unwarranted punishment did not put Križanić off, and he used his years in the Siberian wastes to continue his writings and develop the theme of the need for Slav solidarity. In fact, Križanić admired the Russians' xenophobia, seeing it as a necessary defence mechanism against pushy, arrogant foreigners. Unlike Gundulić, he was no admirer of the Catholic Poles, precisely because they had given away their throne to foreigners. 'The Poles have been called pigs and dogs by some of their queens,' he lamented. 'There are no rulers of Slavic origin anywhere except here in Russia.'[10]

Križanić worked on a theme that was expanded by many Slavophile thinkers in the nineteenth century, namely that Slavs could be subdivided into six groups, Russians, Poles, Czechs, Serbs, Croats and Bulgars. The point, however, was not to play on the differences but to realise their common origin. If only that could be achieved, the Slavs would cease to be 'the laughing stock of all peoples, among whom we alone are cruelly offended'.[11] Križanić believed in the destiny of the Russian Tsar to become the focal point around which the various Slav nations ought to unite. 'The entire Slavic nation looks to you,' he told Tsar Alexis. 'As a father, please take care of and bring together your dispersed children. ... if you cannot, Oh Tsar, in these difficult times make possible their victory and help them to reestablish their ancient kingdoms, at least correct the Slavic language books ... so they start to respect their own honour.'[12] It was fitting that he died in battle against the hated Ottomans, in the ranks of the Polish soldiers fighting to lift the Turkish siege of Vienna in 1683.

Križanić was one of those Croatian intellectuals of the Baroque era who travelled abroad in search of enlightenment. Others left their afflicted homeland with baser motives, such as Marco Dominis, the Archbishop of Split, who defected to the Anglican Church in 1614, moved, so malicious contemporaries reported, by rumours of the generosity shown by King James I towards his Protestant clergy.

The arrival of such a high-ranking prelate, albeit from an impoverished see, caused a great stir in England and titillated the King. By 1617 it was reported that the Archbishop was in great favour in Lambeth and that the bishops had assigned him an income of £600 a year. In the same year, he had printed an apologia for his conversion to Protestantism.[13] It is strange that this slender volume did not awaken the seeds of suspicion about the Croatian Archbishop's motives in such a committed Calvinist as Archbishop George Abbott of Canterbury, for the book says scarcely a word about those Protestant doctrines concerning the Mass and justification by faith alone that formed the kernel of the faith of the Anglican Church. The failure of the Croatian prelate to obtain the preferment in England he had been denied by Rome soon caused him to think again, and to the embarrassment of his English hosts he preached a sermon which appeared to back papal claims in 1622, and which led to his banishment on pain of death. Hastening to Rome, where he hoped his errors would be forgiven, he was surprised to find the Roman authorities unimpressed by his published description of the curia as a body run by 'torturers, cut-throates and bloodie mur-therers'.[14] He was imprisoned and conveniently died, and his body was burned as a lapsed heretic.

Many Croats left their homeland for the West during the Ottoman era in search of inspiration or material gain. Few Westerners travelled in the opposite direction. One of the handful of Englishmen to penetrate Croatia and Bosnia in the mid-seventeenth century and record his impressions was Henry Blount, who wrote a book on his travels in the Balkans in 1636.[15] Blount was disappointingly terse in his account of Croatia, remarking only that in Split, 'the Venetians allow the Turke to take the custome of the merchandize', and that at Salona there was 'not so much as ruine left, excepting a poor piece of Diocletian's aqueduct'.[16] He was not impressed with Sarajevo, which was 'meanely built and not great, reckoning about four score Meskeetoes [mosques] and thwentie thousand houses', although he was struck by the Bosnians themselves, 'vast and almost giant-sized ... which made me suppose them for the off-spring of those old Germans noted by Caesar and Tacitus for their huge size'.[17]

What is striking in Blount's book is the strong impression he leaves of mutual intolerance between the Catholic and Orthodox communities. Whatever the Illyrian visionaries believed on their islands in the Adriatic about the creation of a big Slavic brotherhood, there was clearly little sign of it on the ground. According to Blount, the two com-munities in Bosnia were 'so desperate malicious towards one another, as each loves the Turke better than they doe either of the other'. He went on: 'The hatred of the Greek Church for the Romish was the loss of Belgrado [Belgrade] in Hungary and is so implacable as he who in any Christian warre upon the Turke should expect the least good wish from the Christians in those parts would finde himselfe utterly deceived.' Blount not only pinpointed the fierce antagonism between Catholics and Orthodox on a local level. He also made some acute observations on the way that the Ottomans had whittled away the Catholic Church in their dominions:

> The Turke takes a more pernicious way to extinguish Christianitie than ever the heathen emperours did. ... the Turke puts none to death for reli-gion ... hee rather suckes the purse than unprofitable bloode and by perpetuall poverty renders them low towards himselfe. Hee turnes the Christian churches into Meskeetoes, much suppressing the publik exer-cise of religion, especially of the Romish, so that ... many who profess themselves Christians scarce know what they mean by being so ...[18]

Although Blount appears not to have come across them, other contem-porary visitors to Bosnia commented on the unusal phenomenon of converts to Islam who maintained a vestigial connection with the Catholic Church. Known as *poturice*, they were reported to observe saints' days, visit shrines and read the gospels. 'In this kingdom', one sixteenth-century visitor wrote, 'there is another kind of people called Potur who are neither Christians nor Turks: they are circumcised but are taken to be the worst [believers].'[19] An episcopal report of the same period claimed: 'Many grown up infidels seek baptism and believe in Christ but are afraid to confess this publicly.'[20]

The Poturs were a fascinating example of the compromises people had to strike under Ottoman rule between their private convictions and the external pressure to convert to Islam. For all the Ottoman's much vaunted tolerance of other monotheistic faiths, adopting the faith of the ruling class was the only passport to social acceptability and any kind of position in the government administration. Of course these pressures lessened outside the towns. In large parts of north-west Bosnia and Turkish-occupied Dalmatia there were no towns of any size. Here the Catholic Church died out or was reduced in size simply through the immigration of Serbs and Vlachs, who appear to have spread across Bosnia in large numbers after the Ottoman invasion.

In the shrunken kingdom of Croatia ruled by the Habsburgs it was not Islam but the rising numbers of Serb Orthodox immigrants which continued to agitate the Sabor in the seventeenth century. In the last decade of the sixteenth century, several thousand Orthodox settlers moved into the region of Petrinja, which lay just inside the Habsburg frontier, and were offered by Ferdinand II a charter confirming their rights. Others moved right into the heart of Habsburg-ruled Croatia, erecting a monastery in 1609 at Marcsa, a village near Čazma, for example.

The conflict between Vienna and the Sabor over this immigration became more heated in the 1600s, as the Sabor twisted and turned in its efforts to recover control over the governance of the Krajina. In 1608 the Sabor made an unprecedented demand for the withdrawal of Austrian officers, only to be met with vigorous opposition from the Commander of the Frontier, General Khisl. 'Instead of bothering the Emperor and the Archduke with their unjustfied complaints, they ought to thank God the Vlachs have formed an outer bastion,' he wrote.[21] The Emperor was not impressed with the Sabor's demands either, remarking that what lay behind them was the desire of the Croat nobles to turn the Frontier settlers into serfs. They wished to 'work the Vlachs as cruelly as the Hungarians work the peasants on their estates,' he remarked.[22] The Sabor returned to the fray in 1620 with a bolder demand for the suppression of the Krajina altogether and the incorporation of the land into the territory controlled by the Ban and the Sabor. The Vlachs retorted with a petition of their own in 1627, in which they told the Emperor they would be 'hacked into pieces rather than be placed under the bishop of Agram or any other Croatian noble'.[23] Again the Emperor Ferdinand II (1618–57) sided with the Vlachs rather than the Croat nobles and in 1630 he confirmed the settlers' rights in a landmark document, the *Statuta Valachorum* (Statute of Vlachs). The act marked an enormous advance in the status of the Orthodox settlers, granting them a large degree of internal self-government and permission to elect their own spiritual leaders and temporal judges, called *knezovi*, as well as their own captains, called *vojvode*. The *Statuta Valachorum* struck a heavy blow against the Sabor's hopes of recovering control over the Krajina and of extending the feudal system to include the settlers. As it was unable to undo the Emperor's expression of support for Vlach rights, the Sabor resorted to a policy of containment, with the aim of ensuring that the privileges granted to the older generation of Orthodox settlers would not be extended to more recent Orthodox immigrants from the Ottoman Empire.

The dispute between Emperor and Sabor over the Krajina was one reason why relations between the Habsburgs and the Croats deteriorated in the seventeenth century. Another was disappointment over the Habsburgs' failure to recover any territory from the Turks. In the mid-sixteenth century it was enough for the Habsburgs to hang on to the *Reliquiae reliquiarum*, the remains of the remains of Croatia, about which the Sabor was wont to lament. But by the 1600s the power of the Turks was visibly waning and the great Croat noble families, the Frankopans and Zrinskis, were becoming impatient with the Emperor's unwillingness to push the Ottomans back. This discontent came to a head in the 1660s, after the Emperor Leopold (1657–1705) defeated the Ottomans at Szentgotthard in 1664, only to sign a peace treaty awarding them another small slice of Hungarian territory. This strange act convinced many Croats and Hungarians that the Emperor had done this deliberately, out of a fear that his noble Croat and Hungarian subjects would withdraw their allegiance to him if their ancestral lands were liberated from Ottoman rule.

The 'Conspiracy of Nobles' was, therefore, a joint enterprise of disaffected Croat and Hungarian grandees. But the ringleader was Nikola Zrinski (1620–64), poet, warrior and Ban of Croatia. The untimely death of Nikola in a hunting accident in November 1664 deprived the conspiracy of a leader, though his place was quickly filled by his brother, Petar (1621–71), and his brother-in-law, Krsto Frankopan, who proceeded to hawk the crown of Hungary–Croatia in secret around the courts of Europe. In Venice Zrinski's wife, Katarina, *née* Frankopan, held talks with an episcopal emissary of Louis XIV. It was in vain. The Sun King was just dallying. The King of Poland also shied away from this dubious prize. In desperation the conspirators turned to their mortal enemy, the Sultan, and Zrinski's emissary, Franjo Bukovački, hurried to Istanbul, where he was informed that the Sultan's answer would be relayed by the Pasha of Bosnia. As suspicions about the plot began to leak out in February and March the Ban dithered, frantically assuring the Emperor of his loyalty and at the same time preparing his officers for a rising. On 18 March he took the plunge and issued a proclamation urging the Croats to rebel. The rising was a complete failure, although interestingly the rebels wooed on to their side the Orthodox Bishop of Marcsa, a sign that relations between the Catholics and Orthodox in Croatia were not always as antagonistic as they sometimes appeared. However, the citizens of Zagreb did not join the revolt, nor did the Emperor's faithful *graničari*. The Ban and his brother-in-law then hastened to Vienna in April, insisting that they had never seriously planned an alliance with the Turks, but the Emperor was in no mood for clemency and Zrinski and Frankopan were beheaded at Wiener Neustadt on 30 April 1671. Zrinski's wife, Katarina, was incarcerated in a convent in Graz, where she died in 1673.

The execution was a seminal event, as it destroyed the power of the great feudal families who had exercised so powerful a hold over Croatia since the early Middle Ages. For centuries these two great dynasties had been like regional monarchies. In the 1670s this was swept away, for not only were the two aristocrats executed but their vast properties were confiscated and the lands distributed to foreigners, many of them Germans and Hungarians. The result was that the landowning class in Croatia became more or less foreign, and far less interested in acting as spokesmen for the historic rights and privileges of the kingdom. Without its great lords, Croatia was rendered more easily subjugated by the Austrians and, later on, by the Hungarians.

5

From Liberation to the French Revolution

The wheel of fortune circling around
Does not stop in its revolutions
Who was up is turned down
And who was down is lifted up.

Gundulić, *Osman*[1]

The long rule of the Turks over most of Croatia came to a sudden end in the 1680s. Responsibility for the conflict fell squarely on the Turks. In 1683 the Sultan's Grand Vizier, Kara Mustafa, decided to revive the tradition of conquest of the previous century. Marching an army of 200,000 soldiers out of Bosnia he made straight for Vienna, arriving outside the city on 17 July. What Suleyman the Magnificent had not achieved in 1529, Kara Mustafa hoped to achieve in his own day. It was a miscalculation. At first it seemed as if the Turks might get their way, for the Viennese were unprepared for the assault. The fortifications erected around Vienna in the sixteenth century had fallen into decay, so much so that if Kara Mustafa had stormed the city without hesitation he might have claimed his prize. Instead, the Turks vacillated. Although the Emperor Leopold had fled to Bavaria, a garrison of about 10,000 fended off the besieging Turks for just over six weeks until the arrival of a relieving army of Poles, Bavarians, Saxons, Germans and Austrians under Jan III Sobieski, the King of Poland. The result was a rout, as definitive for the Turks as the Battle of Kosovo had been for the Serbs three centuries earlier, or the Battle of Mohacs for the Hungarians in 1526. The Polish King entered the city to the pealing of church bells and delirious cries of joy from the Viennese. The confused Turks reeled back to the fortress of Belgrade. There, in accordance with the grim traditions of the Ottoman Empire, the Grand Vizier paid the traditional price for presiding over the defeat and humiliation of the Sultan's forces with the death penalty.

The failure of the siege of Vienna in 1683 marked a great turning point in the history of Central Europe and the Balkans. From 1529 the threat of encirclement and occupation by the Turks had hung over

Vienna, posing a question mark over the very existence of the Habsburg Empire. After the siege collapsed, the legend of Ottoman invincibility was broken and an exaggerated fear of Ottoman strength gave way almost overnight to an equally exaggerated underestimation of the resources that still remained at the Sultan's disposal. Although the Ottomans kept much of their European empire until 1913, from 1683 the Turkish empire was saddled unfairly with a reputation as the Sick Man of Europe.

The thirty years following the siege of Vienna were, nevertheless, a disastrous time for the Turks. The frontiers of the Habsburg Empire expanded south and south-east with astonishing speed. Slavonia, most of which had been submerged under the Ottoman yoke for a century and a half, was liberated within a few years. In 1684 Virovitica in central Slavonia was freed. The next year it was the turn of Kostajnica on the northern, Croat bank of the Sava. Shortly after, the Austrians reached Derventa, on the southern, Bosnian bank of the river. In September 1686 Buda, seat of the Ottoman Pasha of Hungary, fell; the following year it was the turn of Osijek, in eastern Slavonia. A year later the Austrians were in Belgrade – the crucial fortress which Hungary had lost in 1521. In 1689 the Austrians penetrated deep into the heart of the Ottomans' European empire, reaching Niš, Skopje and Kosovo. The Turks rallied in 1690 but were unable to roll back all the Austrian conquests, and in 1697 Prince Eugene of Savoy delivered a crushing blow at Zenta, in southern Hungary, not far south of the site of the débâcle of Mohacs.

Finally despairing of a return to the highly favourable borders of 1664, the Ottomans sued for peace. In the Treaty of Sremski Karlovci of 1699 they resigned any claims to Hungary and Croatia, with the exception of the city of Bihać, which, although it had been part of the old Croatian kingdom, was left in Ottoman Bosnia. It was not the end of the frontier adjustments. Another round of fighting in 1716, again provoked by the Turks, led to a second great Austrian victory by Prince Eugene at Petrovaradin (Peterwardein). Two years later, in the Treaty of Požarevac, Austria gained a strip of territory in northern Bosnia on the southern bank of the Sava, the Banat and a portion of northern Serbia, including Belgrade.

But these gains were not permanent. With the death of Prince Eugene in 1736 Austria lost its exceptional commander and in the fighting from 1736 to 1739 the Ottomans recovered some of the territory they had lost and forced Austria to restore the border agreed at Sremski Karlovci. The frontier between the two empires then remained unchanged until the Austrians occupied Bosnia in 1878 and annexed it in 1908.

The wars in Slavonia, Srijem and Bosnia from 1683 to 1699 caused population shifts on a scale that would not be seen again until the Balkan wars of the 1990s. The entire Muslim population of Slavonia fled south into Bosnia. There are no precise records of how many Muslims were displaced, but one Croat historian estimates that the population of Slavonia in 1680 was about 210,000, of whom just under half were Muslim, the remainder including about 70,000 Catholics, 30,000 Orthodox.[2]

The void left by the Muslims was quickly filled. The first to return were Serb and Croat *starosjedioci* (old settlers) who had lived in Slavonia under the Turks but fled during the most intense years of fighting. The normal pattern was that Catholics returned to abandoned Catholic villages and Orthodox likewise. In this way the pattern of settlement under the Ottomans was restored. Thus the village of Pačetin, which had numbered about 100 Orthodox homes before it was destroyed in the 1680s, was resettled again by seventeen Orthodox families in 1697. It was the same story in the east Slavonian villages of Bršadin, Bobota and Trpinj, all of which were mainly Orthodox before the 1680s and which were again settled by Orthodox families in the 1690s.[3]

The old settlers were then boosted in numbers within a few years by immigrants. From Bosnia in the south came tens of thousands of Catholics, who had rallied to the Austrian cause when Habsburg armies penetrated Bosnia in 1689, and then retreated northwards with the Austrians when the Ottoman army returned. At the same time an enormous number of Serbs poured in from the south-east, from the heart of the old Serbian kingdom. The string of Turkish defeats in the 1680s had raised great hopes among the Austrians and among a section of the Serbs that the Turks might be expelled from the Balkan peninsula and the entire region placed under Habsburg sovereignty. The Austrians did their best to ignite an uprising by the Serbs, and issued a proclamation in 1689 urging all Serbs, Albanians and Bulgarians to rise against the Turks, with a guarantee that Serb religious rights would be respected in the event of a Habsburg victory.

The Austrians gained the support of the Serbian Patriarch in Peć, Arsenije Čarnojević, who toured Serbian districts making compromising declarations of support for the Austrian campaign. But the hoped-for Serbian revolt failed to materialise. In spite of valuable backing from the Patriarch, many Serbs were as suspicious of the Catholic chaplains who accompanied the Austrian armies as they were of Ottoman Muslims. They preferred the devil they knew. When the Ottomans rallied in 1690 and the Habsburg armies retreated north across the Danube, those Serbs who had supported Vienna found themselves in an invidious position. Tens of thousands of them streamed out of Kosovo and southern Serbia in a great exodus. The vast human column crossed the Danube in the autumn of 1690 and moved into the empty plains of southern Hungary. Patriarch Arsenije himself led an enormous column of about 30,000 families into Srijem and southern Hungary. The Emperor Leopold welcomed the influx of settlers into the semi-deserted landscape of Slavonia and published an edict in 1691, which was confirmed in 1695, giving the Serbs permission to remain in Hungary and to elect Orthodox bishops and civil representatives. At first this permission was a temporary device. But as it became clear that the Serbs neither wished nor were able to return to Kosovo, the provisions were made permanent. The Serbs made the eastern part of Srijem their own, and the rolling hills of Fruška Gora were soon dotted with the spires of new Orthodox monasteries – many of them unfortunately blown up in the Second World War by the Germans, the Ustashe or even the Partisans. After a period of being based in the village of Krušedol, the Serbian Church made its new seat in Sremski Karlovci in 1712; after the Turks had suppressed the Patriarchate in Peć entirely in 1745, placing the see under the Archbishop of Ohrid, Sremski Karlovci became the Serbs' cultural and ecclesiastical capital – a position it retained until the foundation of an independent Serbian principality in the nineteenth century.

The arrival of Croat and Serb immigrants did not complete the pattern of resettlement in Slavonia. In the mid-eighteenth century the Empress Maria Theresa settled other groups in the region, especially Germans, who it was thought would revive commercial enterprise in the towns. They soon formed a large proportion of the inhabitants in towns such as Osijek and Vukovar. But they also settled in the surrounding villages, and were followed by Hungarian, Slovak and Ruthene peasants. There were in addition small groups of Albanian Catholic refugees, some of whom settled in the village of Hrtkovci.[4] Along with the Jews, who settled mainly in the larger towns, they made eastern Slavonia one of the most ethnically diverse regions in Europe, a character it retained until the Serb seizure of eastern Slavonia in 1991, after which almost the entire non-Serb population was expelled, fled or was killed.

The settlement of Slavonia presented the Habsburgs with an enormous legal tangle over the question of property rights, the solution to which was delayed by continued warfare with Turkey until the 1740s. Although the authorities encouraged peasant immigration, they had no intention of creating a society composed purely of peasant freeholders. Most of the land was awarded, or sold, to foreign German or Hungarian aristocrats, further diluting the Slav element among the nobility of Croatia. Estates were also given to the Churches, both Catholic and Orthodox. As soon as the Austrians reconquered Slavonia, the see of Djakovo (with jurisdiction over Bosnia)[5] was revived and presented with land around the town. The ancient see of Srijem was also revived. However, the influx of Serbs into this region left the Catholics a small minority there, and with only six parishes to start with (later there were ten), no cathedral and no chapter, the see was ruled unviable and was amalgamated with Djakovo in the 1770s. The Orthodox were not left out of Habsburg largesse. The Serb metropolitan gained large estates around Sremski Karlovci in Srijem, and in 1706 around the village of Dalj, in eastern Slavonia.

What did not go to the Churches was distributed to the wealthy landlords and deserving generals from the wars of the 1680s. Prince Eugene of Savoy was rewarded for his exploits with an estate at Bilje in Baranja;[6] after his death it reverted to the crown, which then held it until 1918. The great Esterhazy family of Hungary also gained a large estate in Baranja, at Darda, which it held until the 1840s. Much of eastern Slavonia fell into the hands of four great families. Baron Peter Hillebrand-Prandau, from Bavaria (1676–1767), purchased the great estate of Valpovo in 1721 from the Emperor. Našice and Virovitica were bought in 1732 by Josip Pejačević, whose family had roots among the old Bosnian nobility but had since moved to Bulgaria and then to Hungary. Ilok went to the Odeschalchi family, princes of the Holy Roman Empire, as a reward for their services in defending Vienna from the Turks in the 1680s. The estate of Vukovar, including twenty-three villages and some 31,000 serfs, was bought in 1730 by Filip Karlo Eltz, Prince Bishop of Mainz, and remained in the hands of the Eltz family until the Second World War, when the family returned to Germany. After the fall of Communism in 1992 Count Jakob von Eltz returned to Croatia and was elected as deputy to Vukovar in the Croatian parliament.[7] In the mid-eighteenth century the Eltzs also obtained the hereditary honour of *veliki župan* (high sheriff) of Srijem. These great families rapidly changed the physical appearance of eastern Slavonia by building the enormous baroque and classical châteaux that were so striking a feature of Nuštar, Vukovar, Ilok, Valpovo and other towns, at least until the war ruined some of them in 1991.

The amount of building going on in Slavonia from the 1720s was colossal. In every town the nobility was flinging up mansions, parks and hunting lodges. The Church also invested an enormous amount in architecture; few Church buildings had survived Turkish rule – one of the handful of exceptions was the small romanesque parish church at Bapska. The Christians now did to the Turks what had been done to them – demolished all the mosques and erected their own houses of worship. Thus the Church of the Holy Cross in Osijek was built on the ruins of a mosque. Big towns like Osijek were ornamented with grand monasteries as well as churches. Then there was the army. With the Turks still in Belgrade it was always possible they would attempt to recapture fertile Slavonia. To insure against such an eventuality, the

Austrians in the 1720s began work on building the enormous squat fortress that still dominates the Old Town of Osijek.

Although the Habsburgs had at last redeemed their pledge to recover Slavonia from the Turks, the Croat Sabor was disappointed in two important respects. It still remembered that Dalmatia had been part of the kingdom of Croatia until the fifteenth century, and it was frustrated by the fact that Dalmatia remained in the hands of the Venetians, who expanded their territory in the peace treaty of 1699 to include the Dalmatian hinterland as far east as Knin.

Another matter was the unresolved dispute over the administration of the Krajina. The dispute between the Sabor and Vienna over the frontier had not abated since the *Statuta Valachorum* in 1630. The Sabor remained determined to gain jurisdiction over the whole of Slavonia; the Habsburgs were equally determined to uphold their direct rule over the Frontier without reference to the Croats. After war broke out with the Ottomans in 1683, the Croatian Ban, Nicholas Erdödy, had taken matters into his own hands in 1685 by leading an army south from Karlovac towards the banks of the River Una, on the southern border with Bosnia. This area, which became known as Banija (Ban's land), was then placed under the jurisdiction of the Sabor and the Ban.

Outside Banija, however, most of the the territory recovered from the Turks was joined to the Krajina, to the irritation of the Sabor. To some extent this was an organic development. Much of the fighting on the Habsburg–Ottoman frontier was carried out on an *ad hoc* basis by *graničari*, who were spurred on by the hope of occupying more fertile land. When they moved into a new area, the Krajina moved with them, for when they settled in the districts that had been vacated by the Ottomans they demanded the extension into the new territories of the customs that they had previously enjoyed.

The imperial edicts of 1691 and 1695 offering toleration to the Serb settlers in Srijem and Hungary were not hopeful signs for the Sabor. But when it demanded the abolition of the Varaždin Generalcy, on the ground that this military district in the Krajina had become superfluous, Leopold appeared to concede the point. In 1703 its dissolution was announced. However, the next year the Emperor changed his mind and the plan was dropped. The Sabor returned to the attack in 1714, when it went a step further and called for the abolition of the Krajina in its entirety. Each time the Sabor demanded the Frontier's suppression, the frontiersmen petitioned for their old status to be left untouched. In spite of the support that the Croat Sabor received from Catholic, clerical circles in Vienna, the emperors sided with the frontiersmen. In 1715 the Emperor reassured the Orthodox settlers that 'they will not be turned into peasants'.[8]

The tension between the Sabor and the frontiersmen spilled over into acts of racial and religious intolerance in the Varaždin district, where the Orthodox were in the minority and their bishopric and monastery at the village of Marcsa near Varaždin could be attacked with impunity. The Orthodox staged riots of their own near Varaždin and, in 1728, in the region of Lika. In 1735 there were fresh riots near Varaždin. The worsening conflict over the status of the Krajina inspired the government in Vienna to contemplate a thorough overhaul of the Frontier's government.

A commission under Joseph, Duke of Sacksen Hildburghausen, set to work in 1735 and came up with a list of reforms. They were designed to increase the number of soldiers that could be mobilised, end the unhealthy system of patronage under which the distribution of officers' positions in the Frontier had become a racket, and put down sectarian riots. On the financial side, the connection between the Hofkriegsrat in Graz and the Frontier was to be abolished and responsibility for the Frontier's financial management transferred entirely to Vienna. Inside the Frontier, Hildburghausen proposed draconian new punishments for *graničari* who disturbed the peace and alterations in military organisation to make it more efficient. The commission proposed to keep the Frontier as a vast barracks in which any other activity would be prohibited. There was to be no commercial activity to divert the locals' minds away from the army and no Jews were to be allowed in. Land was to be held strictly by the *graničari*; even the clergy were prohibited from purchasing land. The reforms were acceptable to the frontiersmen, who wanted above all to keep the Sabor and the feudal system at bay. But this ambitious plan of action was never carried out, owing to the start of the unsuccessful Austrian war with the Turks in 1737.

The conclusion of peace with the Turks in 1740 allowed the new Empress, Maria Theresa, to resume the work of reorganising and pacifying the Krajina and putting into effect some of Hildburghausen's recommendations. In 1743 the Hofkriegsrat in Graz was abolished and the business of the Frontier's finances placed under a new military directory, run by Hildburghausen in Vienna. At the same time, in 1745, the Sabor's irritation was soothed by the transfer of the counties of Virovitica and Požega from the Krajina to Civil Croatia, as the portion of Croatia under the control of the civilian authority of the Ban and Sabor was called. The patronage rights of the Inner Austrian Estates to officers' posts was also abolished. A new code of 1754 attempted to put into practice Hildburghausen's determination to keep the Frontier as a vast barracks in which there were no diversions from a life devoted to bearing arms. These flurries of activity on Vienna's behalf did not stop the Orthodox settlers from engaging in violent protests.

In 1754, when the new code for the Frontier was being announced, the Empress caved in to Catholic pressure to abolish the Serb Orthodox bishopric at Marcsa. The suppression of the bishopric triggered an explosion among the *graničari*, about 17,000 of whom marched on Marcsa and occupied the village. The rebels had no real idea what they wished to achieve. Throughout the past century or so, the combination had always been the Emperor plus *graničari* versus the Croatian Sabor. Defying the Empress came unnaturally and the rebels at Marcsa melted away. The following year the Serb bishopric at Marcsa was abolished and the parish given to the Catholic Piarist order.

The remaining years of Maria Theresa's reign, until 1780, saw no more large-scale riots. Inside the Frontier, the rules about keeping the entire region free from commerce began to fray at the edges, although Jews continued to be banned. In the 1750s market towns were set up on the Slavonian frontier, at Brod and Gradiška, and in the 1760s remaining restrictions on commercial activity, such as holding markets, were abolished in Bjelovar, Koprivnica, Gospić, Otočac, Ogulin and Kostajnica.

The reign of Maria Theresa also saw the creation of a *cordon sanitaire* in 1770 on the border of Croatia and north-west Bosnia, from which the region of Kordun received its name. Intended to prevent a feared eruption of plague, the *cordon* consisted of a chain of wooden observation towers manned by *graničari* whose duty was to stop and disinfect anyone, or anything, wishing to cross over from Ottoman territory. The system was quite efficient. Travellers were detained at the empire's frontier for a quarantine period of twenty-one days. Even money and letters were stopped for inspection and disinfected in vinegar baths.

Maria Theresa was more inclined to follow her Catholic conscience than her predecessor, hence the Sabor's success in achieving the suppression of the Orthodox bishopric at Marcsa. Her absolutist tendencies were less pleasing to the Sabor. In 1767 these found expression in the decision to set up the *Consilium Regium Croatiae*, a Croatian Royal Council, which comprised officials nominated by the crown. The Royal Council sat in Varaždin, the seat of the *ban* and *de facto* capital of Croatia from the 1750s until the 1770s, and took away more of the Sabor's competencies. That development was bad enough, but in 1779 the Council was incorporated into the Royal Hungarian Chancellery.

There was little that the Sabor could do to stop its functions from wasting away. It was a conservative body that reacted to events rather than initiating them. Its membership had scarcely altered since the Middle Ages, comprising the bishops, the Magyarised aristocracy, representatives of the Kaptol, the canonical foundation in Zagreb, burgesses from the Royal Free Towns of Zagreb, Varaždin and Rijeka and the peasant nobles of the Turopolje. The speeches and declarations were in Latin, which was the official language of Hungary. But this made its proceedings arcane and utterly incomprehensible to the great mass of the population. The Sabor saw its job in the narrowest of terms: to defend the rights of Croatia as they had been set down in the *Pacta Conventa* with Hungary in 1102, the Hungarian king's responsibilities having fallen to the Habsburgs after Ferdinand was elected king of Croatia at Cetingrad in 1527. The Sabor's work was limited to the formulation of addresses to the emperor and the election of representatives to sit in the Hungarian assembly. From the sixteenth century, the Sabor had sent three deputies to the lower house of the Hungarian parliament and one to the upper house. It had no role over the economy, taxation, foreign policy or any other issue that might have made its proceedings relevant to the masses.

The day-to-day conduct of government in Civil Croatia was the job not of the Sabor but of the county assemblies, headed by the *veliki župan* (high sheriff), nominated by Vienna. He was seconded by a deputy, the *podžupan*, who was elected by the assembly and shouldered most of the practical work. The throng of impoverished 'peasant nobles' did not play much of a role in the Sabor. They voted as a community for the County Assemblies and paid fewer taxes than the common people. Apart from that they lived the lives of peasants.

If commercial and urban life did not exist at all in the frontier, the situation was not very different in Civil Croatia – the result of almost endless warfare and an unfavourable geographical position on the outer periphery of the Austrian Empire. By the late eighteenth century Zagreb had been an episcopal see and a royal free city for nearly seven centuries. Yet the population was still only a tiny 2,800 or so. Varaždin, then the largest urban centre in Slavonia, boasted 4,800 inhabitants out of a combined population in Civil Croatia and the Frontier in 1785 of about 1.1 million. A report from 1799 said the population of the Frontier was as follows: in Karlovac Generalcy there were 182,733 inhabitants; in the Varaždin Generalcy, 101,902; in the Banija, 91,545. Catholics were the majority in Varaždin Generalcy by a 2:1 majority. Banija had a Serbian Orthodox majority while Karlovac Generalcy was fairly evenly mixed, Catholics predominating around Gospić and Otočac and Orthodox dominating the interior of Lika. By 1829 the pace of urban development had inched forward. Varaždin by then mustered about 7,800 inhabitants and Karlovac about 4,000. Zagreb had overtaken Varaždin with a population of about 8,000, though Osijek held the lead with just over 9,200.

The Croat urban population was even smaller than these figures suggest, for only Karlovac was inhabited more or less exclusively by Croats. In Zagreb and Osijek the urban merchant class was mostly German, while many of the nobles who built town houses to attend the Sabor and other social functions were Hungarian or German. The language on the street would have been as much German or Hungarian as

Croatian. There were no regular newspapers or theatres, merely visiting German-language theatre groups. Education made few strides in
eighteenth-century Croatia. At the end of the century there were about
six secondary schools in Civil Croatia and some 500 primary schools.
Zagreb had its academy – the former Jesuit college – where the language of instruction was Latin.

The pace of life in late eighteenth-century Croatia was slow, even by
the standards of the Austrian Empire. Yet the baroque churches that
adorned the villages of Slavonia (at least until the war of 1991), the
classical mansions of the Old Town in Zagreb and the baroque mansions of eastern Slavonia and the Zagorje region pay tribute to the quiet
prosperity of the upper classes during the long reign of Maria Theresa.
Social life in Croatia's small and somewhat provincial world revolved
around the small court of the *ban* and the households of the bishop of
Zagreb, the commander of the Military Frontier and the few great noble
families such as the Erdodys and the Draškovićs, whose enormous
mansion at Trakošćan became a symbol of the power and wealth of
Croatia's Habsburg aristocracy. There were no royal visits in the reign
of Maria Theresa; the problems with the *graničari* made the prospect too
dangerous, although the Bishop of Zagreb knocked down part of the
wall around the Kaptol to make room for a driveway – all in preparation
for a royal visit that never took place.

Zagreb had to wait until 1818 for a visit of several days' duration by
the Emperor and Empress, when in honour of the royal couple the town
was illuminated on the night of 28 June with thousands of candles,
some 8,500 being stuck on the town hall alone.

While Slavonia revived in the eighteenth century under the
Habsburgs, Dalmatia declined under the Venetians. Under the Treaty of
Karlovci in 1699, Ottoman possessions in Dalmatia passed to Venice
with the exception of a tiny stretch of coastline north of Dubrovnik, at
Neum, which remained in Turkish-ruled Bosnia.

The Venetians divided their possessions in Dalmatia into three administrative units – the islands, the coast and the interior, garrisoned by an
army of about 5,000, which was backed up by police. The total territory
contained   about   160,000–180,000   people,   of   whom   about
140,000–150,000 were Catholics and most of the rest Serb Orthodox.
The Venetians inherited little from the Turks that was economically useful and the only settlements of any importance in the new territories
were Knin, Sinj, Klis, Drniš and Skradin. On the coast, the once fine cities
of Dalmatia had long since vegetated under the impact of repeated warfare. The Venetians complained there were so few nobles left that it was
difficult to find enough people to fill posts on the municipal councils.

The downturn in Dalmatia's fortunes, which accelerated after
Venice's consolidation of the region, was not all the fault of the Most

Serene Republic. Austria's expansion southwards, especially between the Treaty of Požarevac in 1718 and the redrawing of the border in 1740, caused havoc to the old caravan trading routes that had once run uninterrupted across the vast Ottoman domains to Split and Dubrovnik, the two big entrepots on the Adriatic coast, where goods were loaded up for export to Italy and the West. In the sixteenth and seventeenth centuries, Turkish and Jewish merchants had dominated the port of Split. In fact the Jews had inspired so much envy that in 1683 the Venetian authorities passed a law forbidding resident Jewish merchants from employing Christian maidservants. The war ended all this. Fewer Turks came to Split; the caravan routes were sliced up by the new state borders, and goods from Austria's newly conquered Balkan domains sailed up the River Tisza to Central Europe and beyond. A second factor that was beyond the Venetians' competence was the destructive legacy of warfare. Parts of Dalmatia had been wrecked by the fighting that had lasted on and off from 1683 to 1718. When the Archbishop of Split, Stjepan Kupili (1702–20), conducted his first diocesan visitation, he lamented that outside the city there was not a single decent house standing.[9]

Most of Bosnia was ruined as well. When a Venetian emissary, Giovanni Pietro Marin, visited the Bosnian Pasha in Banja Luka early in the eighteenth century to sound out the possibility of resuming trade with the Ottoman Empire, he noted sadly that there were not many economic centres in Bosnia worth trading with. According to Marin, Sarajevo had the only lively market place in Bosnia. The rest of the country was deserted, given over to nomadic Morlach shepherds.[10]

But Venetian rule over Dalmatia was catastrophic in its own right as well. The verdict of one modern historian was that:

> the Venetians constructed absolutely nothing [in Dalmatia], neither public works nor the most primitive industry, nor schools, nor one single printing press. ... except for very primitive mills for grinding, pressing and tiling, there was no industry at all, neither tanneries, brick kilns, pottery works or smithies. All manufactured articles were imported. The only exports were oil, wine, figs, salt, fish, string, tallow and wool.[11]

The republic destroyed what was left of Dalmatia's native industries by the imposition of vicious colonial economics. Dalmatia was forced by law to import almost everything from Venice except wood and grapes. And the Dalmatian merchants had to export everything to Venice, with the exception of a few privileged individuals who were granted exemptions. The result was that Dalmatia's industry was reduced to the export of basic raw materials for whatever price Venice wished to pay for them. The main items were salt from the islands of Pag and Rab, olive oil from the other islands, horses, especially from Sinj, salted fish, animal furs (rabbits, martens and a few bears), dried grapes and fruit. There were a few half-hearted attempts to set up new 'industries', such as silk production, but they folded.

Confined to the sale of raw materials for knock-down prices, the once-prosperous Dalmatians were brought by Venice's rule to the brink of extinction. In 1749, a Venetian commission looking at the administration of Dalmatia was sufficiently horrified to warn that the population was 'decreasing every day with the evident danger that it will disappear completely'.[12]

In the latter half of the eighteenth century, Dalmatia was forced to import even agricultural products to keep the local population alive, draining precious supplies of money to Venice and Italy and worsening the province's trade deficit. By the 1780s the situation was catastrophic. At Obrovac in northern Dalmatia in 1780 people were close to starvation and eating grass and roots to survive.

The decay was compounded by a severe outbreak of plague a few years later in 1783. As the province deteriorated, Venice made faint efforts to counteract its own negative policies, freeing some towns, such as Split, from having to send all their exports to Venice and allowing local merchants to tout for business where they pleased. These concessions did not revive the region's economy, however. By the end of the century, Dalmatia had taken on the depressing aspect that it retained under Austrian rule – a desolate, emptied place of ruined, sun-baked towns inhabited by a malarial population reduced often to beggary.

For the most enterprising, the only solution was to emigrate. In 1780 the authorities reported that 4,765 people had packed up and emigrated from Zadar, Sinj, Imotski, Omiš and Skradin in the space of just a few months in summer. Some found new homes far away in the flat green pasturelands of the Austrian-ruled Banat, around Timišoara.

When the Venetians absorbed the lands of the Dalmatian hinterland around Knin in the 1690s, they found themselves in possession of a far more ethnically and confessionally mixed population than they had ruled over before. About 20 per cent of Dalmatia's total population was now Orthodox. The Morlachs grew more numerous the further one went inland from the coast, especially in northern Dalmatia. But they were also numerous near the coast in the region of Zadar, where, of about ninety-two settlements in the eighteenth century, thirty-nine were purely Catholic, seventeen purely Orthodox and the rest mixed. They were present in considerable numbers in Šibenik too. The Venetians, for the most part, regarded the Vlachs and Morlachs as little better than animals, because they slept with their livestock, knew nothing of the ways of the Italians and despised them into the bargain. The attitude of the Croats was more complex. Catholic and Orthodox

Vlachs lived intermingled in the interior. The impression of most Venetian and foreign visitors in eighteenth-century Dalmatia, however, was that the two communities regarded each other with a good deal of hatred.

To the urban Catholics of the coast, the Morlachs were uncivilised newcomers who had arrived on the coat-tails of the Turks and taken their villages. As for the Morlachs, they scorned the Italianised culture of the Croatian cities and prized fighting above work. A noted characteristic of the Morlach was the practice of sleeping with a gun under one's head. Their customs were shaped by their nomadic lifestyle, which did not bring them into any contact with urban, or even village, life. In the summer they worked hard with their flocks. But the greater part of the year was spent doing little except roaming, sitting around the hearth and holding riotous festivals at which prodigious amounts of drink were consumed. Not only did they not live in towns, they also avoided villages, preferring to live dotted around in isolated houses. Although they lived quite near the sea, they were not of it, shunning the Dalmatians' staple diet of fish and avoiding also veal – an antipathy that they learned from the Turks. The Venetians noted with surprise that the Morlachs also had a horror of eating frogs and would not even trade them, regarding any contact with this favourite Italian delicacy with superstitious terror. The Serbian Orthodox Church, to which many, though not all, Morlachs belonged, was a humble affair compared to its Catholic counterpart, and was treated as a second-class organisation by the Venetians. In the 1780s, there were about 2,400 Catholic clergy, another 800 men and women in monasteries and convents, headed by two archbishops in Split and Zadar and four bishops in Trogir, Šibenik, Skradin and Hvar. By contrast, there were only about 220 Orthodox clergy in Dalmatia and one bishop. In other words, there was a Catholic priest, monk or nun for every 50 or 60 Croats and an Orthodox priest or monk for every 180 or so Serbs.

An interesting portrait of the Venetian *ancien régime* in eighteenth-century Dalmatia comes from Alberto Fortis, whose *Travels into Dalmatia* published in London in 1778 provides a voluminous account of the region before the French Revolution. Fortis was most interested in geography, fossils and ancient ruins. In Split he was more agitated by an encounter with a peasant who was demolishing what was left of the Roman ruins of nearby Salona to build cottages than he was by political currents in the city itself. He came into his own with a long account of the Morlachs of the interior, who 'generally call themselves in their own idiom *vlassi* [Vlachs]'.[13] Although he commented on the hostility between Catholic and Orthodox Morlachs, or, as he called them, Latins and Greeks, Fortis detected a stronger antipathy between Morlachs of both confessions and the inhabitants of the coastal cities. 'The inhabitants of the maritime towns ... are no friends to the Morlacchi, who in return look upon them, as well as the inhabitants of the islands, with the greatest contempt,' he wrote.[14]

Fortis believed that the Morlachs' terrible reputation as uncivilised brigands was undeserved. He found them deeply hospitable and for the most part honest, although rough towards their women and superstitious. Wives were frequently beaten up on their wedding day, owing to a strange custom whereby the parents would denounce their daughter's bad qualities before presenting her to the bridegroom, upon which the groom would strike his bride a blow. Following marriage Morlach women usually slept on the floor; the husband got the bed, if there was one. Fortis also noted that when Morlach women went to confession, the priest often gave absolution with several blows of a cudgel. The Morlachs' belief in the supernatural was strong. 'Whether they are of the Roman or the Greek Church [they] ... are as firmly persuaded of the reality of witches, fairies, enchantments ... as if they had seen a thousand examples of them. Nor do they make the least doubt of the existence of vampires.'[15]

On the anniversary of a relative's death, the women would sing dirges beside the grave, asking the dead questions in verse form. People viewed as potential vampires had their ligaments torn when they died, so as to prevent them from rising from their coffins. There were other interesting burial customs. In some areas, quantities of honey were thrown into the coffin of the deceased. Fortis was fascinated by the same-sex unions he witnessed among the Morlachs, in which women would make oaths to each other in front of the church altar, after which they became *posestre* (half-sisters). 'I was present at the union of two women who were made posestre at the church in Perušić,' he noted. 'The satisfaction that sparkled in their eyes when the ceremony was performed gave a convincing proof that delicacy of sentiments is found in minds not formed, or rather not corrupted, by society.'[16]

6

'Still Croatia Has Not Fallen'

Na noge se dižte!　　　　　*Get up from your knees!*
Mač u ruke sada!　　　　　*Sword now in your hands!*
Tudjinstvo nek padne,　　　*May the foreigners fall,*
Slavjanstvo nek vlada!　　　*And Slavdom rule!*

Kukuljević, 'Slavjanke'[1]

The prosperous torpor into which Slavonia sank in the eighteenth century and the wretched torpor into which Dalmatia sank at the same time were ended by the whirlwind of reform unleashed by the Emperor Joseph II, and by the subsequent impact of the French Revolution. The programme of reforms of the Habsburg Emperor centred on curtailing the privileged position of the Catholic Church, allowing Protestants freedom of worship, abolishing feudalism, introducing a more equitable system of taxation and promoting German as the *lingua franca* throughout the empire. The reforms caused uproar in Hungary and Bohemia and aroused the indignation of the ecclesiastical hierarchy and the nobles everywhere.

The reforms predated Joseph's coronation, as he had been co-ruler of the empire since 1765; it was under his influence that the Jesuit order had been dissolved throughout the empire and the Jesuit school in Zagreb converted into an academy. But the storm broke only after his mother's death in 1780. In 1785, in one swoop, Croatia was virtually abolished. Zagreb found itself part of a new unit of local government based in Zala, in Hungary, while eastern Slavonia was merged into a region centred on Pecs, also in Hungary. The post of *ban* was rendered virtually redundant. The Croat nobles and the bishops were astonished. Maria Theresa had tinkered with centralisation through the Croatian Royal Council and its subsequent absorption into the Hungarian Royal Chancellery. But that was nothing compared to this avalanche. The equilibrium of centuries was upset, and in their panic the outraged Croats threw in their lot with the more powerful conservative force of the Hungarian nobility. In a landmark act in 1790 the Sabor surrendered most of its prerogatives to the Hungarian parliament. Henceforth, its jurisdiction was confined to justice and education while all other legislation was entrusted to the joint parliament in Pressburg (Poszony in Hungarian, Bratislava in Slovak), in which Croats had only a few seats. Moreover, the Sabor could now only meet at the same time as the joint parliament. The Croats had decided in haste. They repented at leisure. After 1790 they found that they had made themselves hostages to the rising force of Hungarian nationalism.

The timid and conservative nobles and bishops might have borne with this state of affairs had Hungary remained a conservative force seeking only the restoration of the *status quo ante.* Instead, the Hungarians tried to Hungarianise Croatia, by enforcing the use of the Hungarian language and incorporating Slavonia into Hungary proper.

Joseph's premature death in 1790 ended the programme of radical reforms. But the ferment had scarcely died down before the outbreak of the French Revolution. The turmoil in Paris had little echo in rural Croatia. But in Zagreb and Dubrovnik the local bourgeoisie was soon excited by the events in France, especially when the Croats were called on to fight the French and small cells of Jacobins made themselves evident. One of the channels of subversion in Croatia was the freemasons' lodge. These spread into Croatia partly as a consequence of the Seven Years' War, during which a number of Croat officers found themselves imprisoned in the fortress of Magdeburg with French officers who were certainly freemasons. 'There seems no doubt that the Croatian officers learned the secrets of the craft from their French colleagues, so that on their return to their native land they established lodges of their own.'[2]

When they returned to Croatia these officers found an enthusiastic patron in Count Ivan Drašković, who founded lodges in the 1760s and 1770s in Zagreb, Glina, Varaždin and Križevci. A lodge was later founded at Otočac, in Lika. It was significant that several of these lodges obviously existed for the exclusive benefit of officers serving in the Krajina. It is the only explanation for the foundation of a lodge in a town like Otočac, then a village without even a school. Glina was the headquarters of the 1st Frontier Regiment. These lodges may not have been hotbeds of revolutionary Jacobin thinking, but they did play an important role in disseminating anti-clerical and rationalist ideas among the lesser nobility and the army officers. Certainly that was the opinion of the reactionary Emperor Francis I (1792–1835), under whom all secret societies were forbidden in 1798.

In 1794 the first Jacobin agitators surfaced in Zagreb, erecting a 'tree of liberty' in the middle of the city like the ones to be found in most French towns in the 1790s. It was hung with a placard bearing a long revolutionary poem which started 'Zakaj išli bi Hrvati prot Franzuzu vojevati?',[3] meaning 'Why should Croats make war upon the French?'

The author of this forty-verse hymn to the French Revolution was never discovered. However, it is most likely he belonged to the circle of Hungarian and Croat Jacobins led by Ignjat Martinović, a Franciscan friar from Vojvodina,[4] who was executed in Buda in 1795 for plotting a republican uprising in Hungary.[5] Francis I was horrified to discover this evidence of treason in the quiet backwater of Croatia. The finger of suspicion even touched the Bishop of Zagreb, Maksimilijan Vrhovac. Although by virtue of his office he sat at the apex of the ancient feudal hierarchy, he was an enlightened and progressive cleric. A child of the Romantic movement, he encouraged his clergy to record the folk sayings and oral lore of the peasants in his diocese. Most of all he was determined to promote the use of a standardised literary Slav language, which, in the spirit of the Dalmatian writers of the Renaissance era, such as Bartol Kašić,[6] he thought ought to be called 'Illyrian' rather than just Croatian.[7] After Martinović was arrested in December 1794 he incriminated the Bishop by suggesting he might have written the revolutionary poem that had been hung from the 'tree of liberty'. In the climate of reactionary hysteria the Bishop's enthusiasm for Slavic studies and his patronage of the Illyrian movement rendered him suspicious in the eyes of the authorities.

The scene then shifted to Dalmatia. In 1796 and 1797 large numbers of Croatian soldiers from the Frontier had been employed in fighting the French in Italy. The war ended in failure for Austria, and on 18 April 1797 Napoleon and Francis agreed to exchange Habsburg-ruled Lombardy, which the French had seized, for Venice's possessions in Dalmatia. In May the French took Venice, while on 5 July a Habsburg Croat general, Juraj Rukavina, entered the city of Zadar. In October, the transfer of Dalmatia to Austria was confirmed in the Treaty of Campo Formio.

In Dalmatia and Slavonia the arrival in Zadar of a Croat general aroused great popular enthusiasm and sparked off a campaign of agitation in the Sabor in favour of uniting Dalmatia and Slavonia. These hopes were misplaced. General Rukavina was a Croat patriot, but also a servant of the Habsburg dynasty, which had no interest in stoking the fires of Croat nationalism. To prevent the unification movement from gaining momentum, the Habsburg authorities made it clear that Dalmatia and Slavonia would retain separate administrations. They also ensured that political power in the Dalmatian cities remained in the hands of the tiny Italian-speaking elite, even though Italian speakers made up at most only about 10 per cent of the population.

There was, therefore, a mood of disappointment in both Dalmatia and Slavonia with Habsburg rule by the time Austria entered the Third Coalition against France in 1804–5, alongside Britain, Sweden and Russia. After the crushing military defeat at Austerlitz on 2 December

1805, Austria was forced under the terms of the Treaty of Pressburg of 26 December to cede its recently gained possessions in Dalmatia to France. The treaty was a landmark in Croatian history. For the first time, a revolutionary and progressive, albeit foreign, government was installed on Croat soil. For a few months French rule over Dalmatia was uncertain as Russia occupied the bay of Kotor, in modern Montenegro, as well as the island of Korčula, while British ships hovered in the Adriatic Sea. But by May 1806 the new French commissar for Dalmatia, General Lauriston, had established control over the entire region, with the exception of Dubrovnik. But time was running out for the city-state. By the eighteenth century Dubrovnik was a political and economic fossil. It had been many centuries since the populace had played any part in its government by acclaiming laws outside the palace of the rector (*knez*), but by the eighteenth century even the vestiges of representative government had been discarded. Officially the government of the republic was still divided between several bodies – the rector, the Grand Council, the Minor Council and the Senate. In practice all power was concentrated in the Grand Council, which elected the Senate out of its own members. And the Grand Council was entirely composed of nobles who never married out and hardly ever allowed any new blood in. Even within this tiny noble caste marriage was forbidden between the families of the most ancient nobles of all, the Salamanchesi, and the 'new' nobles, the Sorbonnesi, who had been created after an awful earthquake in 1667 forced the nobles to let in some new members, to make up for the ones who had been killed.

Because the nobles would not allow new members, in the eighteenth century, they began to die out. From about 200 or 300 members in the sixteenth century, the Grand Council was down to between sixty and eighty by the eighteenth century. Another side-effect of the ruling elite's ultra-conservatism, of course, was that the populace and the middle classes ceased to identify with the state, its independence or its famous liberty. Economically Dubrovnik – like Venice – was only a shadow of its former self in the eighteenth century. The value of trade in the Mediterranean had declined; its position as an entrepot between Venice and the Balkans was worth very little now that Ottoman-run Bosnia was so torpid.

Dubrovnik, in short, was a rotten fruit and ready to drop into the lap of anyone who asked politely. On 26 May, General Lauriston and a force of 800 French soldiers did indeed 'ask' for permission from the Senate of Dubrovnik to be let into the city, and the following day the gate was opened, after two senators read out a formal protest. The pretence that the French were only passing through was maintained until 31 January 1808, when they ordered the Senate to dissolve itself. Marshal Marmont, the French governor of Dalmatia, who was created Duke of Ragusa (Dubrovnik) by Napoleon, fell in love with Dubrovnik and the courtly society of its aristocracy. It was, he said, 'ce petit pays, qui jouissait du plus grand bonheur, dont les habitants sont doux, industrieux, intelligents; oasis de la civilization au milieu de la barbarie'.[8]

Marmont's reference to barbarians was apt. From 17 June to 6 July 1808 a combined force of Russians and Montenegrins bombarded the city, killing at least 100 people and destroying Catholic churches outside the city walls in a manner that anticipated that other, more recent Montenegrin assault on Dubrovnik, in 1991. But by the end of July Marmont had arrived in Dalmatia with three regiments and, by the Treaty of Tilsit, Russia was obliged to cede to France Dubrovnik's southern possessions around the bay of Kotor, to the relief of the Catholics who dominated the coast and to the chagrin of the Orthodox who dominated the wild interior. In the town of Budva, the French discovered an enthusiastic and influential supporter in a local Croatian nobleman, Count Miroslav Zanović.

The French got to work immediately, reorganising their new acquisitions after several centuries of decay and decline under Venice. Formally the province was subject to the viceroy of the kingdom of Italy, of which Napoleon was king. The first civil governor, Vincenzo Dandolo, was based in Zadar. The province was divided into four districts, Zadar, Split, Makarska and Šibenik, which were sub-divided into cantons and councils (opchinas). Dubrovnik and Kotor, following their acquisition in 1808, were placed in a separate administrative unit.

The reforms swung rapidly into action. On 12 July 1806 the first newspaper in Dalmatia appeared, the King's Dalmatian, printed in Italian and Croatian, and with two editors, Fr Paško Jukić, a Franciscan Croat, and Bartuo Benincasa, an Italian. The pages on the left were printed in Italian and those on the right in Croatian. The print run of 1,100 was modest, reflecting the sad fact that under Venetian rule almost the entire population had become illiterate. Feudalism was abolished, the system of punishments was modernised and the guillotine made its appearance. There were attempts to reforest parts of Dalmatia that had been reduced to a virtual dustbowl by the Venetian policy of stripping its colonies of their raw materials. Tobacco and potatoes were introduced to widen the range of crops that was grown by the peasants. There were new hospitals and an energetic programme of road-building. In Zadar a college of higher education was established, which was later transferred to a suppressed monastery in Dubrovnik. The college was intended to educate a future class of officials and administrators. Alongside the college, the new government set up seven high schools, nineteen primary schools for boys and fourteen for girls, and under an educational decree of 1807 all families by law had to educate at least one of their children.

The liberal spirit that underpinned the Napoleonic administration of Dalmatia showed itelf in matters of religion. Superfluous monasteries and convents were closed to make way for educational institutions. The Serb Orthodox community was assisted, with the establishment of a permanent bishopric in Šibenik funded from the provincial budget. This budget, which had to be approved by the government of Italy in Milan, was based on peasants' tithes, a pasture tax, the salt monopoly of the island of Pag and other islands and customs taxes levied on imports. The French had little time to oversee the reforms, however. In 1809 Austria declared war again on France, and Habsburg armies under Generals Stojčević and Knežević invaded Dalmatia from Slavonia. For a time, Marshal Marmont was forced to withdraw in order to join Napoleon. But on 5 July 1809 Austria was defeated again at the Battle of Wagram, and after this decisive encounter France was able to extract enormous territorial concessions, which effectively reduced Vienna to the status of a second-rank power. Under the terms of the Treaty of Schönbrunn of 14 October 1809 France's existing Dalmatian possessions were augmented by Carniola, in modern Slovenia, a slice of southern Carinthia and a large part of Slavonia running from Jasenovac westwards to Karlovac.

The Marmont regime in Ljubljana continued to press on with reforms, founding more schools and trade schools. In 1810 a new newspaper, *La Télégraphe*, appeared, French having being declared the official language of administration. In the same year, Marmont despatched an Illyrian delegation to Paris for the Emperor's wedding, headed by the ever faithful Count Zanović of Budva and the Bishop of Ljubljana, in the expectation that the dazzling spectacle of the imperial capital would make the Dalmatians and Slovenes more enthusiastic about French rule. At the same time, 100 youths were selected for training at the officers' military academies at Saint-Cyr, outside Paris, and at La Flèche. Another 100 youths were sent to France to learn trades.[9]

The French regime in Dalmatia crumbled rapidly in the aftermath of the disastrous campaign in Russia, in which many soldiers from the Krajina fought with distinction. In 1813 Austria demanded the return of Dalmatia as the price of neutrality, while Britain seized the islands of Vis and Korčula. On 17 August an Austrian army under General Radivojević attacked from Slavonia without warning, and, after meeting little resistance in an assault on Karlovac, Austria declared war. The Illyrian Provinces melted away. On 15 November Dubrovnik declared its independence and once more, though not for long, hoisted the Libertas flag above the city. In Budva, Count Zanović's house was sacked by a pro-Montenegrin mob. At the Congress of Vienna in 1815

Austria's right to Dalmatia was confirmed and on 3 August the region was declared the Kingdom of Dalmatia, partly to emphasise the fact that Dalmatia would remain separate from Slavonia. Count Zanović was incarcerated in jail in Zadar until 1816, after which he returned to Budva, dying in poverty in 1834. Dubrovnik's brief attempt to re-establish its independence was quashed. The victorious Austrians hauled down the flag of Libertas as soon as they entered the city, which they ensured was included without differentiation from the rest of Dalmatia in their gains of 1816.

The French regime in Dalmatia was heavily criticised as an 'occupation' by historians in the Communist era. For a mixture of ideological and patriotic reasons they refused to accept the notion that a foreign empire could possibly have played a positive role in Balkan or Croatian affairs. It is true that the expansion of French territory in 1809 was a mixed blessing for the Croats, simply because Slavonia was cut into two, gravely disrupting the economies of Zagreb and Karlovac. And it is true that by the end of the French era Dalmatia was being taxed heavily, in order to fulfil Napoleon's injunction that the provinces should all pay for themselves. The cost of supporting a large military force weighed heavily on such an impoverished region. It is also true that the French regime was extremely unpopular outside the circles of revolutionary aristocrats like Count Zanović, owing to the anti-French agitation of the lower clergy among the peasants.

Yet this is not enough to condemn the French experiment. Dalmatia had been brought so low by Venice over the centuries that most of its inhabitants were not in a position to appreciate the enlightened French policies. The newspapers remained unread because no one could read. Even the choice of Croatian words in them was controversial, as the use of the Slav tongue had been suppressed by the Venetians for so long that no one had any idea what dialect to use, although Marmont favoured the usage of Dubrovnik. Squashed and squeezed by their temporal lords for so long, and succoured in their misery only by their priests, it was not surprising that the mass of Dalmatian peasants heeded the clergy's fearful warnings about the 'godless' French, and assumed their reforms were the work of the devil.

The underlying problem of the Illyrian Provinces was that it formed no logical national or geographical unit. It was established as a dagger to point at the heart of Austria. The Croats, Slovenes and Germans in it could not be welded into a nation by a whim of the French Emperor. The Slovenes in the northern part were convinced they were not Croats, or 'Illyrians'. The Croats who comprised the majority of the population were unlikely in the long term to remain satisified with an arrangement that left them divided between two empires. Nevertheless, unpopular, short-lived and somewhat artificial as it was, the Illyrian experiment was significant for the future of Croatia. The flame of Slav nationalism had been kindled and would not be put out, however much Metternich tried to recreate the world of before the French Revolution. The immediate effect of the international decisions of 1816, however, was to turn the clock back. In Dalmatia the Austrians returned power to the Italian minority, as a counterweight against the movement for union between Slavonia and Dalmatia. There were no more attempts to publish newspapers in Croatian. In Slavonia the old conservative order struggled on, though under increasing pressure from Hungary.

It was in this conservative atmosphere that Ljudevit Gaj was born in the town of Krapina, in the hills of the Zagorje, north of Zagreb, in 1809. Gaj's influence on the future course of Croatian and southern Slav nationalism was far-reaching. He borrowed most of his ideas from other people, was not a great writer and ended his political career enmeshed in scandal. Nevertheless, he was a most successful propagandist and, even if his ideas were not his own, it was his energy that made of them a popular movement.

Like many nationalists, he was something of an outsider. Neither of his parents was a Croat. His mother was German, deeply religious and Catholic, and his father was a Slovak. Gaj was fascinated in his childhood by a legend that his home town was the birthplace of the mythical patriarchs of the Slav race, Čeh, Leh and Meh, the founders respectively of Bohemia, Russia and Poland. His burgeoning interest in Croatian history was fed by studies in the local Franciscan monasteries and by his friendship with the local clergy (with the exception of a handful of eccentric landowners, the clergy were then the only educated people in Slavonia who were remotely interested in the question of Croatian history). These early studies bore fruit in his first book on the history of Krapina, which was published in German after he completed his studies in Karlovac.

From 1826 to 1831 Gaj studied in Vienna, where he dedicated himself to writing a more general history of Croatia. In the course of the work he would break off for trips back to Krapina, where he would question aged peasants in the hope of salvaging scraps of oral folklore. In short, Gaj was a budding young Romantic, imbued with that era's fascination with ruined castles and whispered enchantments, and genuinely interested, in a patronising way, in the memories and customs of the peasants. From the start he was affronted by the prospect of Magyar domination and was convinced that Hungarian nationalism threatened to wipe out what little remained of the Croats' own identity, language and culture. 'In an illiterate land such as ours, it seems important, yes, most necessary, to bring all powers to bear upon awakening an effective and noble cultural patriotism,' he wrote in 1827. 'The history of our fatherland has already taught me how much [it] deserves to be lifted out of the miserable Magyar darkness.'[10]

This was not merely an intellectual conviction born out of the study of history books. As a student, young Gaj had been irritated by his education in Varaždin, where the language of instruction was Latin, the ethos was Hungarian and nothing was taught about Croatia, or in Croatian. The problem for Gaj was that, while the history books filled his head with the long-ago glory of the Croatian state, there was little to catch hold of in the present. To the east, the Serbs had preserved a strong sense of national identity across the centuries through the *millet* system of the Ottoman Empire and the organisation of the Serb Orthodox Church. In 1804 the Serbs in the rich arable woodland of Šumadija south of Belgrade had revolted against the rule of the Ottoman janissaries. In spite of setbacks, they succeeded in establishing a semi-autonomous principality, although Serbia nominally remained part of the Otoman Empire. After the resurrection of the Serbian state, a talented linguist, Vuk Karadžić, an official attached to the new prince, Miloš Obrenović, in 1818 published a new standard dictionary of the Serbian language. Karadžić's reform of Serbian was based on the motto 'write as you speak'. It aroused strenuous opposition from conservative churchmen in Sremski Karlovci but was destined to carry the day. With their new state, new prince and new dictionary, the Serbs seemed to Gaj in many ways more assured of a bright future than the Croats themselves.

Hitherto the Croats' contacts with Serbs had been few and far between. For all the similarities between the two peoples and their speech, the fact that the Serbs were Orthodox in religion and wrote with the Cyrillic script while the Croats were Catholic and used Latin letters created a gulf between them. Gaj's interest in Karadžić and the new Serbian principality in the east was quite a new thing. Again in German, he wrote the poem 'Der Zeitgeist unde die Kroatien' in 1827, asking: 'You faithful vassals of Rome, do they also want to rob you of your mother tongue?' The problem was – what mother tongue? Karadžić had the backing of a prince and mini-state for his work; Gaj was an intellectual seeking a patron. There was no agreement at all about what language Croats ought to speak and write in. For centuries it had been little more than a peasant dialect. The upper classes in Dalmatia spoke Italian. In Slavonia they spoke German or Hungarian at home, and Latin at school and in the Sabor. Looking round at the Slav dialects, Gaj had plenty to choose from. In his native Krapina and in Zagreb, the local language was the *kajkavski* dialect, which was close to Slovene. In Istria, on parts of the Dalmatian coast and on most of the islands, the *čakavski* variant held sway, while in Dubrovnik, the rest of Dalmatia and Herzegovina the *štokavski* variant prevailed (*kaj*, *ča* and *što* all meaning 'what').

The language of Dubrovnik was the most attractive choice, as it was the language of the Illyrian writers of the Renaissance, of Gundulić and *Osman*. The cult of Dubrovnik – the bastion of Slav culture, identity and freedom against the invading Turks and Italians – was at its height in the mid- to late nineteenth century; the leaders of the Croat national revival trooped down to Dubrovnik as pilgrims to a shrine, while the plays of sixteenth-century Dubrovnik were then at the height of fashion in the drawing rooms of Zagreb. It was a cult symbolised in overloaded fashion by the picture on the great curtain of the new Croatian national theatre in 1895, which depicted the leaders of the Croatian revival sweeping towards the figure of Gundulić, seated on a throne against a background of the skyline of Dubrovnik and of Zagreb – the one the symbol of Croatia's great past, the other the hope of the future.[11]

Another reason for choosing *štokavski* was that it was close to Karadžić's Serbian, and Gaj was convinced that Hungary could be kept at bay only by the co-ordinated action of all the southern Slavs in the Austrian empire. The biggest drawback to Gaj's linguistic plans was the opposition to *štokavski* in conservative circles, and especially among the clergy, in Zagreb, the capital of Croatia and centre of Gaj's endeavours. Gaj moved in 1829 to Pest, where his shock on encountering the sudden explosion of Hungarian nationalism stimulated his determination to carry through the work of writing a standard Croatian orthography. In the Hungarian capital he came into contact with another influential figure, a pan-Slav Lutheran pastor, Jan Kollar, a Slovak. Kollar shared the idea that was common to the Dalmatian Renaissance writers, that the Slav family of nations could be broken down to a few basic national and linguistic units, Russian, Polish, Czecho-Slovak and southern Slav, and that it was the duty of each to develop and cross-fertilise with the others. It was in this time of enthusiastic endeavour in 1831 that Gaj wrote a famous poem that was to become the anthem of the Croatian national revival of the nineteenth century, 'Još Horvatska nije propala' (No, Croatia has not perished). The lyrics were remarkably similar to a contemporary Polish poem–song, which it seems Gaj adapted to his own uses. Original or not, it served as a triumphant manifesto of the creed of the Slav national movement in Croatia:

> Still Croatia has not fallen
> Our people have not died
> Long she slept, but she's not vanquished
> Her sleep dreary death defied.
>
> Still Croatia has not fallen
> We are in her still alive.
> Long she slept, but she's not vanquished
> We shall wake her and revive

With an orthography printed in 1830 in the Zagreb dialect and the instantly popular 'Još Horvatska' to his name, Gaj returned to Zagreb with the aura of a promising celebrity and was fêted by a circle of gentry and local officials. His entry into Croatian politics was timely. In 1827 Hungary had pushed through an ambitious piece of legislation intended to confirm the subordinate status of Croatia to Hungary, with a law making Hungarian a compulsory subject in Croatian schools. The move provoked uproar in Croatia, where the radicals were determined to promote schooling in Croatian while reactionaries wished to retain education in Latin. In 1832 there were fist-fights in the academy at Zagreb between Hungarian and Croatian students, following an attempt by one of the professors to give lectures in Croatian. Gaj was in his element and immediately applied for permission from the Habsburg authorities to set up a newspaper, *Novine Horvatske* (Croatian News) with a weekly literary supplement, *Danica* (Morning Star), written in the Zagreb dialect.

Growing Hungarian pressure divided the Sabor and encouraged the formation of parties. Until 1848 the Sabor had the same membership it had had since the Middle Ages, comprising the bishops of Zagreb and Senj, the magnates, the high sheriffs of the counties and a few other representives of the royal free cities. The so-called 'peasant nobles' of Turopolje, descendants of the Bosnian nobles who had fled the Turkish invasion in the sixteenth century, were also represented in the Sabor, though as a bloc rather than individually.[12] Such a conservative body, passing the time drawing up petitions in Latin, might have been expected to have been thoroughly reactionary, and hostile to Gaj's Illyrian agitation, with all its overtones of the Napoleonic experiment in Dalmatia. And many of the Hungarian or Magyarised Croat aristocrats were indeed hostile. So were the 'peasant nobles' of Turopolje, who clung to every vestige of their ancient political privileges. Then there was the Church hierarchy. Many of those were not especially pro-Hungarian, but they were appalled by Gaj's linguistic reforms and by the assault he had led on the old Zagrebian *kajkavski* dialect. Many thought the Church had done well to keep the language alive over the centuries in the face of competition from German and Hungarian and were annoyed by Gaj's apparent contempt for their labour. There was a confessional dimension to the Church's hostility. Many clergy were suspicious of the tendency of Gaj's Illyrians to suppress differences between Orthodox Serbs and Catholic Croats. The conservatives' stronghold was Zagreb and the old conservative royal free cities of Varaždin and Križevci.

Gaj's Illyrian supporters naturally included all those elements who felt stifled or impatient with the feudal conservative order, such as the lower clergy, seminarians, students, officers serving the Krajina and the emerging middle class in more economically advanced towns such as Karlovac.[13] The Krajina was a stronghold of Illyrian sentiment, partly because the Illyrians strongly championed the unification of the Krajina with Croatia. But the Illyrians also had aristocratic supporters in the unreformed Sabor, and this fusion of Illyrian intellectuals and progressive nobles formed the basis of the National Party, a great political force opposing the Hungarians and their Croat supporters throughout the nineteenth century.

The most prominent of these aristocratic Illyrians was Count Janko Drašković (1779–1856), lord of the magnificent castle of Trakošćan, whose father had played such an influential role in the spread of freemasonry in Croatia. His political pamphlet *Disertatia* (Dissertations) in 1832 was the first public Illyrian manifesto. Written in Croatian, which was itself a significant point, it demanded the union within the Habsburg Empire of Slavonia, Dalmatia and Bosnia and the restoration of the prerogatives of the *ban* that had been surrendered to Hungary in the 1790s.

The rapid progress of the Illyrians was demonstrated in November 1832 when the new session of the Sabor opened in an atmosphere of high excitement. There were cheers when General Rukavina, the liberator of Zadar, made his acceptance speech as the new commander of the Military Frontier in Croatian, rather than in traditional Latin. Emboldened by the mood, the Sabor instructed its deputies to the joint parliament in Pressburg to raise the threat of rescinding the concessions made in 1791.

In Vienna the imperial authorities under Francis I had decided to allow the Croats to let off steam, in order to put pressure on the Hungarian nationalists, who posed a greater danger.

In May 1833 Gaj even managed to get an audience with the Emperor and, following this apparently agreeable encounter, was given permission in July 1834 to start his new paper. There were great difficulties in securing a printing press and enough money, but on 6 January 1835 the first issue of *Novine Horvatske* (still written in the Zagreb dialect) saw the light of day. The Illyrian ideology of the newspaper was reflected in the bylines of the correspondents, all of whom signed their articles as 'an Illyrian from ...'.

Within a year, the newspaper had adopted the *što* dialect and had changed its title to *Ilirske Narodne Novine* (Illyrian National News). The actual circulation of the newspaper was trifling, a mere 500 copies or so – a fact that reflected both the content of the newspaper and the shortage of Croats who were wealthy and literate enough to take any interest in such a project. But there was no gainsaying Gaj's success in launching the movement of national revival in Croatia. The evidence was everywhere. In theatres, his song 'Još Horvatska' was sung at the end of performances. His ideas took hold almost instantly in the seminaries and in the academy of Zagreb. In Varaždin, Križevci and Karlovac, reading rooms were set up where the public could browse through his ruminations. At home, the Sabor in 1836 and 1839 took up many of the Illyrian causes, calling for the establishment of elementary schools and a Learned Society to promote the use of the Slavic tongue. The Sabor of 1839 also championed the cause that was dearest to Illyrian hearts, the reunification of Dalmatia and Slavonia, as well as repeating the call for the incorporation of the Krajina into Croatia.

Gaj's effusive loyalty to the dynasty at first ensured the favour of Vienna. On a visit to Vienna in 1836, Gaj rejoiced in the discomfort that the Croatian movement was causing the Hungarians and in the manifest support the Croats enjoyed from the imperial court, while in 1839, the Emperor even sent Gaj a diamond ring as a token of his gratitude for the services that the dynasty thought he was rendering. One year later, in a calculated snub to Hungarian ambitions to Hungarianise the educational system in their Slav and Romanian domains, the Emperor indulged the Sabor by ordering 'Illyrian' to become the principal language in Croatian schools.

These were the halcyon years for Gaj and for the Croatian national movement. From nowhere they appeared to sweep all before them. Loyal to the Emperor and empire, demanding only the restoration of those rights the Habsburgs had themselves confirmed in 1527, the movement was on firm ground when it resisted Hungarian claims. By preaching up the 'Illyrian' or southern Slav aspect of the movement at the expense of the more traditional Croatian and Catholic angle, Gaj's followers avoided antagonising the Serbian Orthodox community in the Krajina, even if they failed to interest them very much. In 1841 Gaj made a triumphant visit to Dubrovnik, journeying on to the Montenegrin capital, Cetinje, in the company of Karadžić and returning to a hero's welcome in Zagreb.

In 1841 the Illyrian movement and Gaj's fortunes reached their apex. Although he was to remain the most powerful intellectual influence in Croatia until he was ruined by scandal in 1848, he was never again so wholly in command in the nation's hearts and minds. But the very success of the Illyrian movement galvanised the conservatives into action and in 1841 the pro-Hungarian aristocrats formed their own political party, which advocated the closest possible ties between Croatia and Hungary. At first known as the Madjaroni (Magyarones), they later adopted the name Unionists. From the early 1840s these conservatives were able with greater success to cast the Illyrian movement as a crypto-revolutionary project. By 1842 these complaints were increasingly aired, especially after the appointment of a new *ban*, Franjo Haller, a strong conservative. Thanks to Haller, as well as to a perception in Vienna that the Illyrians were stepping over the line. Gaj's stock fell in imperial circles. There were no more tokens of the Emperor's favour; instead Gaj was compared to Lajos Kossuth, the leader of the radical nationalists in the Hungarian parliament. The axe fell the following year, when, on 11 January, by imperial decree, the use of the word 'Illyria' was banned. The censors got to work in Zagreb, officials of Gaj's National Party came under pressure and the newspaper was forced to change its name to the *Narodne Novine* (National News).

The Illyrian movement did not disappear; it merely changed its name into the National Party. However, Gaj never quite recovered his equilibrium after the loss of imperial favour in 1842, and he began to explore radical notions of union between Croats and Serbs, and even Croatia's detachment from the Austrian empire and its union with the new principality of Serbia – ideas that were beyond the pale for all but a few extremists. In 1845, the ban on the use of the word Illyrian was lifted. The new bout of political activity transformed Croatia's sleepy county elections. In 1845 there was unprecedented violence at the polls as conservative Turopolje 'peasant nobles' and National Party supporters fought pitched battles, and thirteen people were killed after troops sent to restore order after the vote opened fire on the crowd. At the Sabor of that year, as well as the usual call for the union of Croatia, Dalmatia and the Krajina, the *narodnjaki* (nationals) called also for the restoration of Maria Theresa's Croatian Royal Council, the promotion of Zagreb's academy into a university and the elevation of the Zagreb diocese to an archdiocese.[14]

On 28 March 1846 the first opera in Croatian, *Ljubav i zloba*, by Vatroslav Lisinski, was performed in Zagreb. A chair in Illyrian studies was founded in Zagreb academy and an assembly hall for the sympathisers of the National Party was opened in the Upper Town in February 1847. Meanwhile a Croatian cultural organisation, Matica Ilirska, the Illyrian Bee, had received permission from Vienna to start activities, with the goal of encouraging the publication of Croatian classics, especially the great writers of Dubrovnik, as well as publishing works on Croatian history and ethnology. Matica also published an influential periodical, *Kolo* (Circle). The last unreformed Sabor before the revolutionary events of 1848, which met in October 1847, voted for a solidly Illyrian agenda. Goaded by the intemperate speeches of Kossuth in the Hungarian parliament, in which he declared he did not see Croatia on the map and that only a sword could decide between the Hungrians and the Croats, the assembly rejected Magyar linguistic imperialism. Illyrian was declared the national language of the Triune Kingdom of Croatia, Slavonia and Dalmatia (although the Sabor had no jurisdiction over Dalmatia), and Latin abolished at last as the language of the Sabor's proceedings. A second motion demanded the repatriation of all the prerogatives of the Ban and the Sabor that had been surrendered to the Hungarian parliament. The motions generated such enthusiam that crowds gathered outside the building to cheer while women spectators in the gallery threw flowers into the chamber.

The events of the 1848 revolution marked the end of Gaj's career. ironically. as the Year of Revolutions and the opportunity it provided to launch an attack on Hungary in the defence of both Croatia and the Emperor fulfilled so many of his dreams. At the start of the trouble, following the fall of Metternich in March and an attempt by the Hungarian parliament to incorporate Slavonia into Hungary. Gaj raced back from Vienna to Zagreb and, drawing up in a coach in Ilica Street. shouted, 'Revolution! Revolution!' to an enthusiastic crowd outside. But that summer he was ruined by the affair of Prince Miloš of Serbia.

The Prince, a member of the exiled Obrenović dynasty, was travelling through Zagreb on his way to Vojvodina. The government in Belgrade. then under the Karadjordjević dynasty, wanted Miloš killed and let it be known that Serbia's attitude towards the Illyrian movement would depend on Gaj carrying out this request. In the event, Gaj arranged for the Prince to be arrested in Zagreb and imprisoned. However, he was not killed, but released after paying Gaj a sum of money. The scandal was then exposed and it brought to the surface accusations that Gaj was in the pay of foreign powers. The uproar destroyed his reputation. Discredited and isolated, in 1849 he sold his newspaper to the repressive government in Vienna of Alexander Bach, a supreme act of bathos. He was never elected to public office again and by the time he died in 1872, in the office of his newspaper, he was a diminished figure.

Gaj's was an imperfect legacy and later generations disparaged his attempt to forge a new Illyrian patriotism that transcended the old barriers and hatreds between Catholics and Orthodox. Many Croats came to believe that he had bargained too much of Croatia's individual identity away in the attempt to form a common front with the Serbs, only to find that the Serbs were interested not in Illyria, but in Greater Serbia.

He was criticised as a plagiarist. 'If [the Illyrian movement] had not created Gaj it would have created someone else sooner or later. who perhaps would have been a better writer, though that does not diminish his services or the fact that he truly successfully began a work for which he felt a general need.' was the verdict of one historian.[15]

Such writers noted that Gaj had borrowed most of his ideas from his Illyrian colleagues, especially Ivan Kukuljević and Bogoslav Šulek. while arrogating all the glory to himself:

> Gaj was a very complicated personality whose work comprised two great contradictions. On the one side he was the people's tribune, propagating the broadest Yugoslav concepts and and aiming for an all-embracing

political solution to our national question ... and on the other secretly keeping up his ties with the Austrian court and the government in Vienna, giving them declarations of loyalty and accepting from them (and indeed from the Russian Tsar) money.[16]

There is some truth in the charge that Gaj muddied waters with the Illyrian movement and that it was, at the end of the day, an artificial sentiment that could flourish only in the minds of intellectuals and their aristocratic patrons. The average Croat or Serb peasant certainly never came to think of himself or herself as Illyrian, and Illyrianism faded in the era of mass politics, when the peasants got the vote.

7

1848

Poor Ban! The sad end of his life will remain an eternal monument to his love of his nation.

Bishop Strossmayer, 1875[1]

The revolutions of 1848 propelled Croatia into a state of wild excitement. The trouble started in Italy after the election of Pope Pius IX, an alleged liberal, in June 1846. In December there were riots in Habsburg-ruled Milan and in February 1848 martial law was proclaimed throughout Lombardy–Veneto. But the conflagration enveloped Europe only after a republican revolution broke out in Paris in February, sweeping away the government of Louis-Philippe of Orleans, the 'Citizen King'. By the beginning of March the contagion had spread to Bavaria and south-west Germany. In Hungary the nationalist leader of the Lower House of parliament, Kossuth, demanded the replacement of government by committees, with a Hungarian ministry responsible to the Hungarian parliament. On 13 March a crowd of demonstrators, among whom students were prominent, surrounded the imperial court in Vienna, demanding a constitution. There was shooting and four protesters were killed by the police. The middle-class Viennese then demanded the right to set up committees of public safety to restore order in the city.

The career of Prince Metternich, architect of the Congress of 1815 and, along with the Tsar, Europe's self-appointed guardian against the spectre of revolution, was over. He was told he had lost the support of the imperial family and had no choice but to withdraw. On 17 March Vienna conceded Hungary its responsible ministry.

Metternich's resignation, however, only unleashed the pent-up forces demanding radical change. In Milan there were more riots on 18 March, and a republic was proclaimed in Venice. In Hungary Kossuth's radical middle-class supporters and aristocratic champions of Hungary's historic rights joined forces to demand greater autonomy, social reform and the right to crack the whip over Hungary's big Slovak, Serb, Croat and Romanian minorities. However, the Hungarian demands had a knock-on effect throughout their domains. In southern Hungary, the Serbs began to stir; in northern Hungary, the Slovaks; in Transylvania, the Romanians. The Austrians had problems of their own, with the Czechs in Bohemia and the Italians in Lombardy and Venetia. But the Czechs were not prepared to man barricades for long, and by 15 June General Windisch-Graetz had suppressed the revolt in Prague, to the relief of Bohemia's nervous German minority. By August General Radetsky had the situation in Lombardy–Veneto under control and the invading Piedmontese had been driven from the plain. Now Vienna had a free hand to use the grievances of the Serbs, Croats, Slovaks and Romanians in the struggle against revolutionary Hungary.

The news of Metternich's resignation immediately sparked off demonstrations in Zagreb and gave the Illyrians a chance to seize control of local government. On 25 March 1848 a national assembly met in Zagreb at which Ivan Kukuljević, the most prominent Illyrian after Gaj, read out a charter of rights. The demands included the unification of Dalmatia and Slavonia, annual meetings of the Sabor, the now ritual call for the Krajina to be abolished, the exclusive use of Croatian in educational and governmental institutions and the establishment of a Croatian army, or at least of army units that would serve only in Croatia. The assembly also demanded the appointment as *ban* of a popular officer from the Military Frontier, Josip Jelačić.

Jelačić was born on 16 October 1801 at Petrovaradin, near Novi Sad in Vojvodina, to a Croatian father who came from an old Frontier family of Petrinja. His mother was a Bavarian baroness. The family's full name, Jelačić von Bužim, recalled distant origins among the noble sixteenth- and seventeenth-century Catholic refugees from Ottoman-ruled Bosnia and Croatia, Bužim being a small town near Bihać. Jelačić's connections with the Krajina and the Habsburg dynasty began early. At the age of eight, he was received in audience with his father by the Emperor Francis and enrolled for his education in the prestigious Viennese noble academy known as the Theresianum. Jelačić's military career after leaving the Theresianum in 1819 was interrupted in 1823 by a severe illness, which may have been as much psychological as physical, for he was subject to severe bouts of depression throughout his life. Nevertheless, by 1830 he had returned to active service and had been appointed lieutenant-captain of the 7th Ogulin Regiment, after which he was transferred to Italy to serve under the aged General Radetsky in the turbulent regions of Bologna and Ferrara. By 1837, having caught the eye of his superiors as a man of talent, he was sent to Dalmatia, as major of the 48th Infantry based in Zadar, and adjutant to the military governor of Dalmatia, General Wetter von Lilienberg. In 1841 he was made lieutenant-colonel of the 1st Ban's Regiment, based in the Krajina at Glina, and a year later he was made a full colonel. Jelačić was delighted by life on the frontier. Unmarried and uninterested in the trappings of urban life or the court, he was devoted to his troops, enjoying a relationship with the frontiersmen that transcended any of the old divisions between Catholic and Orthodox.

In 1845 he achieved a certain notoriety by conducting a headstrong reprisal raid against the Ottomans of neighbouring Bosnia. Raids by the Ottomans from the Bihać region on the sparsely inhabited Lika region of Croatia were still common in the early nineteenth century, though in the more relaxed conditions then prevailing in the Frontier the Habsburg authorities no longer bothered to do much about them. Jelačić caused something of a scandal therefore when, in reprisal for a raid on Cetingrad, just inside Croatia, he raced into north-west Bosnia from Glina with a company of about 5,000 frontiersmen and sacked the village of Pozvizd, near Velika Kladuša. During the raid Jelačić killed at least eighty men on the Bosnian side but lost about sixty-seven of his own. The authorities in Vienna tut-tutted about such losses, especially as the expedition had been conducted in reprisal for the shooting of a single teenager, sixteen-year-old Sava Vojnović. The more the Viennese officials hissed in disapproval of such antics, the more Jelačić was idolised by the frontiersmen. They considered his behaviour worthy of the highest traditions of the region.

The anonymous author of *Scenes of the Civil War in Hungary* was one of many who became fascinated by Jelačić once they met him. 'Jelačić is of the middling height and size,' he wrote.

> His bearing is upright and truly military: his gait, quick, as indeed all his motions. His face, of a somewhat brownish tinge, has in it something free, winning and yet determined. The high forehead, under the smooth black hair, is very striking. The eyes are large, hazel, and full of expression. He is the mildest and kindest of officers … and while commanding the 2nd Banal Regiment as colonel, there were not so many punishments in it in a year as there were formerly in a month.[2]

The account went on: 'Never was a general more beloved of his troops. Wherever he shows himself in a military village, all, old and young, little boys and aged men, and pretty girls too, all rush out to see him, to shake hands with him and to greet him with one "*živio*" [long may he live] after another.'

'The language usually spoken by Jelačić is German, but he also understands Italian, French, Croatian and he has some knowledge of Hungarian. … he is unmarried, has not much property, lives simply and frugally, applying all that he can spare to the support of his soldiers.'[3]

The author also described the colourful, vanishing world of the old

Krajina in which Jelačić lived and flourished. This was his impression of the average frontiersman.

A high cap, of brown or black felt fur, covers their long shaggy hair. The bearded face is lean, with sharp features and darkly tanned. The spare sinewy body is clad in a short brown jacket, with a half-standing collar bordered with red braiding and wide, dirty-white linen trousers, tied at the ankle. The foot clothing consists in wide, blue-and-white stockings, drawn up to the thigh, and sandal shoes fastened with thongs. Round the waist they wear a wide red or yellow sash ... over the shoulder the long Turkish gun which has a very narrow barrel. These guns are frequently of very beautiful workmanship, enriched with ornaments of gold and silver, and often of considerable value. ... licentiousness is apt to creep in among [the frontiersmen]; but under good leaders, they make the best soldiers in the world.[4]

The author noted also the ancient way of life centring around the *zadruga*, the communal household which the Slavs had brought with them to the Balkan peninsula from their old homeland beyond the Carpathians. 'In general, the eldest of the family, mostly a border soldier whose term of service has expired and who still belongs only to the reserve, is elected by the others to be house father and his wife is the house mother. These are then invested with superintendence over the whole family ... to the number frequently of 60 or 80 individuals, in a single house.'

These extended households, the author wrote, formed the basis of the the Krajina's military organisation. 'Every house must furnish the company to whose district it belongs with a certain number of soldiers in proportion to its adult male population.'

The soldier in the field battalions must go on guard duty the whole of every fourth, or even third week. At his departure, the family to which he belongs supplies him with provisions, which he cooks himself at the post. He takes with him to the frontier musket, sword, cartouche box and cloak.

The guard posts consist of ... huts sunk in the ground. Each of the huts ... contains six or eight men. At every officer's post is set up a signal post with a pitched barrel, which is fired in case of emergency, to alarm the district upon any serious incursion of the Bosnians.[5]

This was the air that Jelačić breathed, a world that in many ways had changed little since the beginning of the eighteenth century. Bound up with the defence of the empire against its Turkish enemies, the officer class of the Krajina had little time to spare for the politics of Civil Croatia.

Indeed, it is hard to imagine Jelačić having got involved in it at all, if he had not been pushed.

However, the Illyrian nationalists needed a respectable figurehead if they were to take advantage of the worsening dispute between Hungary and Vienna. Gaj had always presented the Illyrian movement as anti-Hungarian but loyal to the dynasty, and had played down the movement's radical, populist tendencies. At such a vital moment, the Illyrians needed a *ban* who sympathised with the conservative wing of their movement but who was known to enjoy the trust of the court. Jelačić was not party to these intrigues. On 26 March he wrote to his brother Djuro: 'The night before last, as I was going straight to my respectable bed, someone knocked and gave me the news that the national assembly wanted me to be Ban. ... I shall have no more peace in this world. There I shall be viceroy of the Triune Kingdom without money, without even pocket handkerchiefs and I must travel, equip myself and arrange a household, Good God!'⁶

Jelačić's election by the Sabor followed quickly. Then Gaj and Jelačić set off for Vienna to secure approval from the well-meaning but feeble-minded Emperor Ferdinand. Jelačić was received in audience and left believing that he had won the Emperor's approval. On 8 April he was appointed a field-marshal-lieutenant and made commander of the Military Frontier.

Back in Zagreb the new Ban lent his authority to the Illyrians' programme of moderate reform. A Banal Council was appointed to provide Croatia with an independent executive government. The last remnants of the feudal system were abolished. Lastly, a new Sabor based on a reform of the franchise was summoned to meet on 5 June.

The reform of the Sabor was an epoch-making event, marking the start of its transformation from a feudal assembly of estates to a democratic, representative assembly of the Croatian nation. Until 1848 the Sabor had been dominated by hereditary lords. They had few competencies and their jurisdiction was restricted to the tiny strip of land known as Civil Croatia. But, however moribund, medieval and puny it appeared to be, the Illyrians invested enormous hopes in the Sabor as a last link with the great vanished kingdom of the past, and they were keen to see it transformed into a truly national assembly of all the southern Slavs in the Habsburg Empire.

Jelačić's reforms met such hopes halfway. Under the new rules for the June election, the Sabor would combine both hereditary and elected elements. The magnates retained their seats, but were joined by deputies elected under a narrow franchise based on property and education. To be fair, the electorate still only comprised about 2.5 per cent of the adult male population. Nevertheless, it was the start of the Sabor's slow transformation. The other truly significant reform in these elections was the extent of the constituencies. The Illyrians had not the power to abolish the Krajina, but they insisted on treating it as an integral part of Croatia. Each regiment in the Krajina was told to elect four deputies. And, alongside the Catholic magnates and bishops, the Serb Orthodox bishops were also granted automatic seats.

The ferment in Croatia caused outrage in Hungary. The Hungarians were angry that Jelačić had declined to take the *ban*'s customary oath of allegiance to Hungary when he was in Vienna, and in the middle of May summoned him to Budapest on charges of treason. For good measure they demanded the surrender to Hungarian jurisdiction of the Slavonian counties. Unfortunately for Jelačić, the Hungarian Prime Minister, Count Batthyany, prevailed on the Emperor to support Hungary's historic prerogatives, and the Emperor sent a message to Zagreb ordering the Ban to obey the Hungarian ministry. While Jelačić pondered his response, however, an enormous gathering of Serbs of southern Hungary took place at the seat of the Serbian Metropolitan in Sremski Karlovci. The meeting was addressed in the most belligerent terms by the Metropolitan Josip Rajačić and ended with a list of demands that would have abolished Hungary's jurisdiction over the region. They included a call for the Metropolitan's status to be upgraded to that of patriarch – the title held by the head of the Serbian Church until the mid-eighteenth century – and for the Serbs to be permitted to elect a secular leader over the region, a *vojvoda*. The Serbs had a certain amount of historical justice on their side as there was no doubt they had enjoyed a greater degree of self-government when they trekked into southern Hungary in the 1690s. The meeting marked the beginning of a small-scale civil war in southern Hungary, in which both Serbs and Hungarians treated each other with great brutality.

On 17 May 1848 demonstrations again shook Vienna. The Emperor and the Empress Maria Anna, an Italian who had been made miserable by the conflict between her adopted state and her fellow countrymen, fled Vienna for the safety of Innsbruck. With the empire in turmoil, there was no question of Jelačić going to Budapest to answer charges of treason. Instead, the Croats busied themselves with preparing a more than usually magnificent ceremony of installation for the new Ban. The celebrations began on 4 June, one day before the actual ceremony of installation and the first section of the new, elected, Sabor. Jelačić rode into Zagreb on a white horse, dressed in the *ban*'s traditional costume of white, red and silver and with eagle plumes in his hat. The welcome that he received was magnificent. Cannons thundered and church bells rang the whole day while in the evening there was an open-air feast and a firework display. The ceremony of the taking of the oath took place before an enormous crowd in St Katarina's Square, which later became Jelačić Square, thousands having crammed on to stands put up for the purpose. Bishop Haulik of Zagreb had fled. The timid reformer of the early 1840s had taken off for the imperial court, alarmed by the revolutionary atmosphere around him. Instead, the bishop who administered the oath was the Serbian Metropolitan, who had arrived from Sremski Karlovci with a Serb delegation at the end of May, on a mission to seal the terms of a Serb–Croat alliance against the Hungarians. Rajačić was accompanied during the ceremony by the Catholic bishops of Senj and Karlovac and the Orthodox Bishop of Pakrac. Jelačić read out the ancient oath in the traditional manner before a crucifix and two lighted candles, promising 'before the living God, the Blessed Virgin and all the saints' to serve the Habsburg Emperor – 'Apostolic King of Hungary, Bohemia, Croatia and Dalmatia'. The Metropolitan in turn called on Jelačić to protect 'the august House of Austria, our common good, sweet liberty, our nationality and the honour and glory of the Triune Kingdom'.[7]

As Kossuth's radicals pushed Hungary into rebellion against the Habsburgs it no longer mattered a whit that Jelačić was a traitor in the eyes of Hungary. The new Sabor voted the Ban dictatorial powers and approved his preparations to go to war with the Hungarian rebels in defence of the Emperor. Neither Jelačić nor the Illyrian deputies of the Sabor were motivated by fatuous, blind loyalty to the throne. In return for their support they expected – *demanded* – change. The Sabor's address to the Emperor began with a preamble making it very clear that the Croats did not wish to be seen in any way as supporters of Habsburg absolutism. 'Let Hungary separate from the Habsburg monarchy and consequently from these [Croatian] kingdoms, if it has the inclination and the strength,' it began. 'But Croatia, Slavonia and Dalmatia are independent countries and as such they not only do not wish to loosen the existing bond with Austria ... but rather desire to enter into a still closer connection ... for if our fathers were deterred from a similar step by the fact that the old Austria had an absolutist government, we now for our part no longer see any obstacle to such a connection in view of the transformation of Austria today.'[8]

The address then demanded the cancellation of Hungarian jurisdiction over Croatia, the creation of a Council of State responsible to the Sabor to oversee all legislation in Vienna that referred to Croatia, the union of the Krajina with Civil Croatia, the exclusive use in Croatia of the 'Slav language', the union of Dalmatia with Slavonia and the return of the port of Rijeka from Hungary to Croatia. The deputies were enthusiastic about the coming conflict with Hungary and optimistic about forging closer links with the Serbs in southern Hungary. Many hurled money on to the floor for an army, in a gesture more symbolic than practical, and set to work organising closer links with the Serb rebels in Karlovci. The next two months were consumed with preparations for conflict with Kossuth's rebel army. At the end of July, Jelačić had one last confrontation with the Hungarians in Vienna, which ended in a memorable exchange. 'We shall meet again on the banks of the Drava,' Count Batthyany is reported to have said. 'I will come to find you before that on the banks of the Danube,' Jelačić replied.[9]

The preparations were not complete until the first week of September. However, at 4.30 on the morning of 11 September, Jelačić led an army of about 40,000 frontiersmen out of Varaždin, across the Drava and into the Medjimurje region of Hungary. The first part of the campaign was uncomplicated. The Croats encountered no serious opposition in the Medjimurje as the inhabitants were for the most part Croats. The uncertain status of Jelačić's invasion of Hungary, which was being conducted officially in the name of the Emperor, was resolved on 28 September when Franz Lemberg, the Imperial Commissioner Extraordinary, who had been sent to negotiate in Budapest, was killed by a nationalist mob. The murder finally sealed the rupture between Hungary and the imperial court and Jelačić received the additional confirmation for his campaign that he sought. On 3 October the Emperor proclaimed Jelačić commander-in-chief of the imperial forces in Hungary. The Croatian crusade in Hungary did not go as planned, however. Jelačić's army, which was largely composed of frontiersmen and included as many Serbs as Croats, suffered from all the deficiencies that the Austrians had detected previously among the Frontier troops. They were fearless fighters but expected quick results. They were violent, and prone to rape, loot and kill civilians – actions that antagonised the Hungarian peasants and encouraged them to rally behind Kossuth. The Frontier troops were motivated by an ambition to get to Budapest and teach the haughty Hungarians a lesson. But just as they were approaching Budapest after passing Lake Balaton, revolution broke out once again in Vienna, plunging Jelačić's plans into chaos.

Torn between the desire to carry on to Budapest and the fear that if revolution succeeded in Vienna all would be lost, Jelačić split his army, sending 12,000 back to Croatia and switching westwards with the remaining 27,000 towards Vienna with the goal of recovering the city for the Emperor. After a brief and indecisive encounter with the Hungarians at Schwechat, he reached the outskirts of Vienna at the beginning of October. There however he found himself in a subordinate position to General Windisch-Graetz.

The bombardment of Vienna started on 24 October. The radicals inside the city – surrounded and regarded with hostility by the middle classes – soon capitulated, allowing Jelačić and Windisch-Graetz to enter on 29 October. The Viennese were amazed and amused by the sight of Jelačić's army of yokels, wearing bobtails and dressed in leather sandals. The Krajina Serbs and Croats were no less surprised by the imperial capital, home to the shimmering, distant figure of the Emperor, whom they were brought up to serve but whose residence they surely never expected to see. Many were struck in particular by the height of the cathedral spire, and could not be persuaded that the Emperor did not actually live inside it.

The fall of Vienna ended the revolution in Austria. It did not end the war. In December 1848, Ferdinand abdicated in favour of his teenage nephew, Franz-Jozef. While the imperial armies were distracted by events in the capital, Kossuth's radicals consolidated their control of Hungary. In April 1849 Hungary was proclaimed a republic in the eastern city of Debrecen. The Croats' calculations had been upset. Jelačić's plan had been to diminish the authority of the Hungarians and so increase the freedom of Hungary's Croat and Serb subjects. Far from being the blind servant of reactionary imperialism, Jelačić envisaged a reconstructed empire in which decision-making power would pass to the empire's hitherto ignored and oppressed Slav masses. He revealed his views with frankness to a newspaper interviewer after entering Vienna, saying: 'I do not fear the making of a greater Germany, but I do demand my people's rights. We cannot and will not wait. It is incumbent on us to create a mighty Slavic Austria.'[10] But the longer the war with Hungary dragged on, the less likely the prospect of this 'Slavic Austria' became. With the court locked in a life-or-death struggle with Hungarian republicans, power shifted into the hands of Alexander Bach, a former liberal turned arch-conservative who was interested not in reducing Hungary's powers over the Slavs, but in restoring autocracy.

April 1849 saw Jelačić back in the field in Hungary, commanding imperial forces in the southern part of the country while General Heynau led the field in the north. But the Croatian campaign had run out of steam and Jelačić was now a distinctly peripheral figure in comparison to Windisch-Graetz. His peasant army had been in the field for six months, which was too long, and the initial enthusiasm of the march on Budapest had long been frittered away. On 23 April 1849 Kossuth's reorganised army achieved a significant victory when it retook Budapest, which had fallen to the imperial army the previous year. Austria's inability to crush Hungary, meanwhile, brought about the military intervention of Russia. Tsar Nicholas I's great fear was that the revolution in Hungary would spread into Russian-occupied Poland. The Emperor formally appealed for aid to the Tsar on 1 May, and on the 21st the two emperors met in Warsaw. On 17 June 1849, after moving into Galicia, the Russian offensive in Hungary got under way in earnest. There was no question of what the outcome would be. On 25 June the Russians entered Kosice and in August they took Debrecen. On 13 August, after the fall of Timisoara made it clear resistance would be futile, the Hungarian officers surrendered, not to the Austrians but to the Russians.[11] Jelačić presided over the surrender of his birthplace, Petrovaradin, in the first week of September. But the Russian intervention had changed the equation of the war to the disadvantage of the Croats.

By the time Jelačić reached Vienna again in mid-September 1849 the forces of autocracy under Bach were in the ascendant. It was not an atmosphere in which Jelačić, or his dream of a confederal Slavic Austrian Empire, had any place and he left, overloaded with decorations from a grateful imperial family, but despondent about the future.

Jelačić's worst fears were realised in the peace that followed. In Hungary the repression was absolute. About 500 rebels were condemned to death in 1849 and 1850. Kossuth could be hanged only in effigy, as he had escaped to the Ottoman Empire. But the thirteen Hungarian generals who had surrendered to the Russians and been handed over were executed at Arad – an act that greatly offended the Russians' sense of chivalry. Nine were hanged and four shot. Count Batthyany was shot by firing squad.

Once Hungary was crushed, the rest of the empire buckled under the 'Bach system', which relied heavily on the police and the German-speaking bureaucrats, who received the nickname 'Bach's Hussars'. Throughout the empire the provincial diets and local constitutions were suspended. Croatia emerged from the war in Hungary with little room for manoeuvre and no improvement to its status. The Hungarians mocked Jelačić's achievement with a cruel but accurate jest. What Hungary received as a punishment, they said, Croatia had received as a reward.

In Zagreb, the Ban was tortured by the realisation that he had achieved nothing on behalf of his fellow countrymen. With their Sabor closed and their constitution suspended, the Croats enjoyed less control over their own affairs in the 1850s than at any other period in their history. The bishopric of Zagreb was released from its historic dependence on the Hungarian Church and elevated to an archbishopric. Feudalism had been abolished and was not reintroduced. The Medjimurje region had been detached from Hungary and reunited with Croatia. But these were small points when weighed against life under 'Bach's Hussars'. Instead of Magyarisation, Croatia was subjected to heavy Germanising pressures. The most important Illyrian demand, for the reunion of Slavonia with Dalmatia, had not been achieved. Nor had the expected merger of the Krajina with Civil Croatia. When Jelačić had been appointed *ban* there had been a great coming-together of Serbs and Croats in Croatia and southern Hungary and a setting aside of the religious and historic differences that had impaired relations between them. The good feeling did not survive the war. The decision in 1849 to set up an autonomous Serbian region of Vojvodina in southern Hungary (which was rescinded in 1861) ignited a quarrel with the Croats over borders; Metropolitan Rajačić was angered to find that his seat in Karlovci was cut off from the Vojvodina by the district of Srijem, which remained in Croatia. It was said relations between Serbs and Croats had become worse than relations between Serbs and Hungarians ever were.

The Ban continued to be treated with courtesy by the new regime in Vienna, but what grieved him was the realisation that his advice on Croatian questions was insincerely solicited and invariably ignored. For a man who had spent his life serving the Habsburg dynasty it was a bitter pill. He frequently considered tendering his resignation. 'I have never known such great sorrow and dissatisfaction among our people as now,' his old Illyrian ally, Kukuljević, wrote to him in 1849. 'The keenness of the dissatisfaction has been caused by the way in which Vienna desires to impose a new constitution on us. Our people who have for centuries been accustomed to discussing and adopting laws concerning their lives and their future realise that attempts are being made to deprive them by force of their liberties inherited from their forefathers. ...'[12]

The gloom that settled on Croatia after the war was reflected in Jelačić's private life. In 1849 he married a girl much younger than himself, Sofija, but their only child, a daughter, Anka, died in infancy. One comfort in his premature old age was his friendship with a rising young clergyman of progressive Illyrian views, Josip Juraj Strossmayer, who was appointed to the bishopric of Djakovo in eastern Slavonia in 1849 on Jelačić's recommendation, and who was to carry on the Illyrian campaign to a new, more questioning generation in the latter half of the nineteenth century. But Jelačić's brother was astonished by the Ban's rapid physical deterioration. In 1850 Jelačić was only fifty. But 'he seemed so aged and altered', his brother wrote. 'He could not get over the disappointment that his views were not considered and that he could do nothing for Croatia.'[13] His death on 20 May 1859 unlocked all the latent sympathy most Croats felt for their tortured, unhappy Ban. No sooner was he buried than a committee was formed to erect a monument in his honour and the main square in Zagreb, St Katarina's Square, was renamed in his honour.

After some debate over whether the work should be given to a local artist or not, the commission was entrusted to the then celebrated Viennese sculptor, Anton Fernkorn.[14] The business of raising the money, however, proceeded slowly, and the funds were not collected until 1865. There were fierce arguments over the precise position of Jelačić on his horse and what direction he should face. A myth even grew up that the decision to place him facing north, brandishing his sword in front of him, was a gesture of ill-will to Hungary, though a surviving letter from Fernkorn to the committee from 4 May 1865 confirms that this is nonsense, and that aesthetic reasons alone dictated the Ban's position.[15] The statue was cast in Vienna in June 1866 and exhibited for three months in the imperial capital before it was transported to Zagreb in October. The ceremonial unveiling on 16 November was the most splendid occasion the Croatian capital had seen since Jelačić's installation almost two decades before, and was carried out before the members of the Sabor, a representative of the Emperor, the higher clergy and the current Ban, Josip Šokčević. As the sheet came off, the crowd numbering tens of thousands was heard shouting over the boom of the cannons, 'Slava mu!' – hail him![16]

But the revolutionary left never forgave Jelačić. Karl Marx raged against the little nations that had sided with Vienna against the Hungarian republic, and sneered at what he called 'these dying nationalities, the Bohemians, Carinthians and Dalmatians [who] had tried to profit by the universal confusion of 1848 in order to restore the political *status quo* of AD 800'.[17] Later generations of Croat and Serb Communists took an equally severe view of Jelačić as a reactionary idiot who had helped to crush revolutionary Hungary in order to keep Franz-Jozef on his throne. Writing in the 1950s, the historian Vaso Bogdanov, a Serb from Croatia, pronounced Jelačić the plaything of Croatian reaction, in the form of Bishop Haulik and Baron Franjo Kulmer, the leader of the conservative magnates who had proposed him as *ban* precisely because he knew he was 'politically incompetent and uneducated, limitlessly naive and neither thought with his own head nor had any willpower ...'.[18] And Yugoslavia's Communist leader after the Second World War, Josip Broz 'Tito', agreed with him. In 1945 the statue of Jelačić was boarded up and in 1947 it was taken down. The square was renamed Republic Square. It was only after the fall of Communist rule in Croatia in 1990 that the pieces were located in a cellar and reassembled and Republic Square renamed once more after Jelačić, the fallen hero of 1848.

8

'Neither with Vienna Nor with Budapest'

Today the idea of a Slavic federation in the Balkan peninsula is imposing itself on everyone.

Bishop Strossmayer, 1885[1]

It was said that he had the appearance of a medieval saint and that only in Latin did his sentences flow with power. The English scholar of the southern Slavs, Robert William Seton-Watson, wrote: 'The well-known Italian statesman, Maro Minghetti, once assured the Belgian publicist Emile de Laveley that he had had the opportunity of observing at close quarters almost all the eminent men of his time. "There are only two", he added, "who gave the impression of belonging to another species than ourselves. Those two were Bismarck and Strossmayer." '[2] Seton-Watson continued: 'As the patron and inspirer of thought and culture his influence upon Croatia and the southern Slavs cannot be exaggerated. As Jelačić typifies the military prowess and loyalty of the Croat, so Strossmayer stands for those qualities of faith and romantic idealism for which the best sons of the race have been distinguished.'[3]

His life never lacked controversy. Brilliant and sweet natured when he wished to be, Bishop Strossmayer in several aspects resembled his English contemporary, John Henry, Cardinal Newman. Like him he never quite achieved that position in society for which his intellectual and moral qualities seemed at an early age to single him out. Like him he stood for a more liberal and ecumenical brand of Catholicism than most of his ecclesiastical contemporaries could stomach. Like him he was a 'great hater', as Cardinal Manning said of Newman. When in 1893, aged almost eighty, he met his great political foe and rival for the hearts and minds of Croatia's youth, Ante Starčević, for a ceremony of reconciliation, he confided afterwards to his friend, Dean Franjo Rački, that he wished Starčević was dead. He disliked his ecclesiastical superiors, believing they were tools of the Viennese court, or of Hungary. He carried throughout his life the memory of the tragic Ban. 'This reminds me – now, at the end of my life,' he said, 'of the words of our Ban Jelačić, who, during his illness, very often used to point to his heart. "Hardly anyone", he said, "will ever know how much love this heart had for my people".[4]

Strossmayer and Jelačić had much in common. Both espoused a conception of Croatia's destiny that was high-minded and liberal. Both believed the differences between Croatia's Catholic and Orthodox inhabitants had been manufactured and exaggerated by their rulers, with the aim of rendering both communities more easily ruled by the empire's more advantageously positioned Germans and Hungarians. Both worked to overcome these divisions, looking to the day when the empire would become a commonwealth of free peoples in which the Slavs would express a preponderant influence. Both had courage, Jelačić on the battlefield, Strossmayer at the First Vatican Council, where he was heckled by the bishops for defying Pope Pius IX and for attacking the doctrine of papal infallibility.

Both were men of wide perspective, whose world stretched beyond the confines of Croatia. Jelačić, like most upper-class Croats of his day, spoke German as well as Croatian and moved as easily amid the pomp of the imperial court as he did among the humble villages in the Krajina. Strossmayer was also as much at home in Vienna and Prague as Zagreb and counted among his numerous foreign friends William Gladstone and the liberal Catholic peer Lord Acton.

Yet there were differences. Jelačić had no vanity; in fact, he underestimated himself. Strossmayer could be very vain. 'It would be a great loss to Slavonia if I do not become the bishop of Djakovo,' he declared when the question of his elevation to the episcopate hung in the balance.[5] At the height of the crisis over Bosnia–Herzegovina in 1878, he described himself to Gladstone as 'a divinely appointed defender of Bosnia and Herzegovina'.[6] Jelačić was unquestioningly loyal to the Habsburgs and never deviated from the conviction that Croatia's hope depended on the Emperor being persuaded of the trustworthiness of his neglected Croatian subjects. Strossmayer reflected the disillusion that swept Croatia after the events of 1848–9; he looked on the Habsburgs more as a necessary evil. Jelačić opposed the Hungarians out of principle. When Strossmayer talked of Hungary, he was capable of venom. He told Gladstone: 'The Hungarians are a proud, egotistical and in the highest degree tyrannical race, and my poor nation is persecuted, oppressed and ill treated.'[7]

There was another difference. In Jelačić's lifetime, the Illyrians carried all before them. Their Magyarone opponents were a collection of befuddled nobles who feared change because it was change, and who found allies among dyed-in-the-wool clergymen from the Zagreb hinterland who opposed Gaj for displacing the *kajkavski* dialect. With the support of the 'peasant nobles' of the Turopolje, they could create an affray at the Zagreb county elections. They did not represent a living

Croatia in Austria–Hungary

idea. Strossmayer presented the Illyrian programme to a more sceptical generation. While the pro-Hungarian conservatives still lurked on the right of the political stage, bolstered by the repressive machinery of the state, a more vibrant popular force arose in Ante Starčević's Party of Rights; and they did possess an idea, an idea that Strossmayer was bargaining too much of Croatia's identity away in the interests of forming a common front with the Serbs. The politics of late-nineteenth-century Croatia was dominated by this clash of ideas between Illyrians and Starčević's nationalists, who believed Croatia should remain alone.

Strossmayer's family, like that of Gaj and Jelačić, was not purely Croatian, but a compound of Croatian and German–Austrian. The Strossmayers were from Linz. Josip's great-grandfather came to Croatia with the army, was based in Osijek or, as the Austrians called it, Esseg, where he married a Croat. Josip was born in Osijek in 1815. Educated by the Franciscans in the local diocesan capital of Djakovo, to which he would later return as bishop and where he would spend the rest of his life, he continued his university studies in Budapest and was ordained at the age of twenty-three. As was the custom for Croats from noble or military families, there was no question of his returning at once to provincial Osijek, or even Zagreb. Like Jelačić, Strossmayer took the high road to the Austrian capital where he continued his studies in the prestigious Augustineum seminary. In 1842 Strossmayer returned to Djakovo for five years, to teach in the local seminary. But a man of his intellectual abilities was not to be held in a backwater. In 1847 he returned to Vienna, was elevated to the rank of court chaplain and became a director of the Augustineum, a not inconsiderable achievement for a man of thirty-two. It was clear that Strossmayer was destined for high office in the Church and an influential role in the affairs of the empire, and in the turbulence of 1848 the young court chaplain acted as a conduit between Ban Jelačić and the young Archduke Franz-Josef, who was soon to become emperor. After only two years in Vienna, he was appointed bishop of his home diocese.

To many, not least to Strossmayer himself, it must have appeared the first step before receiving the see of Zagreb at the very least. Yet such was his controversial nature that this first step up the ladder turned out to be the last. There is a great full stop in Strossmayer's ecclesiastical career after 1849, when as an exceptionally youthful bishop of thirty-four he returned to the quiet little town in eastern Slavonia. There he stayed until his death at the age of ninety in 1905, after an extraordinary fifty-five years as bishop. Jelačić spent much of his own money on his beloved soldiers. Strossmayer spent nearly all of the ample revenues of the see of Djakovo on his clergy, cultural projects and the National Party. In 1866 he began work on the great neo-gothic cathedral whose spires, rising like needles above the flat fields of wheat and sunflowers in eastern Slavonia, can still be seen from miles around. He was passionately concerned with helping the Catholics, though not only the Catholics, of Bosnia, drawing on the ancient jurisdiction of the bishops of Djakovo over the see of Bosnia. When Archbishop Mikalović thwarted his plan to have Bosnian Croat seminarians educated in Djakovo, he attributed it to the Archbishop's jealousy on behalf of the Hungarians (who feared any coming together of Bosnia and Croatia). The setback fuelled his dislike of his metropolitan and his contempt of the Magyarones in general.

Strossmayer was too all-embracing in his talents to limit his efforts to ecclesiastical projects. From the fall of Bach in 1860 until 1873 he was the *de facto* leader of the National Party. The term 'Illyria' was not revived in the new era of party politics. Instead, Strossmayer's clerical friend and ally in the National Party, Franjo Rački, popularised the vogue notion of *Jugoslavenstvo* – south Slavism – as the party's programme. The term was publicised in an article of that name published by Rački in 1860 which called for the spiritual unification of the southern Slavs in the Austrian and Turkish empires, and those of Serbia and Montenegro. The aim was 'jednim narodom u duhovnom smislu postati' – to become one nation in the spiritual sense.[8] Rački recognised that Bulgarians and Slovenes had developed their own identities, and made no bones about the fact that the Yugoslav project could only realistically hope to involve Serbs and Croats. With that hope in mind, both Strossmayer and Rački worked to build up a level of trust between the National Party and the new principality of Serbia.

Strossmayer's fall from favour with the Emperor began soon after he entered public politics. In 1861 he was appointed to the 'Ban's conference', a body entrusted with the management of the first Sabor to be held in Croatia since 1848. The great dilemma the new Sabor faced was whether they should side with Vienna or Budapest over the question of participation in the new imperial assembly in Vienna, the Reichsrat. Most of the lesser nationalities in the empire – Hungarians and Czechs included – were against. Strossmayer agreed with them. Along with the majority in the Sabor, he believed there could be no question of joining this new-fangled imperial parliament until the nature of Croatia's ties with Hungary had been settled.

However, Strossmayer's policy of non-cooperation with Vienna brought the Croats no rewards. The boycott of the Reichsrat split the ranks of the National Party while the authorities took punitive measures against them, closing down the National Party organ, *Pozor*, and exiling alleged agitators. But in 1866, when Strossmayer visited Hungary at the head of a delegation from the Sabor to negotiate once more with the Hungarians, it became clear that Budapest would not reward the Croats for ignoring the Austrians. The talks were broken off in any case by the outbreak of the Austro-Prussian war, and within weeks of Austria's defeat at Königgratz the Croats discovered that the Emperor and the Hungarians had already reached an agreement to split the empire between them.

The compromise of 1867 marked the rebirth of the Habsburg Empire as the Austro-Hungarian Dual Monarchy. As in 1848 the Croats had attempted to squeeze capital from the struggle between Vienna and Budapest only to emerge completely empty-handed. Under the compromise agreement Croatia was handed over to Hungary and left to work out whatever form of autonomy was pleasing to Budapest. A new *ban*, Levin Rauch, an ardent Magyarone, was appointed to oversee the working out of Croatia's autonomy inside Hungary under an agreement known as the *Nagodba*. Dalmatia remained in 'Austria', that is, in the lands that were represented in the Viennese Reichsrat.

Under the *Nagodba*, the Croats retained the *ban* as the president of the Croatian government, the Sabor, the supreme court, the Croatian Domobrani (Home Guard) and the right to use Croatian as the language of administration and education. But the deal was worse than it sounded for the most important point was that the *ban* was to be appointed on the recommendation of the Hungarian prime minister, and would therefore be responsible to the Hungarian government rather than the Sabor. The Hungarian leader Ferencz Deak, however, was not hostile to good government in Croatia and did not wish automatically to foist unpopular rulers on to the Croats. For example, from 1873 to 1880 Ivan Mažuranić, a poet and a convinced Illyrian, was appointed *ban* for two terms, presiding over the opening of Zagreb university and numerous reforms to the primary school system, the press and government administration. The remaining disabilities of the Jews and Protestants were abolished. Nevertheless, the most important office in Croatia had been placed in the pockets of the Magyars, and the Croats were reminded of the consequences of this decision when Vienna and Budapest forced Mažuranić out in 1880 and replaced him with less acceptable figures.

The fiscal terms of the *Nagodba* were not generous either. Fifty-five per cent of Croatia's revenues were allocated for the use of the joint treasury, leaving 45 per cent for the domestic budget. In a further blow, Rijeka and the Medjimurje region were detached from Croatia and reincorporated into Hungary, reversing Empress Maria Theresa's decision of 1776.

Strossmayer was appalled by the agreement between Vienna and Budapest. He insisted that Franz-Josef should present himelf in Zagreb for a separate coronation as king of Croatia if he were to go ahead with a separate coronation as king of Hungary in Budapest, a demand the Emperor took no notice of whatever. However, Strossmayer's outspokenness certainly offended the court, so much so that he was threatened with the loss of his right to sit in the Sabor, and went into brief, self-imposed exile in France for a few months until matters had cooled down.

Meanwhile Strossmayer's followers were exposed to the taunts of the pro-Hungarian party, now known as Unionists, that a far more favourable settlement with Budapest could have been achieved if they (the Unionists) had been in charge. The elections in the autumn of 1867 reflected the electorate's disappointment; the National Party won only a handful of seats and the Unionists took control of the Sabor until 1871. Strossmayer returned to the Sabor after the Unionist defeat in that year with a mandate to renegotiate the *Nagodba*. But after failing to achieve a significant revision to the terms in 1873 he withdrew from public politics for ever, although he continued to wield enormous influence behind the scenes.

Strossmayer's disillusion with both Habsburgs and Hungarians in the 1870s turned him back to those cultural and ecclesiastical projects which had always accompanied his none-too-successful forays into politics. Here his efforts were far more effective. In the 1860s he had invested 50,000 forints in the foundation of a new centre for intellectual study and debate in Zagreb, which under his influence was deliberately named the *Yugoslav* Academy of Art and Science. His inaugural address – 'All which is done for the faith is profitable to science and ... all which is done for science is to the advantage of the faith'[9] – encapsulated his optimistic, almost modernist theology. The first president was his friend Rački, a great authority on early Slavonic history and the Glagolitic liturgy as well as a close colleague in the National Party. The new institution, whose statutes were finally confirmed by the Emperor in 1866, brought together not only Croats from Slavonia, Dalmatia and Bosnia, but scholars from Serbia, Slovenia, the Czech lands, Russia and Bulgaria. The academy promptly established itself as the centre of Croatia's reinvigorated intellectual life, publishing a scientific journal, *Rad*, from 1867 as well as invaluable editions on Croatian historical sources and antiquities.[10]

Apart from his work on the Academy of Art and Science, Strossmayer busied himself also with upgrading the status of Zagreb's old academy into a proper university. And to this project he also contributed large sums of his own money and his annual salary as *veliki župan* (high sheriff) of Virovitica. The idea was taken up by the first Sabor after the Bach era in 1861, and after numerous delays the University of Agram (Zagreb) was finally opened in 1874. There were at first only three departments and it was not on a level with the university in Prague. But it was the first institution of its kind in any of the southern Slav lands.

The creation of the Yugoslav Academy of Art and Science recalls Strossmayer's other great cause – the reconciliation of the Catholic and Orthodox Churches, which he regarded as the prerequisite of any serious project of union between Croats and Serbs. As such he bitterly opposed the prevailing trend in the Catholic Church of his day towards narrowing the definition of Catholicism and erecting high doctrinal battlements around the Catholic faith. Having already infuriated the Emperor, he was now set on collision course with the Pope at the First Vatican Council of 1871.

With Italy on the verge of reunification and Garibaldi's armies encircling Rome, the vast majority of bishops shared Pius IX's determination to deliver a ringing statement of defiance, not just against the kingdom of Italy, but against modern civilisation. But Strossmayer was unimpressed. A friend – like Gaj – of Jan Kollar, the Lutheran pan-Slav

Slovak, he despised the Church's persecutory attitude to Protestants as well as Rome's unthinking contempt for the Eastern Churches. The result was a dreadful scene. While delivering his speech against papal infallibility at the Council, he was drowned out by a chorus of Spanish and Italian bishops baying: 'Lucifer! Anathema!' Forced to come down from the pulpit before he had finished his oration, he absented himself from the final session on 18 July when the papal infallibility was proclaimed. He told Dean Rački: 'These Romans employ the same weapons against me which the Germans and Hungarians used against me in order to paralyse my political influence.'[11]

This stressful experience in Rome, following years of strained relations with Vienna and with his own archbishop in Zagreb, pushed Strossmayer into more extreme views, and stirred up in him a romantic reverence for Russia and the other Orthodox nations. 'I need hardly to recommend [the Montenegrins] to you,' he enthused to Gladstone. 'If any people deserve the world's admiration, it is this splendid Montenegrin people, which has taken up its abode like an eagle on a lofty and barren crag in order to buy its freedom.'[12] In 1881 he sent a telegram of congratulation to St Vladimir's university in Kiev that was so adulatory of the Tsar's government – praising 'Russia's glorious international role' – that it simply amazed Franz-Josef. Strossmayer knew he was courting trouble; he even said with a touch of melodrama that it might lead to his being deprived of his see. In the event he was merely snubbed by the Emperor when the bishops were summoned to attend him at Bjelovar during military manoeuvres. But the action wrecked his chances of succeeding to the see of Zagreb when his old foe Archbishop Mikalović died in 1891.

His interest in reconciliation with the Eastern Churches was not reciprocated in the slightest, however. In Orthodox Serbia, where the practice of the Catholic religion was to all intents and purposes forbidden, he was regarded with suspicion bordering on hatred as a subtle spokesman for Rome.[13] In old age Strossmayer gave up wooing the Serbs. He was shocked when the Serbian government threw itself under Austrian influence in the 1880s, an act which betrayed all his hopes of achieving a common front between Croats and Serbs on the basis of *Jugoslavenstvo*. At the same time the rise of an exclusive and aggressive brand of Serb nationalism, in which Croats had no part, depressed him profoundly. The about-turn in his views was so marked that by 1885, when Serbia declared war on Bulgaria, he was delighted that the Serbs were roundly defeated. 'The idea of resurrecting [the fourteenth-century Serb Tsar] Dušan's kingdom is insane and illusory,' he fumed. The Serbs, he complained, were now 'crushing the idea of a Croatian state. We should pray now that they see that the grave which they were digging for others, they were preparing first of all for themselves.'[14] The other great trial of his old age did not concern Serbia. It was the awful knowledge that his position among the Croats had been usurped by his hated rival, Ante Starčević.

Strossmayer's great rival started off as enthusiastic about the Illyrian movement as he was. Born on 23 May 1823 in the village of Žitnik, near Gospić, in the Lika region, to a Croat father and a mother from a Serb Orthodox family, Starčević was just old enough to have become an adult by the time of the great events of 1848. His first formative influence was that of an uncle, Šime Starčević, an enlightened clergyman from the coastal town of Karlobag who became an ardent supporter of the short-lived Napoleonic regime in Dalmatia and published an Illyrian–French phrasebook under General Marmont. The young Starčević drank deep from the waters of the Romantic movement, publishing melancholy poems about ruined towns, dead kings and the national revival, some of which were published in a Serbian review called *Bačka Vila* (Faery of Bačka) of Novi Sad in Vojvodina (one of the few Serb periodicals to take an interest in the Illyrian movement) and in the *Zora Dalmatinska* (Dalmatian Dawn), which was set up to propagate the Illyrian cause in Dalmatia. Alongside most young Croatian students in 1848 Starčević was enthusiastic about the appointment of Jelačić as *ban* and was disappointed by the results.

Up until 1852, Starčević's ideas deviated little from the tenets of the other lights of the Illyrian movement. But in 1852 their paths diverged when the budding young writer published a savage literary assault on the Serbs. 'The Croatians, gentlemen, fought. They were not anybody's slaves,' he declared. 'They did not beg Byzantium for rags. The Croatians have an organised state, their country system ... an army and a navy, they engage in trade. In sum, the Croatians are a nation organised as a state. There is no such evidence for the Serbs.'[15] The assumption that the Serbs had received their medieval state by 'begging' for it from Byzantium was unprecedented from a writer in the Illyrian camp, and drew a shocked rebuke from the discredited figure of Gaj, whose *Narodne Novine* was now financially in the pockets of the Viennese authorities. Rude the assumption certainly was. Yet to an extent Starčević reflected rather than initiated the decline of the Illyrian movement.

The Illyrian movement had begun in the 1830s as a reaction to Hungarian political and cultural pressure. Faced with Hungary's apparent determination to reduce Croatia to the status of a province, it had seemed entirely logical for the Serbs and Croats of the empire to unite against their joint enemy. But after Hungary was defeated in 1849 the Illyrian movement lacked an opponent. Besides, the very premise of the Illyrian movement, the cultural union of all the southern Slavs, was looking increasingly unrealistic. Although a handful of intellectuals on magazines like *Bačka Vila* were enthusiastic, most Serbs had no interest in Illyria. They now had their own Serbian state, centred on Belgrade, where an assertive tone was being set in the 1840s by Ilija Garašanin, the foreign minister. Garašanin's well-known policy document, *Načertanije* (Plan), outlined the new country's foreign policy goals. Garašanin paid no heed to *Jugoslavenstvo*; he thought only in terms of creating an enlarged Serbian state at the expense of the Ottoman Empire; his ambition was for Serbia to expand south to Kosovo and then on to Thessaloniki. He also cast a covetous eye over the Slavs of the Habsburg Empire. It was significant that even Karadžić, a Serb intellectual who had enjoyed extensive contacts with Gaj and the Illyrian leaders, was just as dismissive about the Illyrian concept.

Karadžić cheerfully expounded the view that most of the inhabitants of Slavonia, Dalmatia and Bosnia, with the possible exception of a few čakavski-speaking islanders on the Adriatic, were Serbs, though he admitted that 'those [Serbs] of the Roman Catholic Church find it difficult to call themselves Serbs but will probably get used to it little by little, for if they do not want to be Serbs they have no other choice ...'.[16]

His yardstick was linguistic; those who spoke a language that was similar to Serbian were Serbs, whether they knew it or not. To Karadžić the words 'Croatia' and 'Croatian' were quaint geographical and historic expressions into which some people – irritatingly – read too much. And Karadžić seemed to get his way, for, in 1850, when a group of Croat and Serb intellectuals, including Karadžić, met in Vienna to work out a compromise formula on a common literary language, the results conceded most of the controversial points to the Serbs.

The ideas coming out of mid-nineteenth-century Belgrade – ideas that were utterly at variance with everything Gaj, Strossmayer and the Illyrian party stood for – had a profound effect on the Orthodox inhabitants of Croatia. For centuries they had been called Vlachs, Morlachs, Serbs, Orthodox, even Greeks. As late as 1848 it seemed quite natural for Rajačić, the Serb Metropolitan of Sremski Karlovci, to preside over the installation of Jelačić as *ban* of Croatia, and pronounce his blessing on the Triune Kingdom of Croatia. Just one generation later, such an act would have appeared incongruous, for the rise of Serbia quickly created an alternative focus of loyalty among the Orthodox inhabitants of the Habsburg Empire, a process which was greatly helped by the local Serb Orthodox clergy. They did not become automatically hostile to Croatia, or disloyal to the Habsburgs. But there was a profound shift of allegiance in the mid-nineteenth century and a great homogenisation around the conviction that to be Orthodox was to be Serb. The terms 'Vlach' and 'Morlach' faded away, or took on pejorative connotations. Henceforth their loyalty became conditional on recognition of the separate status of the Serb nation in Croatia. Starčević's polemics about

Serbs may have sharpened the division, but the division was already there.

While the Bach system was in force, these disputes remained the preserve of periodicals read by tiny, if influential, groups of people. But, after the revival in 1861 of the Sabor, Starčević had a platform from which to expound his views, which had hardened against the Serbs and the Austrians in equal measure since the row in 1852. In the elections of that year Starčević stood successfully as a representative for Rijeka. The manifesto he produced marked the birth of what was to become a most influential political force in Croatia, the Party of Rights.

Starčević insisted that Dalmatia, Slavonia, Istria and Slovenia ought to be unified into one state, linked to Vienna only through the person of the Emperor, as King of Croatia. The Emperor ought to sanction Croatia's historic 'rights' by a separate coronation in Zagreb. He ought also to set aside the 'illegal' manner with which the Habsburgs had governed Croatia since 1527. Apart from the inclusion of Slovenia – really a lost cause by 1851 – it was the charter on which Croat nationalists were to campaign until the fall of the empire in 1918 made it redundant.

The Sabor of 1861 released the torrent of frustration that had built up in the Bach years as a result of Germanisation, the continued separation of Slavonia from Dalmatia, and of Civil Croatia from the Krajina. To add insult to injury, Vienna refused to allow the Krajina to send any representatives to the Sabor, as it had done in 1848. In the debate over whether to take part in the new Reichsrat, most deputies followed Strossmayer in supporting negotiations to restore the union with Hungary, on condition that Hungary recognised Croatia's separate identity and self-government. But Starčević, another fiery nationalist Eugen Kvaternik and a third deputy struck out on their own, demanding total independence from both Hungary and Austria. It was an extreme demand that had no chance of being adopted by the Sabor. Yet Starčević made a great impression on Croat public opinion with his bold attacks on Austria. The Croats, he said, must no longer put any faith in Vienna or the Emperor but only in 'Bog i Hrvati' (God and the Croatians). He went on: 'We must remove from the minds of the people the belief thrust upon us by Austria and Russia that we cannot exist in any way except as someone's slaves.'[17] Starčević's agitation resulted in imprisonment in 1863, while Kvaternik was sent into exile. But he had become famous.

The terms of the Austro-Hungarian agreement of 1867 appeared to vindicate Starčević's grim predictions. Strossmayer shared his gloom, but shared disappointment only increased the mutual hostility of the two ageing patriachs and their followers. Starčević retreated to journalism, printing ribald satires against his political opponents, including Strossmayer, in a series of publications, including *Zvekan*, *Hervat* and

Hervatska. He continued to write polemics against the Serbs. A particularly notorious one in 1868, 'Ime Srb' (The Name Serb), asserted that the word Serb was based either on the Latin *servus*, meaning slave, or on the Slavic verb *svrbiti* meaning to scratch. His favourite insult was to label an opponent *Srboslav* – a 'Serbo-slav' – one who believes in a greater Serbian state.

Starčević's close ally in the Sabor, Kvaternik, moved deeper into the revolutionary underworld. In exile after 1863, he roamed through Russia, Budapest, Turin, Paris, Florence and Zurich, seeking allies in the struggle to liberate Croatia by force of arms. After becoming disappointed about the possibility of Russia liberating Croatia, he turned his attention to the revolutionaries of Italy, France and Poland, drawing up unrealistic schemes for a Croatian revolution which he hoped would involve Cavour, Garibaldi or the patron of Italian unification, the Emperor Napoleon III of France. To him 'The Croatian question was the natural corollary of the Italian question,'[18] and after being received by Jérôme Bonaparte in Paris he wrote a book on the subject, *La Croatie et la confédération Italienne.*[19] He had a strange idea that the Šibenik-born Risorgimento writer Niccolo Tommaseo might become Croatia's head of state after the coming war of independence. Poverty and years in exile made him more eccentric. After returning to Croatia at the end of the 1860s, to work in pro-Starčević publications such as *Hervatska,* he resolved on an armed uprising. Unbeknown to Starčević, he travelled down into the Krajina and on 8 October 1872 started a half-baked uprising against the terms of the *Nagodba.* Proclaiming himself the prime minister of Croatia, and insisting he enjoyed the support of France and the Ottoman Empire, he roused about 400 peasant followers to seize control of the village of Rakovica and called to the frontiersmen of the nearby Ogulin Regiment to rise up. The *graničari* did not rise but obeyed Vienna, as they had always done. On 11 October Kvaternik was shot dead and his little rebellion was quashed. The authorities, however, were nervous. They proclaimed martial law and arrested Starčević. As a result the infant Party of Rights was condemned to a virtually underground existence until the 1880s.

In the last years of his life Starčević moderated his attitude towards the Serbs. He was greatly excited by the unification of Bulgaria with eastern Rumelia in 1883, which he wrongly attributed to the benign influence of Russia. Convinced that the Tsar might destroy Austria and adopt the role of midwife to an independent Croatia, he suddenly became much more sympathetic to Orthodox Russia, and in consequence felt it necessary to modify his views about the Orthodox Serbs. The number of his followers was growing rapidly, especially in the university. The students regarded the National Party as a worn-out force, and admired Starčević for suffering for his beliefs and for his refusal to compromise either with Vienna or with Budapest. But many of his newer followers thought his refusal to admit the separate identity of the Serbs in Croatia was old-fashioned. In 1883, in an article called 'Slovenci i Srbi', Starčević resolved that if Serbs and Slovenes insisted on maintaining their separate identity, then let them do so.

The growing moderation in Starčević's views about the Serbs and Strossmayer's disillusion with Serbia proper meant that there was little to divide the policies of the Party of Rights and Strossmayer's followers by the 1890s. Bowing to popular pressure to unite forces against the Hungarians, the two grand old men of the Croatian political stage met for an uncomfortable meeting of reconciliation near Krapina on 20 June 1893. But Strossmayer remained bitter. 'The man is a monstrosity, both in his exterior appearance and internal character,' he wrote to Rački.[20] The Bishop could never forgive his opponent for stealing the affections of the nationalist youth and for the fact that Starčević's party had become the greatest political force in Croatia.

Starčević died in 1895. Strossmayer lingered on until 1905. After Starčević's death his followers split, which was not surprising as the party could not make up its mind whether the main enemy was Vienna, Budapest or Belgrade. The faction which advocated co-operation with the Serbs merged into the National Party and gradually disappeared as a separate force. The opposing faction, led by Josip Frank (1844–1911), a Jewish convert to Catholicism, declared itself the Party of Pure Rights. The Frankists, as they became known, remained faithful to Starčević's earlier tradition of hostility towards the Serbs. But whereas Starčević told the Croats to co-operate 'neither with Vienna nor with Budapest', the Frankists were so consumed with thwarting the Serbs that they ended up becoming the tools of Vienna. After the formation of Yugoslavia in 1918, the Frankists were persecuted as enemies of the state. Not surprisingly, they were wholly unreconciled to a centralised Yugoslav state – the 'Serbo-slavia' Starčević had always dreaded. After the proclamation of the royal dictatorship in 1929 the Frankist heritage was claimed by the Croat Fascists of the Ustashe, led by Ante Pavelić, who governed Croatia under German and Italian protection from 1941 to 1945. There was even a family link, as Frank's daughter Olga had married Slavko Kvaternik, one of the Ustashe leaders.

Pavelić claimed Starčević was the spiritual father of the Ustashe-run Independent State of Croatia (NDH). His enemies among Tito's Communist Partisans, on the other hand, appropriated Strossmayer for their cause. In 1945, when Tito rebuked the Archbishop of Zagreb for the role the Catholic Church had played in the Second World War, he urged the clergy to return to Strossmayer's ideals.

But both men were grossly misinterpreted by the people who later claimed to be their followers. Starčević believed in a united southern

Slav state as much as Strossmayer. His quarrel was really only over the name and the centre of such a state, which he insisted ought to be Croatia, and not Serbia. His belief in Croatia's independence was absolute; he preferred splendid isolation in the wilderness to compromises with Austria or Hungary. It is hard to imagine him bestowing approval on Pavelić's Nazi puppet state, or on Pavelić's surrender of Dalmatia to Mussolini. It is also hard imagine him condoning Pavelić's policy of annihilating the Croatian Serbs simply because they were Orthodox. Apart from the fact that his mother came from an Orthodox family, Starčević shared the anti-clerical sentiments of the radical middle classes of the nineteenth century and he thought a Croat's religious affiliation was irrelevant.

As for Strossmayer, he dreamed that Zagreb and Croatia would be at the centre of the new southern Slav entity, and would have been amazed at the way his name was lent to a Yugoslav project centred on Belgrade, and in which Zagreb was reduced to the status of a provincial capital. He would have been most surprised to see his name invoked by Tito, the persecutor of the Catholic Church.

The ideas of both men were somewhat exhausted by the end of the nineteenth century. They belonged to the age when politics was the preserve of the 2–3 per cent of the male population that was entitled to vote, and when it was conducted in the salon, through newspaper columns and in the homes of the gentry. Neither man lent much thought to economic problems that concerned the great mass of Croat peasants. Starčević said there was no point in discussing any economic problems until the glorious day of Croatia's liberation.

To Stjepan Radić, the torchbearer of Croatian nationalism in the first quarter of the twentieth century, Starčević's programme was somewhat arid, especially the form in which it was carried on by the Frankists. 'Their adoration of Starčević, their limitless faith in Dr Frank and their hatred for the Serbs – these are feelings and passions, not thoughts and ideas,' he wrote. Radić preferred Croats 'of honest hearts and clear minds ... many are sincere friends of Serbs and all adore the Slovenes, but do not claim they [the Slovenes] are mountain Croats, nor that Serbs are Orthodox Croats'.[21]

What mattered to the new generation of nationalists was bettering the economic position of the Croatian peasantry, which they looked on as the uncorrupted life-force of the nation. Start co-operative banks. Open libraries. That was the way they wished to conduct politics.

9

'Our President'

Maybe you'll get the Slovenes, I don't know; maybe you'll get the Serbs too, but I know you won't get the Croats.
Radić to the National Council, January 1918[1]

The last quarter of the nineteenth century was dominated by the policies and personality of Charles Khuen-Hedervary, Ban of Croatia and the devoted executor of Hungarian rule from 1883 until he was relieved of his post in 1903. During his long term of office, Budapest undermined the terms of the *Nagodba* and stepped up its attempts to Magyarise Croatia. He proclaimed his motto as 'Red, rad i zakon' – order, work and the law – but in practice he played on the divisions between Serbs and Croats to increase Hungarian control. He concluded that his Unionist predecessor as *ban*, Levin Rauch, had failed to govern effectively because Croats and Serbs united against him. Khuen-Hedervary decided to break this alliance by singling out the Serbs for special treatment and currying favour with the Orthodox Church. The ambitious members of the Serb middle class who responded to his call were dubbed *Khuenovi Srbi* – Khuen's Serbs.

Khuen-Hedervary perfected the art of manipulating Croatia's tiny franchise to achieve the result he wanted in the Sabor and applied open pressure on the electorate, which included a great number of government employees. Simply, officials who failed to vote for his nominees lost their jobs. He was assisted in his designs by the Emperor Franz-Josef's proclamation in 1881, reincorporating the redundant Military Frontier into Croatia. This had been expected for some time, as the territory on the other side of the Krajina – Bosnia – had been occupied by Austria–Hungary in 1878. The union of the Krajina and Civil Croatia had been a demand of practically every session of the Croatian Sabor since the sixteenth century. But there was no rejoicing. Instead, the sudden increase in the number of Serbs in the Sabor only fuelled the ethnic tension that Khuen-Hedervary had done so much to promote.

The Ban promoted the Serb cause through newspapers, such as the Zagreb-based *Srbobran* (Defender of Serbs), which started publication in the 1880s. Its inflammatory tirades against the Croats reached such a peak in 1902 that they triggered an outbreak of anti-Serb rioting in Zagreb that year.[2] At the same time the Ban clamped down on the Croatian press and forbade even the most innocuous expressions of Croat national feeling. Thus, in 1883, the Hungarian coat of arms was ordered to be placed alongside Croat escutcheons over government offices in Croatia, an action that caused riots in Zagreb. In 1888 Khuen-Hedervary closed down the Croatian National Opera. The last performance, of the opera *Nikola Šubić-Zrinski*, was held in a charged atmosphere. During the scene in which Mehmed Sokolović Pasha, the Ottoman Vizier, offers the Ban Zrinski the crown of Croatia in exchange for the surrender of the Hungarian fortress of Szigetvar, there was a commotion in the audience. A short-sighted youth aged seventeen stood up and shouted: 'Glory to Zrinski and down with the tyrant Khuen-Hedervary.'[3] He was arrested. His name was Stjepan Radić and he was to spend a large portion of his turbulent life, until his assassination in 1928, in flight or under arrest. Inside or outside prison, he dominated Croatian politics as had no one since Jelačić.

Radić was born on 11 June 1871 in the Slavonian village of Trebarjevo Desno, the ninth of eleven children of peasants. That in itself was a distinguishing characteristic. Until then, the leaders of Croat parties had been drawn from the ranks of intellectuals and journalists, the gentry, higher clergy and the officer class. Living in the hothouse world of the officers' mess, the cathedral close or the salon encouraged abstract and philosophical ideas. As a peasant who had educated himself and knew the meaning of real poverty, Radić thought in more practical terms. Setting a new tone, the manifesto of the party that he founded in 1904 with his elder brother Antun declared: 'It became imperative that we should pursue a policy that will not only lead to a united Croatia and its complete independence, but will also provide for all people a better education and general social progress.'[4]

Zagreb was growing rapidly in the last quarter of the nineteenth century. At the time of the *Nagodba* it had housed about 20,000 inhabitants. By the 1890s the population had almost doubled and by 1910 it would double again to 80,000. However the beginnings of industrialisation only increased the Croats' feelings of resentment. The construction of the railways from the 1860s onwards brought home to Croats a feeling that they were a colony of Hungary. For political reasons the lines were built running north to Budapest, instead of running east–west to link the cities of Croatia with each other. The Hungarians also stifled proposals to improve communications between the Austrian and Hungarian lands of the Dual Monarchy, a policy which hurt the Croats. There was no railway at all from Croatia to Dalmatia, and not a decent one from Zagreb to Ljubljana, in Slovenia.[5] When the Emperor came to Zagreb to preside over the opening of the new national theatre in the presence of the Ban in 1895, it was clear the Croats' traditional *Kaisertreu* sentiment was at a low ebb. The imperial visit was marred by a noisy student demonstration in which kerosene was poured over the Hungarian flag in front of the statue of Ban Jelačić and set alight.[6] Radić was not a participant but was viewed – correctly – as the event's real sponsor. He was arrested and, along with a great many Croatian students, was forced to quit Zagreb university and continue his studies in the less repressive atmosphere of Prague. He moved restlessly through Russia, France and Switzerland, returning to Prague to marry his Czech fiancée Marija, and living for a time in an apartment next door to Tomas Masaryk, the future Czechoslovak President.

The Ban's cat-and-mouse game with the Serbs and Croats postponed rather than solved an emerging constitutional crisis in Croatia in the 1890s. In spite of Khuen-Hedervary's attempts to play the two communities off one another, and to patronise the Serbs, a growing number of politicians in both camps decided to resist a policy that benefited only Hungary. In the 1890s the followers of Strossmayer and Starčević[7] had merged into one bloc, which became known as the United Croatian Opposition. The new coalition bloc did not carry all of Starčević's disciples into its fold, but the new grouping still became the largest party in the Sabor.

In Dalmatia, the spread of Slav nationalism was accelerated by economic hardship and by Vienna's policy of vesting political power in the city councils in the hands of a tiny Italian minority. The region eked out a poor existence on wine and shipbuilding. But in the 1890s blight destroyed vineyards throughout Europe. Another blow was a favourable trade agreement reached with Italy that allowed Italy to flood the empire with cheap wine, undercutting the Dalmatian exports. The switch to iron and steel ships then ruined the Dalmatians' second principal industry; there was not nearly enough capital in the region to finance the restructuring of Dalmatia's old wooden ship industry. Nor was there any local money to finance the building of railways. By the turn of the century short lines linked Split to Šibenik and Knin but no further. As a result there were no decent transport links with either Bosnia or Croatia.

Poverty in Dalmatia drove tens of thousands to emigrate to America, and left the Adriatic islands with the half-deserted air they have retained ever since – outside the tourist season. But economic depression exacerbated the militant political convictions of those who remained. Throughout Dalmatia the Italians were displaced by Croats and Serbs from the municipal councils in the 1880s, with the exception of Zadar. As a result the Italians lost control of the Dalmatian Sabor to *narodnjaci* (Nationals) demanding unification with Croatia. An energetic Dalmatian journalist, Frano Supilo, used the more liberal press laws of Hungarian-ruled Rijeka to conduct a strong campaign against Khuen-Hedervary's regime in Croatia proper, through his newspaper *Riječki Novi List* (Rijeka New Paper). It soon became the most influential Croat-language newspaper. A close ally of Supilo's was the former mayor of Split, Ante Trumbić.

Under Supilo's and Trumbić's auspices, on 2 October 1905 forty Croat deputies from the Dalmatian Sabor met in Rijeka to demand the union of Dalmatia and Slavonia. In a historic document, known as the 'Resolution of Fiume', the deputies also agreed formally to recognise the distinct status of the Serbs and guarantee their equality as a nation, a demand that the Serbs had been voicing with growing determination since the 1860s. Ten days later, it was the turn of the Serb deputies in Zadar who agreed to support the union of Croatia–Slavonia and Dalmatia in exchange for the promise of equality. The final joint statement read like a tribute to Strossmayer and was enough to make the blood of any Hungarian or Habsburg official run cold. 'The Croats and Serbs of Dalmatia will work shoulder to shoulder as blood brothers in national and political questions and will endeavour with united forces to realise as soon as possible the union of Dalmatia with Croatia and Slavonia,' it read. 'Both parties will insist on and work [towards the goal] that the names Croatia and Serbia occupy a position of honour ... and that both Latin and Cyrillic scripts will be taught.'[8] After this historic agreement, a Croat–Serb coalition won the elections that year to the Dalmatian Sabor. The events in Dalmatia were then repeated in Croatia. After Khuen-Hedervary returned to Budapest in 1903, the Serbs wriggled out of the government's patronising embrace and formed a new political organisation, the Independent Serbian Party. In 1906 the United Croatian Opposition merged with the Independent Serbian Party to form a big Croat–Serb coalition. This also swept the elections to the Croatian Sabor. Thus in both Dalmatia and Croatia, Croat–Serb coalitions had taken over local government.

The mood of political flux in Slavonia and Dalmatia was fuelled also by an abrupt change of regime in neighbouring Serbia. Since the 1880s Serbia had been a virtual client state of Austria–Hungary – a state of affairs which wrecked any chance of co-operation between Strossmayer's supporters in Croatia and the government in Belgrade. But in 1903 King Aleksandar of Serbia was assassinated by nationalist officers who brought the elderly prince Petar, head of the pro-Russian Karadjordjević family, to the Serbian throne. The manner in which Aleksandar and Queen Draga were murdered – they were slashed to death in the palace – disgusted public opinion in Western Europe. But the liberal and nationalistic ferment of King Petar's Serbia proved attractive to many Croats. To Dalmatia's prestigious young sculptor Ivan Meštrović, King Petar was not a terrorist but 'Čika Pera' (Uncle Pete);[9] in 1911 a number of Croatian artists followed Meštrović's example and exhibited their art in the Serbian, rather than Hungarian, pavilion at the international exhibition in Rome. It was also significant that many of the artists chose Serbian themes for their work.

The political discontent in *fin de siècle* Croatia benefited the Croat–Serb coalition. Radić's party, the Hrvatska Pučka Seljačka Stranka (the Croatian People's Peasants Party) got off to an inauspicious start. Officialdom, acting under Budapest's instructions, was hostile to Radić. That alone ensured he would not get many votes, as government officials formed a strong part of Croatia's tiny electorate before the franchise was widened in 1910. The progressive middle-class followers of Strossmayer were also put off by the anti-urban tone of Radić's programme. There was opposition from the Church, which was competing to influence the same constituency that Radić was addressing. While the bishops were devoted to the Habsburgs, the lower clergy resented this political rival to the Croatian People's Party, which was a clerical front. In its first electoral test in the Petrinja by-election of 1905, Radić's HPSS came third.

The Croat–Serb coalition was tested severely in 1908, when Austria formally annexed Bosnia–Herzegovina. The province had been under Austrian occupation since 1878, but the annexation provoked a European crisis, and raised the threat of war between Austria–Hungary and Serbia, backed by Russia. The Catholics in Bosnia, led by Archbishop Josip Stadler of Sarajevo (1843–1918), were delighted by the annexation. So were most Croats, including Radić, who saw it as a step towards the union, or, as they saw it, reunion, of historic Croatian lands. But the Serbs, not just in Serbia but in the Habsburg Empire as well, were infuriated by the way Vienna had thwarted Bosnia's absorption into Serbia. The annexation crisis altered the whole tone of politics in Croatia. Under Khuen-Hedervary, the Serbs had basked in official patronage. After the coup in Serbia, Budapest and Vienna both became fearful of Serb pretensions towards the empire's southern Slavs. The Serbs' vociferous opposition to the annexation of Bosnia ensured that they were no longer seen as a benign force.

But the new official tone of hostility to the Serbs only welded the Serbs and Croats in the coalition together. In the elections of 1908 the coalition won triumphantly after the Ban made the mistake of trying to win the election without applying the usual police pressures. The coalition won sixty-five seats, the Frankists twenty-four and the HPSS three, Radić winning the seat of Ludbreg, in the Zagorje district, north of Zagreb. The Sabor achieved little, however. The angry authorities prorogued the assembly only a few days after the election.

The Hungarian government's failure to drive a wedge between the coalition drove it to desperate measures. In the autumn of 1908 it staged a series of political trials in Zagreb, involving some fifty-two Croatian Serb politicians, who were accused of fomenting agitation against the empire and of working for the Serbian government. The trials ended in 5 October 1908 with draconian sentences. Thirty-one Serbs were sentenced to jail terms and two leading figures inside the coalition, the brothers Adam and Valerijan Pribićević, received twelve years in prison each.

But the trials were a propaganda disaster for Budapest. Much of the so-called evidence brought against the Serbs was held up to ridicule by the defendants' able lawyer, Nikola Hinković. Far from splitting the coalition, the trials drew the Croats and Serbs closer together. In spite of the bad feeling aroused by the trials, the authorities blundered on. In 1909 an eminent Viennese historian, Dr Heinrich Friedjung, writing in an Austrian newspaper, the *Neue Freie Presse*, accused Supilo, one of the leading Croats in the coalition, of accepting money from Serbia. The charge rang hollow and convinced almost no one. Friedjung's sources were a collection of minutes from a Serb nationalist society in Belgrade, Slovenski Jug. But most people in Croatia, apart from the Frankists, were convinced these minutes were manufactured by the Austrian police. Supilo sued the newspaper for libel and was widely judged the victor when the newspaper agreed to settle out of court.

The elections to the Sabor in October 1910 revealed the extent to which both Vienna and Budapest had discredited themselves in Croatia. This time Radić's HPSS did better under a new, wider franchise, which had been enlarged from 50,000 to 260,000, then about two-fifths of the adult male population, and won nine seats to the coalition's thirty-five. The supporters of the Ban took only eighteen. The Frankists won fifteen.

In the four years preceding the outbreak of the First World War, Croatia became increasingly ungovernable. The expanded electorate was less amenable to the kind of official pressures that had worked under Khuen-Hedervary. The *bans* found it impossible to obtain a majority in the Sabor, so they were forced to dissolve it and call new elections. In 1912 Ban Slavko Cuvaj was driven to desperate measures, dissolving the Sabor, arresting Radić and suspending constitutional government in Croatia. On 8 June he was the object of a failed assassination attempt in the streets of Zagreb by two young nationalists.

The Balkan wars of 1912 and 1913 brought tension between Serbia and Austria–Hungary to unprecedented levels. Bulgaria's error in taking on Serbia, Greece and Romania in the Second Balkan War of 1913 resulted in Serbia nearly doubling in size. This expansion induced a mood of near panic in Vienna, where the General Staff demanded a decisive, short war to bring Serbia to heel. The generals got their chance after 28 June 1914, when the heir to the throne, the Archduke Franz Ferdinand, and his Czech wife, Sophie Chotek, were assassinated by Gavrilo Princip, a Bosnian Serb member of the underground 'Mlada Bosna' (Young Bosnia) movement in Sarajevo. Throughout Croatia and Bosnia, the Catholic clergy thundered loyal denunciations of the Serbs from the pulpits, and in Zagreb and in parts of Bosnia, Serbian shops were attacked by mobs. The empire lurched towards the long-expected war with Serbia, which was declared on 28 July.

Radić was pessimistic about the outcome. 'The only chance for Croatians lies in the total defeat of Austria–Hungary without, however, causing its dissolution,' he said.[10] Victory, he feared, would strengthen the Hungarians. Austria's dissolution opened up a nightmare scenario of Croatia's partition between Italy and Serbia.

Croatia's position was parlous. Lying on the southern edge of the Austro-Hungarian empire, its territory inevitably became a subject of potential trade-offs by the great powers in their attempts to bribe medium-sized neutrals like Bulgaria and Italy into entering the war on their side.

The Croats had good reason to fear that they would be sacrificed on the altar of secret diplomacy. On 26 April 1915 in the secret Treaty of London, the Entente Powers of Britain, Russia and France offered Italy the lands of Gorizia, Slovenia, Istria and the northern half of Dalmatia in return for declaring war on Germany and Austria–Hungary. At the same time Serbia was offered Bosnia, a stretch of Dalmatia's southern coastline up to Cavtat, and a large but unspecified portion of eastern Slavonia. Italy took the bait and entered the war on the Entente side, although its military value to the Entente was questionable.

While the Croatian politicians in Zagreb struggled to keep track of Italian aspirations, a Dalmatian trio comprising Supilo, Trumbić and Meštrović formed the nucleus of what would become the 'Yugoslav Committee' in Florence in November 1914. These three – journalist, politician and sculptor respectively – had given up on Austria–Hungary and decided to lobby for union with Serbia, albeit on the best possible terms for Croatia. Later, they moved to Rome, where they held talks with Serbian ministers between 22 and 25 November 1914. From there they moved to Paris and then to London, where they enjoyed the enthusiastic support of an influential and prolific British writer on Balkan affairs, Robert William Seton-Watson,[11] and his friend Henry Wickham Steed, *The Times*' former Vienna correspondent and future foreign editor.

The Yugoslav Committee was a self-appointed group and its members were aware that the Entente powers would treat them only as one of many tiresome lobbies unless they they were able to demonstrate that they were a representative body.

To bolster their credentials as a kind of government in exile they sent emissaries to London, St Petersburg and the United States and decided to form their own armed force, the Yugoslav Volunteer Legion, which was to fight on the side of Serbia. Supilo went first to London, where Seton-Watson engineered a meeting with the Foreign Office. In February 1915, visiting St Petersburg, he was alarmed to get wind of the details of the forthcoming Treaty of London, none of which was promising for Croatia. (The Russians were busy at this stage in trying to persuade Serbia to surrender their portion of Macedonia to Bulgaria and take Croatia in exchange.) Franko Potočnjak, the coalition candidate who had beaten Radić in the 1905 Petrinja by-election, went to the US. The American visit was important, as about 400,000 Croats and 200,000 Serbs had emigrated there in recent years, many to work in the factories of Chicago and Pittsburgh. 'The Serbian element knew well their duty towards Serbdom and would not move an inch further than that,' Potočnjak recalled. 'They listened with pleasure to the national union ... which they *eo ipso* identified with a powerful Greater Serbia.'[12] Nevertheless, he succeeded in persuading a congress of Serbs, Croats and Slovenes, convened in Chicago, to recognise the committee as their representative body and a Yugoslav National Council was established in Washington.

The Yugoslav Committee was established formally on 30 April 1915 in Paris. In May, without mentioning the Treaty of London by name, it issued a manifesto denouncing any acts of secret diplomacy involving Croatian territory. 'The Jugoslavs form a single nation, alike by their identity of language, by the unanswerable laws of geography and by their national consciousness,' it read. 'To transfer portions of them to another alien rule would be a flagrant violation of our ethnographical, geographical and economic unity.'

While his colleagues restlessly toured Russia, Britain and the US in an attempt to drum up diplomatic support for the committee, Trumbić, the chairman, fostered contacts with political leaders in Vienna, and with one of the leaders of the Croat–Serb coalition in Zagreb, Svetozar Pribićević, the brother of Adam and Valerijan, the Zagreb Trial victims of 1908. Together, they started intense negotiations with Nikola Pašić, the Serbian Prime Minister, in Corfu, which was the seat of the exiled royal government from January 1916, after Austria, Germany and Bulgaria overran Serbia.[13]

The Yugoslav Committee has been criticised by subsequent generations in Croatia as an unrepresentative clique of intellectuals who handed Croatia on a plate to Serbia without securing adequate guaarantees. But it is difficult to see what the alternative to their policy might have been. If the Croatian leaders had stuck by Austria, they would not have saved Austria from military defeat, in which case the Treaty of London might have been realised and Croatia partitioned between Serbia, Italy and what was left of the empire. They were convinced that the only solution for the Croats was to go entirely to one side or the other, and that if the choice was between Italy or Serbia, it should be Serbia. Their biggest problem was that they had few bargaining points in their talks with Pašić and the Serbs. Before his premature death in September 1916, Supilo resigned from the Yugoslav Committee in protest at what he considered an irresponsibly pro-Serbian drift of its activities. 'He no longer has any confidence in the Jugoslav Committee or in the Serbian government,' Seton-Watson noted. 'He fears the promises of the latter ... would prove false and that Pašić would yield to Russian pressure and revert to his old attitude *re* an Orthodox state.'[14]

Pašić had not dropped his 'old attitude'. The leader of the Radical Party was a straightforward Serb nationalist who aimed to create an enlarged Serbian state along the lines of the Treaty of London, by annexing Bosnia, parts of Slavonia and Dalmatia. Although he was in exile on Corfu, he still had a king, an army and the diplomatic support of the Entente powers. The Yugoslav Committee had only their maps, their briefcases and a vague programme.

Nevertheless, the Serbs were won round to the committee in 1917. In London, Seton-Watson and *The Times* pressed the case of the Yugoslav Committee on reluctant Foreign Office officials. Much more importantly, the outbreak of the Russian Revolution knocked the Serbs' main ally out of the war. Once Russia was out of the equation, the prospect of an Entente victory receded. It was at this moment of weakness that Pašić decided to go along with the Croats, put the idea of a Greater Serbia on one side and agree instead to a union of Slovenia, Croatia and Serbia in a Yugoslav state.

Trumbić and Hinković joined a Serb delegation on Corfu and together the two sides on 20 July produced a declaration. The preparatory meeting in Nice between Trumbić and Stojan Protić, a representative of the Serbian government, was an educative experience for the Croats. 'We have the solution to Bosnia,' Protić announced to Trumbić, in one of their discussions. 'When our army crosses the Drina we will give the Turks [Bosnian Muslims] 24 hours, well, maybe 48, to return to the Orthodox faith. Those who won't, will be killed, as we have done in our time in Serbia.'[15] The Croatian delegation fell silent in astonishment. 'You can't be serious,' Trumbić said at last. 'Quite serious,' the Serb replied.

After this ominous reminder of the difference between Croat and Serb political culture, the talks were summarised in an agreement known as the Pact of Corfu. The two sides agreed to work for union and a 'constitutional, democratic and parliamentary monarchy under the Karadjordjević dynasty'.[16] The task of working out the new state's internal organisation, however, was put off and left to the auspices of a freely elected constituent assembly.

The Yugoslav Committee was not the only political factor wrestling with Croatia's future. There was another group in Vienna, where the Dalmatian and Slovene deputies of the Reichsrat were also pondering their options. When the Reichsrat was recalled in the spring of 1917 following the death of Franz-Josef the previous November, the Slovene leader, Monsignor Anton Korošec, formed a club of about thirty-three southern Slav deputies representing constituencies in Slovenia, Dalmatia and Istria. They then issued a manifesto that went beyond the vague plans for the empire's constitutional reorganisation put forward by the new young Emperor, Karl, in May. In its petition, the club demanded the unification into one administrative territory of all the lands in the empire inhabited by Slovenes, Croats and Serbs (whether or not they fell under the auspices of the Reichsrat or the Hungarian parliament). They did not mention union with Serbia, however, and appeared to envisage a role for the Habsburg monarchy, as the self-governing state was to remain 'under the sceptre of the Habsburg–Lorraine dynasty'.[17] A year later Korošec abandoned the Emperor and threw in his lot with the Yugoslav Committee.

Radić was disturbed by the drift of events over which he had no control. He was suspicious of the Croat–Serb coalition, which he considered unrepresentative of the peasant masses, and was especially wary of Pribićević. In 1916 he led his little party into a short-lived alliance with the Frankists against the coalition. But in 1918 he withdrew, disillusioned by the Frankists' continuing faith in the Habsburgs. This he could no longer countenance after the Emperor in his coronation declaration as king of Hungary pledged to uphold the territorial integrity of Hungary, which included Croatia.

In 1918 the empire collapsed. In January, President Wilson produced his 'Fourteen Points'. Intended as the basis of a just peace, they included a call for the autonomy of all the peoples of Austria–Hungary, the rectification of the empire's frontier with Italy and an independent Poland. In February, there was a naval mutiny in the bay of Kotor, on the Adriatic, in which many Croats took part, and in May a meeting of the emperors of Germany and Austria at Spa resulted in Austria being bound still closer to the German war machine. In July events gathered pace as the Czechs and Slovaks formed a National Council, which the British Cabinet recognised as the trustee of a future Czecho-Slovak government, and the Slovenes formed a National Council under Korošec in Ljubljana, in August. On 26 September Bulgaria pulled out of the war, and it was clear the end was not far off. On 4 October the Austro-

The formation of Yugoslavia in 1918

Hungarian armies dissolved as the French and Serbs broke though the Thessaloniki front. Austria–Hungary finally broke with Germany and formally sought an armistice. Four days later, Korošec and Pribićević formed a National Council of Slovenes, Croats and Serbs, based in Zagreb. Korošec was appointed president and Pribićević became one of the two deputy presidents. The Emperor rushed out a proclamation on 16 October promising to reorganise the empire on federal lines and declaring that 'following the will of its people, Austria shall become a federal state in which each racial component shall form its own state organisation'.[18] But this came too late to be treated seriously. Moreover, the proclamation still excluded Hungary. Karl assured the Hungarians that the federalisation of the empire 'shall in no way affect the integrity of the lands of the sacred Hungarian crown'. On 28 October, the Czechs and Slovaks declared independence. The following day, the Sabor in Zagreb, acting as the constitutional mouthpiece of the National Council, formally ended the 800-year connection with Hungary and declared independence.

Although the new state declared independence at the same time as Czechoslovakia, its fate was quite different. The government of the Serbs, Croats and Slovenes had no means to defend its territory and was not recognised by any foreign power. Although Admiral Horthy, the future Regent of Hungary, surrendered the imperial navy to the National Council in Pula when the empire declared an armistice on 3 November, the Italians made use of the confusion to commandeer many of the vessels, blow some up and land troops in Istria and Dalmatia. On 5 November, Italian troops occupied Pula itself and on 14 November they seized Zadar. The following day they moved into Rijeka. The Serbs made no attempt to stop the Italians from taking this important port. In fact, the Serbs used the Italian advance to put pressure on the Croats. Pašić did not want to see the National Council stand on its own feet and worked to prevent foreign powers from granting it diplomatic recognition. At the same time, he refused to accept the right of the Yugoslav Volunteers, now numbering about 80,000, to be termed an Allied belligerent force.

In the territory controlled by the National Council there was social chaos. The peasants rose up throughout Slavonia, looting shops, cutting power lines, uprooting the railway lines, breaking dams in rivers and burning the landlords' estates. Short-lived peasant republics were even proclaimed in the regions round Valpovo, Našice and Donji Miholjac, in eastern Slavonia. Jewish shopkeepers, widely viewed as war profiteers and hated as a pro-Hungarian element, were a prime target. 'First of all they attack the Jews and then the counts and gentlemen generally,' the newspapers noted.[19] The Jews themselves saw with indignation that even the respectable middle class joined in these pogroms. 'Ladies and girls from the best circles went with the mob,' a Jewish paper in Zagreb reported angrily.[20]

While the peasants rioted, the Serbs of Croatia simply ignored the government in Zagreb and clamoured for union with Serbia. They had an important supporter in Pribićević, the council's vice-president. Although Korošec was the council's nominal leader, Pribićević was in real control of events, aided by the police chief of Zagreb. Together they organised demonstrations demanding union with Serbia and attacking Radić and the Frankists. Although the Italian invasion of Istria and Dalmatia had reduced the council's power to bargain with Belgrade and most members now accepted union with Serbia on whatever terms were offered, Radić still held out. After being appointed a member of the proposed delegation to Belgrade to oversee the final negotiations, he made an indignant speech on 23 November 1918 to the council's Central Committee demanding an independent Croatian republic. 'It needs more to make a nation than assimilation of tongues,' he warned. The Croats were rushing into union with Serbia 'like drunken geese in the fog'. 'Long live the republic. Long live Croatia.'[21] He was expelled from the delegation to Belgrade.

The other members journeyed to the Serbian capital on 28 November. There they accepted the terms Pašić had already drawn up. On 1 December, the delegation presented an address to Prince Aleksandar, Serbia's ruler now that his father, King Petar, had become senile. The Prince formally proclaimed the existence of the Kingdom of Serbs, Croats and Slovenes. It ought to have been the end for Radić. In fact, it was the beginning of his meteoric rise.

After Radić's assassination, a myth took hold that the overwhelming majority of Croats had opposed the creation of Yugoslavia from the start, and had been tricked into joining the new state by the Yugoslav Committee and the National Council. There is not much evidence for this. In Zagreb, there was a small revolt by some soldiers on 5 December who refused an oath of allegiance to King Petar. Apart from that incident, the mood in Croatia was one of confusion concerning the intentions of the Serbs. Fear of Italy and its designs on Dalmatia was much stronger. Leroy King, an American sent to Zagreb by the State Department to report on the mood of the former Habsburg dominions, described the atmosphere as peaceful and relatively prosperous in the spring of 1919. 'The vast majority of Croatians are strongly supporting a united Jugoslavia,' he wrote on 20 March 1919, although he warned that 'the city of Zagreb itself has a predominant autonomist sentiment, because the people would like to see Zagreb the most important city in Jugoslavia and do not welcome the idea of being second to Belgrade.'[22] In Bosnia, King said that 'the Serbian party is large and strong and carries the Mohammedans with it, as the latter are not very actively interested in politics. They are quite content to follow any decent leadership if it secures for them their religious and economic rights.'[23] A day later Radić was arrested in Zagreb for publicly demanding a republic. King was not impressed with the degree of opposition that the arrest aroused. He considered Radić a mercurial troublemaker.

There is no reason to doubt the broad accuracy of King's reports in 1919. Yet by 1920, the situation had been transformed. In the elections to a constituent assembly held on 28 November the HRSS (having changed its name to the Croatian Republican Peasants Party) won fifty seats, sweeping the board in Croatia–Slavonia and becoming the third largest party in the Belgrade parliament. It was a stunning triumph, especially as Radić himself had been sentenced to two-and-a-half years in prison in August for republican agitation. In the elections of 1923 Radić's electoral victory was still more striking. This time the HRSS won seventy seats and became the largest opposition party to Pašić's government.

One reason for the dramatic rise of the HRSS was that the franchise had been extended to the entire population: as a party of peasants, the

HRSS naturally benefited from the expansion of the electorate. But another reason was the extraordinarily insensitive manner with which Pašić and Pribićević, who was appointed Yugoslav Interior Minister, had handled the business of unification. The public was insulted by the arrests of Radić and his family and the harassment of his supporters. The middle class was angered when currency union was carried out in such a way as to reduce the value of the savings of the Croats and improve the financial position of the Serbs. The peasants were angered when the introduction to Croatia of a Serbian monarchy put paid to their millenarian dreams of a peasants' commonwealth. The Dalmatians were alienated when, under the terms of the Treaty of Rapallo between Yugoslavia and Italy in 1920, Istria, the islands of Lošinj, Cres, Lastovo and the city of Zadar were handed over to Italy, while Rijeka was detached from Croatia to become an independent state under League of Nations trusteeship. Nearly all Croats were angered by the centralising constitution that Pašić pushed through the constituent assembly on 28 June 1921. The 'Vidovdan' (St Vitus' Day) constitution abolished Croatia's traditional institutions, including the *ban* and the Sabor, and broke up Croatia (and the rest of the new state) into departments, governed in the French style by prefects appointed by the government. The electorate was gerrymandered to over-represent Serbian districts and under-represent the Croats.[24]

Radić's triumphs at the polls in 1920 and 1923 made him the unofficial president of Croatia. But they brought him no nearer to power. He boycotted the Belgrade parliament in protest against the Vidovdan constitution, and this excluded his party from a role in the decision-making process. Worn down by frequent arrests and spells in prison, he toured Vienna and London, visiting Russia in 1924 after the Comintern reversed its decision to support a unified Yugoslavia and came out in support of the right to self-determination of Croatia, Slovenia and Macedonia. The tour was a failure. In London, Radić discovered that no one was interested in his goal of a neutral, peasant republic. In Moscow, although he admired Lenin's New Economic Policy, he was ill at ease with Communism. After signing up the HRSS to the Peasants International, a Comintern front, he was arrested on his return to Yugoslavia. The arrest of the entire HRSS leadership in 1925, including his deputy and close friend, Vladko Maček, nearly broke his spirit and convinced him a dramatic change of course was needed. From jail he dictated a memorandum to his nephew Pavle, a deputy in the Belgrade parliament, which the younger Radić then read out in his uncle's name in the assembly. It was a bombshell. Radić turned the HRSS programme on its head, abandoned both independence and republic, and accepted the hated Vidovdan constitution and the Karadjorjević monarchy. Shorn of its republicanism, the HRSS shortened its name to the HSS.

The volte-face scandalised some of the party faithful and alienated extreme Croat nationalists. But Radić's spell over his followers was such as to persuade many of the wisdom of his course. His deputy, Maček, shared his pacific nature. Many others in the party had also concluded that the course of non-violent resistance and abstention from parliament was getting them nowhere and that Croatia needed to find allies among Serb opponents of the corrupt and dictatorial Pašić government. The results of the U-turn were speedy. Radić was released from prison and, in a gesture of reconciliation, helped organise the first visit of King Aleksandar and Queen Marija to Zagreb in August. In November he entered the cabinet for the first and last time, as minister for education. The experiment in office was a failure and lasted only six months. He had spent his whole life in opposition, much of it behind bars, and was not suited to collegiate government. His new Radical partners were annoyed when he stumped off through Vojvodina and Bosnia, holding rallies and making speeches against the government. He resigned in July 1926 and returned to the opposition benches.

This time, he was less alone. Pribićević, his tormentor for the first half of the decade, had fallen out badly with both the Radicals and with many of his colleagues in his own Democratic Party. Still faithful to the idea of Yugoslavia, he had become convinced that Pašić's corrupt Radicals had ruined it in practice, and that the Croat home-rulers were right after all. A sensational reconciliation took place with Radić, resulting in the formation of a Peasant–Democratic coalition which was committed to transforming Yugoslavia into a genuinely federal democracy. Pribićević's change of course was lasting. So was that of Radić, who was moving away from narrow Croat nationalism towards the idea of leading a common front of Serb and Croat peasants. The Radicals were now more dependent than ever on the support of Serbs in Serbia proper, the royal court, the police and the army.

The alliance between Radić and Pribićević created an incendiary situation. The death of Pašić in 1926, aged eighty-two, meanwhile removed a figure who, corrupt or not, was a force for stability. In January 1928, the new Prime Minister, Veljo Vukičević, tried to draw Radić back into the cabinet and split the Peasant–Democratic coalition. Radić's refusal to dump his new Serbian partners was magisterial. 'The peasant–democratic coalition has been accepted and endorsed by the Croatian and the Serbian nation in Croatia,' he wrote, 'and with such delight and wholeheartedness that that coalition will sooner turn itself into a united party than be broken up.'[25] In consequence, Vukičević formed a government with no Croat representatives, relying on the support of Slovene, German and Bosnian Muslim deputies.

From then on the meetings of the Belgrade parliament became increasingly highly charged, as the pro-government press inflamed Serb opinion with a hysterical campaign against the Radić–Pribićević alliance. At the end of the month there were fist-fights in the assembly between Serb and Croat deputies, during which Lune Jovanović, a deputy for the Serbian town of Kruševac, whipped out a revolver. Radić was banned from the assembly for three sessions, but on his return the atmosphere was worse than ever, and there was more physical violence.

During the Easter recess, Radić and Pribićević went back to Croatia. The two men held huge rallies in Osijek and other towns, where they demanded changes in the constitution and fiercely attacked the Belgrade regime. On their return to Belgrade, events took an even more ominous turn. On 14 June 1928 the newspaper *Jedinstvo* (Unity), which was widely seen as the organ of Prime Minister Vukičević, printed an open invitation for Radić to be assassinated. 'If you think the country is being destroyed, then your first duty would be – and remains – to kill on the same day Svetozar Pribićević in Belgrade and Stjepan Radić in Zagreb.'[26] .

In spite of the murderous undercurrents swirling round Belgrade Radić insisted on continuing to attend sessions of parliament, in order to block the passage of a convention with Italy. The end approached on 19 June, when Radić accused the ruling Radicals of acting less like deputies than like cattle, to which Tomo Popović, a Serb, shouted back that blood would shortly be spilt, and not the blood of Serbs. Puniša Račić, a Montenegrin Serb known for extremist opinions, forwarded a motion calling for Radić to be deprived of his right to sit in parliament for insulting the deputies. The motion was disallowed by the speaker, but the session of the 20th opened amid cries from the HSS benches that their leader's life had been threatened. Račić leapt up again, and made a wild speech asserting that Serbian interests had never been in greater danger than now, and that he would not shrink in using 'other weapons, as need be, to defend the interests of Serbdom'.[27] More shouting followed, during which Ivan Pernar, an HSS deputy, shouted back: 'You robbed the begs [Bosnian Muslim landlords].' Račić then jumped out of his seat, ran over to the HSS bench and pulled out a revolver, which he pointed at Pernar. Some other deputies attempted to grab his hand, but Račić threw them off and the sound of bullets exploded round the chamber. Pernar fell forward, seriously wounded. Račić then raced over to where Radić was sitting, transfixed in his seat. Pavle Radić darted in front of his uncle to try to save his life, but to no avail. 'Ha! I've been looking for you,' Račić shouted, blasting off at the younger Radić, who fell dead to the floor. One of the bullets lodged in his uncle's body. Račić then fled the chamber. Radić managed to walk out of the chamber unaided, but then collapsed in the corridor.

He was not killed. But his constitution had been sapped by a life of constant travel, flight and imprisonment. He was taken back to Zagreb, where he lingered between life and death. Complications set in. After delivering a final confidential briefing to Maček on 8 August, at 8.55 in the evening he died. The man whom the Croatian peasants, especially in his Slavonian heartland, called 'our president' was dead.

That evening Archbishop Bauer was informed that Radić was gone. He immediately gave permission for the great bell of Zagreb Cathedral to be rung – a solemn dignity normally accorded only to deceased bishops. The bells of all the parish churches began to toll in mourning.[28] The next day Radić's body was carried to the Peasants' Hall in Zrinski Square for lying-in-state. The funeral on 12 August ressembled more the funeral of a great monarch than of a one-time republican politician, and about 100,000 people took part in the solemn procession through the streets of Zagreb.

In Belgrade, King Aleksandar used the threat of civil war, a situation that the court itself had done much to ferment, to proclaim a royal dictatorship on 6 January 1929. The King abolished political parties, destroying the foundations of democracy and drawing power even further into his own hands. The Kingdom of Serbs, Croats and Slovenes was officially renamed the Kingdom of Yugoslavia and the country reorganised into nine provincial units, named *banovinas*, which were named after geographical features.

In Croatia Maček assumed control of the HSS. A certain amount of relief that the hated 1921 constitution had been abolished soon gave way to deep disappointment, when it became clear that the new *banovinas* would enjoy no real degree of autonomy. The police began to arrest and harass Croat activists to an unprecedented degree.

Among the politicians who fled abroad in the wake of the proclamation suspending parliamentary government was a young deputy from Zagreb. His name was Ante Pavelić.

Pavelić was born in 1889 in the village of Bradina, near Konjic, in central Bosnia, to parents from Lika who had moved to Bosnia to work on the Sarajevo–Metković railway extension. His origins were humble; in the village where he grew up the only educated man in the community was the local Muslim cleric, and in the evenings young Ante entertained the Muslim begs in the village inn by reading aloud from a book of Croatian folk tales. His Croat nationalism was fired by a trip to Lika with his parents, where, much to his surprise, he heard well-dressed people talking Croatian in the streets of Senj; hitherto he had imagined Croatian was a language of peasants. 'In Bosnia all the great gentlemen spoke only German among themselves, for whoever ate of the Emperor's table spoke the Emperor's language ... even though most of them were Croats, Czechs, Poles and Slovenes,' he later recalled.[29]

At school in Travnik, and later in Zagreb, he became a follower of the ideas of Starčević and the Frankist wing of the Party of Rights. In 1912 he was arrested in connection with the attempted assassination of Ban Cuvaj. But it was in the elections of 1927 that he first achieved national prominence, when he entered the Belgrade parliament as a deputy from Zagreb in a hardline Croat nationalist party known as the Croatian bloc, which was led by Trumbić. The Trumbić–Pavelić bloc won only just over 10 per cent of the vote cast for the HSS – a mere 40,000 votes in Croatia overall. However, it triumphed in Zagreb, where Radić's alliance with Pribićević was not popular. They won especially strong support among hardline nationalists in the university, where Mladen Lorković, son of a prominent old Yugoslav Committee politician, and Eugen 'Dido' Kvaternik, grandson of Josip Frank, and Vlado Singer, a Jewish intellectual, were important activists. Another pillar of the movement was Dido's father, Slavko Kvaternik, a former colonel in the Austro-Hungarian army.

After the assassination of Radić, Pavelić formed an illegal underground paramilitary organisation, the Hrvatski Domobran (Croatian Home Guard). A day after the King suspended parliamentary government on 6 January 1929, he set up the Ustashe Croatian Liberation Movement in Zagreb (an *ustasha* is one who takes part in an *ustanak* – an uprising). The movement had the following aims: 'The Ustashe movement ... has as its aims with all means possible – including armed uprising – to liberate Croatia from alien rule and establish a completely free and independent state over the whole of its national and historic territory.' The declaration went on to say that the Ustashe would 'fight to ensure that in the Croatian state only the Croatian nation would rule ...'.[30]

Pavelić then decided to escape before the police net closed in on him. After crossing the border into Italy he fled to Vienna, and from there he travelled through Romania to Vidin and Sofia, where he made contact with the anti-Serbian Macedonian revolutionaries of IMRO, the Internal Macedonian Revolutionary Organisation. In November 1929 the courts in Belgrade sentenced him to death for publicly advocating the overthrow of the state while he was in Bulgaria – an act that merely increased his popularity in Croatia.[31]

The Yugoslav government exerted all its influence on neighbouring states to curtail his freedom of movement. Expelled by the fearful Austrian government, he moved to the friendlier climate of Mussolini's Italy, where he was allowed to set up training camps for the renamed UHRO, or Ustashe Croatian Revolutionary Organisation.

Although the exiled Ustashe in Italy numbered only a few hundred, Pavelić proved his worth to Mussolini by organising diversions inside Yugoslavia that embarrassed the authorities in Belgrade. In 1932 Ustashe cells inside the country organised disturbances in Zagreb university and, in the same year, a small revolt in Lika. The 'Lika uprising' was not much more than an armed attack on a police station in the Velebit mountains and was put down with ease. But in 1934 Pavelić, 'Dido' Kvaternik and the Macedonians from IMRO put together a more impressive plan. While King Aleksandar was on a state visit to France, in Marseilles, he was shot dead by an IMRO gunman. Mussolini took fright at this *succès de scandale*, had the Ustashe interned and closed down the training camps. Pavelić himself was imprisoned until the spring of 1936. But the Ustashe did not die; it was merely frozen until such time as the leader was released. In Zagreb, Slavko Kvaternik continued to recruit and organise. Outside Italy, the newly formed Ustashe drilled and expanded their organisation as far apart as Vienna, Pittsburgh, Buenos Aires and Hungary. Within a few years, this unlikely group of conspirators was to become the government of Croatia.

10

The *Sporazum*

The unity of Yugoslavia! There has never been such a thing. ... That unification, sir, is unification downwards. It is the illiterates who command the educated; imbeciles who command the intelligentsia.

Ante Trumbić in 1935[1]

Shortly before the assassination of Radić in the Belgrade parliament, Josip Predavec, a Peasants Party official, gave this illuminating account of Croat perceptions of Serb rule:

> Right up to 1918 we lived under the guidance of native Croatian officials. The four main internal departments of government were housed in Zagreb, and in all internal matters, even under the Habsburgs, the Croat people were their own masters. Now, if you want to find those government departments, you must search for them at Belgrade ... you will further find that all the police, the civil service and even the railwaymen on the state system are Serbs. Every post is reserved for the predominant race, despite the fact that the Croatian people are by common consent a century ahead of the Serbs in civilisation.[2]

After the death of King Aleksandar in October 1934 authority passed into the hands of the late King's cousin, Prince Paul (Pavle), who was proclaimed regent for the duration of King Petar's childhood. The change did not at first convince Croats that the situation would change for the better. In 1935, the eighty-year-old Archbishop of Zagreb, Cardinal Bauer, was so distressed by the number of arrests that he travelled to Belgrade to present the Regent with a long memorandum on police outrages. In the same year a French writer, Henri Pozzi, met Trumbić in Zagreb.

The former Yugoslav foreign minister was in a furious mood. 'You are not going to compare, I hope, the Croats, the Slovenes, the Dalmatians whom centuries of artistic, moral and intellectual communion with Austria, Italy and Hungary have made pure occidentals, with these half-civilised Serbs, the Balkan hybrids of Slavs and Turks,' he

fumed. 'They are barbarians, even their chiefs, whose occidentalism
goes no further than their phraseology and the cut of their clothes.' He
also made a menacing prediction: 'Between us and the pan-Serb
camarilla which directs Yugoslavia today, it is not a question of force, for
they are by far the strongest, but it is a question of time, a question of
patience, until the day arrives when accounts will be settled.'[3]

This blistering tirade, from a one-time champion of Yugoslav unity,
throws light on the degree of bitterness felt by many Croats under the
royal dictatorship. Even Seton-Watson, Yugoslavia's devoted foreign
champion, was appalled by the condition of Croatia on his last visit to
Yugoslavia in 1936, although he found a glimmer of hope in the fact
that many Serbs at last were beginning to realise they could not carry
on for ever with the centralised unitarist state.[4]

Yet, as the memory of Aleksandar's death in 1934 faded, it became
clear that a window of opportunity had in fact been opened for a new
political *modus vivendi* between Yugoslavia's two biggest nations. With
the deaths of Radić and Aleksandar, the chief protagonists in both
camps had been removed. Vladko Maček, Radić's successor, although
as tenacious on the subject of Croatian home rule as his predecessor,
was a less volatile personality.

Then there was the character of the Regent. He was certainly an odd-
ity in Serbia's ruling elite. Thin, saturnine and sensitive, he was an
academic Anglophile. A defining experience in his life had been a long
sojourn in Oxford, with which he fell in love after being sent to study at
Christ Church. When he left the university in 1920, he showed no
enthusiasm about hurrying back to Serbia. Instead, he went to live in a
flat in Mount Street, in London, which he shared with the well-known
socialite, Henry 'Chips' Channon. For the next four years Prince Paul
mingled with the world of the Bright Young Things, entering with
gusto into the spirit of the Roaring Twenties. By the time he returned for
good to Belgrade in 1924, accompanied by his new wife, Princess Olga
of Greece, it was clear that he had been altered by his long stay abroad
and had become alienated from his Serbian roots, where artistic leanings were not much appreciated.

For Prince Paul and Princess Olga, returning to Serbia was a let-
down. 'Life here is a dreadful bore, and a monotony, and Paul feels it
too,' Princess Olga lamented.[5] The striking Prince and his lively consort were, however, enlivened by a trip to Croatia. Princess Olga was
delighted by the reception that the royal couple received in Zagreb,
where attitudes had not yet hardened against the Serbian royal
family. 'I had to speak to one lady after another, and nearly the whole
of the time in German, which is the predominant language there. ...
what made a specially good impression is that Paul attempted to kiss
the ring on the hand of the Cardinal [Antun Bauer], and as they are all

very Catholic, it made an excellent impression!'⁶

It was, possibly, a new beginning both for Croatia and for the Karadjordjević dynasty. There was a plan for Paul to set up perma-nently in Croatia as *ban*, and there can be little doubt that the young couple would have been popular. Paul's love of art and his 'European' outlook suited the Croats' image of themselves, and might have dis-pelled the growing conviction in Croatia that Serbs were all barbarians. The Prince's glamorous wife was equally well cut out for the role of Croatia's chatelaine. But it was not to be. The authorities in Belgrade appeared more interested in holding on to the Croats by force than in winning them over by flattery, and King Aleksandar was jealous of the reception that Paul and Olga had received in Zagreb. He may have feared that the young couple would preside over an alternative and more attractive court than his own, and that this might pose a threat to his control over the country. Tentative plans for Paul to go to Zagreb were scrapped and the King's cousin spent the next decade in the polit-ical wilderness, dedicating himself to the purchase of paintings and to pursuing an intense friendship with the art expert Bernard Berenson and his wife. Paul's relationship with his cousin the King was rocky, so much so that in 1933 the Prince and Princess even feared they would be exiled from Yugoslavia. His initial contacts with Croatia were not kept up. Instead, the royal couple spent much of their free time at the royal residence in Slovenia near Lake Bled.

The death of King Aleksandar plunged this aesthete into the lime-light. Although the new Regent made no immediate changes, it was expected he would regard with disfavour the prospect of continued rule over Croatia through a policy of coercion. He looked on the Serbs, and on Belgrade, with a cold eye. 'I don't suppose the desire for possessing pictures would be so great if I lived in a big city with fine museums,' he lamented to Mrs Berenson in 1935. 'But in a town like this, where the vicissitudes of history have destroyed every vestige of tradition, one feels sometimes starved for beauty.'⁷

The main obstacle to Paul's hopes of forging a new deal with Croatia lay at home. His dislike of the Serbs was reciprocated. He had never been part of the Serbian military caste, as King Aleksandar had been, and his authority over the traditional power structures in Serbia, such as the army and the Serb Orthodox Church, was weak, and was seen to be weak.

A second problem for Prince Paul was that his efforts came too late. The cheers he had received in Zagreb in 1924 rang in his ears. But he had not kept pace with events in Croatia since then, nor with the sour-ing of Croat attitudes towards all things Serbian following the murder of Radić. Because the Regent was intimidated by the Serb politicians, and because they distrusted him, change came with painful slowness. In

June 1935 the government of the Prime Minister, Bogoljub Jeftić, was dissolved.

In a symbolic act, Maček, who was still a dangerous terrorist in the eyes of the Jeftić cabinet, was invited for talks with the Regent in Belgrade, where significantly he received a warm welcome from the people of Belgrade. The Regent's invitation was an important gesture, and throughout the next few years Maček kept his lines open to the Regent through the offices of Ivan Šubašić, a moderate Croat member of the Peasants Party with connections at the Belgrade court. But little of substance emerged. A new government was appointed under Milan Stojadinović that promised much but carried out only superficial changes.

The next three years of the Stojadinović government were marked by a policy of vying for the favour of the Fascist powers of Italy and Germany. The old Entente powers, with which Yugoslavia had been in alliance since 1918, were in diplomatic retreat and after the German remilitarisation of the Rhineland in 1936 Stojadinović placed little store on the old alliance with France.

Stojadinović proved quite successful in wooing the Nazis in Berlin and the Fascists in Rome, although his policy puzzled the traditionally anti-German Serbian general public. The main problem with Italy was Mussolini's refusal to surrender Pavelić and his Ustashe to the Yugoslav authorities for trial in connection with the murder of King Aleksandar.

The Italians' efforts to persuade Belgrade that they were taking a tough line with the Ustashe were almost comic. In March 1937 the Italian foreign minister, Count Galeazzo Ciano,[8] theatrically informed the Yugoslavs that Pavelić was 'furious' with him. 'He keeps sending me messages blaming me for Italy's having abandoned the Croatian cause.' To prove the point he picked up a telephone in front of Stojadinović's emissary and called the Italian chief of police. 'Yes, Ciano speaking,' he announced. 'How are things with the Croats? Are they quiet and under control? I don't care. Strengthen the guard.'[9] Ciano kept the Ustashe locked up on the island of Lipari. But he would not extradite them.

There were no problems for the Yugoslav government over frontiers or exiled terrorists with Germany. In March 1938 Stojadinović went to Berlin. The Germans were flattered by his ham-fisted attempts to introduce superficial elements of Fascism into Serbia, by drilling his party followers and encouraging them to wear uniforms and make the straight-arm salute.

The Germans were also amused by the Yugoslav Prime Minister's antics at state dinners. At one party, held in Austria, 'Stojadinović began to dance the *kolo* with the German minister's wife. As the dance gathered momentum he became more and more excited and soon jumped on the food-heavy table. With a crash the table came down and Stojadinović and Frau von Heeren rolled in the wines, tea, ham, salami, cheese and fruit compote. ...'[10]

The Yugoslav Prime Minister supported the annexation of Austria, still foolishly convinced that Hitler posed less danger to Yugoslavia than the restoration of the Habsburgs in Austria. And he also expressed Belgrade's 'boundless admiration' for the way Hitler dismembered Czechoslovakia.[11] In Berlin Hitler repaid his Balkan toady. He assured Stojadinović that he wanted a strong and united Yugoslavia. 'In the Balkans we want nothing more than an open door for our economy,' he said.[12] By then Germany's economic penetration of Yugoslavia was in any case so far advanced that it amounted to a virtual stranglehold. In the mid-1920s Germany had taken only 10 per cent of Yugoslavia's exports, placing it in third place behind Italy and Austria. But by 1936–9 it had soared to 28 per cent, way above Austria (until 1938), with 11 per cent. It was the same with imports. In the mid-1920s 14 per cent of Yugoslavia's imports came from Germany, well below Austria and Czechoslovakia. The figure for 1936–9 was 34 per cent.[13] By the time Yugoslavia tried to extricate itself from Germany's suffocating economic embrace at the end of the 1930s, it was too late.

While Stojadinović was buttering up the Nazis, Maček was busy wooing the Serbs of Croatia. After the murder of Radić, Pribićević had become even more hostile to the centralising policies of the government in Belgrade, and where Pribićević went, his Croatian Serb disciples in the Independent Democratic Party followed.

From exile in Prague and Paris after 1929 he continued to denounce Aleksandar's dictatorship in ever more strident terms. He accused the King himself of masterminding the assassination of Radić. 'Puniša [Račić] was only the instrument,' he told Meštrović in Paris in 1933. 'The bullet was fired by the Great Serbs, and not just at Radić but symbolically at all Croats. I'm amazed you fail to understand that.'[14]

Pribićević died in Prague, a disappointed and embittered man. But Maček continued to build up the alliance between the Independent Democrats and the Peasants Party. The result was that in the local elections in Croatia and Bosnia he was able to win solid results even in traditionally Serb districts. By pledging allegiance to the dynasty and to the existence of Yugoslavia, he reconciled many Serbs in Croatia to the idea of Croatian autonomy, without losing the bulk of his Croatian supporters.

By 1938 Stojadinović had lost the Regent's support. Prince Paul was furious with him for bungling a project that he had set his heart on – a concordat with the Vatican. The Regent considered that the passage of this bill was essential, in order to break down the widespread conviction of Croats that they were second-class citizens. But the Serb nationalists were not interested in disabusing the Croats of this belief. Anti-Catholic feeling remained very strong in Serbia. The bill was opposed with enormous determination as it came before parliament, and there were clashes in the streets of Belgrade in the course of which the Orthodox Bishop of Šabac – one of the protesters – was hit by a policeman's truncheon.

The Regent, sensing that the matter had got out of hand, dropped the concordat but blamed Stojadinović for piloting the scheme ineptly. The last straw was the Regent's discovery that Stojadinović had been negotiating without his knowledge with the Italian foreign minister over the dismemberment of Albania. The two men had put together a curious plan for Serbia to expand south-west into northern Albania and take Thessaloniki in Greece into the bargain, while Italy was to occupy the rest of Albania. Had it been acted on, such a plan threatened to bind Yugoslavia irrevocably to the apron strings of Rome and to undo the Regent's policy of remaining free of foreign policy entanglements.

In the elections held in December 1938, Maček and his coalition partners polled extremely well, especially given the meddling by the police and the government bureaucracy. Maček won just over 44 per cent of the vote – Stojadinović a fraction more. Although the Prime Minister had scraped home, Maček was widely judged the victor of the contest. There could be no mistaking the seismic nature of the swing towards Maček in Croatia and many parts of Bosnia. Yet the government had secured a wafer-thin majority and was determined to remain in office.

The Regent used the first available opportunity to get rid of his unwanted Prime Minister. A chance presented itself when, in protest against an anti-Croatian speech by a deputy in the chamber, several non-Serb ministers withdrew from the cabinet. The Regent refused to allow Stojadinović to form a new cabinet, after which he was forced to withdraw. The Regent then sent for the little-known minister of health, Dragiša Cvetković, a Serb, and charged him with forming a government that would be acceptable to the Croats. The appointment of Cvetković, with a mandate from the Regent to find a historic compromise with the Croats, opened a new chapter in the history of the twenty-year-old Yugoslav state. Cvetković was a colourless individual with no political power-base of his own. He was there, and everyone knew he was there, for the sole reason that the Regent was determined to make a deal with Croatia, which meant with Maček and the Peasants Party.

The talks dragged on for months. Maček was a master in the game of brinkmanship, and when the talks appeared to founder over the issue of control of the police in the proposed Croatian autonomous unit, he kept his options open by making vague pledges to Italian emissaries that he was ready to start an uprising.[15]

While the talks on autonomy inched forwards Maček flirted with both Mussolini and the Serbian opposition parties. But, the more the talks progressed, the more Maček became convinced that Prince Paul was a more reliable negotiating partner. Once the prize of home rule was in his grasp he proved determined to haggle over every village. The Croats felt that the *banovinas'* borders had been drawn up in a discriminatory way, to ensure that Serbs formed a majority in most of them. Many Croats in the Srijem region of eastern Slavonia had been put in the Danube Banovina, where they were in the minority. Dubrovnik and the bay of Kotor had been placed inside the Serb-and-Montenegrin-dominated Zeta Banovina. The Croats of western Herzegovina had been put within the Sarajevo Banovina. Maček was determined to win autonomy not only for the two Croat-dominated *banovinas*, the Sava and the Primorska (coastal), which embraced most of Slavonia and Dalmatia, but for Croat enclaves lying in other *banovinas* as well.

After a week of haggling over maps in the company of a team of experts, Cvetković and Maček finally reached a complete *sporazum* (agreement) on 20 August 1939, which received the Regent's approval on the 22nd and was published the day after. The new Croatian Banovina included all the old Sava and Maritime *banovinas* with the addition of Dubrovnik and the bay of Kotor, about one-third of Bosnia and a large part of the Srijem region.

The agreement on competences was less comprehensive. The new *banovina* was to have a unified parliament and the post of *ban* was to be restored, though with the *ban* being made responsible to the Croatian Sabor, not to the joint parliament in Belgrade. Foreign affairs, foreign trade, the army, the post, the railways and certain key main roads remained the responsibility of Belgrade. Outstanding disagreements concerned the new *banovina's* budget and the police, who – confusingly – remained under the auspices of both the military in Belgrade and the *banovina* in Zagreb.

Altogether, the Croats had good reason to be satisfied. Only the Ustashe and the Communists were angry, the Ustashe because they wanted total independence and the whole of Bosnia, and the Communists because they insisted the *Sporazum* was a deal concocted by the Crotian and Serbian 'bourgeoisie' against the interest of the workers. For the Bosnian Muslims, the agreement was a disaster that marked the ruin of their entire political strategy since 1918. The leaders of the principal Muslim party in Yugoslavia, the Yugoslav Muslim Organisation, had lent important parliamentary support to the Belgrade government over the passage of the 'Vidovdan' constitution in 1921. In return the Serbs had agreed to respect the historic borders of Bosnia within Yugoslavia and had refrained from plans drastically to expropriate the holdings of the old Muslim begs (landlords). Now it availed them nothing as Travnik, ancient seat of the Ottoman pashas of Bosnia, along with Mostar, the capital of Herzegovina, both disappeared into the new Croatian Banovina. Šubašić, the messenger boy between Maček and Prince Paul, was appointed *ban* of Croatia. In exchange for the agreement on autonomy, Maček, somewhat reluctantly, agreed to join the cabinet, assuming the post of deputy prime minister.

The *Sporazum* might have solved, at least for a decent interval, the crisis in relations between Serbs and Croats that had threatened to wreck the Yugoslav state since its creation. Like the Austro-Hungarian arrangement of 1867, it solved the problem of the two largest nations in the state at the expense of the smaller fry. The Serbs lost control over the internal affairs of Croatia. But the division of Yugoslavia strengthened their hold over the Albanians of Kosovo, the disaffected Slavs of Macedonia and two-thirds of Bosnia. It was a more promising agreement than the *Nagodba* of 1868 put forward by the Hungarians.

But it was never given a chance to get off the ground. The agreement remained the brainchild of a Serb prince who was drawing on the dictatorial powers assumed by King Aleksandar, and who was out of step with Serbian opinion. It was the product of a government that was frightened by the unfavourable shift in the balance of power in Europe. Within Croatia, many were fearful that their newly won autonomy would be abolished by Belgrade once the external threats to Yugoslavia disappeared. Maček was convinced that the Serbian establishment – the army, the Church and the majority of politicians in Belgrade – were not reconciled to Croat home rule, felt the terms had been far too generous and were only waiting for an opportunity to get rid of the unpopular Regent. Then again, some Croats who supported the exiled Ustashe were too embittered by the experience of the previous twenty years to accept any kind of autonomy, however far-reaching. They regarded Maček as a traitor.

The outbreak of hostilities between Germany, France and Britain in September 1939 confronted the Regent with a terrible dilemma. His sympathies lay with Britain, where he had received part of his education and for which he cherished fond memories. He had family ties to the British royal family. His sister-in-law was Princess Marina, the Duchess of Kent, and he knew King George VI and Queen Elizabeth well. The Serbs' ties were with the Versailles powers, England and France, and they were congenitally anti-German, but the Croats' ties were with Austria and *Mitteleuropa*. So preserving the fragile agreement between the Regent's quarrelsome Serbian and Croatian subjects meant keeping Yugoslavia out of the German conflict with Britain and France.

At first, this seemed possible. Hitler was not interested at the beginning of the war in taking on Yugoslavia. It did not fall inside the sphere of the planned expanded German Reich, did not contain valuable oil fields, like Romania, and was not strategically vital, like Greece. The policy of currying favour with Berlin pursued by Stojadinović had borne fruit. It had soured briefly when the Regent got rid of his prime minister, but enough good feeling remained for Prince Paul and Princess Olga to head off for a sumptuous state visit to Germany in June 1939 which ended in a banquet given by Hitler.

But the delicate balance that the Regent was striving to maintain could not be kept up indefinitely. As the countries of Europe were forced to choose their side, staying neutral became an increasingly difficult act. The Serbs became more anti-German. The Croats became more determined not to go to war on behalf of Britain and France – the godparents of royal Yugoslavia. Maček was convinced that in the event of war the Yugoslav army, dominated by Serbian officers, would withdraw to pre-war Serbia, leaving Croatia to become a battleground. The conflict raging outside made it difficult to put the *Sporazum* on an even footing.

A visit by the Regent and his wife to Zagreb in January 1940 to shore up support for the monarchy and the *Sporazum* proved rather disappointing. The royal couple expected a warm reception following the promulgation of home rule. Instead they found that the Croats had gone cool on them, although the visit did not lack splendour. On arrival in Zagreb by train, the royal couple drove in an open carriage through the streets to the Upper Town, halting outside the ancient church of St Marks, opposite the Ban's Palace, where they were greeted by Bauer's successor, Archbishop Alojzije Stepinac. Later, the royal couple deigned to visit the humble village of Kupinec, where Maček lived with his family. The atmosphere of the visit overall was strained, although it seemed to improve towards the end. 'At the outset the attitude of the population was reserved,' the British Consul wrote. 'But they gradually melted to such an extent ... that some resemblance could be found to the conquest of Paris by King Edward VII.'[16]

The outbreak of war between Germany, Britain and France exacerbated a competition between Rome and Berlin for influence over Yugoslavia, while the British attempted desperately to woo Yugoslavia to the side of the Allies. The Italians were the most interested party, and were deeply concerned that the Germans might stop them from annexing Dalmatia in the wake of Hitler's annexation of the rump Czechoslovakia. In March 1939 Count Ciano had noted that the Duce was 'anxious about the Croatian problem, fearing that Maček may proclaim independence and put himself under German protection. ... on my advice he has decided to discuss the Croatian problem with the Germans. He said, frankly, that a change in the Yugoslav *status quo* in Croatia could not be accepted by us.'[17]

In the summer of 1939, the Italians began to ponder more closely the idea of sponsoring an independent Croatia under Italian influence and ruled by a member of the Italian royal house of Savoy. Berlin encouraged these aspirations. The negotiations between Maček and the Yugoslav government over autonomy were faltering at this point, and Maček played up the threat of an uprising for all it was worth in order to push Belgrade along. 'Maček no longer intends to come to any agreement with Belgrade,' Ciano reported on 18 May. '2. He will continue his separatist movement. 3. He asks for a loan of 20,000,000 dinars. 4. Within six months, at our request, he will be ready to start an uprising.'[18] A few days later in Berlin he told Foreign Minister Ribbentrop: 'An internal revolt in Croatia would not leave us indifferent. Ribbentrop approves, but I can see that he really prefers to maintain the Yugoslav status quo. [SS Chief] Himmler, on the other hand, tells me definitely that we must hurry and establish our protectorate over Croatia.'[19]

At the end of May 1939, as the plan to set up an independent Croatia under Maček seemed near fruition, Ciano described the planned agenda. '1. Italy will finance Maček's revolt with 20,000,000 dinars. 2. he undertakes to prepare the revolution within four to six months. 3. he will quickly call in Italian troops to ensure order and peace. 4. Croatia will proclaim itself an independent state in confederation with Rome, it will have its own government but its ministries for foreign affairs and defence will be in common with Italy. ... Mussolini is taken up with the idea of breaking Yugoslavia to pieces and of annexing the kingdom of Croatia.'[20]

The suave Italian aristocrat was no match for Maček, a consummate dealer, for all his affectation of simple peasant ways. For the Croat leader, hints of rebellions and foreign intervention were a useful tactic with which to blackmail Belgrade. And it worked. By August he had reached his agreement with Cvetković and there were no more meetings with visitors from Rome fixing the date for an uprising. Instead, to the dismay of the Italians, Maček entered the Yugoslav cabinet. The Italians were piqued and turned promptly from Maček to the exiled Ustashe agitator, Pavelić. His organisation had been suppressed in Italy since the assassination of King Aleksandar in Marseilles in 1934 and had languished in exile. Now it was allowed to reorganise and about 700 Ustashe members were released from internment in camps throughout southern Italy. In January 1940, Ciano agreed to meet Pavelić for the first time. He was not impressed by the Ustashe, whom he referred to privately as 'a band of cut-throats'.[21] But he was prepared to use them to advance Italy's aspirations in the Adriatic.

Throughout the summer of 1939, Germany had been egging the Italians on to act unilaterally in Croatia. But after war broke out in September, Germany changed tack and dampened down suggestions of an Italian attack on Yugoslavia. Instead, Berlin decided to force Belgrade to join the Axis camp with Germany and Italy. Throughout 1940 Berlin attempted to prod Yugoslavia into declaring its hand, while the Regent continued to evade making hard and fast commitments. What sank the policy of neutrality was the bungled Italian invasion of Greece at the end of October. The Italians greatly underestimated their opponents in their eagerness to rival the Germans, and by January 1941 Greek forces were not only repelling the Italian invaders, but were pressing on into Italian-occupied Albania. The prospect of an Italian military débâcle in the Balkans made a German invasion of Greece likely. The second blow to the Regent came in March 1941, when Bulgaria signed the Tripartite Pact of September 1940 (by which Japan had joined the Axis), enabling German forces to enter Bulgarian territory. Under German pressure the Regent agreed to meet Hitler on 4 March at the Berghof, the Führer's Alpine villa above Berchtesgaden. During the talks, Hitler applied his formidable powers of persuasion and promised in particular to guarantee Yugoslavia's frontiers.

The Regent tried to wriggle out of making a commitment with evasive words, but there was no escape. Two weeks later, the Yugoslav Foreign Minister, Aleksandar Cincar-Marković, was summoned to Berchtesgaden. Returning to Belgrade on 19 March, he briefed the Regent, Maček and the other members of the Crown Council on Germany's demands. They started with Yugoslavia's immediate adherence to the Tripartite Pact. In exchange, Germany was to guarantee Yugoslavia's frontiers. No German troops were to be based in Yugoslavia, nor were they to be allowed to cross the country. This was an important concession although its value was reduced by Germany's insistence that this clause had to remain secret and could not be included in the published draft.

The Regent was appalled by the choice he was faced with. 'My sister-in-law has married into the British royal family, my wife is a Greek princess, it is not difficult to guess where my heart lies,' he complained.[22] Nevertheless, there was no doubt that, for all his English sympathies, the Regent believed it was necessary to sign the pact to avoid the greater peril of invasion and civil war. The Regent formally had no vote, but the majority of the council supported his views. There remained only the business of signing on the dotted line. Cincar-Marković departed once more for Germany and Yugoslavia signed the pact on 25 March. The Regent, worn out by his endeavours, left by train for a brief holiday at Brdo, in Slovenia, on the afternoon of the 26th. His family remained in Belgrade. Maček returned to Zagreb.

As foreign policy was one of the areas left entirely within the competence of the government in Belgrade, Maček and the HSS had little impact on these events, beyond supporting the Regent's decision to sign the pact. Maček exercised no influence whatever on the events that followed fast on Cincar-Marković's return from Germany. As soon as the news of Yugoslavia's adherence to the pact was published, huge crowds took to the streets of Belgrade and other cities in Serbia, shouting 'bolje grob nego rob' (better the grave than slavery) and 'bolje rat nego pakt', (better war than the pact). The demonstrations were the signal for the Regent's enemies in the armed forces, supported by the British Embassy in Belgrade, to launch a putsch and replace him with an anti-German government. Shortly after 2am on 27 March, a group of coup plotters under air force generals Borivoj Mirković and Dušan Simović took over the radio station in Belgrade, the War Ministry, the General Staff and the Post Office.

Mirković recalled the event in a speech in 1951 in London. He said the idea of a coup had been in his head in 1938, and that he had discussed the possibility quite openly with most of the top generals, including Milan Nedić, the war minister. All of them had approved of the scheme but only Mirković agreed to take responsibility for the leadership of the country if it succeeded.

> I could not decide at what exact time I should take command or start the coup. I thought about this while awaiting the return of the signatories [Cincar-Marković and Cvetković]. My plan was all carried in my head – nothing was put on paper. At 2 o'clock in the afternoon of 26 March I definitely decided for the following night and went to the office of General Simović from where, later, I issued my orders.
>
> At 1am a slight drizzle began to fall and through the open windows of [General] Simović's office I was listening to the trucks and lorries loaded with my soldiers going to their positions and in the various parts of Belgrade. The whole coup was undertaken and completed like a flash of lightning. ... I felt I had fulfilled the wish of my people and my conscience was entirely clear. I sent for General Simović at 3.30am and asked him to come to General Staff headquarters. I turned over to him full command. ...[23]

The seventeen-year-old King knew nothing of these events, although he supported them entirely. Indeed, he was surprised to switch on the radio at 9am and hear someone impersonating his voice, proclaiming that he had taken royal power into his own hands.[24]

The Croats were oblivious to these developments. That morning Maček was awoken in Zagreb by his son with the news of the coup. He was then told to meet the Regent's train at Zagreb railway station. Hastening to the station, he found the Regent still in bed in the sleeping car, confused by reports of the putsch in the capital. Maček suggested that the Regent should remain in Croatia, and that the army units based in Zagreb should be mobilised in his support.[25] He said that this would strengthen the Regent's hand against the plotters in Serbia.

The Regent declined, not least because Princess Olga and their children were in Belgrade and he felt it was his duty to be with them. At Zemun station, outside Belgrade, he was detained the moment his train drew in at 7.10pm. He was ordered to sign papers abolishing the regency and then sent into exile in Greece. In the British Embassy there was a champagne celebration in honour of the fall of the man who had kept Yugoslavia out of the war.

In London, the British Prime Minister, Winston Churchill, declared that Yugoslavia had found its soul. He neglected to add that British secret agents in Belgrade organised by the SOE (Special Operations Executive) had played an active part, especially since the fall of France in June 1940, in helping Yugoslavia to find its soul. They had paid out considerable sums of money to enemies of the Regent in Serbian political parties and to various ultra-nationalist Serb associations, such as the Order of White Eagles. The payments were so liberal that some Serb politicians opposed to Prince Paul 'expressed surprise and regret to the correspondents of the Greek newspapers that the British Embassy had never offered them any money'.[26]

The coup confronted Maček with an awful dilemma. He felt a sense of personal loyalty to the Regent, who had ended his persecution by the authorities in 1935 and had worked tirelessly to overcome the hostility between Serbs and Croats. Maček was aware that the coup plotters were drawn from the same circle of Serb nationalists who had opposed the concordat with the Vatican in 1937 and the *Sporazum* of 1939.

The problem was that the Prince had gone back willingly to Belgrade. That gesture lent the coup legitimacy. To refuse to join the next government involved the risk of plunging the country into bloodshed. To add to the confusion, General Simović was on the telephone within hours, urging Maček to join the new government and reassuring him that the *Sporazum* was quite safe. Not only that, he went further, promising to extend the Croatian Banovina's competences.

Like Prince Paul, the Peasants Party leader was in an impossible situation. Although he appeared to be offered many choices, they were all poisoned chalices. 'I and all the Croats were convinced the coup against Prince Paul was launched because the agreement [on autonomy] "gave too much away to the Croats",' he recalled. 'Nevertheless, not to join Simović's government would mean automatically siding with Hitler. ... we were certain Hitler would finally lose the war and that we Croats must at the end of the war be on the side of the democracies. We could not have foreseen that the war would not be won by Hitler or by the West, but by the Communist Soviet Union.'[27]

After securing agreement from General Simović, the new Prime

Minister, that the Banovina would be respected and that the new government would immediately try and reach a new agreement with Germany, Maček went to Belgrade and joined the new cabinet.

The putsch was a boon for the Allies, as Hitler was forced to postpone the invasion of Russia in order to divert armies into the Balkans. But it was a disaster for Yugoslavia. Neither Maček nor Prince Paul was entirely blameless; for all his professed affection for English ways, the Regent had continued to govern Yugoslavia using King Aleksandar's highly undemocratic prerogatives. By appointing a cipher like Cvetković as prime minister he alienated the entire Serbian political class and made the agreement with the Croats dependent on his remaining in power. By excluding the teenage King from all deliberations of government he left him vulnerable to the intrigues of the Regent's opponents. Maček also made some mistakes. His intrigues with the Ustashe and with Mussolini in the 1930s compromised his reputation. He was repaid with Mussolini's undying enmity. As for the Ustashe, they destroyed his organisation when they came to power.

It was the end of the road for all of them. Maček spent the war on the political margins, at first in detention at his home village of Kupinec and later in detention at the Ustashe concentration camp at Jasenovac. He fled Croatia shortly before the arrival of the Partisans in 1945 and never saw his country again. He died in Washington in 1964. In the spring of 1996 his remains were brought back to Zagreb for reburial.

Prince Paul spent his remaining years after the war in various parts of Africa before dying in Paris in 1976; to the end of his life he continued to be pilloried in the British media as a traitor and as a German sympathiser. In exile, his relations with the Serbs got even worse. The nationalist émigrés never forgave the man who was responsible for the *Sporazum* with the Croats, and on his death in 1959 the Serb Orthodox clergy in Paris refused to conduct a requiem for his soul, which had to be performed instead in a Russian Orthodox church.

King Petar and General Simović enjoyed power for only a few days, before fleeing abroad for a lifetime in exile. The destiny of Yugoslavia passed into the hands of men of a different stamp: Pavelić, Tito and Mihajlović.

11

The Ustashe

A reign of slaughter has come to pass.

Bishop Mišić of Mostar, 1941[1]

The storm came soon enough. On 6 April 1941, Germany declared war on Yugoslavia. At 6.40am the sirens wailed in Belgrade as the Luftwaffe bombed the city, killing thousands of people. German armies streamed into Yugoslavia from Bulgaria in the east and from Hungary in the north. The invasion was backed up by Hungarian, Bulgarian and Italian troops. Maček, who had been staying in the Hotel Bristol with the other Croat ministers, fled to Vrnjačka Banja in southern Serbia with the rest of the government, while the King and General Staff set up base at Zvornik, in eastern Bosnia. As the Germans rolled south, the government moved on to Nikšić, in Montenegro, to Athens and eventually to London. But two days after war was declared, Maček decided to return to Croatia, after a final leave-taking of the King at Zvornik. Maček returned to find Croatia in a state of chaos, over which he proved able to exert little influence. Šubašić had fled with the King. On 8 April, he made a radio broadcast from Zagreb in which he assured the nation he would remain at its side throughout the coming storm. His advice was vague and, by calling on Croats to be 'disciplined', the Peasants Party leader did not make it clear whether he opposed or supported the invasion. Anti-Serb mobs, furious at being dragged into war with Germany by the Serbs, had taken to the streets and were wrecking Serb shops and businesses. The Yugoslav army offered the Germans no resistance and its collapse produced a mood of spontaneous public exultation in many Croat towns, where the Germans coasted in to a warm welcome. 'A wave of enthusiasm pervaded Zagreb at this time,' Maček recalled, 'not unlike that which had swept the town in 1918.'[2]

Overnight, power slipped from the Yugoslav state and from the Banovina to the Ustashe. Unlike the Peasants Party, they knew what they wished to achieve and wasted no time. On 8 April, as soon as the German invasion began, Ustashe supporters in the Yugoslav army garrison in Bjelovar revolted against their officers and proclaimed Croatia's independence. On 10 April, as the first German tanks arrived in Jelačić Square in Zagreb, Slavko Kvaternik, a former colonel in the Austro-Hungarian army and Pavelić's most important supporter in Croatia, proclaimed the establishment of the Nezavisna Država Hrvatska (Independent State of Croatia), known generally by the letters NDH, on Zagreb Radio. 'I appeal to all Croats, wherever they are but especially all officers and the armed forces in Zagreb, that they and the entire armed forces should swear allegiance to the Independent State of Croatia and its leader. Bog i Hrvati – Za Dom Spremni [God and Croats – Ready for the Homeland].'

Minutes later there was another broadcast on Zagreb Radio by Maček. German officers had arrived in his home in Kupinec and ordered him to consign authority over the Peasants Party publicly to the Ustashe. Maček agreed and told his supporters to 'co-operate sincerely with the new government'. To the Serbs it was an act of treason, as the Yugoslav army had not yet surrendered. But Maček was surrounded by German soldiers and later claimed he had had no choice.

The Italians moved quickly to ensure that Pavelić – their candidate – gained control in Croatia as soon as possible. As soon as Mussolini had been informed of German plans to invade Yugoslavia, he had summoned Pavelić from his home in Siena for a first face-to-face encounter in Rome, to brief him on his tasks. There was, as yet, no question of treating him as a head of state, so the dictator of Italy met the future dictator of Croatia in the dining room of the Villa Torlonia, the private residence of the Mussolini family in Rome. The Italians feared that the German invasion of Yugoslavia would get in the way of their own plans for Dalmatia, which is why Mussolini was so eager to get Pavelić to Zagreb. He was concerned in case the Germans should give Croatia to Maček, who had double-crossed them in 1939 and joined the Yugoslav cabinet. Italy's paranoia was unnecessary. The Germans remained sensitive to Italian territorial ambitions in the region.

The exiled Ustashe were surprised by the upturn in their fortunes. Since the assassination of King Aleksandar in 1934, they had been in disgrace in Italy. The training camps had been closed down and most of the 700-odd Ustashe in Italy imprisoned on the island of Lipari. From October 1934 to March 1936, Pavelić himself had been in jail. Following his release he had lived in comfortable but supervised retirement in Siena with his wife Mara and their three children, Višnja, Mirjana and Velimir. The other Ustashe were not so lucky. Colonel Kvaternik's son, Eugen 'Dido', spent almost the entire period from 1934 to 1940 in Italian jails. He heard the news that Germany had attacked Yugoslavia in bed when he accidentally tuned in to the BBC news on the radio.[3]

The Ustashe leadership were still in the dark when their followers in

The Independent State of Croatia

Croatia seized power. According to Dido Kvaternik, the Italian exiles heard about it on Zagreb Radio: 'Dr Pavelić was a bit thoughtful. When I asked him what he thought about the news, he answered, "Well, look, the Ustashe are taking power".' Kvaternik still had no idea that his own father had proclaimed Croatia's independence and had named Pavelić as *poglavnik* (leader). It was only at 9pm, when he strolled over to the Pavelić villa, that he found out what had taken place: 'Mrs Pavelić greeted me with the words "Have you heard the latest?" When I answered that we had heard the news from Zagreb Radio on the local Ustashe taking power, she answered: "But how! Croatia is free already. Your father proclaimed it in the name of the Poglavnik." On my asking: "In the Poglavnik's name?" she answered proudly: "Yes, in the Poglavnik's name".' She added: 'Now do you believe we are going home?'[4]

In Zagreb on 12 April, Colonel Kvaternik formed a provisional government. The following day, Pavelić, Dido Kvaternik and the other exiles crossed the Italian frontier and headed for Zagreb. Kvaternik recalled seeing, in the Serb village of Moravica, the worried faces of the local peasants as their convoy charged through.[5] There was a warmer welcome in Karlovac, where Pavelić presided over a council of local Ustashe leaders. At five o'clock on the morning of 15 April he reached Zagreb, stepped out of his car, barked a quick greeting to the waiting guard of Ustashe troops and delivered a short speech. 'Ustashe! We have won. We won because we had faith. We won because we held out. We won because we fought. Ustashe! We won because we were always *za Dom Spremni*.'[6]

Two days after his arrival, he formed his first cabinet, dividing the posts between the Ustashe faithful who had remained in Yugoslavia, and the exiles. Slavko Kvaternik was appointed deputy *poglavnik* and head of the army. His son assumed control of police and internal security. Andrija Artuković, a Herzegovinian, became the first interior minister. Mladen Lorković, son of a well-known pro-Yugoslav politician at the turn of the century, became foreign minister, and Mile Budak, a writer, the minister for education.

The first acts of the NDH made it clear that the new state was to be a carbon copy of Nazi Germany. There was no pretence at democratic government. The *sabors* summoned by Pavelić had no authority, met only occasionally and were composed of hand-picked nominees from the pre-1918 Croatian Sabor and Ustashe officials.

Instead, the Poglavnik governed through decrees issued from 17 April, which prescribed the death penalty for a huge range of offences against 'the honour and interests of the Croatian nation'. On the 26th the use of Cyrillic was forbidden. On the 30th a decree protecting the 'Aryan blood and honour' of the Croatian nation forbade marriages between Jews and Croats. In June, a decree forbade Jews to shop or to trade with non-Jews. On 10 October the anti-semitic legislation was completed by a decree confiscating Jewish goods. Other decrees passed in the summer required Jews to wear yellow stars, compelled the conversion of non-Catholics to the Catholic Church and ordered the erection of detention centres for political and racial undesirables. To speed up the trial and punishment of offenders, special courts were set up at the end of April. These lent an appearance of legality to what was, in fact, a policy of eliminating the new regime's political and racial opponents through persecution.

An important role in establishing the Ustashe regime's credibility among Croats was played by the Archbishop of Zagreb, Alojzije Stepinac. Stepinac had succeeded to his see in 1937 with the approval of the Serbian court, where it was incorrectly believed that he would act as a pro-Yugoslav force on the bench of bishops. The court laboured under this misapprehension because in the First World War Stepinac had fought with the volunteers of the Yugoslav Legion against the Austro-Hungarian army on the Salonika front. After his ordination in 1930 Stepinac rose fast in the hierarchy, being appointed coadjutor to Archbishop Bauer in 1934 with the right of succession to the see, when he was only thirty-six. In spite of his youthful Yugoslav credentials, Stepinac had matured into a convinced opponent of Serb domination. He strongly supported the Peasants Party and let it be known that he had voted for Maček in the elections of 1938. The Archbishop lent his reputation to the Ustashe regime without hesitation and quickly gave Pavelić his public blessing. Two days after the NDH was proclaimed, he called on Kvaternik and on 16 April he was received by the Poglavnik himself – before Yugoslavia had officially surrendered on the 17th.

The circular Stepinac distributed to his clergy twelve days after the meeting with Pavelić was euphoric. 'The times are such that it is no longer the tongue which speaks but the blood, through its mysterious union with the earth, in which we have glimpsed the light of God,' he wrote. 'We are convinced, and expect, that the Church in the resurrected state of Croatia will be able to proclaim in complete freedom the uncontestable principles of eternal truth and justice.'[7]

The chaplain to new Croatian army, Dragutin Kamber, recalled his own ecstatic joy on the formation of the NDH. 'The creation of the NDH was greeted by the enormous majority of Croats with indescribable delight,' he wrote in 1945.

I doubt you could have found 1 per cent of Croats who did not approve of it to the bottom of their souls. Pavelić was the hero of the day, the new and only programme, the realiser of ancient desires, the hope and guarantee of future days, the avenger of a tortured past ... an almost mystical being, a minor demi-god, the greatest Croat of all time, the most beloved and respected being besides whom Tomislav, Starčević, the Radićs (not to mention Maček) paled, just as stars pale beside the sun. ...[8]

The Vatican was more reserved than Croatia's hysterical clergymen. When the Poglavnik journeyed to Rome on 18 May to sign an agreement on the NDH's frontiers with Italy, Pius XII received him politely but he did not grant the NDH recognition. Instead, the Holy See conducted diplomatic relations through an Apostolic Visitor, Ramiro Marcone, who was accredited to the Croat bench of bishops, not to the NDH government.

The question of the new state's frontiers demanded attention as soon as the Ustashe seized power. The Ustashe's policy since its foundation in 1929 had been to unite all 'historic' Croatian lands in one state. By this they meant Slavonia, Dalmatia and Bosnia. The extremists also wanted to include Montenegro and the Sandžak region.

There was no controversy about Bosnia, as Italy and Germany were eager to punish the Serbs by awarding Bosnia to Croatia, part of Vojvodina to Hungary, Macedonia to Bulgaria and Kosovo to the Italian puppet state of Albania. But, as Pavelić had arrived on Mussolini's coat-tails, it was obvious there would be a serious crisis over Dalmatia, where the NDH's territorial demands clashed with those of its Italian sponsors; Pavelić turned out to be more slippery than the Italians had bargained for. He was conciliatory but evasive, pleading with Mussolini and Ciano not to ruin his regime in the eyes of the Croatian public by demanding too much too soon. In private, he boasted: 'We'll hold on, clear things up here and then throw the Italians into the sea.'[9]

The Poglavnik enlisted German support as a counterweight against Italian demands. Hitler was impressed by the Croats' pro-German reputation and was cordial to Pavelić at the four meetings they held during the war. But the Führer was not prepared publicly to contest Mussolini's ambitious projects in Dalmatia. The question of Croatia's frontiers was left to a meeting between Ciano and Ribbentrop in the Imperial Hotel in Vienna on 21 and 22 April. The Italians demanded the cession of the entire former Yugoslav coastline, from Rijeka (which they already held) south to the bay of Kotor. Next, Italy wanted to bind the rest of Croatia to Rome through a personal union under the House of Savoy. Thirdly, Montenegro was to become an independent state once more, under an Italian sovereign. The Italians toyed with the idea of installing Queen Elena of Italy in this post, as she was the daughter of King Nikola, Montenegro's last independent ruler.[10]

Ribbentrop believed that the Italian demands would ruin Pavelić and insisted on the proposals being watered down. Moreover, even the Italians were not united over their aspirations: the King and the army leaders opposed an adventurous policy in Dalmatia. Under a compromise, Italy settled for direct rule over a smaller portion of Dalmatia and a 'sphere of influence' over a much bigger belt of territory, running the length of the former Yugoslav coast and penetrating deep into Bosnia. Germany's 'sphere of influence' comprised the rest of the NDH – Zagreb, Slavonia and northern Bosnia.

Mussolini did not give up hope of gaining the rest of Dalmatia, but fell back on a twin-track policy. Ciano noted on 24 April, 'one that involves a continuous stretch of territory from Fiume [Rijeka] to Cattaro [Kotor] and one limited to historic Dalmatia. This last-named portion should be integrated by political contract which would put practically the whole of Croatia under our political control.'[11]

On 25 April, Ciano and Pavelić formalised the deal in the Italian-occupied Slovene capital, Ljubljana. 'A hell of a day,' Ciano recorded laconically in his diary. 'I see Pavelić surrounded by his cut-throats. He declares that the solutions proposed by us would have him thrown out of his job.'[12] The outcome of the haggling over land was the Rome Agreement between Italy and the NDH signed on 18 May. Italy received the port of Sušak, near Rijeka, the island of Krk, and a stretch of northern Dalmatia, running from Zadar (which it already held) to Split. Croatia – for the time being – kept the coast south of Split. The fate of the city of Split itself and the other Adriatic islands was put on hold. Croatia was to become a monarchy under a member of the House of Savoy, but not under King Victor Emmanuel himself.

The Italians wanted to keep the NDH weak. Croatia was forbidden to build a navy. In the Italian 'sphere of influence' Italy's armed forces enjoyed priority over Croat military and civilian authorities. The Italians behaved as if their 'sphere' was destined in a very short time to become part of metropolitan Italy, and undercut the NDH's authority as much as possible. They were still terribly afraid Germany might take Croatia under its wing completely and spoil Italy's plans in Dalmatia. Ciano found the Duce in a towering rage about Dalmatia on 10 June. 'The Germans recognise our rights on paper [but] in practice they take everything and leave us only a little heap of bones,' Mussolini raged.[13]

The NDH had no territorial problems with the Germans in the eastern portion of Slovenia that was annexed to the Reich. The NDH government did, however, have a problem with Hungary over the Medjimurje region, which Hungary occupied in 1941. The Hungarians proved uninterested in reaching a frontier agreement with the NDH and held on to the Medjimurje until the end of the war.

The Rome Agreement struck a terrific blow to the NDH's popularity. Until then, the new regime had been credited with sending the Serbs packing. Now the government had to wrestle with the consequences of handing over large tracts of indubitably Croatian territory to Mussolini. Pavelić justified his acts to his hand-picked Sabor on 21 May. No enslaved nation had ever been freed with songs, but only with bloodshed and arms, he said, in a negative aside on the pacifist tactics of the Peasants Party.[14] He thanked Germany and Italy for their support for Croatian independence and vigorously defended the agreement with Italy. Although Pavelić brazened it out, the loss of Dalmatia was an enormous shock to the public. Dido Kvaternik blamed the agreement for the steep rise in support for the Communist Partisan movement in Dalmatia and for the loss of support of most Croat intellectuals.[15] The agreement also exposed a split – the first of many – in the ranks of the NDH hierarchy, between Pavelić and the Kvaterniks, who feared Pavelić's pro-Italian leanings and hankered for a more independent foreign policy.

Pavelić followed up the frontier agreements with his first visit to Hitler at the Berghof in Bavaria, accompanied by Artuković, Lorković and Ivan Werner, the Mayor of Zagreb. At the meeting the Führer devoted his attention to the NDH's ethnic mixture, and remarked that Croats made up barely one-half of the new state's population.

Contrary to the views of his army commanders in Yugoslavia, who mostly advocated a conciliatory policy towards the Serbs, Hitler said the NDH would have to persecute the non-Croat population in the NDH for at least fifty years. The visit was followed by another important visit to Venice on 15 May, at which Pavelić signed Croatia up to the Tripartite Pact of Germany, Italy and Japan.

Pavelić's next task was to mollify the Italians by choosing a new king for Croatia from the House of Savoy. The choice fell on the Duke of Spoleto – a decision of the King of Italy, who said he chose the Duke on account of his good looks and intellectual qualities. The King was soon disappointed.

'When we looked for him to give him the good news we managed to find him only after 24 hours in a Milan hotel, where he was hiding in the company of some young girl,' Ciano noted on 8 May.[16] By November, King Tomislav II of Croatia, as he was styled, was still in Italy and showing no sign of departing for his kingdom.

'He frequents restaurants and gets tight,' wrote Ciano in disgust. 'A few nights ago, in a restaurant near the Piazza Colonna, he put a twisted towel around his head in imitation of a king, amid the applause of the waiters. ... He is a fine man to be a king!'[17] As the fortunes of Mussolini's Italy and Pavelić's Croatia declined in tandem, any pretence that the King was about to depart for Croatia was dropped.

The Poglavnik needed no encouragement from Hitler to follow an intolerant policy towards non-Croats. As soon as the first racial decrees were passed in mid-April, the NDH embarked on a campaign of persecution of Jews, gypsies and Serbs. It disappointed the German commander in Croatia, General Edmund Glaise-Horstenau, who – unlike Hitler – believed the violent alienation of the Serbs would prove counter-productive.

Complementing the persecution of Serbs and Jews was a policy of wooing Bosnian Muslims. Following the teachings of Starčević, the Ustashe leaders believed the Muslims were ethnically pure Croats who needed to be brought back into the fold. To do this, they were quite prepared to stress the biconfessional nature of the NDH – much to the confusion of the peasants in Croatia proper who had been brought up on folk tales of heroic battles with the 'Turks', as Muslim Slavs were called.

At a speech in Križevci, Budak, the new Education Minister, explained: 'This is an Islamic state, where our people are of the Islamic faith. I stress this because I need to, so that you understand we are a state of two faiths, Catholics and Muslims.' He added: 'We Croats can be happy and proud that we have our own [Christian] faith but we must be conscious of the fact that our Muslim brothers are the purest of Croats, just as our blessed late teacher Ante Starčević told us. ... This is something we must build up, as we build up the NDH.'[18]

An important Muslim from Bihać, Džaferbeg Kulenović, who had been a minister under Stojadinović and Cvetković, was appointed deputy prime minister of the NDH. Other Muslims won posts in the cabinet. Pavelić was not concerned with whether the Muslims were Ustashe supporters. Hamdija Hadžić, the NDH Ambassador to Hungary, for example, had been a member of the Peasants Party. Meštrović's circular art pavilion in the centre of Zagreb was converted into a mosque and surrounded by three enormous minarets.

The Jews were easily dealt with. By 1941 they numbered about 14,000 in Bosnia and 23,000 in Croatia, and were easy to round up, as they were concentrated in urban centres. Some 11,000 lived in Zagreb alone, mostly Ashkenazi. About 8,000 lived in Sarajevo, most of whom were Sephardic, Ladino-speaking descendants of the Jews expelled from Spain by Ferdinand and Isabella in 1492. The Jews were quickly rounded up and transported to camps for extermination, either in Croatia or in Germany. Some were hidden by Bosnian Muslims, or escaped to the Italian zone of Dalmatia, where Zagreb's writ did not run, or fled to the forests, where they joined the Communist rebels. Most were caught and by the end of the war, over 80 per cent of the Jewish population in Bosnia and Croatia had been killed.[19]

The NDH's anti-semitic zeal was paradoxical, as the leadership contained several people of Jewish descent. Mrs Pavelić was partly Jewish, as was Dido Kvaternik, through his mother Olga, the daughter of Josip Frank. The SS was suspicious of the sincerity of the Ustashe's commitment to extirpating the Jews, noting that the NDH's anti-semitic laws allowed Jews to gain 'honorary Aryan' status if they contributed to the 'Croat cause'. In 1943 the SS complained that at least 5,000 Jews were still alive in the NDH and that thousands of others had emigrated, by buying 'honorary Aryan' status.[20] They directed that those caught should henceforth be transported directly to German concentration camps, rather than being left to the NDH to deal with.[21]

Fifty years after the end of the war, a Croat from Split provided this account of the diverse attitudes to the persecuted Jews in his home town, and the fate of two Jewish families he encountered:

At the end of 1941, during the Italian occupation, a family of five members arrived from Belgrade in Sustjepanska Street (then Via Stefano) next to our flat. According to what they had declared, they were Filip Majić, a lawyer, then aged about fifty-five, his wife Vuka, sister Ruža, a doctor, a daughter Lena and her daughter Mila. We knew they were

Jews and that they had false papers but no one spoke about it. At the same time, in the flat below, another Jew from Belgrade arrived, Simo Benvenusti, with his sister. They declared themselves as Jews. We all saw each other every day and were on good terms, and as it was forbidden to go out after 6pm my father used to sit with Mr Fici (as we called him) late into the night with some wine, playing cards.

And so it was until the fall of Italy in 1943, when the Partisans came into Split for about fifteen days. Then came the Germans and the NDH. Among other things the Jews were then ordered to report, with threats against those who failed to do so. Simo Benvenusti and his sister presented themselves and were taken away. We never heard of them again. Filip Majić and his family did not report, as they had declared themselves as Croats. Everyone in the vicinity knew they were Jews but we trusted no one would report them. We were mistaken. Across the way from our house lived an Austrian woman who was married to one of our people, and she reported the whole case to the Germans, with an additional accusation against my father for having a radio and listening to the news from London.

One afternoon, while Mr Fici was with us as usual, two SS men, from the Prinz Eugen Division and armed to the teeth, burst in. The atmosphere while they searched the flat from top to bottom cannot be described. They found nothing except our ordinary radio but they then demanded our papers, and Mr Fici gave them his identity card with the name Filip Majić on it. They asked my father whether he was a Jew, to which my father said they were not Jews, but Croats. ... but they stayed a while, not believing what they had heard. At last they left, after warning that they would check the matter out. Fortunately they never returned. Probably they had left Split. Mr Fici was speechless for a long time and the whole family terrified. ...

Time passed and the war ended. ... I discovered the truth about the Majić family, which had returned to Belgrade. From Belgrade a lawyer by the name of Isak Levi got in touch, alias Filip Majić, thanking my father for his courage. ...[22]

The Serbs were a more difficult target. Altogether, of the 6.3 million inhabitants of the NDH, about 30 per cent were Serbs and only just over 50 per cent Catholic. The Ustashe solution was to weld the Catholic and Muslim communities together. But this still left a lot of Serbs especially in Bosnia. Faced with this potentially disloyal fifth column, the regime decided on a dual policy of mass killings and mass conversions to Catholicism.[23]

The government made no secret of its intention to get rid of the Serbs. At a speech in Nova Gradiška in June 1941, one of the new ministers, Milovan Žanić, declared that the NDH had no room for these (Serb) 'settlers' from the east. 'I say this openly, this state, this our homeland, must be Croat and nothing else. Therefore those who have moved in must go. The events of centuries, and especially of the past twenty years, show all compromise is impossible. This must be the land of the Croats and no one else, and there are no methods that we Ustashe will not use to make this land truly Croatian, and cleanse it of the Serbs who have endangered us for centuries. ...'[24]

Deportations started within weeks of the Ustashe coming to power. On 4 June an agreement was signed between Croatia and Germany for the transportation of Serbs to Serbia. The original plan was for about 20,000 Slovenes from the German-ruled portion of Slovenia to go to Croatia, while a corresponding number of Serbs would go to occupied Serbia. But in the end the Slovenes were sent to Serbia, not Croatia, while the Croats forced as many Serbs on to trains bound for Serbia as they could. The transportations were carried out under such wretched conditions that the German authorities in Serbia complained. They had decided to set up a puppet regime in the rump of Serbia under the former Yugoslav Minister of War, General Milan Nedić, and did not wish to be overwhelmed by waves of refugees. The Germans later demanded a complete halt to the operation, although about 300,000 Serbs had been deported or had fled to Serbia by the end of the war.

The process of mass 'conversions' was equally violent. In a circular to his clergy, Archbishop Stepinac had insisted that conversion had to be voluntary and might only follow religious instruction. But the authorities took no notice of this. Nor did the Serbs. In some villages Serbs demanded baptism from the local Catholic clergy to escape persecution. On occasions, the Ustashe used the prospect of mass conversions to lure Serbs into a trap. The most notorious example took place at Glina, where hundreds of Serbs made their way to the parish church in the autumn of 1941 only for the doors to be locked and the would-be converts burned alive. High-ranking Serb Orthodox clergy, those who had not been deported, were earmarked for liquidation. Bishop Irinej of Dalmatia was interned by the Italians in Italy and the Serb Orthodox bishops of Zagreb, Zvornik-Tuzla and Mostar were deported to Serbia. But the bishops of Dabar and Banja Luka were beaten to pulp. The body of Bishop Platon of Banja Luka was thrown into the river outside the town. Bishop Sava of Gornji Karlovac was thrown off the top of a mountain.[25]

There were mass killings in dozens of towns and countless villages throughout the sprawling territory of the NDH in the spring and summer of 1941. Precise figures are hard to come by, but there were numerous reports of killings in villages at the end of April; of 184 Serbs killed near Bjelovar, 250 at Blagaj in the Kordun on 6 May, 300 in Glina, 140 in Ljubinje in eastern Herzegovina, 150 near Gacko in eastern Herzegovina, 1,200 at Grabovac, near Petrinja, as well as numerous other killings in a host of settlements in north-west Bosnia. At least 20,000 Serbs were killed in these pogroms in the summer months of 1941. On top of these local killings, the regime set up centres for the detention and extermination of the NDH's enemies modelled on Nazi death camps. There were several camps for 'undesirables' in the NDH, at Kerestinec, Stara Gradiška and elsewhere, but none achieved the notoriety of Jasenovac, which was set up in the summer of 1941 in a quiet village south of Zagreb on the old border between Croatia and Bosnia. The camp was not just a death camp; there were plenty of Croat political prisoners interned there in varying degrees of comfort. Maček himself was imprisoned there for about six months from the autumn of 1941 to the middle of March 1942, after which he was sent back to Kupinec under house arrest. But the camp became infamous chiefly as an extermination camp for Serbs, Jews and gypsies, who were often killed in the most brutal manner. Mental as well as physical torture accompanied the killing. The camp commander, Vjekoslav Luburić, was a sadist who enjoyed taunting his prisoners about the date and method of their forthcoming liquidation. The executions were frequently messy affairs, carried out by guards with clubs or hooks bound to their wrists.

After the war, the Communist authorities told the UN Reparations Committee that the total number of war dead in Yugoslavia was about 1.7 million, of whom about 600,000 had perished in Jasenovac. However, a leading contemporary Croat historian, Ivo Banac, has reached a figure of about 120,000 victims in all the NDH-run camps.[26] Others have settled on 80,000 victims in the camps of all nationalities, with Serbs making up about 50,000. The future president Franjo Tudjman caused a furore in the 1970s when he insisted that only about 60,000 victims had perished in all the NDH camps put together. He also insisted that many of the victims were left-wing Croats, gypsies and other non-Serbs.

One recent Croatian publication, which draws on the work of both Croat and Serb historians, estimates the total number of casualties in Yugoslavia during the war at 947,000, of whom 487,000 were Serbs, 207,000 Croats, 86,000 Muslims and 60,000 Jews. According to this account, 78 per cent of all Yugoslav Jews were killed in the Second World War, 8.1 per cent of Muslims, 7.3 per cent of Serbs and 5 per cent of Croats. This account sets the total number of concentration camp deaths at 215,000, although this figure includes Serbs killed in Serbia by the German occupation authorities.[27]

The figure of 600,000 Serb deaths in the NDH is probably much too high, as it does not tally with the ethnic composition of Croatia and Bosnia after the war, which would have had a very small Serbian population if such a huge number of Serbs had been killed. On the other hand, Tudjman's figure was misleading, as it ignored the vast number of Serbs who were certainly killed in local pogroms in villages rather than in the camps themselves. There is no doubt that the NDH intended to exterminate the Serb population and failed only because it lacked the means.

The NDH was not an insignificant military power. It had no navy, owing to the terms of the Rome Agreement, and the air force was modest as well, consisting of about thirty small commercial aircraft. But the army was large, divided into two groups. The Ustashe proper constituted the elite. The home guard, the Domobrani, was much larger. Together they mustered about 110,000 troops by the end of 1942 and about 130,000 in 1943.

On 23 June 1941, two days after the German assault on the Soviet Union, Pavelić even volunteered several thousand soldiers for service in the German invasion. In a public address the Poglavnik declared that Croats 'cannot remain peaceful observers in this great and fateful hour, but burn with a desire to take part in the battle to destroy the greatest enemy of humanity and Croatdom'.[28] Altogether about 8,000 Croatian legionnaires joined the German assault on Russia, many of them recruited with promises of double pay and rapid promotion. It was an unwise decision for a state which exercised an uncertain hold over its own territory, and reflected the desperate ambition of the Poglavnik to be seen to be keeping up with Mussolini and with Francisco Franco, the dictator of Spain, who was then setting up the 'Blue Division' to fight against Stalin.

In spite of this considerable armed force, the NDH lost territory almost continually from the summer of 1941, until by the end of the war the authorities held only the larger towns and cities. One factor was the indifference, or hostility, of the Croat left, the HSS and most Croat intellectuals to the NDH. The second was the armed resistance of the Serbs to the NDH, in so-called 'Chetnik' formations (after the bands who fought against Ottoman rule) and then later on in the Communist-led Partisan units. The third was the interference in the NDH's affairs by Germany and Italy, which in Italy's case amounted to outright sabotage. The fourth was a chronic shortage of weapons in the NDH, resulting from the lack of arms factories and supplies. Finally, the NDH's hierarchy was racked by debilitating power struggles that weakened the morale of the Ustashe faithful.

Among Croats, the problem the Ustashe confronted was the movement's lack of a broad popular base. Unlike the Nazis, the Ustashe had no strong grass-roots organisation before taking power. Pavelić, Artuković, Dido Kvaternik and most of the other Ustashe leaders had been out of the country since 1929 or the early 1930s. In Italy the

Ustashe had been interned and the organisation suppressed from 1934 until 1940. In Yugoslavia, the movement had been illegal from the moment it was founded in 1929. Ustashe supporters had become used to a conspiratorial, underground existence. After they took power, the conspiratorial habits of a lifetime proved difficult to shake off. Pavelić was paranoid about his personal security and took up residence in a secluded villa in the exclusive Tuškanac district of Zagreb, shielded from the public by a wall of security guards. Although the Pavelićs were devout, they never attended services in public churches, but heard Mass at home, conducted by their domestic chaplain. The Poglavnik and his wife were fearful of poisoning, and Mrs Pavelić supervised everything that went into her husband's mouth. On his infrequent trips outside Zagreb, it was noticed that the Poglavnik would never eat or drink. Years spent in exile abroad had alienated the Pavelićs from their Croat roots. Mrs Pavelić had become immersed in Italian society during exile, sent her children to an exclusive private school and when back in Zagreb associated mainly with Italian diplomats or with a few old friends from the pre-1929 era. The local Ustashe complained that she denigrated her own people in comparison to Italians, even calling Croats 'trash'.[29]

The Ustashe were cut off from their fellow countrymen because they were mainly drawn from a few areas, such as Lika and western Herzegovina. Pavelić grew up in the village of Bradina, near Konjic in central Bosnia. But his family was from Krivi Put, in Lika. Budak was from Sveti Rok, a Croat village near Gračac, in the parched mountains of northern Dalmatia. Artuković was from Klobuk, in western Herzegovina. Several other Ustashe leaders came from nearby villages, especially from Siroki Brijeg. Few of them knew much about Slavonia – the heartland of Croatia and the richest, most populous region. It was a hindrance to the regime that Slavonians were not represented in the NDH hierarchy, with the exception of Ivan Werner, the Mayor of Zagreb. The Zagrebians did not take to the Ustashe. There had always been a degree of contempt – and fear – in the relations between the capital and the country peasants, and to the inhabitants of the capital the Ustashe were the latest in a long line of *torbari* (basket-carriers), or *dotepenci* (carpet-baggers). In Germany and Italy, Fascists capitalised on the widespread public disillusion with the old democratic parties. But most Croats had not rejected their old parties. In Zagreb, many working-class people remained attracted to the Communists. Among the intelligentsia, sympathy for the underground Communists had been far more widespread than sympathy for the underground Ustashe. In the Catholic countryside of Slavonia, the Peasants Party had been the only important political party for more than twenty years.

A mark of the Ustashe's lack of a popular base was its inability, or unwillingness, to stage the kind of impressive mass rallies that were the hallmarks of the regimes of Hitler, Mussolini and Franco. As a result, the Poglavnik remained an unknown quantity to most Croats, glimpsed occasionally at military parades in his Nazi-style uniform, or heard on the radio. With his almost expressionless face and huge ears he was not inspiring to look at. The rest of the NDH hierarchy was little better. Colonel Kvaternik was in his sixties when the Ustashe took power, and his taste for uniforms and Habsburg flummery inspired more derision than respect. Dido Kvaternik was undoubtedly intelligent, but he evoked more fear than affection.

In the Church, steadily accumulating reports of atrocities committed against Serbs, Jews and gypsies alienated the bishops. Among the clergy, attitudes to the NDH were divided. The NDH authorities believed that most of the parish priests were reliable, but that the episcopal bench was of dubious loyalty. Only a few bishops were real enthusiasts for the Ustashe, among them Archbishop Šarić of Sarajevo. Some were prepared to co-operate with any regime, such as Bishop Bauerlein of Djakovo, who was equally friendly in turn with Serbian royalists, the NDH and then the Communists. Bishop Alojzije Mišić of Mostar, in Herzegovina, was appalled by Ustashe violence in his diocese. In 1941 he sent a circular to his clergy forbidding absolution to any who took part in the killings of Serbs. 'A reign of slaughter has come to pass,' he fumed to Stepinac. 'Men are captured like animals, they are slaughtered, murdered, living men are thrown off cliffs. ... in the town of Mostar itself, they have been bound by the hundreds, taken in wagons outside the town and then shot down like animals.'[30]

After Stepinac heard this and other bishops' reports at the episcopal conference of 1941 his enthusiasm for the NDH waned. On 20 November he drafted a letter to the Poglavnik containing parts of Bishop Mišić's horrific report from Mostar plus those of Jozo Garić of Banja Luka and Ivan Šarić of Sarajevo. He expressed confidence that the worst of the atrocities was over and that they were the work of individuals acting at their own behest. Nevertheless, the letter was a challenge. 'No one can deny that these terrible acts of violence and cruelty have been taking place, for you yourself, Poglavnik, have publicly condemned those which the Ustashe has committed,' he said.[31] 'The Croatian nation has been proud of its 1000-year-old culture and Christian tradition. That is why we wait for it to show in practice, now that it has achieved its freedom, a greater nobility and humanity than that displayed by its former rulers.' In a later letter to Pavelić, he brought up the concentration camps: 'Jasenovac camp itself is a shameful stain on the honour of the NDH.'[32] But he remained naive about politics and about the nature of the regime. When he asked Meštrović whether he thought Pavelić knew anything about the killings of Serbs, and Meštrović replied that of course Pavelić knew everything, the Archbishop went pale and burst into tears.[33] He would not denounce the NDH in public, but in private he helped victims of the regime, including Jews.

Amiel Shomrony, secretary to the last Chief Rabbi of Zagreb, Miroslav Freiberger, recalled:

> I took part in many actions to save Jews in the war with the help of the Kaptol [the Archbishopric]. In that way we managed to get many children out to Hungary and from there to Palestine. ... besides that, the Archbishop personally saved a lot of people and children by hiding them. He gave the community flour every month and financially supported Jews who had been left without any means of support by the persecution.... [34]

The right wing and the clericals were held back from opposing the NDH by their conviction that Croatian independence was a good thing, even if the form that it took under Pavelić was not. The left was less restrained. The Communist Party had remained strong in parts of Croatia, in spite of persecution under the royal regime and the Banovina. Zagreb was more industrialised than Belgrade and the factories had a long tradition of industrial militancy, articulated though the URS, the Udruženi Radnički Savez (United Workers' League). Communism was strong in intellectual circles, among writers and in the theatre world. After Croatian and Slovenian parties were reorganised in 1937 as separate sections within the Yugoslav Party, after the new Party leader, Josip Broz, returned from Moscow, suspicions that the Communists supported a centralised Yugoslav state subsided.

The future nuclear physicist Ivan Supek recalled: 'Most intellectuals were communists and we all supported the idea of a popular front. We had an old tradition of social democracy which came from Vienna ... the Ustashe had no roots in Zagreb. The Jews were very established in Zagreb and people could not understand why they had to be imprisoned. People had compassion for the Serbs as well. Zagreb was too cosmopolitan to accept the Ustashe.'[35] Left-wing intellectuals began slipping out of Zagreb to the countryside to join the first anti-government rebels. Others remained in the city to organise acts of terrorism, setting fire to the main sports stadium, blowing up the central Post Office and assassinating Ustashe soldiers. The most celebrated act of sabotage took place in July 1941, when Partisans threw grenades at open-topped lorries carrying Ustashe officers, and twenty-two were killed. In reprisal, many prominent left-wing writers and journalists were arrested and killed, including the writer August Cesarec and Božidar Adžija, editor of the URS trade union newspaper.

The persecution of the left-wing intellectuals hastened the flight of the intelligentsia to the Partisan side, and in 1942 Croatia's best-known writers, the aged Vladimir Nazor and the youthful Goran Kovačić, slipped out of Zagreb to join the Communists hiding in the woods in the south. The left-wing writer Miroslav Krleža remained in the city, where he was shielded from persecution by Budak. But he stayed in contact with his Communist friends in the forests. The loss of these influential voices from the world of culture meant little to Croatian peasants, but it did dent the NDH's prestige in the cities and undermined the government's attempt to portray the Partisans as an anti-Croatian force.

The regime was in a quandary over what to do with an artist with an international reputation like Meštrović. As a founding member of the Yugoslav Committee and a close acquaintance of the late King Aleksandar, he was hated by some of the NDH hierarchy. But Budak cherished hopes of winning over such a famous figure to the service of the regime and insisted that he should remain unharmed. After being arrested and imprisoned for four-and-a-half months, without warning he was taken to Pavelić's office, where the Poglavnik apologised for imprisoning him and for giving away so much of his Dalmatian homeland to the Italians. 'Thank God you don't look bad,' Pavelić told him. 'I know as a Croat and a Dalmatian you must be livid about Dalmatia, but what could I do, when Mussolini was threatening to take everything up to Karlovac?'[36] In spite of Dido Kvaternik's opposition, he insisted on Meštrović being allowed to leave the country.

Armed revolts against the NDH by Serbs in rural areas were a more serious problem to the regime than the defection of the intellectuals and occasional acts of terrorism in Zagreb. In the first year of the war the regime's most dangerous opponents were the so-called Chetniks, Serbian irregulars under the loose command of a royalist officer, Colonel Draža Mihailović. After the shock of the collapse of Yugoslavia and the flight of the King to London had subsided, the Serbs in the NDH started a series of uncoordinated revolts that spread like wildfire. In July fighting broke out in eastern Herzegovina, Gračac in northern Dalmatia, Lapac in Lika and around Bihać and Drvar in north-west Bosnia. The Ustashe was not able to quench the rebellion and Glaise-Horstenau became so alarmed that on 13 November he told Berlin that only about one-third of the NDH remained in the hands of the government. The German commander blamed the Ustashe for this chaos. He criticised the excessive influence in the NDH government of the returning exiles, attacked the persecution of the Serbs and warned of the rapid demoralisation of the Croats. He condemned the arrest of Maček and noted that the Muslims in Bosnia were starting to turn against the Ustashe.

One reason for the Chetniks' initial success was Italian support.

Whenever they ran into trouble, they were able to find sanctuary in Italian-ruled Dalmatia, where the Ustashe had no authority. Some Ustashe leaders, including Dido Kvaternik, advocated hunting down the Serbs inside the Italian zone, but Pavelić was unwilling to provoke the Italians. Although the Germans were dismayed by the NDH's persecution of the Serbs, they were shocked by the way the Italians cosseted the Chetniks. 'The Italians are putting the Croats under such pressure that there is no semblance whatever left of a free state,' wrote Goebbels in April 1943. 'Possibly, they are merely trying to prove the Croatian state cannot survive. But there's a much easier way of doing that than supplying arms to the opposition. ... the reign of terror which the Italians have established in some sections of Croatia baffles all description.'[37]

The fighting inside the NDH and the fear of losing German support persuaded the Ustashe leaders that a change of policy was needed to placate the NDH's enraged Serbs. At a meeting of the puppet Sabor on 23 February 1942, Pavelić announced the establishment of a new religious organisation, the Croatian Orthodox Church. As the Ustashe had murdered several Serbian Orthodox bishops, they had trouble finding clergy for this body. But they found a head for the new Church in an émigré Russian priest, Grigorije Maksimov (1861–1945), who was discovered living in a monastery in the Fruška Gora region of Srijem when the war broke out. He took the title of metropolitan and the name of Germogen. His formal enthronement, on 7 June 1942, in the former Serbian Orthodox Church of the Transfiguration in Zagreb, was given enormous publicity by the regime, and took place in the presence of an armed guard, the speaker of the Sabor, Mayor Werner of Zagreb and several government ministers. The following day Germogen made an oath of allegiance to the Poglavnik. The Ustashe intended the Croatian Orthodox Church to comprise three bishoprics, based at Bosanski Brod, Petrovac and Sarajevo, as well as the Metropolitan in Zagreb. In the event, the authorities could not find bishops for the posts. It was not until 1944 that Spiridon Mifka, an eccentric Croat who had converted from Catholicism to Orthodoxy as a student, was enthroned as bishop of Sarajevo.

The Croatian Orthodox Church was not a success. Abroad, its credentials were eyed with suspicion by the rest of the Orthodox communion, although the clergy in pro-Axis Romania and Bulgaria were more sympathetic. At home, although the Church had recruited about seventy clergy by the end of 1942, mostly based in parishes in Srijem, it had no legitimacy in the eyes of the Serbian community, which regarded its priests as traitors. The quality of the clergy was often poor. One letter of complaint to Germogen, for example, claimed that the priest in Vlasenica in eastern Bosnia was a former prisoner and inmate of a mental institution. He was accused of drunkenness and had allegedly boasted publicly of the number of people he had killed. The Church was not treated seriously by the Croatian authorities, in spite of the pomp of Germogen's enthronement. When the Metropolitan attempted a visitation of Srijem, he was coldly told not to bother, as 80 per cent of the Serbs in the Vukovar region had been rebaptised as Catholics.[38]

As part of the policy of conciliating the Serbs in 1942, the Ustashe tried to enlist the Chetniks against a rival force of left-wing rebels, known as Partisans. In March 1942, NDH and Chetnik military chiefs held meetings in Knin in northern Dalmatia to discuss the possibility of joint action. But it came to nothing. The Chetniks hated the Communists, but they hated the NDH more.

The Chetniks started with all the advantages. They enjoyed a great deal of support among the Serbian peasants, especially in Serbia proper. Their leader, Mihailović, was recognised by the exiled royal government in London as its official representative in occupied Yugoslavia and was given military support by the Allies. In spite of this, his movement was steadily sidelined in 1943 by the Partisans, led by Josip Broz 'Tito', the half-Croat, half-Slovene leader of the Yugoslav Communist Party.

Tito's Communists got off to a slow start in organising an insurrection, owing to conflicting instructions from Moscow before the invasion of the Soviet Union in June 1941. Once the Soviet Union was attacked, the Yugoslav Communists stopped calling the war an imperialist war, and on 26 June the Party proclaimed that it had formed a general staff for what it called its National Liberation Partisan units.

Its first military operation was a disaster. In eastern Serbia in August and September 1942 Tito's Partisans occupied the town of Užice and attempted to set up a republic on Soviet lines. The local Serbs rejected this revolutionary experiment, which was run with a good deal of terror, and they made no effort to prevent the Germans from sweeping into Užice and driving the Partisans eastwards into Bosnia. Tito learned his lesson from the Užice fiasco. In Bosnia the Partisans toned down their Communist rhetoric and concentrated on appealing to the patriotic instincts of all the ethnic groups in Yugoslavia. Their attachment to Yugoslavia and determination to get rid of the NDH made headway with the Serbs. Their attacks on the 'Great Serbian hegemonism' of the pre-war royal regime went down well with Muslims and Croats.

The Partisans' military strategy was to attack the Germans without any regard to reprisals against civilians. It was a risky policy, inviting terrible revenge attacks on towns and villages. But it did raise their reputation at home and abroad.

The Chetniks, meanwhile, were hampered by indiscipline and the loathing they inspired among non-Serbs. They made a terrible error in

Croatia and Bosnia, alienating the Croats and Muslims as completely as the Ustashe had alienated the Serbs, by carrying out ghastly massacres. During an assault on the Muslim town of Foča in eastern Bosnia in August 1942, for example, the Chetniks slaughtered hundreds if not thousands of civilians. At the same time, they were in a fearful muddle over whether they should resist the Germans and Italians, or just wait for the end of the war and an Allied victory in Europe. Mihailović's bedrock of support was in Serbia proper, and after the Germans had exacted a terrible reprisal for the killing of some German soldiers in the town of Kragujevac in October 1941, executing a large number of schoolchildren, the Chetniks abandoned terrorist actions in an attempt to protect the civilians of occupied Serbia from similar atrocities. It was an understandable policy, but it led to Partisan accusations of collaboration.

After the flight from Užice, the Partisans managed to overrun large chunks of Bosnia, pushing south-west as far as Livno and north-west as far as Bihać. There, a few hours' drive from Zagreb, on 26–27 November 1942, they staged their first big wartime congress. The Anti-Fascist National Liberation Council of Yugoslavia, known by its acronym, Avnoj (pronounced Avnoy), was designed to present to Yugoslavia and the outside world the Partisans' status as the leading anti-German resistance movement in the region, as well as their ambition to control the government of Yugoslavia after the war. The pronouncements of the Bihać assembly fell short of a detailed blueprint on the future government of Yugoslavia. But there were important gestures in the direction of federalism in a vaguely worded call for the 'freedom and fraternal unity of Serbia, Montenegro, Croatia, Slovenia, Bosnia–Herzegovina and Macedonia'. The mere mention of Macedonia, which Serbian nationalists insisted was southern Serbia, made it clear that the Communists were not going to restore the centralised state set up after the First World War. The reference to Bosnia suggested that the carve-up of Bosnia between Serbs and Croats in the 1939 *Sporazum* would be rescinded.

While the Partisans were holding their assembly in Bihać, Pavelić was returning from the Ukraine, where he had met Hitler for a second time on 23 November 1942. The Führer had a number of complaints concerning the course of events in Croatia. One was that the spreading rebellion inside the NDH was disrupting the German war economy, preventing the transport of goods and minerals to the Reich and drawing off much-needed German military manpower. The second complaint was that too many Jews had been left untouched in the NDH inside the Italian 'sphere of influence', around Dubrovnik and Crikvenica. On his return, the Poglavnik decided that the entire military and security apparatus needed shaking up. Slavko and Eugen Kvaternik were removed from their posts and went into exile in Slovakia, a decision which Dido Kvaternik claimed contributed to the breakdown of the newly formed NDH army and police.

The first half of 1943 was a period of stalemate for the NDH vis-à-vis its Chetnik and Partisan enemies. Although the Ustashe were unable to subdue the Partisans and Chetniks in Bosnia, they could neither combine, nor defeat the Ustashe on their own. The Domobrani were not effective as an offensive force but were numerous enough to keep the Ustashe in control of the larger towns. Around Zagreb, the government's authority was unchallenged. In Zagreb itself, Partisan terrorist actions did not endear them to most of the city's inhabitants. Reports of Chetnik atrocities against Croats and the government's efforts to persuade the population that the Partisans were murdering Catholic clergy encouraged people to rally to the regime.

Concerned that his Balkan protégé was losing ground, Hitler determined on a further big offensive in January 1943, called Operation Weiss, which the Partisans called the Fourth Offensive. German troops were ordered into the Lika region and north-west Bosnia. However, the outcome was inconclusive as Tito succeeded in negotiating a truce with the Germans that enabled him to evacuate his forces south-east across the River Neretva into Montenegro. The respite was only temporary. In May 1943 some 60,000 German troops backed up by about 40,000 Croat auxiliaries launched what the Partisans called the Fifth Offensive. This time it appeared there would be no escape, as the Germans had Tito virtually surrounded on the banks of the River Sutjeska in central Bosnia. But in an escape that passed into legend the Partisans evaded the German net and slipped across the Sutjeska into eastern Bosnia, dragging thousands of wounded soldiers with them.

Despite the failure of the attempt to destroy the Communist rebellion inside the NDH, Pavelić was encouraged by the fall of Mussolini in the summer of 1943. On 25 July, after the Allied landing in Sicily had shattered public confidence in the regime, the Fascist Grand Council with the support of King Victor Emmanuel dismissed the Duce. The arrest and confinement of Mussolini enraged Hitler but delighted Pavelić, who saw it as a wonderful opportunity to tear up the Rome Agreement and take control of Italian-occupied Dalmatia. Goebbels was most impressed with the Croats' resolve. 'The Poglavnik has issued a sharp declaration against Italy,' he wrote on 10 September 1943. 'He stated that at last he was in a position to create a free Croatian state, together with Dalmatia. The Führer has already promised him that. He now rejects Italian suzerainty. What a pity one doesn't observe that kind of spirit in other nations.'[39]

Goebbels was wrong. The collapse of Italy helped the Partisans far more than the Ustashe. They collected huge quantities of arms from the retreating Italian soldiers. The mood in the former Italian-occupied zone of Dalmatia was pro-Partisan and hostile to the Ustashe for handing them over to Mussolini. As a result, the Partisans, not the Ustashe, raced into Split when the Italians moved out, although the Germans drove them out again in the so-called Sixth Offensive.

The Poglavnik experienced another big setback at the end of 1943, when the Allies switched support from the Chetniks to the Partisans. Churchill had become dissatisfied with the Chetniks' lack of fighting resolve and was intrigued by the reports of the Partisans' robust tactics. The change of course took place after he had despatched two special envoys to Yugoslavia, Bill Deakin and Fitzroy Maclean.

Maclean parachuted into Partisan territory on 17 September 1943 near Mrkonjić Grad in north-west Bosnia and made contact quickly with Tito and the other Communist leaders: Eduard Kardelj, a Slovene; Aleksandar Ranković, a Serb; and Milovan Djilas, from Montenegro.

In their talks, Tito was coy about his political agenda for post-war Yugoslavia and about the future position of King Petar. Maclean had no doubts that Tito intended to create a Soviet-style state in Yugoslavia but he was captivated by Tito personally and convinced of the Partisans' military superiority to the Chetniks. He was unimpressed by the captured Domobrani he saw. 'Generally, they took the first opportunity of deserting or of letting themselves be taken prisoner,' he wrote.[40] After seven weeks with the Partisans, Maclean reached Cairo, where he sent a report on Yugoslavia to Churchill, which arrived before Churchill met Stalin and Roosevelt at the Allied leaders' summit in Tehran. Maclean recalled saying that the Partisan movement was undoubtedly Communist, but that 'as a resistance movement it was highly effective and that its effectiveness could be considerably increased by allied help, but that whether we gave such assistance or not, Tito and his followers would exercise decisive influence in Jugoslavia after liberation.'[41]

At Tehran, Churchill lectured Stalin on the need to support Tito rather than the Chetniks, claiming the Partisans were holding down thirty German divisions. Stalin was sceptical, as he was better informed about events in Yugoslavia than was Churchill; he told the British Prime Minister that there were not more than seven German divisions in Yugoslavia. Nevertheless, he agreed to start supporting Tito. However, before withdrawing liaison officers from the Chetniks' headquarters, Mihailović was to be given one last chance to disprove charges of collaboration with the Germans by blowing up the railway between Belgrade and Thessaloniki. Maclean later wrote that he reminded Churchill of Tito's Communist intentions.

'Do you intend', [Churchill] asked, 'to make Jugoslavia your home after the war?'

'No. Sir.' I replied.
'Neither do I.' he said. 'And that being so, the less you or I worry about the form of government they set up, the better.'[42]

The British mission to the Chetniks was withdrawn finally in May 1944 on the grounds of Chetnik collaboration with the Germans. As a result, the Partisans obtained some 60,000 tons of supplies dropped by air by Allied aircraft. At the same time Tito received invaluable diplomatic support by being acknowledged as leader of the resistance in Yugoslavia. Although Britain continued to recognise the exiled government in London, and officially sought only to press King Petar to 'include' Tito in his cabinet, in fact the King and his government were politically marginalised from this point. It was Tito who had the army and the territory. The King now had only his crown to bargain with.

On 30 November 1943 the Partisans held a second assembly of the Avnoj at Jajce in central Bosnia. This council, subsequently held by Communists to mark the birth of the new federal Yugoslav state, formally recognised the existence of Partisan-run local governments in Croatia, Slovenia, Serbia, Macedonia, Bosnia and the Sandžak, known as National Liberation Councils.[43] King Petar was forbidden to return to Yugoslavia until elections had taken place at the end of the war. The cession of territory to Italy in the Treaty of Rapallo in 1920 was pronounced null and void and the land in question declared part of Yugoslavia. Finally, Tito was made a marshal of Yugoslavia.

Most of the 'liberation councils' were nominal affairs, as the Germans were still very much in control of the terrain in Serbia, Macedonia and Slovenia. In Croatia it was very different. There the local Partisan government, known by the acronym Zavnoh (Zemaljskó Anti-fašističkó Vijeće Narodnog Oslobodjenja Hrvatske), was an alternative government, controlling a large swathe of territory and running its own schools, ministries and newspapers, *Vjesnik* and *Naprijed*.

Vladimir Dedijer, a Serb Partisan, was tremendously impressed by a visit to the left-wing Croat mini-state, which was based in the summer of 1943 in the old Lika town of Otočac before moving to Topusko, south of Zagreb. The first public meeting of Zavnoh in Plitvice, he wrote in his diary, had 'had a tremendous impact' on the Croat public. 'They are crossing to our side in droves.' Further north, in the Serb stronghold of Korenica he noted that 'when the name of Tito or of the Communist Party is mentioned, a great roar arises. Five full minutes of clapping and chanting.'[44]

In the Partisan state in Croatia the old and the new coexisted in an odd fashion. In Otočac Dedijer was fascinated by the sight of the Croat peasants on a Sunday morning, all dressed in their traditional black hats and trousers and white smocks. At the same time he noted that the peasants were singing hymns to the far-away Soviet Union which were obviously modelled on traditional ballads:

> From Banija to Russia
> The red banner waves
> The red banner waves
> Under it Stalin drinks wine
> Oh Stalin our pride
> May your glass be filled with fortune.[45]

The Croat Party leader, Andrija Hebrang, was a forceful, ambitious character. Born in Virovitica, he grew up in eastern Slavonia, and was an early convert to Communism, joining the Party in 1920, aged twenty. As the repression of the Communists intensified in the late 1920s, he was frequently jailed. Arrested again when the NDH was proclaimed in 1941 he was imprisoned in Stara Gradiška with his future wife Olga until 1942, when the Ustashe authorities exchanged him and Olga for some Ustashe prisoners being held by the Partisans. Hebrang had become an important figure in the Croat section of the Party before the war. Once out of prison he rose rapidly to the top again and was made secretary of the Central Committee, presiding over the first Zavnoh congress in June 1943.

From the start, there were serious problems between Tito and Hebrang, and between Hebrang, Djilas, Ranković, Kardelj, Bakarić and Moše Pijade, a Jew. They soon decided that Hebrang was a convinced nationalist as well as a Communist, who wanted to run an independent Croatian state. Tito was annoyed, for example, that Zavnoh posters urged people to support 'the complete freedom and independence of Croatia' and made little or no mention of Yugoslavia. In September 1943 Hebrang angered Tito again when Zavnoh declared that Istria, Fiume and Italian-occupied Dalmatia were part of Croatia without waiting for Avnoj to give the lead.[46]

In 1944 Hebrang's relationship with the rest of the Yugoslav Communist hierarchy got worse, and Tito grew more convinced that Hebrang was planning to keep Croatia independent after the war. Hebrang would not back down. He stressed the Partisans' heritage from the 'illustrious Strossmayer' and from Radić as well.[47] He made overtures to the Peasants Party and to the Catholic Church, criticised moves to introduce divorce and suggested that religious education in schools might be maintained after the war. Tito was outraged by the olive branch Hebrang held out to the Church and was suspicious of the implications of his defence of Croatian independence. In the summer of 1944 he ordered Hebrang to stop holding Partisan 'people's courts'. In

September he exploded when Zavnoh set up a Croatian press agency, called TAH. 'Halt immediately the work of your so-called telegraph agency,' he informed the Croat Party leader. 'You are entering with all your might into separatism.'[48]

In the summer of 1944 Tito sent Kardelj to report on the situation. When he returned, Kardelj denounced Hebrang in no uncertain terms, claiming that he hated Slovenes and Serbs and saw Yugoslavia only as a 'necessary evil'. Tito dared not attack Hebrang openly in case this split the Croatian Party, but decided instead to lure him out of Croatia.

Tito's entry into Belgrade on 20 October 1944 with the support of the Red Army strengthened his hand against Hebrang. Churchill had become very dissatisfied with King Petar's quarrelsome cabinet-in-exile and had forced the King to dismiss Purić, a hardline Serb, and appoint Šubašić, the former Ban of Croatia, as Yugoslav prime minister. Churchill hoped that Šubašić would effect a reconciliation between the royal government and the Partisans. Once he was installed in office, Šubašić obediently hurried off to the Allied-controlled island of Vis in the Adriatic on Churchill's orders to meet Tito on 14 June 1944, and, on 1 November, just after Tito entered Belgrade, he reached an agreement with him on the terms of a coalition government. The terms were a complete victory for Tito. Avnoj was recognised as the provisional executive government. Tito was made prime minister and it was agreed that the King would not be allowed back 'until the people pronounced their decision'.[49]

Once Tito's control had been officially endorsed by the royal government, he decided to get rid of his Croatian rival. Hebrang was removed from his position as head of the Party in Croatia and brought to the more hostile environment of Belgrade, where he was made president of the planning commission in the Yugoslav government.

In the old Serbian capital he was isolated. Vladimir Bakarić, a fervent Tito loyalist, was installed as head of the Croatian Party. Nicknamed 'Vlada mrtvac' (Vlado the corpse), he was a far less charismatic figure than his predecessor. Under Bakarić, Zavnoh continued to stress its commitment to Croatian sovereignty and statehood.[50] In practice the Croats ceased to act unilaterally and many of Zavnoh's functions were quietly transferred to the new federal government in Belgrade.

In Zagreb, time was running out for the NDH. A German Abwehr intelligence report quoted the anonymous predictions of several Croat ministers. They told the Germans:

> Our powers are limited to tormenting ourselves with the problem of provisions and with increasing our monthly currency supply by two-and-a-quarter billion, which contributes to the hopelessness of the course of inflation. ... our peasants are abandoned to the rage of the

Partisans and Chetniks. ... if we were an occupied country it would be easier for us and no one could force us to pass for a 'government'.[51]

As the military situation deteriorated, the atmosphere of panic in Zagreb unleashed a power struggle inside the NDH hierarchy between a faction which hoped to reach a deal with Russia and the Allies before it was too late, and those who wanted to soldier on to the end with Hitler.

In July 1944, Pavelić had Mladen Lorković, Foreign Minister from 1941 to 1943, and Ante Vokić, the War Minister, arrested at a cabinet meeting on charges of plotting a pro-Allied coup. The two ministers were killed by the Ustashe in prison at Lepoglava, north of Zagreb, just before the regime collapsed. The war went on. Split fell for the second time to the Partisans, a week after Tito entered Belgrade. The Ustashe fought on for another six months. But they had no future. They had no ammunition and no hope once Germany was certain to be defeated.

The end came in the spring of 1945. On 14 February Mostar fell. For several weeks the relative stability of the eastern front engendered a mood of renewed optimism in Zagreb, but in April Tito launched a final crushing offensive in Srijem, into which he hurled vast numbers of troops. The casualties on both sides were enormous but on the 13th Vukovar fell and on the 16th Valpovo followed. As the Partisans inched westwards, there was talk of falling back on a more easily defended frontier, to be called the 'Zvonimir line', running from Senj to Zagreb. But nothing came of this desperate plan. Instead, as Nazi Germany writhed in its death throes, Pavelić decided that the army should retreat towards the Austrian and Hungarian frontier and surrender to the Allies rather than the Partisans.

The end came on 6 May, when Pavelić was informed that Germany was about to surrender and was given command over the remaining Axis forces in Croatia. The same day Partisan forces entered Karlovac. There was a last-minute plea by some Ustashe to Archbishop Stepinac to take over what was left of the state as regent, in the style of the sixteenth-century Ban and Bishop Petar Berislavić, who had rallied Croatia against the Turks. The Archbishop would have nothing to do with it. Some of his bishops were already packing their bags and fleeing the country. The Archbishop was determined to sit it out.

As the NDH army surged northwards to the Austrian frontier, Pavelić and his son Velimir, driving in a big black Mercedes, branched off from the main throng and headed north-west into Slovenia. They had to drive fast, as the roads were already partially blocked by advancing Partisan forces, and they had to dodge heavy gunfire. But they slipped through and on 8 May, the day Germany surrendered and the first Partisans reached Zagreb, the Poglavnik crossed the old Yugoslav

frontier at Maribor into Austria and headed for Salzburg, where Mara
and their other children were waiting for him.

Evading his captors, he and his family slipped into Italy and from
there to Argentina. Out of reach of Allied retribution, he survived
several assassination attempts carried out by Tito's secret police and
died in his bed in Spain in 1957. But he had left behind him a country
that was prostrate. The first experiment in independence had ended cat-
astrophically, drowned in bloodshed. It seemed unlikely there would be
another.

12

'My Conscience Is Clear'

We Communists did not want any opposition, none whatsoever.

Milovan Djilas[1]

As the remnants of the NDH's army fled towards the Austrian frontier with an enormous number of civilians in tow, the first Partisan troops entered the deserted streets of Zagreb on 8 May 1945. The population stayed indoors. One reason was Partisan radio warnings about continued fighting in the streets with the rump of the Ustashe. Another was a certain wariness about the Partisan Second Army, which contained many Serbs and Montenegrins who had fought as Chetniks before taking advantage of an amnesty offered by Tito in 1943 to any Chetniks or Domobrani who wanted to join the Partisans. But a few days later, when the 10th Zagreb Corps marched triumphantly into the city, an enormous crowd of hundreds of thousands streamed into Jelačić Square and crowded around the statue of the Ban to give this most Croatian of Partisan units a hearty welcome.

Many people, of course, remained fearful of the new regime. Throughout the war the population in the government-held towns had been subjected to a diet of anti-Communist propaganda, portraying all Partisans as killers and as sworn enemies of Croatian independence and of the Catholic Church. It was different in the Italian-occupied areas of Dalmatia and Istria. There almost all the Croats regarded the Partisans as liberators from Mussolini's rule, Italianisation and the Chetniks. At Makarska, peasants greeted the Partisans with shouts of 'Long live the Virgin Mary and the Communist Party.'[2]

The first task awaiting the Partisans after the entry into Zagreb was to eliminate the NDH army, then fleeing towards the Austrian frontier. The Ustashe and the Domobrani were desperate to get out of the country. Many were convinced that the West would not hand them back to the Communist allies of Stalin's Russia. Between 14 and 16 May this column, several hundred thousand strong, was massing on the banks of the River Drava, demanding the right to enter Austria.

The Ustashe overestimated the anti-Communist feelings of the British and the Americans. They did not know that the Allies had decided to hand them back to Tito to do as he wished. Tito for his part wanted to annihilate as many of the Ustashe as possible. Now that control over the whole of Yugoslavia was within his grasp, he was determined not to allow the NDH to recoup its strength in exile, or filter back into the country as an anti-Communist fifth column. On 15 May he informed the Yugoslav First Army that:

> a group of Ustashe and some Chetniks, a total of some 50,000 men, is reported by the Third Army in the Konjice–Šoštanj area, towards Dravograd. It includes Pavelić, Maček, the Croatian government and a huge number of criminals. They are attempting to cross at Dravograd and give themselves up to the British ... you must move your forces most urgently ... to concentrate for an attack aimed at the annihilation of this group.[3]

On the other side of the River Drava, a small, lightly armed British force of about 150 was watching the arrival of the Croatian army with concern. The British were confused. They had only a small force on the Austrian border with which to confront the Ustashe army. They resolved on a policy of deception. The Croats were to be disarmed and put on trains, but not told of their destination.

On 15 May the confrontation came to a head when the Croats attempted to cross into Austria at Bleiburg. They were now in a dire state. From the rear they were being attacked by the advancing Partisans, who were trying to cut off the tail of the column of refugees and soldiers as it headed north. The Croats might have marched through the 150 British troops and moved into Austria, but they parleyed. The British commander at Bleiburg, Brigadier Scott, later recalled the lengths to which the Croats were prepared to go to avoid falling into Partisan hands: 'They suggested that they might go to America or Africa and I told them that the ways and means for such a movement were completely non-existent and that if they moved anywhere they were bound to starve. Starving, they insisted, was an infinitely preferable course to surrendering to Tito.' The Brigadier bluffed the Croats and told them that if they attempted to move into Austria, 'they would not only be attacked by the Yugoslavs, but by all the weight of British and American air forces, land forces and anything else I could get my hands on, in which case they would unquestionably be annihilated'.

The NDH troops agreed to surrender to Allied forces on condition that they were interned outside Yugoslavia, and in a bewildered state they were packed on to overcrowded trains, which rolled straight back into Yugoslavia. The Partisans killed as many of the soldiers as they could, executing the Croats and Slovenes as they got off the train and throwing the bodies into the quarry at Kočevje. a village on the Slovenian side of the frontier. The executions were carried out in such haste. however. that some of the soldiers survived and crawled out of the pits at night.

The question of how many Croats were killed at Bleiburg is difficult to estimate. Like the question of how many Serbs were killed in Jasenovac. it is hedged around with propaganda. Some Croat nationalists insisted that up to 200,000 were killed. Others have put the final death toll from Bleiburg at 30,000.

Not all the victims were Croats. Many were Slovenes associated with the Bela Garda. an anti-Communist militia in Slovenia which collaborated with the German and Italian occupying forces. After the war. Djilas said the Partisans had been surprised by the decision to return the Croats to Yugoslavia. as it was obvious that they would be massacred. Tito himself became disgusted by the orgy of killings that followed the Partisan victory. According to Djilas. he exploded with anger at a session of the Central Committee, declaring that as a result of the slaughter 'no one is afraid of capital punishment any longer'.[4]

While the Partisans in Slovenia were killing off the remnants of the NDH army. the people of Zagreb awaited the arrival of Tito and the new Croat government under Nazor, Bakarić and Franjo Gaži. one of the left-wing leaders in the Peasants Party. The new civilian government had replaced Zavnoh. and was established in liberated Split on 16 April.

Few people in Zagreb knew much about Tito at that time. Maček said that the first time he ever heard about him was at the begining of 1943. when the newspapers published a reward for his capture.[5] That the leader of the Partisans was a Croat was certainly a reassuring sign. which ensured he was greatly preferable to Mihailović's Chetniks. He spoke with a strong accent that betrayed his origins in the region of Zagorje. the heartland of Croatia to the north of Zagreb. Yet to what degree Tito considered himself a Croat is debatable. He was born Josip Broz in 1893 in Kumrovec. a village on the border between Croatia and Slovenia. to a mixed marriage – his mother was Slovene and his father Croat. He had spent much of his youth far from home. fighting in the Austro-Hungarian army and later in Russia. caught up in the ferment of the Bolshevik Revolution. From 1928 to 1934 he had been imprisoned for Communist activities in Lepoglava. in Zagorje. and in Ogulin. in Lika. under the royal government. On his release. he spent three years in Moscow. After assuming leadership of the Communist Party of Yugoslavia in 1937 his duties had taken him all over the country. The beginning of the war found him in Zagreb. The latter part of 1941 he spent in Belgrade. For the remainder of the war he moved with his Partisan army between eastern Serbia. Bosnia. Montenegro and Croatia. until the entry into Belgrade in November 1944. The only extended period he had remained in Croatia had been in the 1920s, as a trade union activist in Zagreb, Sisak and Kraljevica.

In the semi-autobiographical *Tito Speaks*, he spoke fondly but briefly of the land of his birth. He recalled with affection his mother baking *štruklje* (cottage cheese pie) and the peasants of his village sitting around the hearth, recounting legends of the peasants' revolt led by Matija Gubec in 1573 and the wicked 'Black Queen' who crushed the peasants with great cruelty, Countess Barbara Erdody. But the overwhelming impression is one of restlessness and a hatred of authority, whether it was the parish priest at St Rok's in his childhood, the Austrian Emperor of his youth or the Yugoslav King when he was an adult.[6]

Time and time again he would set off on the back of a hayrick for Kamnik or Ljubljana in Slovenia, or for Trieste, in search of work. No matter how often he was dragged home by failure to find a job he would soon be off again, this time to the Czech factories of Bohemia, or to German-speaking Wiener Neustadt. The phenomenon of Croat nationalism passed him by, as he matured from rebellious Austro-Hungarian into Socialist internationalist. His favourite books as a young man were *Sherlock Holmes* and the writings of Jack London and the Russian radicals. His musical tastes were those of the Viennese coffee houses. He was not indifferent to his Croat heritage; he insisted he took the *nom de guerre* Tito from the eighteenth-century Croat writer, Tito Brezovački. But he placed little stress on it.

None of his wives was a Croat. His first, Pelagia Belousova, was Russian. His second common-law wife, Herta Hass, was an ethnic German from Maribor, in Slovenia. His wartime companion, Davorjanka Paunović, was a Serb from Belgrade and his post-war consort, Jovanka Budisavljević, was also a Serb, from the Lika region of Croatia. He rarely referred to himself as a Croat in public, and after the war ended he resided in Belgrade. In his conduct of Communist Party business there was nothing that betrayed any special sympathy with Croat interests. He endorsed the creation of separate Communist Parties in Slovenia and Croatia in 1937, but he did so as the faithful executor of the Comintern's policy towards suppressed nationalities, not as a supporter of regional rights. He had denounced the creation of the Croatian Banovina in 1939 as a ploy to co-opt the Croat bourgeoisie into government, just as he had denounced the 'second imperialist war' in 1939 – until Germany attacked the Soviet Union two years later.

He inherited from his Croat background a profound dislike for the old Serb-dominated 'Versailles Yugoslavia', although the six republics organised in 1945 enjoyed only limited decision-making powers in the first two post-war decades. He stamped on Moše Pijade's plan to create a separate Serb province in Croatia in 1942.[7] He was also determined to acquire for Yugoslavia as much Croat- and Slovene-inhabited land in Austria and Italy as he could lay claim to, although whether this was evidence of his territorial greed or a genuine interest in 'liberating' Croats and Slovenes is, again, debatable. Success in this venture was mixed. The Partisans occupied Trieste and part of southern Austria around Klagenfurt in 1945. In Trieste they presided over a brief reign of terror, not only against the Italians but also against Slovenes suspected of right-wing sympathies. But the attempt to gain these territories for Yugoslavia collapsed in the face of fierce Allied opposition – to the enormous relief of Trieste's Italian majority and the Austrian majority in Klagenfurt.

The Zagrebians' curiosity about their new master was soon to be satisfied. Tito arrived in the city on 21 May and delivered a speech to an enormous crowd in St Mark's Square, outside the old palace of the *bans* in the Upper Town. His speech was the first opportunity the Zagrebians had to find out what kind of a state was going to replace the NDH.

If they expected a harangue, they were mistaken. Tito was at his most conciliatory and flattering. He spoke of his joy at being back in 'our beloved Zagreb' and said he was speaking 'as a Croat'. He tried to dispel any fears that the end of the NDH meant the return of the old, hated Yugoslavia.

'We have done away with the form of government created in the aftermath of the Treaty of Versailles, when a clique of the Great Serbian bourgeoisie imposed the centralised system on us, a system in which other nations were entirely deprived of their rights,' he said. 'Today no one will be able to object that this or that nation is being oppressed.' The period from 1918 to 1941 had been 'a bitter and terrible lesson, and not only for the Serbs', he added.[8]

Tito went on to explain that although the new Yugoslavia would resemble 'a conglomerate of small states' there would be no place for reactionary nationalism or petty disputes between Serbia, Croatia and the other republics. The arrival of Socialism rendered such disputes not only unnecessary but unthinkable. In fact, the borders between the new republics would scarcely be noticed. They would be like 'white lines in a marble column'.[9]

In spite of Tito's advice, the exact position of the 'white lines in a marble column' generated a fair amount of controversy. The debate was heated up by an announcement in the spring of 1945 from the provisional government of Vojvodina that the province would be attached to Serbia.

This was controversial, as it reopened a dispute over Srijem, which had belonged the Croat Banovina of 1939 and which Hebrang had insisted ought to remain in Croatia. The majority of the population in Srijem was Serbian, but the western districts of Vukovar, Ilok, Vinkovci

Changes to Croatia's borders 1939–45

and Županja were mostly Croat, and historically the region had been part of Slavonia. Another question mark hung over Dalmatia, where supporters of autonomy inside Croatia had clashed with Hebrang the year before. South of Dalmatia, the Montenegrins laid claim to the bay of Kotor, which had formerly belonged to the city-state of Dubrovnik, and where the population was a mixture of Catholic and Orthodox.[10] The last area of dispute was Istria, although this was a dispute of a different kind, pitting Yugoslavia against the West rather than Croatia against Slovenia.

With Tito's support, Bakarić fended off the more unfavourable claims made against Croatia, in particular a Bosnian suggestion to swap Dubrovnik for Bihać. On the eastern frontier with Vojvodina, a border commission under Djilas got to work, applying economic and ethnic criteria. The eastern tip of the old Croatian Banovina around Šid and Ruma was awarded to Serbia on ethnic grounds, while western Srijem stayed in Croatia. Baranja was awarded to Croatia on the ground that it formed a natural hinterland to Osijek. The result of the dispute over Istria favoured Croatia. Although Yugoslavia was forced to give up the city of Trieste after a brief period of occupation, the rest of the peninsula, including the mainly Italian town of Pula (Pola in Italian), went to Croatia, apart from the small strip of land awarded to Slovenia. The Croat portions of Bosnia, including the old Ustashe heartland of western Herzegovina, however, were lost to the new republic of Bosnia–Herzegovina, and the bay of Kotor went to Montenegro.

During the six months that followed the Partisan entry into Zagreb, Tito suppressed non-Communist political organisations and created a one-party state throughout Yugoslavia. In Serbia there was little opposition. This disappointed many foreign governmental observers, especially in the US, who had confidently predicted a royalist uprising in Serbia against the Partisans. Seton-Watson, on his last visit to Yugoslavia in 1936, drew this comparison between the two peoples. 'The fact is that in Serbia it has always been a tradition to vote for the government of the day,' he wrote. 'Very different is the situation in Croatia. There the peasant masses have a long tradition not of subservience to the government of the day, as in Serbia, but on the contrary, of opposition at all costs.'[11] Although support for the Partisans was weak in Serbia and most of the rural population remained attached to the monarchy, the rising against the Partisans in Serbia that many foreign observers had predicted never took place.

In Croatia non-Communist political activity was more difficult to suppress, although Maček's flight abroad a few days before the Partisans reached Zagreb rid the regime of a potentially troublesome foe.[12] The Peasants Party had been accustomed to persecution. The Church was stronger and more disciplined in Croatia than in Serbia, and was stiffened in its opposition to Communism by the strong support of the Vatican.

The Communists' first task was to ease out of office the non-Communist ministers who were included in the Yugoslav cabinet following the Tito–Šubašić accord. This at first might have appeared problematic, as there were several non-Communists in the new Yugoslav government formed in March 1945, as well as three regents, who under the terms of the Tito–Šubašić agreement exercised the prerogatives of the King pending a final constitutional settlement. Apart from Šubašić, who was made foreign minister, there was another Croat in the cabinet from the ranks of the HSS, Juraj Šutej, and Miroslav Grol, leader of the Serbian Democratic Party, who was appointed deputy prime minister. Two other 'non-Communists', Sava Kosanović, a Serb, and Drago Marušič, a Slovene, were really fellow travellers. The ace held by the Communists was that they acted in unison against their rivals throughout Yugoslavia, whereas the non-Communist parties in

Serbia and Croatia were too divided by their experience in the war to form a united front.

Alongside a sharp divide between the Serbian and Croatian parties, there were deep splits in the parties themselves. In Croatia the Peasants Party was split into three factions, which greatly undermined its chances of revival. In the centre, Šubašić attempted to steer a course between the Communist-led Popular Front and the opposition. On the left, Gaži advocated working inside the Popular Front. At the other end of the spectrum, Stjepan Radić's widow, Marija, tried to uphold the party's independence and its traditional anti-Communist stance.

Šubašić's tactics weakened the ability of the Peasants Party to present a united front; they did not, however, endear him to the Communists, who got rid of him – and all the other non-Communists – as soon as they were no longer useful. On 19 August Grol gave up the struggle and resigned. In October Šutej and Šubašić also were forced out of the cabinet, shortly after the provisional government set a timetable for elections to be held for a constituent assembly in November. The Foreign Minister had attempted to leave the country in September for talks with Maček, who was then in Paris giving interviews to the newspapers accusing the Communists of aiming for a dictatorship. The Communists at first gave Šubašić permission to depart, then withdrew it. Unable to leave the country, Šubašić saw that his position as foreign minister had become absurd. He resigned, and withdrew from politics, a disappointed man. Before his death he apparently wrote a letter to Maček, asking to be forgiven for the mess which his intrigues had partly helped to bring about.[13]

Once Šubašić and Grol were out of the cabinet, the Communists had a free hand to deal with their less important opponents. The three regents were simply ignored from the start, and King Petar relieved them of their responsibilities in August 1945. As the election grew closer, non-Communist candidates encountered more obstacles and intimidation. 'We Communists did not want any opposition, none whatsoever,' Djilas recalled. 'In the summer of 1945 when the draft of the elections was discussed, we deliberately included provisions that rendered it impossible for the opposition to participate.'[14]

Supporters of Mrs Radić, the most significant opponent of the Communist-run Popular Front, were intimidated by the new Communist-run secret police, OZNa, which was later known by the acronym UDBa. When Mrs Radić's newspaper, *Narodni Glas*, was suppressed at the end of September she decided to boycott the election in protest. The left wing of the Peasants Party under Gaži, meanwhile, surrendered its separate identity by agreeing to merge with the newly formed Popular Front, a Communist umbrella organisation which purported to harness a broad spectrum of progressive interests.

As a result the voters on 11 November were presented with a single list of candidates. The election was a farce. Voters were given rubber ballots, which they were told to drop in one of two urns, one representing the Popular Front and the other the non-existent opposition. The balloting was supervised by Popular Front officials, who could see, and hear, if the ballot was being dropped in the opposition urn. Not surprisingly the Popular Front won over 95 per cent of the votes in Croatia, as in the other republics. The Constituent Assembly quickly scrapped what was left of the Tito–Šubašić agreement. On 29 November the monarchy was abolished and Yugoslavia proclaimed a people's republic.

Some non-Communists tried to save their parties' independent existence by joining the Popular Front. But most were weeded out within a few years. The fate of Dragoljub Jovanović was illustrative. The leader of the Serbian Agrarian Party was a convinced left-winger who had supported the Partisans in the war. He was elected to the Constituent Assembly in 1945 on the Popular Front ticket. He was highly popular in his Pirot constituency and the Communists recognised him as a man of integrity. Nevertheless, in 1947 he was arrested on trumped-up charges and sentenced to nine years' imprisonment.

Tito's only concession to the pre-war regime was to place a few harmless and respectable relics of the old literary and political establishment in symbolic posts: in Zagreb, Nazor was rewarded for his services to Zavnoh with the post of president of the new Croatian People's Republic; in Belgrade, Ivan Ribar, father of the Communist youth hero, Ivo Lola Ribar, became spokesman of the federal parliament.

Nazor was incomparably the greatest Croat poet of his time. His ode to Croatian independence, *Hrvatski Kraljevi* (Croatian kings), written between 1904 and 1912, had moved an entire generation. He was a convinced Christian. For a short time, while the Partisan government of Croatia was based at Otočac, he tried to act like a real president and make decisions. The Communists, who wanted only a figurehead, did not like that, and Djilas was sent to explain to him that he must not interfere in politics. After that he gave up.[15] He never appeared to regret entering Tito's service. He was old, surrounded by officials who kept him in the dark, and either he did not know, or he did not want to know, about the terrible purges that were going on around him.[16]

By the early 1950s the only political arena in which Communist control was less than 100 per cent complete was local government, where it seems that a few hostile elements clung on to menial positions in some of the more far-flung village councils. After the elections of 1952, the Party-controlled press launched a fierce campaign against the way the vote had been conducted in some areas, claiming that 'reactionaries' in several local councils had been elected to office.

Tito's political radicalism was matched in the economic sphere. In August 1945 a vast amount of land was expropriated by a law confiscating the holdings of 'collaborators' and all those larger than 35 hectares (about 86 acres), with a few exemptions for the Churches.[17] In Vojvodina the property of several hundred thousand ethnic Germans, who had been expelled for collaboration, was confiscated in its entirety. So was the land of about 200,000 Hungarians, although unlike the Germans the Hungarians were not expelled *en masse*. The property was handed over to a land fund, which then distributed much of it to landless Serb and Montenegrin families from Lika, Montenegro and Bosnia. But at the same time part of the confiscated land was set aside for the first agricultural collectives and enormous pressure was soon applied on the peasants to join them, especially in Vojvodina and Macedonia.

In both his economic policy and his suppression of the non-Communist opposition, Tito was far more headstrong than his East European comrades, who struggled on with coalition governments and mixed economies until 1947, or in some cases until 1948.

He was equally brutal in his handling of the Churches, the Catholic Church in particular. According to a report submitted to Anthony Eden by the writer Evelyn Waugh, who was attached to Partisan headquarters in Croatia in Topusko for several months from July 1944, the OZNa executed a large number of clergy after liberation on flimsy grounds:

Trials by OZNa take place in secret, the names of judges, accusers and witnesses are not disclosed; a prisoner is never acquitted in a judicial sense; he is sometimes set free ... and finally shot after the third or fourth period of liberty. When executions have taken place a notice is posted giving the names of the victims and some general charges, such as 'Ustasha', 'enemy collaborator', or 'denouncer'.

Waugh was convinced that the active pro-Ustashe sentiments of a minority of clergy, concentrated in Bosnia, were being used by the Partisans to stigmatise the entire clergy and eliminate potentially troublesome clerics whose real crime was anti-Communism, or even excessive local popularity:

Any priest prominent as an opponent of Communism is condemned as a traitor ... even priests who lacked all interest in politics incur condemnation, simply by their prestige. Fr Petar Perica, a Jesuit of Dubrovnik, shot by the OZNa in November 1944 devoted himself entirely to the spiritual life [yet] an influential partisan spokesman told the writer of this report that he had been the instigator of Ustashe massacres. ...

Of the fourteen priests killed to date in Dubrovnik, only three concerned themselves with politics, the others were singled out for their popularity, for example Fr Marjan-Blažić, a blind preacher, Fr Bernadin Sokol, a musician. ... to have influence with the younger generation is especially culpable. The Croatian clergy has already been depleted by killings by Chetniks, Germans and Italians. It is steadily being depleted by partisan killings.

Waugh was a devout Catholic. The first British Ambassador to post-war Yugoslavia, Ralph Skrine Stevenson, was keen to keep the wartime alliance of the British and the Partisans alive. As a result, Waugh's account was simply dismissed as propaganda. Stevenson wrote to Eden on 2 May 1945: 'I cannot accept the general conclusions which he draws in the report.'[18]

In Zagreb, Archbishop Stepinac had remained at his post. Several other bishops had fled, breaking their canonical oaths, among them the Archbishop of Sarajevo and the Bishop of Banja Luka. Stepinac was taken into 'protective custody' as soon as the Partisans reached Zagreb.

On 2 June 1945 one of his suffragans, Bishop Salis-Seewis, called on Tito in his stead and assured him of the Church's willingness to work alongside whatever civil authority was established. Tito spoke sooth-ingly on this occasion, downplaying fears of organised retribution against the clergy. 'Speaking as a Catholic and a Croat,'[19] he told Salis-Seewis that he hoped the clergy would return to the ideology of Strossmayer and the ideas of southern Slav unity. He said that he blamed the Catholic Church for being inclined more to the Italians than to the Slavs and compared it unfavourably with the Orthodox Church in this respect.

The next day, Stepinac was released from detention and on 4 June visited Tito himself. The meeting did not go well, and the Archbishop came away convinced that Tito wanted the Church in Croatia to loosen its ties with Rome. He may have misunderstood Tito's words, though there was no mistaking the fundamentally hostile position of the new authorities towards organised religion.

The Yugoslav Communists opposed the Church not only on dogmatic grounds but because they looked on the Catholic and Orthodox Churches as the main props to the kind of Croat and Serb nationalism that was irreconcilable with a wider Yugoslav nationalism. In the long term the Communist ideology and punitive land reforms undermined and impoverished the Orthodox Church, and some Orthodox bishops would also suffer persecution.[20] But in 1945 the Serbian Church was still in a mood of euphoria over Serbia's liberation from German occupa-tion by fellow Orthodox Slavs from Russia, and its position seemed relatively secure. The Serbian Patriarch, Gavrilo, had been imprisoned in German concentration camps and his patriotic stock was high. The position of Archbishop Stepinac was quite different. He headed a Church which had lent considerable support to a defeated and utterly discredited Fascist regime, and, although he was not accused of personally advocating or encouraging war crimes, he was compromised by association.

The Archbishop, for his part, was shocked by the wave of trials and judicial executions that began in earnest in June. Some of the victims had little cause to expect clemency. They included several NDH government ministers who had been apprehended in Croatia, or repatriated to the Yugoslav authorities while attempting to escape through Austria, and notorious war criminals such as Fr Filipović, a Franciscan friar from Herzegovina, who had become a concentration camp attendant at Jasenovac. But the war guilt of other victims was more questionable. The Muslim Mufti of Zagreb was shot soon after the Partisan victory and the Bishop of Dubrovnik 'disappeared', and was certainly killed. Germogen, the Metropolitan of the quisling Croatian Orthodox Church, and Spiridon, the Croatian Orthodox Bishop of Sarajevo, were also executed almost immediately. The Partisans took rapid and brutal revenge on Catholic parish clergy who were thought or known to have supported the wartime regime, especially in Bosnia, which had borne the brunt of Ustashe persecution and where the new republic's regime was made up mostly of Serbs and Muslims.

There was savage retribution in May in Široki Brijeg, the village in western Herzegovina that had produced several Ustashe leaders and where the local Franciscan community was seen as an Ustashe seminary. Shortly after Partisan troops arrived, fourteen friars were doused in petrol and set on fire. Several others were taken away and shot.

In this tense atmosphere, Stepinac received permission in July to go ahead with the annual procession to the Marian shrine of Marija Bistrica, north of Zagreb. But Church–state relations were already tense and the authorities appeared angry that 40,000 pilgrims dared to go, complaining afterwards that the crowd included the families of Ustashe fighters. Stepinac defended the participants, saying many were distraught wives and children of soldiers who had gone 'missing' at Bleiburg. Already it appears that Stepinac had resolved on confronting Tito's regime. It was not only the killing of clergy that aroused his indignation. He was also implacably opposed to the introduction of civil marriage, the confiscation of Church property, the abolition of religious education, the promotion of atheism in schools, the suppression of religious houses, and most other items on the Partisan agenda.

On 20 October the simmering quarrel burst into the open when the Archbishop published a strongly worded pastoral letter. In it he declared that 273 clergy had been killed since the Partisan take-over, 169 had been imprisoned and another 89 were 'missing', presumed dead. The letter was so controversial and daring that many Catholic clergy would not read it out from the pulpits. Tito was furious and – for the first time – publicly attacked the Archbishop for failing to speak out against the Ustashe massacres of Serbs in the war. On 25 October he wrote a signed editorial in the Party newspaper *Borba* accusing Stepinac of 'declaring war' on the new Yugoslavia.[21] The rest of the media took their cue from Tito and launched a vociferous campaign against the Archbishop as a Fascist sympathiser. There is no doubt that it was the Archbishop's opposition to Tito, not his record during the NDH, that condemned him. Djilas, then in the inner circle of the Party leadership, recalled: 'He would certainly not have been brought to trial for his conduct in the war ... had he not continued to oppose the new Communist regime.'[22] On 4 November the Archbishop was attacked by a stone-throwing crowd of Partisans in the village of Zaprešić. Shaken by the display of violence he withdrew to his palace and did not appear in public again.

The authorities did not arrest the Archbishop, however, until they had caught the Chetnik leader Mihailović in a cottage near Višegrad in eastern Bosnia at the beginning of March. They executed Mihailović in June. Once the regime had dealt with its principal opponent among the Serbs, it returned to settle its accounts with its principal enemy among the Croats. In September 1946 Stepinac was indicted to appear at the trial that was already under way of the former NDH police chief Erih Lisak, the Archbishop's secretary Ivan Šalić, and about sixteen other clerics and former NDH officials.

There was a long list of accusations against the Archbishop. The principal ones were that he had called on 'the criminal Pavelić' on 16 April 1941 before the Yugoslav army had surrendered, and had then issued a circular to his clergy two days later urging them to support the NDH. He was accused of celebrating Mass at the opening of the NDH's toy Sabor and of presiding over the forced conversion to Catholicism of thousands of Serbs 'who had knives at their throats'. He was also accused of secretly meeting Lisak after the Partisan entry into Zagreb.

The Archbishop was reluctant to answer specific charges, claiming repeatedly in the courtroom (and for the rest of his life): 'My conscience is clear.' A respected defence lawyer was appointed by the state, Ivo Politeo, who answered many of the accusations Stepinac himself would not deign to rebut, such as the oft-heard charge that the Archbishop had allowed the Church to be used for the glorification of the Ustashe state.

'Why is it never mentioned that, as soon as Pavelić took power, Stepinac never sang the *Te Deum*, let alone in the cathedral?' Politeo asked.

Why is it not recalled that only once in four years of occupation did the Archbishop serve Mass in the cathedral, and that only in 1943, when the Italians organised a ceremony in memory of the Duke of D'Aosta?

And on that occasion it was not the Archbishop nor any one of the clergy who received Pavelić at the church door but the sacristan. Is that the behaviour of an Archbishop towards a self-styled head of state whom he had recognised, supported, and with whom he had collaborated?[23]

Politeo also cited Stepinac's numerous sermons in which he had condemned racial and religious intolerance, in particular the Archbishop's address at the feast of Christ the King on 25 October 1942, when he had declared that:

> all men and all races are the children of God.... all without distinction, whether they are Gypsies, Blacks, civilised Europeans, Jews or proud Aryans, have the same right to say 'Our father who art in heaven'. For this reason, the Catholic Church has always condemned and does condemn, all injustice and violence committed in the name of theories of class, race or nationality. One cannot exterminate Gypsies or Jews because one considers them of an inferior race. ...'[24]

Politeo reminded the court that the Archbishop had no automatic influence over the Church press during the war, many of whose publications had come under the authority of other bishops of the religious orders. He did not deny that Stepinac had received Lisak in his palace after the Partisan victory, but insisted that Lisak had gained the interview under a false identity.

It was a respectable case. But, although the trial was not quite a Stalinist show trial, the guilty verdict undoubtedly had been decided in advance. Stepinac was sentenced to sixteen years' imprisonment and was taken to Lepoglava, where, only months before, the Ustashe had imprisoned and murdered many of their own opponents.

Once Tito had Stepinac under lock and key, he closed in on Hebrang, his most dangerous rival within the leadership of the Communist Party. The Croatian Party's former leader had languished in the hostile atmosphere of Belgrade since 1944, where he fought an unsuccessful rearguard battle on behalf of Croatian interests. He opposed the new borders of Croatia that were drawn up by Djilas, especially the loss of Srijem, shouting that Croatia's historic borders ran up to Zemun, just north of Belgrade;[25] he opposed the unfavourable exchange rate forced on the Croats after the abolition of the kuna currency used in the NDH; he opposed the show trials of various so-called economic criminals that began in Croatia in 1946;[26] and he appears to have opposed the suppression of non-Communist parties.[27]

Tito evidently feared and hated the man, and in 1946 made a ferocious attack on both Hebrang and Sreten Žujović, a Serb Communist, at a Central Committee session from which the two men were absent. 'What leaders of Yugoslavia they would make,' he hooted. 'One an Ustasha, the other a Chetnik.'[28] In April Hebrang's slide towards disgrace was confirmed when he was excluded from a government delegation to Moscow to discuss economic affairs, which, as the Minister for Industry and architect of Yugoslavia's first five-year plan, he felt entitled to have led.

In January 1948, two months before Tito's quarrel with Stalin burst into the open, Hebrang was abruptly demoted to the position of minister of light industry. That was the start of his final downfall. In April he was placed under house arrest. In May he was expelled from the Communist Party, which opened the way for his formal arrest. In the meantime, Ranković got to work concocting a case that presented Hebrang as an Ustasha double-agent who had been recruited during his time in the NDH jail in Stara Gradiška in 1942. At the Fifth Party Congress in July, just after Yugoslavia was expelled from the Cominform, Hebrang's fate was sealed when Bakarić announced that the Party was investigating his Ustashe ties.

Andrija Hebrang was never seen in public again. A veil of silence fell over his fate, which was lifted only partially with the release in 1952 of a book entitled *Slučaj Andrije Hebranga* (The Case of Andrija Hebrang), written by Mile Milatović, the Serb head of the UDBa who had been in charge of investigating Hebrang after his arrest.

Written in the typically hectoring and denunciatory style of Communist literature in the 1950s, the book made an unconvincing case for Hebrang's suicide after he was allegedly confronted with the proof of his wartime work as a double-agent. It is almost certain that Hebrang was killed in secret, and that the authorities feared to grant him a public platform in court, in the way that they had given one to Stepinac.

Because Stalin had cited the arrest of Hebrang as evidence of Tito's anti-Soviet stance, Hebrang has been associated with the Stalinist cause in Yugoslavia, and with the fall of the 'Cominformists' who supported Stalin against Tito. And perhaps it is possible that Tito genuinely feared that Hebrang would be used by Stalin against him during the dispute in 1948. But it would be a mistake to assume that Hebrang fell from grace because he was a Stalinist. It is much more likely that Tito eliminated him because his political moderation and obdurate championship of Croatia's special position within Yugoslavia both angered and embarrassed him. Hebrang most probably within a year or two would have been eliminated even had there been no quarrel between Tito and Stalin. There is little evidence that he advocated a conciliatory line towards the Peasants Party and the Church simply because that was then the Kremlin's line, and more that he did so from conviction.[29]

The break with Stalin in 1948 did not lead to a relaxation of conditions inside Yugoslavia, least of all in Croatia. The fear that Yugoslavia could be penetrated by Stalin's agents heightened the campaign to root out class enemies and nationalists, and the UDBa assumed an ever more pervasive role in the country's life, at least until 1952. There was no let-up in the barrage of anti-Western rhetoric. Instead, Tito attempted to disprove Stalin's charges of ideological deviation by accelerating the drive towards full-blooded Communism. In spite of the passive resistance of the peasants to a deeply unpopular policy, the authorities speeded up the collectivisation of agriculture after 1948 using more or less coercive methods, and the number of state farms grew from 1,318 in 1948 to 6,797 in 1950, by which time one-quarter of the farmland in Vojvodina had been taken into state ownership.[30]

Most Yugoslav businesses had been taken over in December 1946, but in April 1948 the job was completed when the government nationalised all the smaller businesses which had slipped through the loop, including all the immovable property of foreigners. The persecution of the Church continued, especially in Croatia and Bosnia, and the parish clergy did not have Archbishop Stepinac's international reputation to shield them from the worst consequences. In 1948 Bishop Petar Cule of Mostar, successor to Bishop Alojzije Misic, who had complained so strongly to Stepinac about the Ustashe persecution of the Serbs, was arrested on charges of wartime collaboration. He was sentenced to eleven years' imprisonment, and in far worse conditions than Stepinac.[31] By the early 1950s some dioceses had been decimated by arrests and killings. In Senj diocese, of 151 priests before the war, only 88 survived in 1951, and half the parishes had no clergy.

13

Croatian Spring

Do you want 1941 all over again?
Tito to the Croat Communist leaders, 1971

For most Croats, the first signs of the revival of independent political activity appeared around 1967, when a reform movement began within the Croat League of Communists which some called the Croatian Spring and others Maspok (short for *masovni pokret*, or 'mass movement'). Like Alexandar Dubcek's movement in Czechoslovakia, it started within the ruling Communist Party, only to gather a popular, nationalist momentum all of its own. Like the Prague Spring, the reform movement in the Croatian Party was crushed from outside, and with it died any hope of political reform within the Communist system.

The first signs of a thaw in Communist rule in Yugoslavia appeared much earlier than 1967. The break with the Cominform eventually forced Tito – against his instincts – to abandon the hardline policies he had forced on the country in 1945. After the Soviet-inspired economic blockade threatened Yugoslavia with collapse, Tito turned to the West for help and accepted loans. Naturally they came with a price, and Tito had to tone down his anti-Western propaganda and stop supporting the Communists in the civil war in Greece. At home, the fear that peasant resistance to collectivisation might spark off a rebellion that could give Stalin an excuse to invade forced him to slow down, and eventually abandon, the whole policy.

Inside the Party's ruling clique, Djilas led the demands for a change of direction. The former leader of the extreme left had undergone a real conversion, which would end with him becoming an anti-Communist dissident. In 1950 he argued that the Soviet-style command economy should give way to factories which were collectively owned and run by local workers, an idea that became known as self-management. 'It occurred to me that our whole economic mechanism might be simplified by leaving administration to those who worked in the enterprises, the state only securing for itself the tax,' he recalled.[1]

The degree to which self-management introduced a true democracy into the workplace was exaggerated. Nevertheless, Tito's decision to bless the whole self-management ideology had serious consequences; once it was conceded that individual enterprises had a right to run their own affairs, the republics naturally demanded the same rights at state level. Djilas' influence peaked in 1952. At the Sixth Party Congress in November the Yugoslav Communist Party changed its name to the League of Communists and abrogated its 'leading' role in society for a mushier 'guiding' role. Party and state functions were separated and non-Communists encouraged to attend Party meetings.

Djilas fell from grace the following year after he published searing attacks on the new Communist ruling class in the newspaper *Borba* which went way beyond what Tito could stomach.[2] After that the reforms of the Sixth Congress were not followed through and the conservatives in the Party, with Tito's support, went on to the offensive. One example was private property. In March 1953 collective farms were abandoned and peasants allowed to take out of collectives the holdings and machinery they had put in. By the end of 1953 there were only 1,152 collectives left. But then the Party hardliners sabotaged the reform, forcing through a reduction in the maximum permitted size of holdings from twenty-five to thirty-five hectares to only ten.

The Croatian leadership after Hebrang's fall made little contribution to the reform debate. Jakov Blažević, the public prosecutor in Stepinac's trial, and Dušan Dragosavac, a Serb, were hardline figures from rural Lika. They had risen to power over the ruins of Hebrang's vision of a Croatian road to Socialism and had no wish to see his ideas rehabilitated. Većeslav Holjevac,[3] the popular Mayor of Zagreb, was one of the few supporters of Hebrang's *nacionalna struja* (national wing) who were still in public office. Bakarić supported mild changes but he was far too timid to stick his neck out. In the argument over private property, for example, he opposed reducing the maximum level to ten hectares, saying it would make farms hopelessly inefficient. But when he was overruled he retreated into silence. Another example was his reaction to the fall of Djilas. In 1953 Djilas had dinner with Bakarić and was astonished to discover the degree to which he had moved away not only from Stalinism but from basic tenets of Leninism as well. Yet only a year later Bakarić was placed in charge of the commission that roundly condemned Djilas as a heretic.[4]

However, in the mid-1950s a new generation of Croat Communists was rising through the ranks, who were less fearful, and perhaps less cynical, than Bakarić. They were led by Miko Tripalo, head of the youth wing of the League of Communists in the 1950s before becoming head of the Party organisation in Zagreb in the early 1960s. In tandem with Tripalo was Savka Dabčević-Kučar, who was a far more popular figure. The backgrounds of Tripalo and Dabčević-Kučar were very different from those of peasants and industrial workers, such as Blažević and Dragosavac. Tripalo's grandfather had been deputy in the Dalmatian Sabor under the Habsburgs and his father had been a substantial landowner in Sinj. Young Tripalo had joined the Partisans at the age of fifteen, inspired more by Croat patriotism and a belief in social reform than by Marxist theories of class war. Dabčević-Kučar was another youthful Partisan from a well-known family. Her father had been one of the students who burned the Hungarian flag when the Emperor Franz-Jozef visited Zagreb in 1895. These relative youngsters had grown up under Tito, and found it easy to reconcile a rather naive and optimistic belief in the Yugoslav community of nations with a vigorous Croat patriotism. They resented what they thought was Bakarić's cringing attitude to Belgrade and the Serbs in general.[5]

One sign of the slow thaw in Croatia was the funeral of Archbishop Stepinac. In December 1951 Stepinac had been freed from prison and sent back to his home parish of Krašić, under a form of house arrest. He was lodged in the parish presbytery and permitted to say Mass in the adjacent church. He refused to leave the country, although the government had made it plain it wanted him to retire to Rome. 'They will never make me leave unless they put me on a plane by force and take me over the frontier,' he said following his release. 'It is my duty in these difficult times to stay with my people.'[6] On the rare occasions that foreign journalists were permitted to enter the guarded village, he made it clear that prison had not effaced his conviction that he was entirely innocent. 'I tried to save, and did save, thousands of lives,' he told a Swedish visitor in 1954. 'As for the massacres in the churches, what could I do?' He still feared he would be bundled out to the Vatican and that 'the gates of Yugoslavia would be locked behind me. That is why I stay, even if it means dying in Krašić.'[7] In February 1960, stricken with illness and embittered by his internment, the Archbishop's ordeal came to an end. He had been ill with a rare blood disorder and his last years were distressing. Towards the end his lungs became inflamed, making even breathing difficult. The burden of continual police surveillance had begun to tell on his nerves.

His death was a relief for Tito. He had been furious with the Pope for making Stepinac a cardinal in 1952 and broke off diplomatic relations with the Vatican. The furore over the Cardinal's hat died away. But it was still assumed Stepinac would be buried in semi-secrecy at the parish church in Krašić, befitting his status as a disgraced figure. That was what the bishops expected, and the dead Cardinal was laid out in the village church in episcopal robes, staff and mitre. But at the last minute Tito had a change of heart. The surprised parish priest of Krašić was informed two days after the Archbishop's death that Stepinac was to be buried in the cathedral in Zagreb and with all the honours due to a prince of the Church. The public was not informed of the change, perhaps for fear of triggering a demonstration by angry Serbs. But the foreign diplomatic corps in Yugoslavia was invited to the service, which gave it the character of a state funeral. The Church was permitted to toll bells throughout Croatia and to hang out black mourning flags from the churches. By the standards of his predecessors, Stepinac was buried in discreet style. There was no splendid tomb, merely a simple tablet with a shallow relief of the Archbishop in prayer, executed by Meštrović.[8] Nevertheless, Stepinac's funeral was a belated gesture of reconciliation by Tito to his most controversial opponent and it went some way to reconciling Croats, most of whom remained practising Catholics, to a Communist system which most of them found alien. In one sense an era closed with Stepinac's death. While he lived, the rancour of Croatia's civil war lived with him. When he died, some of the fury of that era was buried with him. Under his successor, Franjo Šeper, the Church gave up its role as a bulwark of opposition to Communism and retreated to the political margins, where it could pursue its pastoral work in a more relaxed atmosphere.

The year after Stepinac's death was accompanied by political turbulence. In 1962, fear of economic collapse caused the first serious public debate within the Party since the early 1950s about such fundamental matters as the nature of a centralised economy, the exchange rate, the amount of money that enterprises should be forced to surrender to Belgrade and the role of the banks. The problem was the policy of pouring investment and heavy industrial plant into underdeveloped republics, such as Bosnia and Montenegro, which had placed an intolerable strain on the economy as a high percentage of these new enterprises were loss-makers. The economic debate opened up a public conflict between Serbia and the less developed republics on one side, and Slovenia and Croatia on the other. The Serbs, championed by Ranković, defended the centralised system and the concentration of fiscal and political power in Belgrade. The Croats and Slovenes, led by Bakarić and Kardelj, wanted greater autonomy and the liberalisation of prices. As Croatia and Slovenia were the major exporting republics, they wanted the exchange rate of the dinar lowered, in order to boost foreign trade. They wanted changes in the laws under which most of the hard currency earned by Croat and Slovene firms went to the banks in Belgrade. As they were the republics with the most profit-making enterprises, they wanted cuts in the amount of money enterprises handed over to Belgrade for general distribution. The Serbs attempted to forge a coalition of poorer republics against Kardelj and the Croats but did not succeed. Macedonia, for example, was economically disadvantaged, and stood to benefit from the policy of centralised finances. But the Macedonians still sided with the Croats, as strong memories of

Serb domination before the war counted more than purely economic considerations.

Tito sat on the fence. He made a sharp speech against the revival of 'bourgeois' ideas in Split in 1962, sided with the centralising faction and appeared to condemn the reformers. Kardelj – Ranković's rival to succeed Tito – was affronted by this public rebuke, vanished from Yugoslavia without permission and turned up in London, claiming he was on holiday. Tito was hurt rather than angry by this show of independence and Bakarić rushed to London to effect a reconciliation. In spite of Tito's reluctance to countenance any dilution of the Party's power, many of Kardelj's proposals for the reform of the pricing system and the exchange rate were adopted, and the republics were granted greater control in the field of economics.

The second conflict between Ranković and the Serbs on one side and the Croats on the other involved the politically charged issue of tourism. Milka Kufrin, one of the younger generation of Croats in the federal government, launched a campaign to open up Yugoslavia's beautiful coastline to foreign visitors. As most of these beaches were in Dalmatia, the issue was more important to Croatia than the other republics. Tito was sympathetic and set up a Ministry of Tourism in 1963, with Kufrin in charge. He followed her advice and agreed that foreigners ought to be able to holiday in Yugoslavia without visas, a most unusual practice for a Communist country. The issue again pitted Serb hardliners against Croat reformers. Ranković insisted that tourists posed a threat to Yugoslavia's state security, and the UDBa systematically harassed foreign visitors, particularly when they made the mistake of pointing cameras at such apparently sensitive objects as railway stations and bridges.

Ranković displayed his power by intimidating Kufrin personally. In 1964 he informed her that he had received a dossier from the UDBa that accused her of a range of sexual and political crimes, including espionage and impropriety with her driver. But he forbade her to inform anyone – even Tito – about the allegations. A year later, when Kufrin finally revealed to Tito on Brioni what had taken place, he was shocked. He showed his displeasure with Ranković by ostentatiously insisting that Kufrin should accompany him to Belgrade on his private Blue Train.[9]

While Ranković was the Vice-President of Yugoslavia and unofficial heir to Tito, change in Croatia could only come about slowly, if at all. But at the beginning of 1966 Tito got rid of his deputy. Ranković had groomed himself as Tito's successor too obviously, alienating the other pretenders as well as the 'Old Man' (as his colleagues called him). His strong identification with Serb national interests in the rows about the economy, tourism and Kosovo alarmed not only the Croats, but all the smaller nationalities which had improved their status under Tito. Bosnian Muslims, Macedonians, Slovenes, Croats and the much persecuted Albanians looked at Ranković and detected a vein of old-fashioned Serb chauvinism under the Communist rhetoric. His image was intertwined with that of the UDBa, whose powers had mushroomed during the conflict with Stalin in 1948 and which was the object of particular dread outside Serbia.

In fact, Ranković rather resented the roles Tito had assigned him and Kardelj. When Tito asked him to 'sort out', that is, smash, a strike, he complained: 'Oh yes, when something needs a theoretical explanation, then it's you, comrade Bevc [Kardelj's nickname], but when it is a question of getting your hands dirty, then it's you go, Marko!'[10]

In the early post-war years, Ranković's services had been indispensable. But by the mid-1960s he was starting to look out of touch. The threat from the Soviet Union had faded, rendering his obsession with surveillance unnecessary. The tourist industry that he had opposed was starting to bring in millions of dollars in foreign currency. Tito was becoming irritated by Ranković's obsessive persecution of Albanians in Kosovo, whom Tito wanted to draw into the Yugoslav community. But far more important than any of these was the discovery that Ranković's UDBa was bugging Tito's private residences in Brioni and in Belgrade.

Tito ordered a thorough investigation of UDBa activities and for the results to be debated at a Party plenum. Significantly, he did not appoint any Serbs to the committee running the investigation, which was headed instead by Krste Crvenkovski of Macedonia. The results confirmed that Tito's private residences had been bugged without his knowledge. The President was alarmed also to learn that UDBa had personal files on about a million people in Croatia, a ludicrously high figure, almost a quarter of the republic's population. The commission did not accuse Ranković of preparing a coup against Tito, but several members, including Tripalo, were convinced that Ranković had tried to make sure no one could challenge his succession in the event of Tito's death. A few days before the Central Committee plenum was due to begin on 16 July on the island of Brioni, Ranković flew in for a private visit. Tito told him he would not be punished if he went quietly. As a result, the outcome of the plenum was decided in advance. Ranković accepted responsibility for the listening devices and Tito graciously accepted his confession. Ranković was then 'advised' to resign his posts. He was not punished, but he remained a political non-person until his death.

The downfall of Ranković, the living symbol both of UDBa power and of Serbian domination, caused an enormous shock throughout Yugoslavia. Among the Serbs, not just the Serb Communists, Ranković's fall was seen as a national calamity that signified their loss of control over Yugoslavia.[11] In Croatia, for exactly the same reason, the fall of Ranković was a cause of general jubilation, and it boosted the fortunes of Tripalo and his supporters. Bakarić was in a peculiar position. He was no friend of the Serb hardliners, but he was too closely identified with the purges of the 1940s and 1950s to welcome any real democratisation.

The first major conflict was initiated not by the Croat Communists, but by the Croatian Writers' Club, in the shape of the *Declaration Concerning the Name and Position of the Croatian Language,* which appeared without any warning on 7 April 1967. The background was a row over a new Serbo-Croat dictionary between Matica Srpska and Matica Hrvatska, the two venerable Serb and Croat cultural organisations. Matica Hrvatska had been a moribund institution for twenty years after the war, during which time it published very little. But in the mid-1960s it was revived, thanks to an influx of energetic new members. Among them were Holjevac, the popular former Mayor of Zagreb, and Franjo Tudjman, a former general.

Tudjman's evolution from orthodox Yugoslav Communist to Croat nationalist dissident reflected the disillusion of a great many Croat Partisans of his generation. Born in 1922 in the village of Veliko Trgovišće, the same Zagorje district as Tito, north of Zagreb, he had grown up in a left-wing Peasants Party family. When the war broke out he naturally enough joined the Partisans and had entered Zagreb in 1945 with the victorious 10th Zagreb Corps. Although he was raised to the rank of general, a spell in the Defence Ministry and at army headquarters in Belgrade left him disenchanted. In the old Serbian capital he ran up against the elitism of the Serbian officers, and he was annoyed at the way the Croats' contribution to the war effort was downplayed, and the entire nation commonly stigmatised as Ustashe. He became convinced that the Serbs were using the issue of the number of war dead in the NDH as a political football to keep the Croats down. He returned to Zagreb a disappointed man 1961. There he become the director of the Institute for the History of the Workers' Movement of Croatia, where his research confirmed his growing conviction that the Serbs had manipulated the figures of the Ustashe victims for their own political purposes.

When the first two volumes of the Serbo-Croat dictionary were published at the beginning of 1967, the Croats were annoyed to find that the dictionary had throughout presented Serbian expressions as the standard ones, while Croatian expressions were either not included at all or classed as dialect. The *Declaration* retorted by attacking the alleged growth of a semi-official Serbo-Croat language that owed much more to Serbian than to Croatian influence. It complained about the growth of a 'state language ... which in practice means the Serbian literary language, because of the dominant influence exercised by the administrative centre of the federation'. It added: 'The Croatian literary language is disregarded and is reduced to the status of a local dialect.'[12]

The *Declaration* demanded constitutional provisions to establish the equality in the status and use of four, instead of three, languages, namely Slovene, Croatian, Serbian and Macedonian. The petition was signed by the twenty most important cultural institutions in the republic, as well as Matica Hrvatska, and about 140 of the country's most prominent writers. Among them was Krleža, Croatia's leading writer and a member of the Croatian Central Committee to boot. In Belgrade, there was consternation. About fifty members of the Serbian Writers Association announced that, if there was to be an official divorce between Serbian and Croatian, they would insist on separate schools for the several hundred thousand Serbs in Croatia and the exclusive use of the Cyrillic script in Serbia itself.

Krleža's association with such a controversial document gave it enormous political significance. Although he was less well known abroad than Andrić, Krleža was by far the most important living writer in Yugoslavia. The argument over the *Declaration* revived memories of earlier quarrels in the late 1930s, when Krleža had engaged in bitter polemics with Djilas. During the war, Krleža had refused to follow Nazor into the woods to join the Partisans and had even been received by Pavelić, thanks to a round-about connection with Budak. As a result, Tito refused to see him alone in 1945. But, since then, Krleža had firmly supported the Party and had become a valued ornament to the regime. Tito was shocked by Krleža's move and summoned Tripalo to his residence in Belgrade, at Užička 15, to ask him to try to change Krleža's mind. But Krleža would not budge. He feared people would laugh at him. 'Everyone will say – "Look at that old fool, now he pretends he did not know what he signed".' he said.[13] Instead he resigned from the Croatian Central Committee. However, Holjevac and Tudjman were expelled from the Party for supporting the *Declaration* in Matica Hrvatska.

The ferment set off by the *Declaration* merely encouraged the reformers. Their hand was strengthened in 1968 when Dabčević-Kučar was appointed head of the Party in Croatia while Tripalo joined the federal Party presidency as one of the representatives of Croatia. The reformers' complaints boiled down to two principal points: that there were too many Serbs in the army, the police and the Party in Croatia, and that too much money, especially hard currency, was being exported to Belgrade.

There was no denying either problem. In Croatia the Serbs comprised about 12 per cent of the population but about 60 or 70 per cent of the police force and about 40 per cent of the Party membership. The army's officer corps was overwhelmingly Serbian, though Croats were better represented in the air force and the navy. The second complaint, about money, was also rooted in hard fact. In spite of several timid attempts at reform, and for all the talk of 'self-management', the Yugoslav economy remained highly centralised. It was true that enterprises were allowed to run themselves, but they could keep only 10 per cent of their profits. The rest went to Belgrade and was pooled between the less developed republics and regions. Profitable enterprises found it extremely difficult to build up any funds of their own to reinvest. The expansion of tourism in Croatia merely highlighted the problem, as most of the foreign tourists stayed in large hotels that were owned by the big Belgrade-based banks and firms. Belgrade, it was said, got the money, while Dalmatia got the traffic.

Tito was perplexed by the anger of his young Croat protégés. He positively believed in the redistribution of wealth between the republics, to try to iron out the glaring north–south divide in the living standards of the pre-war kingdom. At the same time he understood the logic of the Croat demand to keep more of the hard currency they had earned through tourism and the money sent home by *Gastarbeiters* – 'guest workers' who took advantage of the lifting of travel restrictions in the late 1950s to work in Western Europe, mainly in the expanding industrial cities of West Germany. He also appreciated the Croat reformers' stand after the Soviet invasion of Czechoslovakia in August 1968. Although Tito had supported the invasion of Hungary in 1956, convinced that Imre Nagy was presiding over a real counter-revolution, he felt differently about Alexandar Dubcek's experiment in Socialism with a Human Face. Along with Nicolae Ceaucescu of Romania, he strongly opposed Moscow's use of force and mobilised the territorial defence units to warn the USSR against any attempt to interfere in Yugoslavia. Dabčević-Kučar and Tripalo naturally supported the Dubcek regime with real conviction, and rushed to the island of Krk to break the news of the invasion to Mrs Dubcek, who was there on holiday. They also strongly supported Tito's decision to set up territorial defence units around the country, which they saw as a step away from the concentration of military power in Belgrade. Some of the Serb generals, on the other hand, remained sanguine about the prospects of a Soviet attack and kept insisting that the danger to Yugoslavia still came from the West, not from the East.[14] The polemics over the invasion inclined Tito to trust the Croats rather more than the traditionally more Russophile Serbs and Montenegrins.

Although Tito at first supported the reformist leaders in Croatia, others did not. The opposition did not come from the Party leadership in Serbia, which was then in the hands of two urbane intellectuals, Latinka Perović and Marko Nikezić, but from Serb and Montenegrin hardliners in the army, headed by the Federal Defence Minister, General Nikola Ljubičić.

They had allies in the rigidly conservative Party leadership of Bosnia. More than any other Yugoslav republic, Bosnia was run on the lines of a police state by an uneasy combination of Serb and Muslim officials. The Bosnian police force was notoriously heavy-handed. Although Tito praised the Bosnian Party for allegedly solving the national question, the relations between the Serbs, Muslims and Croats remained tense and the carnage of the war had not been forgotten.

A third source of opposition to the reformers came from the old guard in Croatia itself. Bakarić at first lent support to the reformers' ideas, but he later concluded that the movement was dangerous. It was an opinion shared by the other old men who had run Croatia in the 1950s, Milutin Baltić and Dragosavac – the two most prominent Serbs in the leadership – and Blažević, a Croat. The hardliners were not all hoary old men. They had a youthful ally in Stipe Šuvar, a sociology professor at Zagreb university who emerged early on as a vitriolic opponent of the reform movement and of Matica Hrvatska in particular. At every opportunity the conservatives grabbed Tito's ear and insisted that Dabčević-Kučar and Tripalo were leading Croatia towards a counter-revolution that would bring back the Ustashe.

The first public clash took place in 1969, when Miloš Žanko, a Croat who was deputy speaker of the federal assembly in Belgrade and a close ally of the hardliners, published two series of dramatic articles in the Belgrade Party newspaper *Borba* in February and November. The second set in particular, entitled 'There Is a Method in This Nationalist Madness', painted a lurid picture of the alleged revival of Fascism in Croatia. This attempt to whip up a campaign against Dabčević-Kučar's leadership of the Croatian Party failed. She promptly called the tenth Session of the Croatian Central Committee on 15 January 1970. There the majority strongly backed her leadership and went on to the counter-offensive, accusing Žanko of harbouring a 'unitarist' agenda.[15] Bakarić agreed, hinting at a sinister campaign by closet pro-Soviet 'Cominformists', while Tito telephoned Dabčević-Kučar during the session to express his support for her leadership.[16] In May Tito joined the offensive against the hardliners with a tough speech in the Istrian resort of Opatija. 'Your Tenth Session was constructive,' he said from the podium, while Dabčević-Kučar basked in his praise in the audience. 'And no one has the right to object to you discussing your own problems in the way you feel is best. ... do not listen to the ones attacking you; they are going for me as well.'[17]

Dabčević-Kučar's victory on the Central Committee was less significant than it appeared. Although Žanko was condemned, other hardliners remained at their posts, just waiting for an opportunity to launch a counter-attack. But the public perception in Croatia was that Dabčević-Kučar had won her fight and the result of the Tenth Session caused a tremendous stir. Rallies were held in favour of the new leadership, and it was then that the *masovni pokret* really took off. In the restaurants of Zagreb songs that had not been sung since the end of the war wafted up to the rafters, while folk singers belted out the patriotic ballads that the Communists had pushed underground. The old red-and-white chequerboard flag, which had been rarely displayed since the early 1950s, was hoisted once more at public rallies, alongside the Yugoslav red star. The cult of Stjepan Radić revived rapidly. A statue to the Peasants Party leader was unveiled in Metković, while students mounted a plaque outside his former home in Zagreb. In Šibenik, plans to erect a monument to the victims of the Ustashe were cancelled, and the council decided instead to put up a statue to the eleventh-century Croat King Petar Krešimir IV.[18] There was talk of putting up a statue to Jelačić, on the site of the old one that had been removed in 1947.

The 'Croatian Spring' affected three main areas of public life. One was the Party itself, where the reforming Communists under Tripalo and Dabčević-Kučar fought for control of the apparatus against Bakarić, Dragosavac, Baltić, Blažević and Šuvar. The second arena was Matica Hrvatska, where more radical nationalists under Holjevac, Tudjman, Marko Veselica, Vlado Gotovac and Šime Djodan were creating a vibrant powerhouse of popular nationalist agitation. The members of Matica were like Tractarians, pouring out pamphlets and booklets which popularised their ideas about the renewal of Croatia's nationhood, culture and economics. The third wing of the movement was Zagreb university, where preparations for the 300th anniversary of the establishment of an academy gave the reformers a platform to spread their views. In a sign of the way that the wind was blowing, the Party's candidate for the post of university pro-rector, Damir Grubiša, was defeated in the election by Ivan Zvonimir Čičak, a rank outsider and an avowed liberal. At the same time, the students formed the first independent students' association in Yugoslavia, the Croatian League of Students, under Dražen Budiša. In time the students emerged as the spearhead of Maspok's most extreme wing.

The Church was not an integral part of Maspok, which, at the end of the day, was an internal battle for the heart and soul of the Communist movement. But it was, of course, greatly affected by the sudden liberalisation of public life, and its newspaper, *Glas Koncila* (Voice of the Council), rapidly became a mass-circulation newspaper with several hundred thousand readers, advocating not only greater freedom for the Church but greater freedom within it as well.

In the summer of 1970 it seemed as if the Croat reformers were safe. But only a few months later the Serb hardliners were back on the offensive. One cause of discord was the constitutional changes proposed by Tito and Kardelj. They were intended to ensure an orderly succession after Tito's death, and centred on a proposal to set up a collective presidency. They also included plans to decentralise power further to the republics and provinces, and, as both Vojvodina and Kosovo were in Serbia, the promise of greater autonomy to the provinces caused a tremendous outcry in that republic, where the Croats were largely blamed for all real and imagined dangers to its integrity.

While the Croat and Serb Party leaders exchanged accusations, the secret police artificially created an air of crisis by dropping hints that some of the Croat reformers were in secret contact with the exiled Ustashe, and were planning to set up an independent Croatia under Soviet patronage. The notion that Tripalo, the Kremlin and Pavelić's followers were all engaged in a joint plot against Tito was an absurd smear, but it had the desired effect of putting the Croats once again on the defensive and of contributing to an atmosphere of instability. Moreover, some of Tripalo's younger colleagues would not restrain themselves and, by rejecting the Serbs' accusations with passion, confirmed Tito's own dawning doubts about the wisdom of the course that Tripalo was following.

In his memoirs, Tripalo recalled being summoned by Tito in the spring of 1971 and told to calm things down, especially among the intellectuals. According to Tripalo, Tito offered him 'functions I could not dream about' if he would help put the genie back into the bottle. Tripalo said he agreed with Tito that nationalism was growing in Croatia, but insisted that the cause of this nationalism needed to be addressed. 'That nationalism, which has deep roots, is feeding off dissatisfaction with two key problems, the social economic position of Croatia ... and the relation between Serbs and Croats in Croatia,' he said.[19] Tripalo reiterated the complaint that, although Serbs made up less than 15 per cent of Croatia's population, they held 40 per cent of the Party posts and a much higher percentage of the posts in the army, the police, the secret police, the army officer corps and the companies. Tito agreed that the high profile of the Serbs was a problem, though one that needed to be handled sensitively. He showed his confidence in Tripalo by supporting his bid to represent Croatia in the new collective Yugoslav presidency and by suggesting he join the National Defence Council as well.

At the same time, however, the agitation in Croatia in the Church, the university, Matica Hrvatska and the Party reached a peak. The first experiment in independent journalism, *Književni List* (Literary Paper), started in 1969. However, *Književni List* went too far. In the July 1969 issue Bruno Bušić, a young student working at Tudjman's institute for working people's studies, broke the taboo on discussing the number of Serb war dead. In a prominent article he claimed that the real number of people killed in the NDH camps was closer to 60,000 than the

600,000 claimed by the Serbs.[20] This was too much for a large section of the Croatian Party to stomach and *Književni List* was closed. Bušić fled abroad.[21]

But since then more and more national and regional publications had joined the reformist camp, including *Dubrovnik, Kolo* and *Glas Slavonije* of Osijek. The principal Croat daily, *Vjesnik*, had swung behind the reform movement, as had Zagreb Television. However the most influential product of the Maspok newspaper boom was a completely new publication, *Hrvatski Tjednik* (Croatian Weekly), first put out in April 1971 by Matica Hrvatska and edited by Gotovac, with a sister publication devoted to economic issues, *Hrvatski Gospodarski Glasnik*, edited by Marko Veselica.

Hrvatski Tjednik was a real phenomenon – a mass-circulation newspaper with an enormous audience that went way beyond the confines of the Communist Party and made a national reputation for Tudjman and Djodan, among others. It left few stones in Croatian public life unturned, be it the designs on the postage stamps or the (lack of) Croatian words used on the railway timetables. It homed in on Croatia's alleged economic exploitation, on the need to redefine Croatia in the constitution as the national state of Croats (and not the national state of the Croatian nation and the state of the Serbian nation in Croatia) and on the position of Croats in Bosnia.

Many of the economic articles came from Djodan's pen. He hammered away on the issue of Croatia's relative economic decline, starting with the assertion that the republic's share in Yugoslavia's total industrial product had dropped from 35 per cent in 1925 to 19 per cent in 1965.[22] The blame was placed on the tight restrictions on holding foreign currency, the artifically high exchange rate for the dinar, which hampered foreign trade, and the excessive burden placed on Croatia (and Slovenia) by heavy compulsory contributions to the federal fund for underdeveloped regions.

Another favourite theme of *Hrvatski Tjednik*, which concerned the new Party leadership as well as Matica Hrvatska, was the demographic change. While Croatia's birthrate was the lowest in Yugoslavia, it was widely reported that 10 per cent of the adult Croat labour pool was working abroad by the late 1960s. Djodan claimed that half the Yugoslav *Gastarbeiters* were Croats.[23] He said that the rate of emigration – at about 5 per cent in the late 1960s – was outstripping the rate of natural increase in the Croatian population: 'If the rate of increase and the rate of emigration continue in this way, the situation may become extremely dangerous for the very existence of the Croatian nation.'[24] *Hrvatski Tjednik* commented with alarm on the fact that, while the percentage of Croats in Yugoslavia had fallen steadily over the years from 28 per cent in 1918 to about 21 per cent, Serbs were continuing to move into Croatia, apparently attracted by wages that were still higher than those in Bosnia or Serbia.

Towards the end of 1971 *Hrvatski Tjednik* dropped a bigger bombshell, by opening up the question of the Croats in Bosnia. Their position had not really been discussed at all since the war. As a group, they were linked (much more than Croatian Croats) with the Ustashe, and the areas where they lived in greatest concentration, such as western Herzegovina, had been visibly ignored by the authorities when it came to building new roads and industries. In November, *Hrvatski Tjednik* reported in minute detail on the national composition of the Bosnian Party membership, the judiciary, the heads of Bosnian enterprises and government officials, and came up with the unsurprising conclusion that Croats were drastically under-represented in comparison to Serbs and Muslims. Although Croats made up roughly 20 per cent of Bosnia's population, they made up only 12 per cent of the Bosnian Party's membership, whereas the Serbs, who comprised 42 per cent of Bosnia's population, supplied 60 per cent of the Party membership.[25]

On 4 July 1971 Tito summoned the Croat leadership to his residence in Zagreb, the Villa Zagorje. By now he had become deeply worried about Matica Hrvatska, *Hrvatski Tjednik* and the big public gatherings Dabčević-Kučar was holding in Croatia, where too many Croat flags were being waved and the language was straying far beyond the lexicon of self-managing Socialism. He castigated the alleged rebirth of the Ustashe, a new cult of Maček and of the pre-war Peasants Party, the growing audacity of attacks against him personally and even the demands for the return of the statue of Ban Jelačić to its old place on Jelačić Square (then renamed Republic Square). He went on to remind them of the danger of a Russian invasion. 'In some villages the Serbs are drilling and arming themselves,' he said. 'Do we want to have 1941 all over again? That would be a catastrophe. Do you realise that if disorders take place, others will at once be there? I would rather restore order with our army than allow others to do it.'[26] In spite of this tirade, the meeting ended amicably enough with a hug for Dabčević-Kučar. It followed a pattern repeated several times in the era of the Croatian Spring: Tito would arrive from Belgrade, incandescent with rage and full of ideas that had been put into his head by the Serb generals, the secret police and the Party officials in Serbia. After seeing matters for himself, he would go away mollified and apparently convinced that matters were less serious than he had first thought.

Until the summer of 1971, Tito defended the Croat reformers against their detractors. But as summer turned to autumn his doubts accumulated. One of several unpleasant surprises he received was when he returned to Croatia in September. After he got off the plane at Zagreb airport he stood to attention for the Yugoslav national anthem, 'Hej

Slaveni'. As he was about to move off, however, the band struck up again and played the Croat national anthem, 'Lijepa Naša Domovina'. Tito froze and stood to attention again, but the Federal Defence Minister, General Ljubičić, who was standing beside Tito, was visibly furious.[27]

Tito swallowed his surprise and after this discomfiting start, continued his visit. Most Croats thought the President was still on their side and they gave him a tremendous welcome when he made a brief walkabout in Zagreb with Tripalo. And, at a speech in the Esplanade Hotel, Tito once again rounded on those spreading tales about the Croat leadership. But only a few weeks later he had once again changed his mind, and he summoned Dabčević-Kučar to his hunting lodge at Karadjordjevo in Vojvodina to warn her about the dangers of counter-revolution.

In October this strange oscillation in the moods of the President was displayed once again, when Tito returned to Croatia to oversee military manoeuvres. Again he arrived full of foreboding, having been inundated with reports about the rebirth of Fascism. Again he went home mollified after inspecting matters for himself. His wife, Jovanka Broz, played an ambiguous role in these intrigues. She was a Serb from Lički Osik, near Gospić, on the ethnic confrontation line between Serbs and Croats. Sometimes she stoked up the campaign against the reformers, saying that she had received panic-stricken letters from her relatives in Lika.

At other times she told the embattled Croat leaders to stand up to the 'Old Man' because she said he was always changing the republican leaderships when he felt like it.[28] That October Tito visited some Serb villages in Lika for himself, and again he came away convinced that fears about the Serbs' safety had been greatly exaggerated. The local Serbs had shown little concern about the political ferment in Zagreb, he reported. He departed once more for a trip to the United States.

Between October and December the battle between the old guard and the reformist leaders in Croatia spilled out into the open. The trigger was a meeting of Croatia's trade unions, at which the hardliners under Baltić staged a startling coup. Prominent figures in the reform movement, including Veselica, editor of *Gosposdarski Glasnik*, lost their posts. The surprising outcome suggested that the workers of Croatia were less interested in nationalism than the students and the professional middle classes. It cast doubt over Dabčević-Kučar's leadership and caused a predictable uproar in the university, where the radicals of the Croatian League of Students were directing the agenda and were bent on a decisive confrontation.

On 22 November about 3,000 students crowded into the assembly hall of Zagreb university and backed a call by the vice-president of the students union, Goran Dodig, to go on strike. The nominal goal of the strike was to alter the disadvantageous laws on hard currency. In reality the strikers were attempting to force Dabčević-Kučar and Tripalo into taking a more aggressive stance, and to show that the reformers enjoyed greater nationwide support than their opponents. Dabčević-Kučar significantly – perhaps foolishly – said she understood the strike's 'progressive' motives. The student protest spread within days to campuses in Split, Rijeka and Dubrovnik, with demands not only for the reform of hard currency laws but for the sacking of Dragosavac, Josip Vorhovec, Baltić and other hardliners.

Before Tito left for the US, he despatched Kardelj to Croatia to report on the situation. Kardelj had arrived in Zagreb on 15 November, a week before the students' strike, where he held a meeting with Dabčević-Kučar, Tripalo and Bakarić. He scolded them soundly, telling them that Croatian nationalism was 'a child's toy' compared with its counterpart in Serbia and he warned them that the din in Croatia was awakening the Serbian leviathan. Kardelj said that it was a mistake to rely on the seeming moderation of the Party leaders in Serbia like Perović and Nikezić. In his opinion they were only mildly opposed to Great Serbianism and 'this [Great Serbian] tendency was very strong in the intelligentsia and should not be underestimated in the other structures, such as the army and the state security'.[29]

In America Tito was embarrassed and enraged by the reports crossing the Atlantic. On top of the demand for a change in the law on the management of hard currency, he heard that the students in Zagreb were demanding a separate Croatian army and a seat for Croatia at the United Nations. When he returned home he consulted with Kardelj. Tripalo in retrospect became convinced it was Kardelj who urged Tito to crush the Croat leadership. As Tito's most likely successor and a known opponent of Serbian 'unitarism', Kardelj was certainly alarmed that the Croats might ruin his chances with their imprudent demands, while as a Communist he was appalled by the manner in which the Croatian Party was allowing itself to be carried along on a tide of popular nationalism.

But Kardelj's was only one of many voices that influenced Tito in the autumn of 1971. The Party leaders of Bosnia were terrified of both the liberal and the nationalist elements of the Croatian reform movement and furious about criticism of their treatment of Bosnian Croats. The army was openly threatening; Tito was warned that his reputation among Serb officers was dropping on account of his indecisiveness towards the Croat leaders. The hardliners in Croatia around Bakarić, Blažević, Dragosavac and Šuvar were clamouring for intervention. Then there were foreign elements, especially the Soviet Union, which was viewing events in Yugoslavia with a proprietorial eye. The

Russians had long ago accepted Yugoslavia's special position in the Socialist bloc but made it clear they were not ready to see all – or part – of Yugoslavia leave the Communist camp. During Brezhnev's visit to Yugoslavia in September 1971, Tito was lectured by the Soviet leader for three hours, and was virtually ordered to remove 'anti-Soviet' elements from office. Ominously, no one from the Croatian leadership, not even Bakarić, was allowed to join the Yugoslav delegation.[30]

Once the students went on strike the removal of the leadership appeared inevitable, even though Dabčević-Kučar halted the strike by a televised appeal on 28 November (the strike folded two days later). In Zagreb detachments of police from Bosnia began to appear in the streets, while outside the city two army bases, at Jaska and Dugo Selo, were put on a state of maximum alert, tanks revving in case they should be needed to put down trouble in the capital.

It was obvious that Dabčević-Kučar's leadership was doomed even before the entire Croatian Party leadership was summoned abruptly to meet Tito at Karadjordjevo at an extraordinary session of the Croatian and the Yugoslav Central Committees on 1 December. The choice of the venue, the old hunting lodge of the Serbian royal family, was not promising for the Croats. Dabčević-Kučar and Tripalo had little time to agree on their strategy before they set off in a column of black limousines in the driving rain, though before they left they agreed that they would resign if Tito asked them to, but would not be party to the violent suppression of the ideas that they had championed. To avoid disturbances, the public was not informed of the real reason for the session at Karadjordjevo; the official reason given for the meeting was that it was to discuss the next five-year plan.

The meeting turned into a Communist marathon that lasted about twenty hours, with only short breaks for meals. The moment that Tito started to speak it became clear he expected the Croat leaders to resign their posts. He denounced the students' strike in the strongest terms but reserved his harshest words for the editorials in *Vjesnik* and above all for Matica Hrvatska, which he accused of running a state within a state and of seeking a restoration of the NDH. He took issue with the Croatian leaders' obsession with 'unitarism' and said: 'If it is the unitarism of Versailles Yugoslavia, I too, it goes without saying, am resolutely opposed to it. But if it is a matter of the unity of our country, of Yugoslavia as an indivisible whole, then I am in favour of such "unitarism" and of such a united Yugoslavia.'[31]

Of the nineteen members of the Croatian delegation, eleven defended the leadership. Bakarić stabbed his younger colleagues in the back, enthusiastically supporting Tito's view that Croatia was in the grip of counter-revolution. His view was strongly supported by Baltić, Dragosavac and one of the younger hardliners, Milka Planinc.

The enlarged session of the Yugoslav Central Committee began on 2 December. This time the heads of the other republics joined in the attack, with the exception of Crvenkovski of Macedonia. 'If they destroy you we are finished also,' he told Tripalo.[32] There were no formal sackings but Dabčević-Kučar left the hunting lodge knowing that the reformist leadership in Croatia was finished. Tripalo knew he was also finished, though he claimed he wrung a concession from Tito before he left Karadjordjevo that there would be no mass arrests if the leadership resigned, and was to accuse Tito of betraying him in this respect.[33]

On 7 December Bakarić publicly disowned his colleagues for the first time in a speech at Virovitica. In Zagreb Dabčević-Kučar summoned a meeting of the Croatian Central Committee for 12 December at which Milka Planinc was deputised to preside. At the meeting, Planinc read out the resignation of Tripalo as Croatia's representative on the state presidency.

Dabčević-Kučar announced her own resignation in grovelling terms. 'Tito's criticism of the *masovni pokret* as an organisation of doubtful tendencies we accept without reserve,' she said. 'As Communists we express our willingness to engage in the battle against Croatian separatism and chauvinism, as against all other counter-revolutionary, anti-Socialist and self-managing forces....'[34] Her close allies followed. On 11 December Srećko Bijelić resigned as head of the Party in Zagreb, and on the 22nd Dragutin Haramija also resigned as prime minister.

The subsequent purge turned out to be much more savage than anyone had expected. Once Tito had turned against the Croat Party, there was no stopping him. On 18 December he told a meeting of union leaders in Belgrade that the Croat counter-revolutionaries had brought Yugoslavia to the brink of civil war, and he continued to stump the country preaching the same message into the new year. Dabčević-Kučar and Tripalo were given absolutely no chance to join the battle against 'separatism and chauvinism'. In May they were expelled from the Party. They were not imprisoned, but like Ranković they became political non-persons. The lower-ranking officials fared much worse. On 21 December police occupied the university and 352 students were arrested. The student leaders, Čičak and Budiša, were sentenced to three and four years' jail respectively.

Matica Hrvatska was shut down and the chief offenders in that organisation, Tudjman and Gotovac, were sentenced to two and four years in prison respectively. *Hrvatski Tjednik* and *Gospodarski Glasnik* were also closed. The editor of *Vjesnik* was sacked and the other newspapers, Radio Zagreb, the judiciary and local government were purged of reformers from top to bottom. Once again the clergy also lived in fear of arrest and imprisonment. By May of the following year, one Party report said that 'political measures' had been taken against more than

1,600 Party members in Croatia; 892 members had been expelled and 280 had resigned.

The Croatian Spring went too far, and lost the crucial support of potential allies in Slovenia, Macedonia and even in Vojvodina and Montenegro. But the legacy of the suppression of Maspok, and the manner in which it was suppressed, was disastrous not only for Croatia but for Yugoslavia. In spite of the charges hurled against them, Tripalo and Dabčević-Kučar were harbingers not of Fascism but of an enlightened, liberal brand of nationalism. They believed that the national aims of the Croats and the other Yugoslav nations could be harmonised in a looser Yugoslav community. Their faith in an intelligent reformulation of Socialism that empowered rather than disciplined people was sincere. When they fell, an entire generation that included the majority of the most talented people in Croatia went to prison or into exile, or was forced into obscurity. As in Czechoslovakia, highly qualified people were obliged to undertake absurdly inappropriate jobs for the next twenty years to survive. In the place of the Maspok generation came time-servers, police spies and nonentities whose main talent was often a proven ability to spy on and denounce their colleagues. In his old age, Tito was unable or unwilling to see that the likes of Šuvar were not the people to carry Yugoslavia, or Socialism, into the next generation.

The atmosphere between Serbs and Croats was poisoned by the events of 1971. Croatia's new rulers justified their take-over by appealing to the threat of genocide and extermination that had apparently hung over the Serbian community in Croatia. Those expelled from public life in 1971 often blamed the Serbs for their lot. 'When we were swept out of power, Croats tended to view that as a victory for Serbia, which was not completely true,' was the opinion of Tripalo many years later in 1989.[35]

The exodus of Croats from the Party accelerated, making the organisation even more lop-sided in its ethnic composition than it had been before. The knock-on effect outside Croatia of the fall of Maspok was also disastrous, for events in one republic invariably had an echo in the others. In Serbia, the liberal regime of Perović and Nikezić was unseated in 1972 and their successors paved the way for the revival of a raucous brand of Serbian nationalism in the 1980s. Similar purges swept away Crvenkovski in Macedonia and liberal Communists in Slovenia.

Throughout Yugoslavia, policemen and bureaucrats tightened their hold on the reins of power. If Tito thought he had saved Communism by destroying *Maspok*, he was wrong, for the cure killed the patient.

1 (*above*) Fragment from the past: plaitwork above the doorway of the Church of the Holy Cross, Nin.

2 Slav hero: Grgur of Nin, by Meštrović.

3 (*left*) Defenders of the faith: St Donat's Church, Zadar.

4 The ramparts of Christendom: Frankopan fortress at Kostajnica, on the Bosnian-Croatian border.

(*clockwise from above*)

5 A land of warriors I:
an eighteenth-century print of a Croat.

6 A land of warriors II:
an eighteenth-century print of
a Morlach.

7 The Emperor's man: a print of Ban
Jelačić's entry into Zagreb in June 1848.

8 A nation mourns: the funeral of Stjepan Radić in Zagreb in August 1928.

9 Turbulent priest: Alojzije Stepinac.

10 Hitler's henchman: Ante Pavelić inspecting troops at Zagreb airport in November 1942.

11 Death in Venice: Pavelić and Slavko Kvaternik in Venice for the signing of the Rome agreement on the NDH's frontiers in May 1941.

12 Propaganda war I: a Ustache poster from 1943, 'What do you prefer, peaceful work or Bolshevik violence!'

13 Propaganda war II: a Partisan poster from 1944, 'Everyone into battle for the freedom of Croatia!'

Živjeli **IZBORI**
za **USTAVOTVORNI SABOR**
IZRAZ DRŽAVNOSTI I
SUVERENITETA
navoda
Hrvatske!

14 (*above*) The rebels in the forest: a Partisan 'congress of cultural workers' near Topusko in June 1944.

15 Propaganda war III: a Communist election poster in 1946, 'Long live the elections for the constituent assembly, the expression of the statehood and sovereignty of the people of Croatia!'

KARDINAL
ALOJZIJE STEPINAC

NADBISKUP ZAGREBAČKI

16 (*left*) A national cult: the memorial to Cardinal Stepinac, 1960, in Zagreb cathedral, by Meštrović.

17 Tito's faithful lieutenant: Vladimir Bakarić in conversation with his master.

hrvatska
demokratska
zajednica

18 (*right*) Croatia sees the light: an election poster for Tudjman's HDZ in 1990.

19 The return of the Ban: the restored statue of Jelačić in the centre of Zagreb.

20 Martyred town: the devastated centre of Vukovar in 1992.

21 Wars of religion?: an eighteenth-century monastery in Kostajnica, destroyed by the Krajina Serbs in 1991.

22 Welcome to Krajina: 'Vukovar year one'. A banner in November 1992 celebrating the first anniversary of the Serbian capture of the town.

23 Broken bonds: the old bridge at Mostar, destroyed by Bosnian-Croat artillery in 1993.

24 Keeping faith with the past: Croats celebrating the centuries-old Sinjska Alka festival in Sinj in 1994.

25 Operation Storm: Croat troops near Biograd bombarding Serb positions in Benkovac in August 1995.

26 Sweet taste of victory: Croat soldier celebrating recapture of the Krajina 'capital' of Knin in Operation Storm.

27 Escape from Hell: Croats fleeing Serb-held Drniš are reunited with their relatives in Šibenik in 1993.

28 (*right*) Ready for war again: a Church in Dubrovnik being boarded up in readiness for Bosnian-Serb shelling in August 1995.

29 The great exodus: Serbs streaming out of Croatia near Petrinja after the fall of the Krajina.

30 Tudjman and his defence minister Gojko Šušak during the election campaign in October 1995.

31 Mr and Mrs Tudjman voting in the election of October 1995.

32 *The History of the Croats*, 1932, by Meštrović.

14

'Comrade Tito Is Dead'

The whole people has declared for unity, and the leadership which is not able
to see that will lose the confidence of the people, and ought to lose it.
Slobodan Milošević, 1984[1]

The announcement by the federal presidency in the spring of 1980 ended four months of speculation about his illness. 'To the working class, to the working people and citizens, to the people and nationalities of the Socialist Federal Republic of Yugoslavia – Comrade Tito is dead.' It went on: 'On 4 May at 15.05 in Ljubljana the great heart of the President of the Socialist Federal Republic of Yugoslavia ceased to beat.' As the Blue Train carried his body from the Slovene capital through Zagreb to its final resting place in the House of Flowers in Belgrade, Croats caught their last glimpse of the man who had ruled them for thirty-five years. It was a suitably regal end for a man whom the great English historian A. J. P. Taylor considered 'the last of the Habsburgs', ruling over different nations by playing them off one against another and reining in their nationalist hostilities.[2]

In Croatia the twilight of Tito's long reign was marked by continued political repression and relative economic prosperity. It was characteristic of Tito that he gave with one hand and took with the other. After purging the Croat Party of nationalists he then mollified many of those same nationalists' grievances with the new Yugoslav constitution in 1974. The competences of the federal government were reduced to defence, foreign policy and a few economic instruments, Serbia lost more authority over the autonomous provinces of Vojvodina and Kosovo, and the right to nominate officials to federal bodies was surrendered to the individual republics and provinces.

The leaders of the Croatian Spring were dispersed. Holjevac had died in 1970. Tudjman was jailed, as were many others. Tripalo and Dabčević-Kučar retreated into silence – the price for not being sent to jail. The authorities in the mid-1970s remained vigilant against the faintest hint of criticism. In a telling move the magazine *Praxis* was closed in 1975. The magazine, which had started in the mid-1960s, had given its name to a large circle of Marxist philosophers, some of whom were somewhat inaccurately labelled dissidents in the West. Not all were Croats, but the editor, Rudi Supek, was a Croat and the journal was based in Zagreb and printed in Sisak. The Praxis group bitterly opposed anything that smacked of bourgeois nationalism and had very poor relations with the Party leadership under Dabčević-Kučar and Tripalo. For that very reason they were patronised by Šuvar and the ultra-orthodox Communists who took over Croatia in 1971–2. Yet, even though Šuvar publicly praised the Praxis group, the magazine was shut down in February 1975.[3]

Repression was so efficient and opposition so splintered that Croatia appeared uncommonly calm from the early 1970s to the mid-1980s. In 1985 one foreign observer even remarked that 'the Croatian front of the national question has been unusually (and perhaps deceptively) quiet for the past 13 years, which is why the Croatian factor is conspicuous by its absence from the discussion of current national-question issues'.[4]

Yet, under the calm surface of the 'silent republic', as Croatia was nicknamed in the Yugoslav media in the early 1980s, there were disturbing trends. The Party in both Croatia and Slovenia was contracting in size and getting old. In 1971 about 20 per cent of the Yugoslav Party were citizens of the Socialist Republic of Croatia; at the time Croatia contained 21 per cent of Yugoslavia's population. A decade later, Croatia's share of the total Yugoslav Party membership had shrunk to 16 per cent and the proportion of members aged twenty-seven or less had dropped from 27 per cent to 21 per cent.[5] In fact, Croatia's disengagement from Yugoslav Communism was more marked than these figures suggested, as a high proportion of members of the League of Communists of Croatia were Croatian Serbs. On the basis of nationality alone, Croats were already under-represented in 1971, when they made up almost 20 per cent of the Yugoslav population but only 17 per cent of the Yugoslav Party membership. By 1981 only 14 per cent of Yugoslav Communists were ethnic Croats. At the other end of the spectrum, Serbs made up almost 40 per cent of the Yugoslav population and almost 50 per cent of the Party in 1971, and 36 per cent of the population and 47 per cent of the Party in 1981.[6]

Tito's death excited speculation in the Western press about the possible break-up of Yugoslavia, predictions of the revival of Croat nationalism and of ethnic tension between Serbs and Croats. These predictions proved exaggerated. Foreign commentators failed to appreciate the degree to which Tito had already handed over the day-to-day management of the country to his subordinates long before he died. The slogan *Posle Tita biće Tito* (after Tito, there will be Tito), or its Croat version *Nakon Tita bit će Tito*, was an accurate summary of their programme. Tito continued to appear on the front pages of the newspapers as if he were still president, in a conscious effort to keep his memory alive. The President's guard of honour continued to march up and down outside his Belgrade address at Užička 15, even though there was no one to guard. Until the late 1980s the moment of his death was solemnly observed throughout the country by wailing sirens – the signal for many people to stop dead in their tracks until the noise stopped. His departure did not lead to any relaxation of pressure against troublemakers, as former activists in the Croatian Spring discovered. Tudjman had already been sentenced to two years' imprisonment in October 1972 for talking to foreign journalists, which was later reduced to one year. But in February 1981 he was sentenced to three years' imprisonment – a tougher sentence than before – for the crime of 'creating the conviction in public opinion at home and abroad that in the SFRY the position of the Croatian nation is not equal with other nations'.[7]

Tudjman's crimes involved several interviews he had given to foreign news media after his release from prison, between 1977 and 1980. In the first, to Swedish television in 1977, he blamed the high emigration rate of Croats from Yugoslavia on 'the brutal suppression' of the Croatian Spring in the early 1970s.[8] A year later, he told an émigré newspaper, *Hrvatska Država* (Croatian State), that contrary to the official line, 'in all the camps in Croatia during the war, 60,000 people lost their lives and these were not only Serbs but also Croats, Jews and gypsies and other anti-Fascists.... that is a huge and terrible number and a crime ... but I am against this number being multiplied 10 times to 600,000 in Jasenovac alone, solely and only to exaggerate the collective and permanent guilt of the Croatian people.'[9] In May 1980 he had given another incriminating interview to Radio France-Internationale, in which he was cited as complaining that, whenever Croats raised questions concerning their status in Yugoslavia, it 'is immediately generalised as nationalism, separatism, and even Ustashe-Fascism, and then even Croat revolutionaries are accused of being connected with various pro-Fascist elements, which is absolutely senseless'.[10]

Tudjman was one of several veterans of the Croatian Spring who had been imprisoned already in the early 1970s, only to return to jail in the early 1980s. Vlado Gotovac was another. The former editor of *Hrvatski Tjednik* spent four years in prison at Stara Gradiška from 1972 to 1976. In 1981 he was arrested for the same crime as Tudjman – talking out of turn to foreign journalists – and was sentenced to two more years in prison, with an additional four-year ban on public speaking or publishing. Not all the victims of the crackdown of the early 1980s were Maspok veterans. One who was to make a name for himself a decade later as leader of the extreme-right Party of Rights was Dobroslav Paraga, a twenty-year-old student when he was imprisoned in 1980 for three years for organising a petition demanding an amnesty for political prisoners.[11]

The Party in Croatia was especially vigilant in dealing with political dissidents, but it also continued to crack the whip over its members for such insignificant-sounding offences as church attendance. Marija Car, of Duga Resa, was expelled from the Party in 1983 for having her child baptised. Although she was not a believer and said she consented to the baptism only to please her family, the Party authorities upheld her expulsion following her appeal.[12]

The Party kept the media under intense scrutiny. In 1982 the editor of the weekly magazine *Danas* was forced out for writing an article which allegedly questioned the role of the Party in society. In April 1983 most of the editorial board of *Karlovački Tjednik* were similarly removed for political reasons. Two months later the literary organ *Književne Novine* suffered the same fate.[13]

Repression was not confined to Croatia. In Bosnia the authorities reacted harshly when six Croat children from the village of Medjugorje in western Herzegovina reported seeing visions of the Virgin Mary on 24 June 1981. The parish priest, Fr Jozo Zovko, was arrested and sentenced to three-and-a-half years in jail for anti-state activities, while lesser sentences were dished out to two other clergy. The village was closed off by the police to stem the flow of pilgrims rushing to the spot and it was not until 1984 that the potentially rich pickings from foreign religious tourists persuaded the Bosnian authorities that the young visionaries were not somehow linked to exiled Ustashe. Three years later Bosnia's first non-Communist president, Alija Izetbegović, was one of thirteen Muslim intellectuals tried for Islamic agitation, in Izetbegović's case for writing an allegedly fundamentalist tract, *The Islamic Declaration*.[14] In fact, all the republics were eager to prove that Tito's death did not signal a change of course, and they were broadly supported in this by the West, which wanted no change in Yugoslavia's pivotal position between Nato and the Warsaw Pact.

But was impossible to preserve the *ancien régime* in aspic, however much the Party pretended that Tito was still alive, and locked up opponents. The old guard were dying. Kardelj had predeceased Tito. In January 1983 Tito's most faithful lieutenant in Croatia, Bakarić, also died after a long illness. The departure of Tito's intimates, who had shared the privations and glories of the war and the battle against Stalin, robbed the Party of a certain aura. The humdrum figures who stepped into their shoes, such as Stane Dolanc of Slovenia, did not have their authority.

But the greatest threat to the regime was not political dissent or the death of the grand old men of the revolution but economic collapse. The late 1970s was a time of *la dolce vita* for most Yugoslavs, symbolised by an enormous rise in the number of private cars, prestige goods such as washing machines and televisions, foreign holidays, shopping expeditions to Rome and Trieste and a very sharp rise in consumption of imports. The whole country looked like a building site as returning *Gastarbeiters* poured their hard-won savings from the factories of West Germany into chalet-style villas. The fascinating and intricate folk costumes of the peasants, which had survived the Communist revolution, rapidly disappeared from everyday use as even village women donned cheap imitations of Western fashions and 'beehive' hairdos. It was this sense of economic well-being that had anaesthetised the population to political repression. But the boom of the 1970s had been supported by enormous foreign loans which were increasingly difficult to obtain. In the early and mid-1970s the national debt remained stable at just under $5bn. But in the last five years of Tito's life it ballooned to just under $20bn.[15]

As Tito tottered towards the grave no one wished to be so impolite as to address this problem. At the Eleventh Party Congress in 1978, not one word in the official addresses was devoted to the approaching crisis. Instead the speechmakers reeled off a list of the achievements of the Yugoslav economy under Socialism: 'At the beginning of the 1950s the average income was half the world's average whereas today it is 20 per cent higher. ... Industrial production fourteen times higher in 1977 than in 1947. ... some 3 million inhabitants have moved from the villages into towns. ... agricultural yield per hectare is two times higher than before the war. ...'[16] And so it went on.

And even after Tito's death, when Yugoslavia was unable to service the interest on its loans and the country experienced a severe balance of payments crisis, the Party refused to admit there was a crisis. It was only in the autumn of 1981 that a federal commission was set up at last to examine the crisis. By that time inflation had soared from the pre-1976 level of about 15 per cent to over 50 per cent.[17] The commission recommended big spending cuts, which were carried out after agreements were signed with the International Monetary Fund (IMF) in 1983 and 1984. In spite of that, inflation reached a record 70 per cent in 1985.

The debt crisis, which was made worse by the rise in oil prices in the mid-1970s, forced Yugoslavia to agree to stand-by arrangements with the IMF, which insisted on repeated devaluations of the dinar as a condition for assisting the federal government with servicing a gross debt of $19bn by 1983. At the same time at home the federal government introduced desperate measures to service the foreign debt, by passing a foreign currency law appropriating 76 per cent of the hard currency earnings of export firms. This hit Croatia especially hard. Ante Marković, a senior figure in the Croatian Party who was later to become the last prime minister of Yugoslavia, complained that Croatia would be left with only $300m, although the republic needed $1.1bn to sustain its industrial production.[18]

As boom turned to bust and consumers were hit by severe shortages of goods and power cuts, the Party's authority among the public sank. The results were marked on the shopfloor with an upsurge in strikes. A more insidious disease was absenteeism. The newspaper *Komunist* estimated in 1982 that about 500,000 of Yugoslavia's 5.5 million workforce were absent each day, while the others worked an average of less than five hours a day.[19]

The media were the first to strain at the ideological straitjacket, playing on divisions between the republics and between Party factions in each republic over how to deal with the crisis. For the first time since the Communists took power, it became common in print to accuse the Party of incompetence and even of corruption. In Belgrade the magazine *Student* pushed out the frontiers of acceptability. In Croatia *Start* led the way. There were still limits to this relaxation of control. *Start* combined mildly pornographic centrefolds with investigative reports and interviews that seemed daring, as they involved bishops and moderately unorthodox writers. But 'nationalism', as the Croat reformers of 1970–1 had understood it, remained out of bounds. It became permissible to publish shots of naked women or to show erotic films in the cinemas; in fact Zagreb became the Yugoslav publishing centre for a burgeoning industry in pornography, led by the monthly magazine *Erotika*. But to interview Dabčević-Kučar or any other victims of the purges of the early 1970s, or to revive the economic arguments popularised by Djodan, was not permitted.

The cautious path of the chastened inhabitants of the 'silent republic' was not followed in Slovenia and Serbia. The Slovene Party had also been purged in 1972 of suspected liberals. But the repression in Slovenia was never anything like as severe as it had been in Croatia, and in 1986 Milan Kučan, a closet liberal, took over the leadership.

The easing of political tension under Kučan was accompanied by the rise of a radical art movement with political connotations, known as *Neue Slovenische Kunst*. A set of attitudes rather than a style or a programme, *Neue Slovenische Kunst* challenged the political establishment through music, art, fashion, theatre and literature that was youth-orientated, satirical and self-confidently nationalistic. The flagship was Laibach, a rock band which rapidly acquired an international following.

The use of German or Habsburg names (Laibach was German for Ljubljana and *Neue Slovenische Kunst* German for 'new Slovene art') was a calculated taunt against the German-hating Serbs. Laibach deliberately set out to cultivate a Teutonic, even neo-Nazi, image, allegedly to draw comparisons between Communism and Nazism. 'The very choice of a German expression to denote the current is a kind of provocation,' wrote a puzzled foreign observer. 'That same irony surfaces in Laibach, a quasi-rock group whose members wear brown shirts and Nazi-style regalia and sing in German ... .' Other new Slovene bands were just as outrageous, such as Borghesia, which drew on sado-masochistic and transvestite imagery in its concerts, and Pankrti, whose name means 'bastards', and which specialised in abusive language.

Some of the movement's followers may well have been Germanophile racists, motivated mostly by hostility to the growing numbers of Bosnian *Gastarbeiters* in Ljubljana. But the movement's main thrust was in tune with political currents emanating from the rest of Western Europe – iconoclastic, environmentalist and anti-army. Unlike the older generation of right-wing émigrés, *Neue Slovenische Kunst* did not hate the Communist state and the Yugoslav army, but affected to despise them. In the long run their barely suppressed giggles were much more dangerous than the old-fashioned anti-Communist propaganda of exiled right-wingers had ever been.

The ferment in Slovenia caused by *Neue Slovenische Kunst* and its affiliates, a new homosexual group Magnus, the feminist and partly lesbian group Lilit, and a burgeoning Green movement, found public expression in a weekly magazine, *Mladina*. Once an uninspired organ of the Communist Party's youth wing, it soon evolved under Kučan's benevolent gaze into a bumptious organ combining comment, investigative journalism, pop news and cartoons, run by a team of Young Turks who took pleasure in infuriating the Party's old guard.

Kučan's leadership tolerated the excesses of *Mladina* as the magazine was blazing a trail for many ideas with which Kučan discreetly concurred. The new Slovene leadership's agenda included many items that would have been quite familiar to Tripalo and Dabčević-Kučar, starting with a reduction in the amount of money handed over to the federal government for redistribution among the less developed regions and a cut in the military budget.

The generals of the Yugoslav army looked on developments in Slovenia with frank hostility and rapidly lost confidence in Kučan's ability, or even willingness, to keep a lid on affairs. Matters came to a head in May 1987, when the army used its judicial prerogatives over the civil courts to arrest an army conscript and three journalists from *Mladina*. One of them was Janez Janša, Slovenia's future defence minister.

The arrests followed the publication of a sensational article entitled 'Night of the Long Knives', which detailed an alleged plan by the military to introduce martial law in Slovenia and arrest people suspected of conducting anti-army and – as they saw it – anti-Yugoslav agitation. The arrest of the 'Famous Four' as they came to be known sparked the first hostile public demonstrations in Slovenia since the Communists had taken power. To many Slovenes, the arrests brought home the unacceptable degree of power the military courts enjoyed. Far from cowing the Slovenes, the army's behaviour merely stimulated opposition to the one-party system and to the army.

In Serbia the challenge to the *ancien régime* came from another angle. To the Serbian public, the privileged positions of the army and of the Communist Party were not a hindrance but a precious guarantee of the unity of Yugoslavia, and of the Serbs' place in it. There was no interest – outside a tiny circle of pro-Western intellectuals in Belgrade – in environmental waste, civil rights, gay rights, feminism or any of the issues with which Slovenes were wrestling. What rallied Serbs was the almost universal conviction that, following Ranković's removal, Serbia's position had been undermined in Yugoslavia, and that this downward trend had been confirmed in the constitution of 1974.

The Serbs' feelings of resentment focused on Kosovo. In the Middle Ages, Kosovo had been the political and ecclesiastical centre of the Serbian kingdom, and long after the Ottoman invasion it remained ethnically Serb territory, until the failed revolt against the Turks in the 1680s sent tens of thousands of Serbs fleeing northwards into the Habsburg Empire. The empty villages were then repopulated by mostly Muslim Albanians. But the Serbs never abandoned hope of recovering Kosovo. After the coalition of Balkan states defeated Turkey in 1912, Serbia retook Kosovo, and after the First World War the government in Belgrade set up a special ministry of colonisation, to repopulate the area with landless Serbs and Montenegrins. In the Second World War the Albanians, who were still a majority in the region, revolted against Serb rule, expelled the colonists and joined Italian-ruled Albania.

Tito's Partisans fought their way back in at the end of the war, but concessions were made to the Albanians to defuse the threat of insurgency. Kosovo was returned to Serbia, but enjoyed limited autonomy. For the first twenty years after the war this caused few problems for the Serbs, as Serbs then dominated the local Kosovo League of Communists. But after the fall of Ranković ethnic Albanians took over the local Party structure, and Serbs began to emigrate, alleging discrimination. The 1974 constitution, which devolved more power to Yugoslavia's republics and provinces, strengthened the Albanians' position. At the same time, the high Albanian birthrate left the Serbs outnumbered by more than nine to one by the early 1980s.

Serb fears that the Kosovo Albanians would use the constitutional gains of 1974 to demand full republican status were compounded in 1981 when a student riot at Priština university turned into a pro-independence demonstration by tens of thousands of people, chanting 'Kosovo republic'. The federal government imposed martial law, sent about 580 activists to prison and imposed a new, supposedly more pro-Yugoslav leader on the local League of Communists, Azem Vlassi. But Serbs continued to emigrate, and whether this was the result of Kosovo's poverty or of harassment by Albanians remained a contentious issue.

The Serbs began to agitate for a reduction in the autonomy of Kosovo and Vojvodina as soon as Tito died. At the Serbian Party congress in 1981 two of Serbia's leading politicians, Ivan Stambolić and Draža Marković, made combative speeches, insisting they would not be blackmailed into silence over Serb rights in Kosovo even if their opponents raised the bogey of Great Serbian nationalism.[20] Three years later, it was the turn of another rising star on the Central Committee of the Party in Serbia, Slobodan Milošević, to articulate the same message. 'We have got to free ourselves of the complex about unitarism,' he told the Central Committee session. 'We don't have any reason to bow our heads before anyone. On the contrary, we have every reason to say what we think. After all, we are fighting for Socialist self-management....'[21]

Stambolić and Marković promoted a more assertive agenda for the Serbs with Milošević's support. But much more radical spirits were stirring in Serbia's intellectual powerhouse, the Serbian Academy of Arts and Science (Sanu). The most influential Sanu academic, the writer Dobrica Ćosić, enjoyed enormous stature among ordinary Serbs, largely for having broken with Tito in 1968 over the handling of Kosovo. Ćosić had matured into an embittered nationalist, nursing strange conspiracy theories about Tito. 'Only about in 1965 did we discover that Tito hated Serbs. Prior to that he had managed to hide that hatred,' he told one confidant.[22]

From about 1982, Ćosić, Antonije Isaković and a young writer and former journalist, Vuk Drašković, began to publish novels in Serbia which were unashamedly 'revisionist' in their treatment of the war, the Communist-run labour camp for political prisoners on the Dalmatian island of Goli Otok and the Chetnik movement.[23] The reaction from Zagreb, by then the centre of Communist orthodoxy, was one of horror: Stipe Šuvar, the dominant personality in the Croatian leadership, formed an ideological commission of some 140 film editors, journalists, writers and politicians, which drew up a document which fiercely attacked 'freethinkers who denounce and insult not only individuals they don't like but the League of Communists, the leadership, politicians, the order, the regime, all the time moaning that they are persecuted, have no freedom to think, talk and act ...'.[24] But Sanu was not afraid of Šuvar, and from Belgrade came more shrill attacks on what they mocked as Šuvar's *Bela Knjiga* (white book). Far from pulling in their horns, Serb writers in the autumn of 1984 for the first time began openly to attack the cult of Tito.[25]

In 1984 the campaign waged by Sanu appeared to many observers, especially in the West, to be liberal rather than nationalist. The following year, however, this view of Belgrade as the centre of a new pro-democracy movement, and of Zagreb as a last bastion of decrepit Stalinism, began to change. In December 1985 Drašković injected a vicious tone into the already strained relations between Zagreb and Belgrade by accusing Croatia's Communists of committing 'cultural genocide' against the Serb community.[26] The use of the word 'genocide' was a sinister novelty.

A much bigger bombshell in 1986 was an anonymous Serbian pamphlet which emanated from Sanu known simply as the *Memorandum*. This document, though never completed or officially published, was widely circulated. Much of it was devoted to a calm assessment of Yugoslavia's economic travails, and to promoting the kind of centralising solutions favoured by the Yugoslav 'integralists' of the pre-war period. What caused a furore, however, was the venomous tone of certain chapters, which insisted that the entire Serbian race was threatened by a sinister anti-Serb conspiracy. The language was extreme and unheard of in a published work since the war. 'The physical, political, legal and cultural genocide of the Serbian population in Kosovo and Metohija is the worst defeat in its battle for liberation that the Serbs have waged from 1804 until the revolution in 1941,' it said.[27] The *Memorandum*'s discussion of the position of Serbs in Croatia was as inflammatory. After noting that the proportion of Serbs in Croatia had declined since 1948 from 14.48 per cent to 11.5 per cent, it concluded: 'But for the period of the existence of the NDH, Serbs in Croatia have never been as threatened as they are now.' Although no one admitted to writing these chapters of the *Memorandum*, they were believed to reflect Ćosić's opinions.

In fact there was little to support the *Memorandum*'s portrait of a community facing quiet annihilation. In Croatia as a whole the Serbs continued to enjoy disproportionate representation in the Party, the police, the judiciary, the state enterprises and the prison services. Nor was there much evidence that the Serbs were losing ground in those rural areas where they traditionally formed the majority.

There were eleven districts in Croatia which had an absolute Serb majority after the war in the regions of northern Dalmatia, Lika and Banija. They were Knin, Benkovac and Obrovac in northern Dalmatia; Gračac, Titova Korenica and Donji Lapac in Lika; Vrginmost, Vojnić, Glina, Dvor and Kostajnica in Banija. A twelfth district, Pakrac, in western Slavonia, had a relative Serb majority. In seven of the districts, the percentage of Serbs had increased between 1971 and the last Yugoslav census in 1991. The percentage of Croats had dropped in ten and increased in only one, Vrginmost, where the Croats had edged up from

22 to 24 per cent[28] (though this differential was accounted for by the increase in the number of people declaring themselves simply as Yugoslavs in the census).

In the Serb heartlands of eastern Lika, for example, the Croat community had practically died out, as a result of displacement in the war and resettlement in the flatlands afterwards. So it was that several ancient Catholic parishes in the area had become extinct, and small former Croat-majority towns, such as Udbina, had become entirely Serbian.

Far from withering away, the Serb-majority districts of Croatia were becoming more compact and ethnically more homogeneous than ever before. The only argument in support of the *Memorandum*'s position was the overall decline in the total population of both Lika and Banija since the Second World War. But this was the result of a whole range of factors, starting with the Ustashe persecution of Serbs in the war, the simultaneous flight of the Croat minority to safer areas, the post-war government policy of resettling Serb families from barren Lika in prosperous Vojvodina and the overall Communist strategy of discriminating against the countryside in favour of the urban communities.[29] To attribute the phenomenon of rural depopulation to an anti-Serb conspiracy was absurd.

The *Memorandum*'s wild language caused a storm throughout Yugoslavia. At the same time the Serbian media fanned a mood of deep suspicion about what was going on in Kosovo by publishing reports of alleged sexual assaults on Serbs in the province. Two reports gained special fame. One claimed that Tatijana, Abbess of Gračanica, outside Priština, had been raped by an Albanian policeman; another that a Serb farmer, Djordje Martinović, had also been raped by Albanians, and a bottle forced into his anus. None of the rape stories was ever substantiated.

The campaign by Sanu, and the way it was taken up by the media and the Orthodox Church, wrong-footed Stambolić. He did not approve of this kind of nationalist frenzy and he strongly disliked the *Memorandum*, whose contents were a surprise to him. 'A war manifesto for the commissars of Serbdom', was his private opinion of the document.[30] To the great disappointment of the Sanu writers, and of most of the public, Stambolić condemned the paper as a nationalist and chauvinist document.

Stambolić was unwilling to mobilise Sanu and the Serb Orthodox Church in a crusade over Kosovo. So was Dragiša Pavlovic, the Party leader of Belgrade. But it left them looking vulnerable and out of step with public opinion. The Party leader of Serbia since 1986, Slobodan Milošević, stepped into the breach. Milošević was an undistinguished, though successful Party apparatchik, typical of the cadres who had taken over throughout Yugoslavia after the purge of liberals and nationalists in the 1970s. He had an unusual family history, as both his parents had committed suicide. Milošević had successfully risen through the ranks of the state industries, becoming head of the biggest Serbian bank, Beobanka, and then of the fuel corporation, Tehnogas. But he owed his rapid promotion in the Party to his close personal connections with Stambolić.

Until 1987 Milošević displayed no particular concern for the plight of the Serbs in Kosovo or in Bosnia and Croatia.[31] But as Stambolić lost face over the Kosovo crisis, he cultivated ties with Ćosić and Sanu, with the frustrated Party cells in Serb enclaves in Kosovo and with key generals, above all with General Ljubičić, the federal Defence Minister, who were unhappy with the drift away from a centralised state and fearful for the future of the army – and its privileges. Without Stambolić noticing, Milošević quietly established strong ties with the bosses of Serbia's state television station and took control of the principal Serbian newspapers, *Politika* and *Politika Ekspres*.

The first sign of a breach appeared on 24 April 1987, when Milošević descended on Kosovo's biggest Serb enclave, Kosovo Polje, a suburb of the province's capital, Priština. A group of angry local Serbs swarmed round the tatty local council offices, where Milošević held talks with local Serb and Albanian officials, including the Kosovo Party leader, Azem Vlasi, shouting that Albanian police were assaulting them. Milošević strode out to meet them and made an emotional speech showing that he supported the demonstrators, and shouting: 'Niko ne sme da bije narod' – No one has the right to beat the people. His action was spontaneous and unprecedented, as he appeared to be encouraging a mob to take on the official Party structure, which in Kosovo was mostly Albanian. It was most unusual for a Yugoslav leader of his rank to encourage a demonstration by one ethnic community against another in such obvious terms. But what made the gesture incendiary was the way it was broadcast on the main television news programme at 7.30pm. That made Milošević a popular hero overnight.

Back in Belgrade, Stambolić was nonplussed. He had expected his protégé to calm things down, instead of which Milošević had poured oil on the flames. The Kosovo Serb militants from Božur, a local nationalist pressure group run by a former boxer, Bogdan Kecman, took Milošević's comments as a green light and within weeks were threatening to send tens of thousands of Kosovo Serbs to Belgrade to occupy the park opposite the federal parliament. Stambolić was alarmed, especially as several other members of the Yugoslav presidency still thought he, rather than Milošević, was trying to engineer a crisis in order to bully them into agreeing to change Kosovo's status. 'They all thought I was trying to organise a Serb exodus from Kosovo, to show I was the only one who could stop it,' he recalled.[32] In the end, only 500 Serbs turned up and Stambolić refused to talk, so one of the leaders of the Croatian Party, Ivica Račan, was sent instead to listen to the Serb demands. But Milošević used the occasion to taunt Stambolić. 'Why are you so afraid of the streets and of the people?' he asked.[33]

The Kosovo Serb demonstration in Belgrade was smaller than its organisers had threatened, but that it took place at all was a humiliation for Stambolić. He now began to suspect that important figures in the secret police and the army were trying to discredit him. Against his will, an extraordinary plenum of the League of Communists of Serbia was summoned to discuss the Kosovo crisis that September. Stambolić's neglect of the grass roots then became terribly obvious as Party cells began forwarding motions of no-confidence in him, accusing him of failing to defend Serb interests throughout Yugoslavia, and in Kosovo in particular. In the run-up to the plenum, Stambolić discovered – too late – that his ambitious underling had the support of the Serbian media and the army. Politika and Politika Ekspres rallied to Milošević. So did General Ljubičić. At the Eighth Plenum in September, Stambolić's policies were condemned and Milošević emerged as Serbia's new ruler. A few days after the plenum, Stambolić was invited to a meeting at the Palace of the Federation in New Belgrade with Ljubičić and Milošević, where Ljubičić simply ordered him to resign, though not immediately, to avoid a scandal. He did so on 14 December, making way for retired general Petar Gračanin, one of Milošević's nominees.

Milošević called his take-over an 'anti-bureaucratic revolution', an inaccurate term for the replacement of one bureaucracy by another. But there was no denying that his bureaucrats were much more dynamic and aggressive than their predecessors and the ripples from the Eighth Plenum were soon felt among the Serbs in Vojvodina, Kosovo and Montenegro. After purging the Party apparatus in Serbia of Stambolić supporters, Milošević revived the Party's mass following by turning Politika and Belgrade Television into soundboxes for a kind of frantic, provocative nationalist sloganising that had never been seen in Communist Yugoslavia. The media campaign was accompanied by enormous public rallies – 'happenings of the people', as they were called – where speakers whipped up the crowds into a fury about the Albanian leadership in Kosovo and the old-fashioned Serb Party bosses of Vojvodina. But the rallies were also a useful lever against the Party leaderships in other republics. Although they opposed changes being made to Tito's 1974 constitution, Milošević played on their fear that the huge rallies in Serbia would erupt into violence to break their resistance.

The 'happenings of the people' culminated in rallies of about 150,000 in Niš in southern Serbia on 24 September 1988 and of about

50,000 in Novi Sad in Vojvodina the following day. Confronted with this furious mob, some of whom hurled cartons of yoghurt at the building of the pro-government newspaper, *Dnevnik*, the government of Vojvodina resigned, and was replaced by Milošević supporters. The 'Yoghurt Revolution', as it was jokily tagged, did not stop there. In November it was the turn of the republic of Montenegro, where the government was overturned with the same methods. There, a new team under Momir Bulatović, a youthful Milošević supporter, took over.

In Vojvodina and Montenegro the old oligarchies were seen as repressive, so these mini-revolutions were popular. Many wanted closer ties with Serbia and its dynamic-sounding leader. Kosovo was different. There, almost 90 per cent of the 2 million population were Albanian and they had strong memories of Serbian persecution under the royal government and under Ranković. Although Vlasi had been installed as leader at Belgrade's behest, he resisted Serbia's pressure to agree to a reduction in autonomy. Under the slogan 'Let's keep the cadres', the Albanians staged big rallies of their own in defence of the Kosovo Party leadership.

Milošević was not perturbed by the Albanian counter-demonstrations. On 19 November, while addressing a giant rally of about half a million Serbs in Ušće Park in Belgrade, he subtly raised the stakes by hinting that a civil war might break out if Serbia did not get its way in Kosovo. Half a century ago, he intoned, Yugoslavs had gone to fight terror and hatred on the barricades of Spain. Kosovo, he added ominously, was not nearly as far away as Spain. The fervour of the Serbian public about Kosovo soon persuaded the other republics to give way rather than follow the former leaders of Montenegro and Vojvodina into oblivion. Support for Vlasi evaporated and he was forced out of the Party leadership of Kosovo and out of the Federal Central Committee. Milošević then imposed an Albanian of his own stamp on the Kosovo Party, Rahman Morina, a former policeman who had spent most of his working life in Belgrade. Albanian strikes and protests against Morina's appointment racked the province, and claimed the lives of at least sixty unarmed demonstrators over the next few months, most of them shot by Serbian riot police bussed into the province to cow the population. But the battle for Kosovo was over. It remained only to prepare a new constitution for Serbia, stripping the two provinces of their autonomy.

The leaders of Croatia, Bosnia, Slovenia and Macedonia thought they had bought time by appeasing Milošević over Kosovo. So did Šuvar, then the federal Party leader. They were mistaken. As soon as Kosovo, Vojvodina and Montenegro had been dealt with, Milošević turned his attention to the Serbs of Bosnia and Croatia, and to what he called the 'counter-revolution' proceeding in Slovenia. The Slovene Communists followed events in Kosovo with alarm, fearing a precedent for themselves in the toppling of Vlasi's popular regime. Taking the opposite course from Milošević, they decided to close ranks with the public by embracing the cause of the opposition. On 11 January 1989 they allowed the first non-Communist party, the Democratic Alliance led by Dimitri Rupel, to hold a public congress in Ljubljana's civic centre. The move was condemned in Belgrade and widened the breach between Slovenia, the army and Serbia.

Milošević, meanwhile, pressed on with demands for Šuvar to resign as leader of the federal Party. Šuvar had little room for manoeuvre. The great enemy of the Croatian Spring had no popular following in his home republic, or in Slovenia. At the same time, his dogged defence of Tito's 1974 constitution turned him into a hate figure in Serbia.

At the end of February, he fell into a carefully laid trap. The Albanian miners at the Trepča zinc mine in Titova Mitrovica, in Kosovo, went on strike against the new regime, barricaded themselves in the shaft and threatened to blow up the whole plant unless Morina was removed and Vlasi restored to office. The students of Priština university at the same time locked themselves into the city's main sports stadium. Šuvar hurried down to Kosovo to cool matters down and agreed to go down the Trepča mineshaft, simply to persuade the Albanian strikers to come out. He later claimed he was invited to do so by the Serbian leadership, but as soon as he went down the mine the Serbian media launched a terrific campaign against him as the willing tool of Albanian 'counter-revolutionary nationalism and separatism'.

It appeared that Kosovo was in the grip of chaos. In fact, Milošević was streets ahead of all of his opponents. As riots in Kosovo reached a peak on 27 February, Morina abruptly resigned. Without delay the Serbian media went into action, calling for massive protests against this apparent Albanian victory. State-owned factories throughout the republic were closed, and the workers bussed to the capital for a 'spontaneous' demonstration.

By the afternoon of the 28th several hundred thousand Serbs were buzzing round the centre of Belgrade outside the federal parliament. Inside the deputies felt intimidated. The half-furious, half-delirious crowd outside reduced any debate they might have to irrelevance. Many wondered whether they would get out alive, and hoped Milošević would do something to calm the crowd down. Late in the evening Milošević, strained and white, strode out of the building and announced through a loud hailer that 'all those acting in their own political interests against Yugoslavia will be arrested'. The deputies got out safely, but the price was a total capitulation to Milošević's demands. Vlasi and fourteen other Albanian officials were arrested the following

day on charges of fomenting 'counter-revolution'. 'Emergency measures' just short of martial law were proclaimed in the province. while
federal army tanks and riot police were sent to put down demonstrations. As the tanks rumbled around Kosovo, Milošević savoured his
political triumph in a grandiose ceremony in Belgrade's Sava Centre,
where on 28 March he was formally proclaimed president of the new,
reunited Serbian republic.

Slovenia was left isolated within Yugoslavia. Alone of all the republican leaders, Kučan had publicly supported Vlasi's fight to remain in
power, even attending a public rally in the Cankarjev Dom civic centre
in Ljubljana in defence of the miners of Trepča. The lesson was that the
Slovene agenda for Yugoslavia – political and economic liberalisation,
greater devolution of power to the republics, closer ties to the West and
a reduction in army influence – could not succeed against Serbia's
opposition. The choice Slovenia then faced was to concede to Milošević
or leave Yugoslavia. For all his talk of Yugoslavia, Milošević seemed to
want to provoke the Slovenes into seceding, and in November he
imposed an economic blockade on Slovenia, as punishment for the
republic's support for the Albanians.

Milošević then turned his attentions to Croatia, where the busy journalists of Belgrade Television and *Politika* soon uncovered evidence of
persecution of local Serbs. TV viewers in Serbia were soon treated to
programmes on decaying Serb villages with unpaved roads and ruined
churches, whose neglect was the result of spiteful Croat discrimination.

Croatia's 600,000 or so Serbs had traditionally formed the bedrock of
support for Tito's Communists and were not all automatically cannon
fodder for the Serbian media's divisive rhetoric. In Lika, Kordun and
Banija memories of the Partisan war were still strong and many Serbs
were reluctant to give up on *bratstvo i jedinstvo*. However, the old
Chetnik strongholds in northern Dalmatia, around Knin, Obrovac and
Benkovac, were more receptive to the new line from Belgrade. And it
was there that the first demonstrations against the Croatian government began in July 1989, on the occasion of the 600th anniversary of
the Battle of Kosovo.

The Kosovo battle anniversary fell on a convenient date for
Milošević. Months after the Albanian leadership had been toppled, he
was able to present himself as the man who had reversed the defeat of
1389 and reclaimed the Serbs' heartland for the *nebeski narod* –the
heavenly nation, as Serbs were wont to describe themselves. In the
months building up to the event the Serbian Church whipped up a great
deal of public interest in the event – and in itself – by transporting the
relics of Prince Lazar around Serbia's ancient monasteries.

Huge crowds, starved of the romance of history and of contact with
religion during Tito's rule, flocked to these old shrines to gaze on the

tragic hero of 1389. But the day itself belonged to Milošević, not to Prince Lazar. Hundreds of buses converged on the undulating plain of Gazimestan outside Priština where Lazar had fallen, transporting a crowd that may have been a million strong to the gigantic dais where Milošević was expected to speak.

It was the greatest gathering in the history of Yugoslavia. Around the Serbian leader stood a gaggle of black-robed Serb Orthodox bishops. Behind him skulked a few Croat and Slovene Party officials, their presence ignored and indeed, on this day of pure Serb triumphalism, unwanted.[34] As the towerblocks of modern – mostly Albanian – Priština shimmered in the distance, Milošević declared that, although Serbia had succeeded in engineering the changes it wanted without violence, a violent outcome to the political battles of the future could not be guaranteed. 'Six centuries on [from 1389] again we are in battle and confronting battles. They are not armed, though that cannot yet be excluded. ...' The Serbs on the plain roared their approval. The rest of Yugoslavia pondered this ambiguous message.[35]

The Kosovo celebrations heightened the mood of euphoria in Serbia. The leader's jowly face was now everywhere – on the fronts of buses, in railway stations and in most shop windows. But the furore inevitably had an echo in Serb districts of Croatia, where the Kosovo battle was celebrated with enthusiasm around Knin. The appearance of crowds dusting down the old royal pre-First World War Serbian flag startled the Croatian Party leadership, and fourteen local Serbs were arrested. They picked out a leader of the Kosovo agitation in Knin, a lawyer, Jovan Opačić, and sentenced him to forty days in prison. In Makarska, there were fights between Serbs and local Croats. Serbian tourists in Dalmatia complained that they were insulted and that cars with Belgrade numberplates were vandalised.

In Serbia, the intellectuals of Sanu under Ćosić's leadership adopted Opačić as a mascot, and sent petitions to the federal authorities demanding his release. Ćosić worsened the conflict by telling an Italian newspaper that Croatia had received the region of Istria unjustly. Tito had 'occupied Istria and given it to Croatia', he said.[36] It was a dangerous precedent, openly suggesting that the borders of the republics settled under Tito were wrong. The Croats detected the revival of the old alliance between Serbian Chetniks and Italian Fascists against the Dalmatian Croats. Sanu would not let matters rest. In September it urged the federal Central Committee to look into what it insisted was the deteriorating position of Croatia's Serbs. At the Serbian Writers' Club in Francuska Street, there were calls for the Serbs in Croatia to be allowed an autonomous province.

After hammering away for months at the counter-revolution in Slovenia, the Serbian President delivered a few lethal blows to the federal government. In an act of brazen theft, without the permission of the federal government, Serbia removed half the supply of money in the Yugoslav National Bank that had been set aside for all six republics for the following year. The theft of 1.8bn dinar, worth about £700m, made the federal Prime Minister, Ante Marković, a Croat who was trying to persuade Western governments to invest in Yugoslavia, look a fool. The robbery of the National Bank snapped the Slovenes' patience. In December Kučan held a referendum on independence which produced a resounding vote in favour of leaving the federation.

In January 1990 the eight Leagues of Communists assembled in Belgrade for the last time at an extraordinary Party congress. But there was no chance of a compromise at this stage between the Slovenes and the Serbs. Milošević insisted on a more centralised organisation and a return to the Leninist practice of 'democratic centralism' in the Party. The Slovenes would settle for nothing less than turning the League of Communists, and Yugoslavia, into a loose association. Neither side got their way. Although the Slovene delegation walked out, Milošević was unable to commandeer the rump and the congress was adjourned, never to reassemble. The following month, the Slovene Communist Party was abolished, to be reformed as a Social Democratic party, and the way was open for multi-party elections planned for April. It was the end of the Yugoslav Communist Party. Strangely, it was the Slovenes, not the Serbs, who were most upset. One of the departing Slovenes was in tears. As she left the congress, a voice was heard shouting from the Serbian benches: 'And close the door behind you!'

15

God in Heaven and Tudjman in the Homeland

You know, we were on the verge of an uprising. They're a crazy nation. I am a psychiatrist, they're a crazy nation, I'm telling you, they're crazy.
Croatian Serb leader Jovan Rašković on the Serbs
of Benkovac, 1990[1]

On 28 February 1989 Franjo Tudjman and a small group of veterans from the Croatian Spring had gathered in the Writers' Club in Zagreb, off Republic Square, to hammer out a programme for a new political movement in Croatia. Four months later on 17 June, after various delays that were caused by the obstructive tactics of the police, the new group at last received permission to hold a founding party congress at the Borac sports centre, in the suburb of Staglišće. The forty-eight founders met in an atmosphere of trepidation that the proceedings would be broken up by the police, though in the event there was no interruption. They named the party the Hrvatska Demokratska Zajednica (Croatian Democratic Union), or HDZ, and elected Tudjman as their president.[2]

That Tudjman and his co-conspirators were able to organise such a movement illustrated the extent to which Croatia's political landscape had changed since the trials and persecutions of the early1980s. The changes going on in Slovenia played an important role. It was, simply, impossible to maintain one-party rule in Zagreb while the Slovenes, less than twenty miles away to the west, were allowing a host of lobby groups and parties to operate without any restrictions at all. In December 1989 the Croatian Party congress, rather to everyone's surprise, elected Ivica Račan, a forty-five-year-old undoubted liberal, as the Party leader. Račan lived up to his reputation as a moderniser by announcing within only a few weeks of taking office that the republic would hold multi-party elections in the spring, around the time of the elections in neighbouring Slovenia. At the extraordinary Party congress in Belgrade in January 1990, Račan had thrown his weight behind the Slovenes and had refused to take part in the congress after the Slovenes walked out. After that, he had to march in step with Ljubljana. In February he changed the name of the League of Communists in Croatia to the cumbersome-sounding League of Communists of Croatia – Party of Democratic Change.

The break-up of the Yugoslav Communist Party at the extraordinary congress unchained the veterans of the Croatian Spring who had spent the previous seventeen years in silence, or in jail. Dabčević-Kučar imagined that she would be swept back into power on a tide of nostalgia as soon as people were free to speak their minds. It became clear that, while many Croats remembered her with affection, there was a tinge of disappointment that she had not been prepared to suffer for her ideas. The grovelling speech she made before she resigned stuck in many people's memories.[3] She had not gone to jail. Tudjman, on the other hand, had gone to jail twice. She was slow in forming a coalition with like-minded politicians, such as Tripalo. It was not until April 1990 that the 'Coalition for a National Agreement' was on the road. Ivan Supek recalled: 'We were too late by April. In the previous three months Tudjman had won the support of the people and the Church. That was decisive. And Tudjman was an old Communist. He knew how to manipulate people.'[4] There was one other big difference. Dabčević-Kučar was too much a child of the Communist revolution to reach out to the Croatian émigré community in Canada and the US, some of whom were descendants of exiled Ustashe. She was frightened to meet them.[5] Tudjman was not. He might have marched into Zagreb in 1945 with the Communist five-pointed star on his cap, but he had burned his boats since then. He was not afraid of the émigrés and was tempted by their big wallets. As soon as the HDZ was formed he made trips to Canada and the US to drum up support for his movement, in spite of the risk this carried of being tarred with the Ustashe brush.[6]

Tudjman recruited several supporters from members of the diaspora who returned home after the relaxation of Communist rule. At the top of the list was Gojko Šušak, a Toronto-based Croat from western Herzegovina. Šušak's circumstances were modest, although he was regularly and incorrectly reputed to possess fabulous wealth. He had graduated from McDonalds academy in Chicago and earned a living in Canada as a decorator. The Zagreb snobs looked down on him and his ilk. The popular satirical writer Tanja Torbarina dubbed him 'pizza man' in her column in the popular weekly Globus, and the tag stuck. But the 'pizza man' was adept at tapping the purses of the tight-knit Herzegovinian community in the Americas, delivering millions of dollars' worth of contributions to Tudjman's campaign.

A year after that secretive meeting, Tudjman presided over the HDZ's first party congress on 24–25 February 1990. This time the turnout was much more impressive. About 2,500 supporters, not just from Croatia, but from Vojvodina in Serbia, Montenegro, Hungary and the Americas, crammed into the Lisinski concert hall, sang 'Lijepa Naša Domovina' and gave Tudjman a rapturous reception. With only two months to go before the poll, Tudjman – and not Dabčević-Kučar – had already emerged as the Communists' principal rival. He appeared totally confident of winning. 'Today we are here,' he told his supporters, 'but soon we'll be in the other assembly, in St Mark's Square [the site of the Sabor].'[7]

Tudjman based his campaign squarely on the national question. He paid little attention to economic questions, beyond stating that the dinar earned in Croatia would stay in Croatia, meaning there would be no more generous subsidies for Kosovo, or for the army. The declarations passed by the HDZ party congress illustrated a preoccupation with nationalism. They concentrated on demography, on the need to found a Croatian news agency to rival the Belgrade-based Tanjug agency and on the national anthem. They resolved to erect 'monuments to all those who had sacrificed their lives on the altar of the homeland in the battle for freedom and independence'.[8] With an eye on his growing – and potentially generous – constituency in exile, Tudjman tackled the subject of the NDH without much apology to its victims. The NDH was 'not only a quisling organisation and a Fascist crime, but was also an expression of the Croatian nation's historic desire for an independent homeland', he said.[9] The peculiar phraseology, suggesting that the Ustashe was the malevolent manifestation of a benign impulse, highlighted the delicate balancing act he was trying to perform between the different political factions in his party.

It was no easy task. In Šušak, Tudjman had a line to the militantly right-wing anti-Communist diaspora. But other, equally important colleagues came from the heart of the Partisan Communist establishment, including Josip Manolić and Josip Boljkovac, elderly veterans of Tito's secret police. There were ageing Maspok martyrs, such as Djodan, and younger ones too, such as Stipe Mesić, who had been mayor of Orahovica in Slavonia in the early 1970s until he was purged for nationalism.

If Tudjman was all things to most Croats, the price was the deep alienation of the 600,000-strong Serb community. Since the war and especially since the crushing of the Maspok experiment, the Serbs had been a pillar of Communist Party rule in Croatia. In their rural strongholds in Banija, Lika, Kordun and northern Dalmatia they formed an insular and defensive community, obsessed with the threat of a revived NDH. Tudjman's talk of Croatia's past glories and independence was anathema to them. They were particularly hostile to the red-and-white Croatian flags his supporters waved at HDZ rallies, which they insisted was the Ustashe flag. In fact the old chequerboard symbol had been the

official coat of arms of the Socialist Republic of Croatia and had faded
from use on election posters and other propaganda only in the 1950s.
No matter. The Serbs had now decided it was the footprint of the
Ustashe.

The great stirrer of Serbian hearts was Jovan Rašković, a psychiatrist
from Šibenik general hospital. Born in 1929 in Knin, into a family with
Chetnik sympathies in the war, he was just old enough to remember the
Ustashe regime. Knin by 1990 was a town of some 40,000 people, of
whom 90 per cent were Serbs. Drab and slightly derelict compared to
the Dalmatian coastal resorts, it was an important communications
centre, lying on the junction of the railway connecting Zagreb and the
Dalmatian cities of Split and Šibenik. It was also the headquarters of a
large Yugoslav army base.

In the spring of 1990 Rašković formed the Serbian Democratic Party
(SDS) along with a group of Serb nationalists, many of whom had
helped organise the Kosovo battle anniversary celebrations in Knin the
previous year. Rašković was not a protégé of Milošević, whom he distrusted as an unregenerate bolshevik. But he had close ties to Ćosić,
who had been a guest at his villa in the quaint seaside village of
Primošten. Rašković's attitude towards Croatia was full of contradic-
tions. Although he was an avowed Serb nationalist, he had married a
Croat and once said he wanted his grandchildren brought up as Croats
'so they won't have the complexes I've got'.[10] He was a fiery orator
against the resurgence of the Ustashe. At the same time, he admitted 'a
free Croatia is the condition for resolving the psychological frustrations
of both the Croat and Serb nations'.[11] He was obsessed with applying
psychiatry to politics and liked to trot out the theory that the Serbs'
oedipal complex drove them to destroy their leaders, while the Croats'
'castration complex' left them permanently frustrated.[12] His view of
Tudjman was just as contradictory. He accused the HDZ of harbouring
Ustashe sympathisers, but admired Tudjman personally as an honest
politician. 'He is a tough politician of clear conceptions who represents
what most Croats accept. Tudjman is the kind of character who speaks
quite openly about his intentions, and we like that ... there's no ideological fog when you're talking with Tudjman,' he said.[13] He opined
that Tudjman was 'Croato-centric', but no Ustasha. His real hatred was
reserved for the Communists, especially the long-dead Bakarić, 'the
political liquidator of the Serbs', who had worked 'falsely, slyly, perfidi-
ously and persistently, every day', to eliminate Serb schools, language,
churches and newspapers from Croatia with the help of a team of
treacherous Serbian careerists.[14]

Choleric and purple-faced from the heart trouble that was to kill him
in 1992, Rašković stumped round the villages of the old Krajina in the
election campaign, waving Serbian flags, entrancing the crowds and

declaring that if Croatia sought greater independence from Belgrade, Croatian Serbs would demand autonomy from Zagreb. Rašković was determined not to play the role of a latter-day Pribićević. But he was vague about what the SDS really wanted. He himself had lived in the heart of Croatian society, practising for thirty years in Šibenik hospital and relaxing at the weekends in the thoroughly Croat environment of Primošten. His weakness was that he loved the crowds, while they looked on him as an Old Testament prophet. But between his fiery words on stage and his real convictions there was a wide gap. Tudjman was to exploit this with devastating effect after the election.

The quiet spadework of building up a party organisation for the SDA was left to Rašković's younger lieutenants. One was Jovan Opačić, the noisy lawyer arrested for encouraging nationalist agitation during the Kosovo battle celebrations. But the most important of the young acolytes was Milan Babić. A portly, chubby-cheeked dentist from Knin and a former member of the Croatian Central Committee, he was, unlike his leader, soft-spoken and casually dressed – he favoured black-leather bomber jackets. But his demure manner and ready smile concealed a strain of fanaticism. Unlike Rašković he did not blink at the prospect of bloodshed, or at the use of ruthless and totalitarian methods to achieve his aims.

The run-up to the elections in Croatia was marked by steadily worsening ethnic tension. As it became clear that Račan's Communists might lose, more and more Serbs and Croats rallied around the opposing poles of the SDS and the HDZ. The Yugoslav army leadership, under General Veljko Kadijević, was firmly convinced the HDZ would win. Kadijević recalled: 'At a meeting of the army leadership with the leadership of the Socialist Republic of Croatia a month before the multi-party elections we told them openly that they [the elections] will bring the Ustashe to power in Croatia....'[15]

The army and the Serbian leadership began to work out their strategy, based on the likelihood of Croatia falling under the control of a hostile, non-Communist government. Two short-term measures were to take away weapons from the Croats and give them to Serbs. Thus, a few weeks before the elections took place in Slovenia and Croatia, the army silently removed the weapons of the territorial defence units from stores all over Croatia. The distribution of military supplies in Serb strongholds in Croatia was a joint effort of Milošević and Kadijević. Milošević's right-hand man in the business of liaising with the militants in Knin was Mihajl Kertes, a key figure in the overthrow of the former anti-Milošević leadership in Vojvodina. The army also distributed weapons in the Knin region. Shortly before the election the official Yugoslav news agency Tanjug reported the unexplained 'disappearance' of a train carrying arms at Dalmatinsko Kosovo, a village near

Knin. According to the report the train had halted at the village before nightfall – it did not say why – and the next day had been emptied of its cargo. There was no suggestion that an inquiry would be held nor any comment on this astonishing theft from the generals.

Tipping the balance of power on the ground was a provisional device. The Serbian leadership and the army were also considering a political strategy. Western journalists were to make much of an alleged struggle between Milošević, the champion of a Greater Serbia, and the army, supporting the 'old' united Yugoslavia. There is no evidence for any such disagreement. Both Kadijević and Milošević were in complete agreement that the old federation was finished and that the future lay in a smaller Yugoslavia that would unite all Serbs in one state, and which would be based on Serbia and include Montenegro, Bosnia, Macedonia and parts of Croatia.

Milošević's close ally Boris Jović noted a passing exchange with the Serbian President just after the Croatian election. 'Conversation with Slobo,' he wrote in his diary on 28 June 1990.

> He agrees with the idea about the ejection of Slovenia and Croatia, but asks me whether the army is ready to carry out such an order.... the problem I see is what to do with the Serbs in Croatia, and how to ensure a majority in the [Yugoslav state] presidency for such a decision. Slobo offered two ideas; the first was that the cutting off of Croatia be carried out in such a way that the municipalities of Lika, Banija and Kordun, which have created an association, should stay on our side, and people should later decide on whether they wanted to stay or leave [Yugoslavia]; second, that members of [the] presidency from Croatia and Slovenia be excluded from the vote on this issue. ...[16]

Carried along by euphoria, Tudjman was oblivious to the extreme danger of the army, Serbia and the Croatian Serbs allying against them. HDZ supporters exuded an almost religious triumphalism. 'God in heaven and Tudjman in the homeland' was the message written on placards at many HDZ rallies. The party's official slogan was a knowing, confident catchphrase, 'Zna se', meaning 'It's known'. The Communists campaigned under a laborious, melancholy slogan, 'We are thinking seriously', and with posters depicting Račan with a worried expression on his face and gesturing madly at an object unknown. Tudjman's posters were far more arresting. The most familiar showed an intense-looking woman staring mesmerised at a ball glowing in the dark. Lying in the middle of the ball, like a glowworm, was a symbol of the HDZ – a fat letter 'H' decorated with early medieval Croat plaitwork.

The ethnic tension was not felt in Knin, which was overwhelmingly Serb, nor in the Zagorje region round Zagreb, which was thoroughly

Croat. The danger lay in the mixed regions, where the two communities were balanced and where the election was an ethnic headcount. One of the hottest zones was the town of Benkovac, in northern Dalmatia. There the 34,000-strong population was about 60 per cent Serb and 40 per cent Croat. The Croats had fared poorly under the Serb-dominated local council. They were declining in numbers and felt bitter about their relative exclusion from local government, justice and the police. Their plight became a *cause célèbre* for some Croat nationalist academics, who pointed out that although Croats made up 40 per cent of the population in Benkovac, they held 18 per cent of the jobs in local government and only 12 per cent of posts in local state enterprises.[17]

The Benkovac Croats looked to the HDZ and Tudjman as potential saviours, and were furious when groups of local Serbs broke up the first public meeting of the Benkovac branch of the HDZ on 17 March. Tudjman was not a man to duck such a challenge, and promptly headed off for Benkovac to stage a march with Croat flags flying. To the Serbs it was one provocation too many and during the march one of their hotheads pulled out a pistol and fired a shot at the HDZ leader. The HDZ extracted maximum mileage from the event. Within a few days, videos entitled *Firing on Croatia* were being hawked by vendors in Republic Square in Zagreb. It was not an auspicious start to the election and Benkovac was to be the source of a great deal more trouble as soon as the poll was over.

Three days before the vote, on 19 April, Tudjman addressed his last pre-election rally, in the Adriatic city of Šibenik. He boasted that he had been asked by foreign journalists whether the HDZ would succeed in winning 40 per cent of the votes. 'We will win 70 per cent or 90 per cent,' he announced.

In the end, the foreign journalists were more accurate. The HDZ emerged the largest single party but failed to gain the confidence of the majority. Instead, the party won just over 40 per cent. Račan's Communists made a respectable showing of about 30 per cent in the country, which justified his attempt to remodel the party on the principles of West European social democracy. The left took a large number of votes from the Croatian Serbs, who were divided between their old allegiance to the Communists and the newer attraction of the SDS. It also did well among the urban Croat middle class, many of whom were identified with the Communist *nomenklatur*, and who were less nationalistic than the peasants or industrial workers. The left polled well in Istria and the industrial port of Rijeka, which had been reclaimed from the Italians by Tito's Partisans at the end of the war, and where tension between Serbs and Croats was not a serious issue. Dabčević-Kučar's Coalition of National Agreement trailed in third place.

Almost until voting day, the Communists insisted they would win a majority. They banked on popular fears of a traumatic confrontation with the Serbs and with Belgrade if Tudjman won. 'Polls in the Croatian newspaper *Vjesnik* give the pro-Yugoslav League of Communists a comfortable 10 per cent lead over their nationalist rivals in the Croatian Democratic Union,' was the prediction of the London *Independent*.[18] The Communists had arranged an electoral system appropriate to such an outcome, setting up a system of representation under which the party that won most votes gained an absolute majority of seats. The Communists had also decided that the post of president would not be directly elected, but would be in the gift of the parliamentary majority. Thus the Communists, in their timidity and greed, granted Tudjman and the HDZ what amounted to a parliamentary dictatorship.

The results triggered an explosion of public jubilation among Tudjman's fans in Zagreb, who poured out of their homes to celebrate, roast meat on the street, wave flags and drink. The result was, in the words of one speaker at a post-election rally, 'a new Jerusalem'. For Tudjman it was a belated vindication of decades spent in disgrace or in prison, and at his first post-election press conferences he sounded a triumphant and vengeful note. He railed against the over-representation of Serbs in the police, media and officialdom, and engaged in a sparring match with Belgrade TV's presenter, Mila Štula.

His complaint did not lack foundation, but the obsessive way in which he harped on the subject made a poor impression on the foreign press. They were already pondering a remark he had made at a rally in the Zagreb suburb of Dubrava on 17 March, where he had declared: 'Thank God my wife is not a Jew or a Serb.'[19] He compounded this image problem by repeating his view that Bosnia and Croatia formed one natural geographic and economic unit. It suggested he hankered for a slice of Bosnia only hours after winning control of Croatia.

The first rumblings of trouble took place a fortnight after the election on 14 May, during a football match in Zagreb between the two cities' premier teams, Red Star Belgrade and Zagreb Dynamo. The match turned into a pitched battle on the terraces between the club supporters, thousands of whom spilled out of the stadium to carry their fight on to the streets, upturning cars, burning kiosks and smashing shops. A sixteen-year-old youth was stabbed. Some of the Serbs shouted: 'We will kill Tudjman.' The affray was so serious that the riot police were called in and helicopters used to transport the Serbian players out of the city. What disturbed Croats was not only the fight, which was almost a premonition of civil war, but the impression that the Zagreb police behaved more aggressively towards Croatian supporters than towards their Serbian counterparts. It brought home an uncomfortable fact; for all Tudjman's parliamentary majority, he was not in control of the real power structures in Croatia, least of all the police.

The first and last democratically elected Sabor of the Socialist Republic of Croatia met on 30 May amid flag-waving, cheering, booing (for the Socialist deputies) and the tolling of church bells. During the campaign Tudjman had tried to forge an alliance with the country's powerful Catholic hierarchy, making a highly publicised visit to the Marian shrine of Marija Bistrica, north of Zagreb. The new authorities wanted to set a solidly Catholic tone for the the opening of parliament. There was a solemn Mass in Zagreb cathedral, at which the Croatian Primate, Cardinal Franjo Kuharić, presided, taking as his text 'Let hatred die away'.

It was a pious hope but a most inaccurate prophecy. From there the scene shifted to the Sabor in St Mark's Square in the Upper Town, where the deputies duly elected Tudjman the first president of Croatia. The old man stood stiffly to attention in the chamber for a rendition of 'Lijepa Naša Domovina', proudly wearing a sash embellished with the until recently frowned-upon red-and-white colours. One detail spoiled the day of celebration. The five seats reserved in the Sabor for Dr Rašković and his colleagues from the SDS were empty. Nor were there present any bishops of the Serb Orthodox Church, although they had been invited. The boycott was followed up by a telegram from Rašković, explaining their absence. The Serbs, it read, would not work in a parliament whose leaders characterised the SDS's activities as terrorism.

In the weeks following the election Tudjman busied himself with the writing of a new constitution, and indulged his historical tastes with the renaming of streets and squares[20] and settling the precise arrangement of the national flag. The first moves were made to establish a new Croatian news agency, Hina, to rival the old Belgrade-based Tanjug, and a new Croatian airline to compete with the Yugoslav company, Jat.

There were new – or rather revivals of old, pre-war – words too, as lexicographers got down to the business of purging the language of imports from Belgrade. Radio Zagreb became Croatian Radio, and Zagreb Television Croatian Television, or HTV. A ceremonial guard of honour for the President in Ruritanian fancy dress was soon strutting up and down outside the Ban's Palace in the Upper Town.

Perhaps no project appealed to Tudjman's historical fancies and taste for ceremony more than the restoration of Ban Jelačić to his old place on Zagreb's main square. The symbol of the city of Zagreb the day it was unveiled in 1866 had been boarded up in 1945 and covered with an unappealing figure representing Socialist womanhood. On the night of 25 July 1947 the statue underneath was dismantled, allegedly on the recommendation of the Zagreb Conference of Anti-Fascist Women.[21] No one ever admitted to having ordered this act of vandalism, though the ultimate culprit was certainly Tito, who detested the cult of Jelačić and slavishly followed the orthodox Marxist line that Jelačić was the reactionary servant of Habsburg absolutism. The pieces were then stored for the next four decades in the basement of the Yugoslav academy under the friendly eye of the curator. Fernkorn's work was pieced together, and the ceremonial unveiling of the restored statue by Tudjman at night, surrounded by coloured flares that lit up the façades of the surrounding buildings, was one of those operatic setpieces the new President both enjoyed and excelled in.

The Communist regime vanished or made its peace with the new without so much as a squeak. General Martin Špegelj, retiring commander of the Fifth Army, which encompassed Slovenia and most of Croatia, had been a life-long Communist. Yet, soon after the election, he accepted Tudjman's invitation to become Croatia's defence minister. In the media, the weekly magazine *Danas* remained true to the reformed Communists. The Split-based daily *Slobodna Dalmacija* remained an independent voice, as did several local newspapers. The editor of *Danas*, Dražen Vukov-Colić, scathingly pronounced Tudjman 'Croatia's answer to Le Pen'.[22] But the important national media – *Vjesnik* and the radio and television stations – adapted to the new regime almost overnight. The new government were soon determined to control the media almost as much as the old Communists, and much more so than the Račan-era Communists had been. The new HDZ bosses were strong nationalists with an intolerant streak. Milovan Šibl, director of the new Croatian news agency Hina, was typical of the new group. 'Many of these journalists are of mixed origins,' he scoffed, referring to the anti-HDZ press, 'one Croat parent, one Serb. How can such people provide an objective picture of Croatia? ... They hate Croatia. ... The only place you can read the truth about President Tudjman is in Hina news.'[23] Antun Vrdoljak, Tudjman's right-hand man at the television station, was equally forthright. His stated goal was to turn the republic's television into 'a cathedral of the Croatian spirit'.[24]

The broad outlines of the new constitution were discussed in the Sabor at the end of June. The draft document granted enormous executive authority to the president, deleted references to Yugoslavia, reaffirmed Croatia's status as a sovereign state and abolished the word 'Socialist' in the republic's title. The most controversial point to the Serbs was not the abolition of Socialism, or even the powers granted to the president, but the paragraph on the republic's ethnic composition. Under the old constitution Croatia had been 'the national state of the Croatian nation and the state of the Serbian nation in Croatia', and official scripts were Latin and Cyrillic. The new constitution declared Croatia the homeland of the Croatian nation alone. The Serbs were relegated to the rank of a national minority, along with Hungarians, Italians and other ethnic smallfry. The official script was Latin.

The new constitution was a *sine qua non* for HDZ supporters, who were determined that 600,000 Serbs in Croatia would not enjoy a higher status than 120,000 Croats in Serbia and were convinced that the Serbs' ascendancy in Croatia could be toppled by a few strokes of a pen. To the SDS and Milošević the constitution was an absolute godsend – all the proof they ever needed that Tudjman's talk of 'Croatia's young democracy' masked an agenda to restore the NDH and cart the Serbs off to another Jasenovac.

The SDS grew in size after the election. Almost overnight Serbs began to leave Račan's party, now that the ex-Communists were no longer in power. Most Croatian Serbs gained their information from the Serbian newspapers, *Politika* and *Politika Ekspres*, which fanned the flames of hysteria about a new Ustashe government in Zagreb. To rural Serbs the new constitution was a tremendous bogey, even though most of them would have been hard put to recount the finer details of the old one.

Building on this mood of Serbian anger, Babić and Rašković struck back at the hated constitution. On 1 July in Dalmatinsko Kosovo, near Knin, Babić proclaimed a union of SDS-controlled local councils in Lika and northern Dalmatia. He threw down a challenge to Tudjman's policy of centralising authority in Zagreb, and took the first step towards the creation of a Serbian mini-state in Croatia. The union of Serbian communes also marked the rise to power of Babić in Knin and the beginning of the fall of Rašković.

The Serbs' rapid progress towards *de facto* independence in Croatia exposed the weakness at the heart of the new government in Zagreb. Confronted with this challenge, Tudjman could do nothing. The territorial defence forces had been disarmed. The police in Croatia was a doubtful force. At least half were ethnic Serbs and hostile to the HDZ.

The Yugoslav army, led by an overwhelmingly Serbian officer corps, controlled bases scattered throughout Croatia. The federal Defence Minister, General Kadijević,[25] although he was of mixed Croat–Serb parentage, identified strongly with the Serbs, bitterly opposed Croat and Slovene 'separatism' and openly despised the federal Prime Minister, Ante Marković, who was a Croat. Kadijević's deputy, Blagoje Adžić, the acting Chief of Staff, was a Bosnian Serb, a large part of whose family had been wiped out by the Ustashe in the war. The Serbs in Knin were strategically well placed to disobey Zagreb. The town was perched up in the Dinaric mountains, and backed on to solidly Serb territory in Bosnia. There was a large army base whose commander from 1991 was Colonel Ratko Mladić. Also a Serb, his family, from Pavelić's home village of Bradina, in central Bosnia, had been decimated by the Ustashe. His sympathy for Babić and the SDS could be counted on.

Tudjman was aware of his weakness, and hurried ahead with the removal of as many Serbs as possible from key positions in the police force in Zagreb and other cities. At the same time he tried to buy off Serb discontent by offering the SDS the post of vice-president of the Sabor, and raising the wages of Serb police who remained in the ranks. This was clearly going to be difficult in areas like Knin, where wild rumours had spread that Tudjman intended to rename the old Communist *milicija* as the *redarstvo*, a word with NDH connotations. In the first week of July the Knin police chief, a portly forty-year-old with a walrus moustache named Milan Martić, emerged as the most militant opponent of Tudjman's new police uniforms, whose cap bore badges with the Croat flag. On 4 July Tudjman sent Boljkovac, his Interior Minister, to talk to the Serb police in Knin. Tudjman hoped that Boljkovac's age, conciliatory manner and old Communist connections would calm the Serbs and believed their opposition to the new government might be bought off with higher salaries. He had no idea just how much rage was boiling up in Knin; the mission nearly ended in Boljkovac's delegation being lynched by a furious crowd of Serbs gathered outside the hall. Inside, the atmosphere was scarcely reassuring. Martić informed the Interior Minister in a most aggressive manner that the police would never wear the new uniforms. Boljkovac returned to Zagreb empty handed. He left a town on the brink of armed insurrection.

There was a last attempt to pull back from the brink. A few days after Boljkovac's abortive trip, Rašković invited himself to talks with Tudjman and his special adviser, Slaven Letica, in Zagreb. Tudjman was genial, promising to consider any proposal for Serb autonomy within Croatia. Rašković seemed distraught. He confided that he found it increasingly difficult to control the Serbs, whom he described as mad. 'I'm telling you, they're crazy,' he said.[26] It was routine for such conversations to be recorded. What ruined things was the decision (which Rašković blamed on Letica)[27] to publish the stenograph of the conversation in the magazine *Danas*. It appeared that Rašković despised his own supporters. The stock among the Serbs of hardliners like Babić, who were not interested in talks with Tudjman, rose instead.

Babić soon decided to turn his union of Serbian districts into an institution that resembled the government of a proper state. Knin's local radio was renamed Serbian Radio Knin. Babić also announced that an open-air mass meeting of Croatia's Serbs would be held at the village of Srb, high up in the Dinaric mountains, on the border between Croatia and Bosnia. The Serbs from rural areas responded massively to the invitation and about 120,000 turned up to hear Babić announce the birth of the Serbian National Council.[28] Standing beside him Rašković proclaimed that a referendum on Serb 'sovereignty and autonomy' in Croatia would go ahead at the end of August.

The enormous rally on the mountainside at Srb and the announcement of a referendum filled Tudjman with anxiety. He was loath to give the Yugoslav army an excuse to intervene and overthrow his government. The army's hostility towards the multi-party system had been demonstrated by the affair of the territorial defence force. Serbia, Montenegro, Macedonia and Bosnia were still under the old one-party Communist system. On the other hand, the creation of a Serbian province in Croatia would be a catastrophe. Tudjman resorted to bluff. On 4 August the Interior Ministry simply sent a telegram to the local authorities in Babić's Serbian National Council informing them that the referendum was illegal. This toothless threat failed to impress, and on 17 August trouble started again in Benkovac, where groups of Serbs rioted outside the police station, claiming that the Croat authorities were coming to take away the guns stored inside.

As soon as unrest began in Benkovac, Tudjman decided to deploy the few resources he had to stop the Serb rebellion from spreading. That afternoon, two helicopters took off for Knin carrying members of a new, loyalist 'special' unit of the police. The plan was to land in Knin and seize the town hall and police station. They had to act fast to stop the army from getting in the way, and so gave a false explanation of the helicopter's mission to Yugoslav air-traffic control. As the craft flew towards the Dinaric mountains, the army spotted the deception and sent two MiG fighters to intercept them. There was no conflict. The helicopters were ordered to turn back, or be blown out of the air.

On the ground in Knin, news of this footling 'invasion' created pandemonium of a sort that suited Babić very well. The Mayor went on to Serbian Radio Knin and declared 'a war situation', whatever that meant. Weapons were divided among most of the male population who, under Martić's directions, blocked the roads and rail lines in and out of the town. Boulders were thrown on to the tracks, while barricades of logs were flung across the winding roads between Knin and the Croat towns of Sinj and Drniš to the south. It was immediately apparent that Milošević's gun-runner Kertes had done his job well. While the Croat police had only pistols, the peasant folk of Knin were well prepared, and not only with old machine guns hidden under the floorboards from the Second World War.

Although no one died, the bungled assault on Knin marked the beginning of the Yugoslav wars. The media in Zagreb affected disdain for the Knin rebels, portraying them as drunken hillbillies. They mocked the Serbs' wooden barricades, dubbing the revolt a *balvan revolucija* or 'log revolution'. But in Belgrade the media set out to create a mood of hysteria. Inflammatory commentaries accused Tudjman of plotting to butcher what they inaccurately called the *goloruki narod* (bare-handed people) of Knin. Stirring commentaries about the revival of Fascism in Croatia were interwoven on the television with gruesome footage of Second World War atrocities committed by Pavelić's Ustashe.

Tudjman had soon to admit that the *balvan revolucija* was not a local dispute in the mountains but a small war that had virtually severed road and rail communications between northern Croatia and Dalmatia. That evening he went on the air. He no longer said the Serb referendum would not go ahead, but appealed to the Serbs not to hold it. He promised to guarantee the Serb rights and, in a side-swipe at his tormentor in Belgrade, accused Milošević of attempting to destabilise the republic. 'Milošević's plan is not only the Kosovo-isation of Knin, not only bloodshed but the destruction of Yugoslavia,' he said.[29]

The Serbian National Council under Babić regarded this appeal with contempt. The fading figure of Rašković still maintained that the Serbs wanted only equality, not a separate state. But Rašković was only the head of the SDS. Executive power in the new Serbian statelet was in Babić's hands. The referendum went ahead with no interruption in the Serb districts. As a democratic exercise it was a farce – the 40 per cent of people in Benkovac who were Croats were not asked their opinions, for example – but the predictable near-100 per cent vote in favour of autonomy gave Babić the legal figleaf he wanted. On 25 August he proclaimed the birth of the Autonomous Province of the Serbian Krajina. The name appealed to the collective memory of the Croatian Serbs, although it was a strange choice as Knin had never been part of the old Habsburg *Vojna Krajina*.[30]

Less than a week after the furore in Knin the Sabor reassembled in a mood of confusion and impotent anger. While they thundered, the Krajina spread its tentacles into the Serb hinterland of eastern Lika, eastern Kordun and Banija. Local Serb councillors who belonged to Račan's Communists were pressurised into resigning by Babić's militants, or crossed over on their own accord into the SDS. The revolt in Knin concentrated minds in the Croatian government on the problem of the lack of weapons. As a result, in the autumn and winter of 1990 the new Defence Minister, Martin Špegelj, embarked on a spending spree that was designed to radically improve the police's ability to respond to such insurrections.

Finding the money and processing the payments were not a serious problem. The purchases were not made in cash but through the Croatian banks and state enterprises, which had big enough accounts to conceal Špegelj's bills. It was months before the federal government, the army or the secret police found out what was going on. Špegelj's main partner was the future Croatian Prime Minister Franjo Gregurić, then head of the big foreign trading concern, Astra.

Getting hold of the weapons was not difficult either. Before the spring of 1991 there was no international embargo on the export of weapons to Yugoslavia or to any of its constituent republics, so all that was needed on Croatia's part was a certain secrecy as regards Belgrade.

Špegelj found many partners in eastern Europe, the Middle East and the Far East, but the most important was Hungary. There the new right-wing government under President Josef Antall looked favourably on Croatia, partly for historic reasons, and with disapproval on Serbia, owing to the worsening position of the Hungarian minority in Vojvodina. On a visit to the Hungarian defence ministry in Budapest on 5 October 1990 Špegelj was delighted both by the warmth of the reception and by the favourable price the Hungarians set for Kalashnikov machine guns, at 280 Deutschmarks a piece. 'When I heard that I almost jumped for joy, as this was an exceptional offer, below every world price,' he recalled. 'During the war [of 1991] we were buying Kalashnikovs for 700 marks or more.'[31] Špegelj spent a total of eleven million marks on his trip to Budapest, ordering anti-aircraft defence systems, rocket-propelled grenades, mines and vast quantities of ammunition as well as some 30,000 Kalashnikovs.

Špegelj and his hosts agreed that the weapons would be delivered in three loads. The first, on 11 October, was the smallest, comprising two lorries loaded with 450 boxes of Kalashnikovs and which crossed into Croatia from Hungary near Virovitica. The second delivery followed shortly afterwards in eight lorries which also entered Croatia directly from Hungary. However the third consignment, in December, arrived by sea on a boat loaded up in the Black Sea and officially destined for a state in Africa. Instead the boat docked suddenly in Dalmatia where its contents were rapidly unpacked under Špegelj's instructions.

By December 1990 Špegelj's purchases had transformed the capabilities of the Croatian police and partly undone the effects of the army's confiscation of the republic's territorial defence supplies. Špegelj was convinced the time was now right to use force against the rebels in Knin and drew up a plan to retake the town. Much to his dismay, however, he found little support either for his arms purchases or for his plan to retake Knin inside Tudjman's cabinet. The President himself was loath to use force and affected an attitude of boredom or irritation whenever Špegelj attempted to explain his military projects.

Tudjman's closest colleagues, Manolić and Boljkovac, also closed ranks against him. Manolić simply echoed Tudjman's opinions. Boljkovac exasperated Špegelj beyond measure. A natural optimist with an incurably sunny disposition, he would not be shaken from a conviction that talks, talks and more talks were the solution to the crisis with the Serbs. Although he had left the Communists and joined the HDZ, he remained a Yugoslav at heart. To Špegelj's annoyance he repeatedly said: 'We must not do anything that might irritate Belgrade. That might hinder us getting a confederation in the coming talks.'[32]

One of many things Boljkovac feared might 'irritate Belgrade' was Špegelj's weapons purchases. And in this matter, Tudjman sided with

Boljkovac. As a result, at the end of February 1991, Tudjman informed Špegelj that he was no longer in charge of purchasing weapons. The brief was passed to Gregurić, Šušak and Hrvoje Šarinić – the latter a university professor with absolutely no experience in defence matters. Under this trio, the purchase of weapons slowed to a trickle for several vital months.

The revolt in Knin also affected the political temperature in the other republics, where the local population looked on the Serb insurrection for the most part with disapproval and a degree of fear. The Serbs' bullishness frightened the Slovenes, the Bosnian Muslims and the Macedonians. In Slovenia the Serbs were too few to start a revolution with barricades. But the army's interference in Knin strengthened the Slovenes' determination to leave Yugoslavia, and the government in Ljubljana soon announced it would hold a referendum on 'disassociating' Slovenia from Yugoslavia at the end of the year.

Macedonia and Bosnia were also touched by the revolt in Knin. Voters in the republics went to the polls on 11 and 18 November, disturbed by the ease with which the Serbs had set up a statelet for the 600,000 Serbs in Croatia, at the same time that Belgrade was closing down the provincial parliament for the far more numerous and far more compact 2 million Albanians of Kosovo.

The elections in Bosnia and Macedonia were vital tests of whether the idea of Yugoslavia still had any popular support outside Serbia and Croatia. The two republics owed their existence to the Avnoj councils of 1942 and 1943, and Tito had enjoyed great popularity in both of them. If Yugoslav-orientated parties could win an election anywhere, it ought to be there. That was the calculation of the Communists in Bosnia and of Ante Marković, the federal Prime Minister. Marković launched his own political party, Savez Reformskih Snaga (League of Reform Forces), in the old Partisan stronghold of Kozara in northern Bosnia. His efforts to steer Yugoslavia towards a free-market democracy enjoyed strong support in the West. At home, his vision of a free-enterprise economy in which the national question would be subsumed by the drive for prosperity appealed to the young. They were the keenest watchers of Yutel, the new Yugoslav television station Marković set up in October 1990.[33] In Bosnia and Macedonia no one doubted that their poor, multi-faith and multi-national republics stood to lose out most if Yugoslavia dissolved.

In the event, both the Communists and Marković's reformists flopped in the elections in Bosnia and Macedonia. In Macedonia, nationalists demanding independence emerged as the largest single party, although a reformed Communist who was sympathetic to Marković, Kiro Gligorov, topped the poll for president. In Bosnia most voters rallied to the three ethnic-based parties, the Muslim-run Party of Democratic Action (SDA), the Serb Democratic Party (SDS) and the Croat

Democratic Union (HDZ), which won votes in almost exact proportion to their ethnic composition in the republic. As the population of Bosnia was then about 44 per cent Muslim, 31 per cent Serb and 17 per cent Croat, the SDA took most seats.

The SDS was the sister party of Rašković's organisation in Croatia, and was just as extreme. By coincidence, it was also headed by a psychiatrist, Radovan Karadžić. The SDS soon formed a Serbian National Council similar to the body in Croatia, and based in the Serb stronghold of Banja Luka, north-west Bosnia. Within a few months it had set up 'Serb autonomous provinces' along the lines of the Krajina.[34]

The crushing defeat of pro-Yugoslav parties in the Bosnian and Macedonian elections came as a great surprise. The election that followed in Serbia was entirely predictable. On 9 December, after Milošević had casually renamed the League of Communists of Serbia the Serbian Socialist Party, he trounced a collection of old-fashioned Chetniks, royalists and exceedingly faint-hearted liberals. His principal rival, Vuk Drašković, a nationalist, royalist author[35] with flowing locks and a powerful oratory, won only a third of the number of votes obtained by Milošević. The old Communist apparatus had not lost its nerve in Serbia, had successfully identified itself as the guardian of the Serb 'national interest', controlled the media and basked in the public endorsement of the army, which threatened the opposition in outrageous terms. General Kadijević had warned that the army might use force if 'aggressive anti-Socialist forces' – a thin codeword for Drašković – triumphed in the vote.

The election of Tudjman and Izetbegović and the re-election of Milošević, Gligorov and Kučan did not offer much of a clue to whether Yugoslavia would dissolve, be recast as a confederation or remain in its present form. Communism appeared to have triumphed in Serbia and Montenegro while 'nationalism' had broadly won everywhere. But nationalism of what kind? In Croatia Tudjman had won the election on the issue of statehood. But the term was far less revolutionary than it sounded to foreign ears, as the 1946 and 1974 Yugoslav constitutions had used the words 'states' and 'republics' almost interchangeably.

At Christmas the Croatian parliament adopted the controversial new constitution, but there was no question of 'sovereign' Croatia withdrawing from participation in the federal government. On the contrary, the HDZ was determined to make its influence in Belgrade felt by replacing Šuvar with Mesić in autumn 1990 as Croatia's representative in the Yugoslav presidency. Both the Croats and the Slovenes were aware that the West Europeans and the US opposed the break-up of Yugoslavia and were keen to distance themselves from that unpleasant word 'secession'. Croatia and Slovenia wanted also to harmonise their positions with the Macedonians and the Bosnian Muslims, whose ambitions did not stretch beyond remodelling Yugoslavia into a looser federation.

For a few weeks over Christmas, Milošević and the army chiefs digested the new arrangement of forces created by the republican elections throughout the country. But at the beginning of January 1991 the army abruptly sent an ultimatum addressed to both Croatia and Slovenia, ordering them to disband their paramilitary police units, and backed it up with a threat that on 23 January the Fifth Army would be placed on combat level if there was no sign that the police had been disbanded. It was significant that the ultimatum was directed only at Ljubljana and Zagreb, not at Knin, and that there was no mention of the Serb paramilitaries prowling round northern Dalmatia, Lika, Kordun and Banija.

The ultimatum was one-sided. But it was based on fairly accurate information from the secret police, the army and the customs officials that the Slovenes and the Croats were illegally importing weapons for the use of their paramilitary police forces. There was little Belgrade could do about this; it was impossible to halt the influx of machine guns stashed in the boots of cars, hidden under the floorboards of lorries or stowed under tons of frozen meat in containers. The fall of Communism in Eastern Europe had released huge supplies of surplus weaponry much of which gravitated south into the restless republics of north-west Yugoslavia.

The army ultimatum provoked alarm in Zagreb. There was a rush on the shops as housewives started panic-buying. Patriots clutching candles occupied Jelačić Square for vigils. The university emptied as students hurried home to their home towns and villages, fearing the outbreak of war. However, Tudjman was learning on the job. His flamboyant election rhetoric now a distant memory, he was determined to avoid a conflict with the army while his forces were still poorly equipped. Hurrying to Belgrade to meet General Kadijević on the 25th, he capitulated, promised to disband the special police and even to allow the army to arrest those Croat nationalists it saw as a particular danger.

He returned to Zagreb, exhausted, and announced that the crisis was over. But it was not. The army and Serbia felt cheated by Tudjman's unexpected climbdown and as soon as he reached Zagreb the secret police in Belgrade produced another trump card – a grainy black-and-white video that showed General Špegelj, seated in a dingy kitchen discussing the import of weapons and plans for an insurrection with a couple of younger men. General Špegelj could be overheard saying that, if push came to shove, the Yugoslav army officer corps in Croatia would have to be eliminated. The video was a great coup for the secret police, Kos. Špegelj was stunned to discover that one of his closest confidants, Vladimir Jagar, was a Kos agent.

The video was broadcast several times on one day alone on Belgrade Television, in case anyone should miss it. It was a tremendous blow to Tudjman. Just as he thought he had defused the situation, the atmosphere was stoked up to boiling point. Mesić insisted – without a shred of conviction – that the video was a fake. The Slovenes tried to take the wind out of the Serbs' self-righteous indignation by releasing an army memorandum allegedly calling for the overthrow of non-Communist governments throughout Yugoslavia. But the furore over the video could not be dispelled so easily. The army issued a demand for Špegelj to be arrested and handed over. This time Tudjman was defiant. Humiliating oral promises were one thing; handing over his Defence Minister for court martial was another. Špegelj went into hiding for a few months and in a tart letter to the Yugoslav President, Borisav Jović, a close ally of Milošević, Tudjman accused Belgrade of using the army as 'a truncheon against any nation that opposes a centralised Yugoslav state'.[36]

January's alarms brought Kučan and Tudjman close together in a fearful alliance against Milošević and the generals. It also drove them to spell out exactly what it was that they sought, both to answer Serb accusations of separatism and to soothe the worries of the West. On 12 February Tudjman and Kučan hammered out a five-point declaration after a meeting of the two presidents on the island of Krk. The first point, and the main one, was that Yugoslavia could survive only as a voluntary league of sovereign republics. The second point was that such a league would be viable only if all the member republics subscribed to parliamentary democracy, a free-market economy and a wide range of civil and human rights. The two republics set a deadline of 30 June for a solution to be reached, and declared that they would seek international arbitration from the UN if there was no agreement by that date.

By the end of February, Yugoslavia was drifting steadily towards war, though no one could pinpoint exactly how, or when, it would start, or what form the response of the federal army would take. Kučan and his right-of-centre Prime Minister, Lojze Peterle, were finalising Slovenia's departure date from Yugoslavia. The Slovene Defence Minister Janez Janša, the former *Mladina* journalist arrested in 1987, was organising the republic's former territorial defence force into an army. Tudjman was reeling from humiliations inflicted almost daily by the army, Milošević and Babić's rebel statelet. If Slovenia were to leave Yugoslavia, there would be no question of Croatia staying. But if Slovenia and Croatia were to leave, Gligorov and Izetbegović had made it clear that Bosnia and Macedonia would not remain. And if Croatia and Bosnia were to leave, Milošević, Babić and Karadžić had made it clear there was no question of those republics taking their Serb minorities with them. As Yugoslavia teetered on the edge of an explosion, Babić made his next move. He exported the *balvan revolucija* from the mountains of Lika and northern Dalmatia to the very centre of Croatia, to the lush flat pastureland of Slavonia. On 2 March, his forces took over the police station in Pakrac.

16

'Serbia Is Not Involved'

Karadžić: *What's going on with the bombing?*
Milošević: *Today's no good for aviation, there's a meeting of the European Community*
Milošević discusses the war in Croatia, September 1991[1]

Pakrac was a typical dingy Slavonian market town of about 10,000, with a small square in the middle. Two baroque churches, one Orthodox and one Catholic, faced each other over a bank of trees. Up the road was the once fine but now rather decayed palace of Lukijan, the Serb Orthodox Bishop of Slavonia. The Serbs' choice of Pakrac was not accidental. In Slavonia as a whole, the Serbs made up only about 15 per cent of the population. Pakrac was the only Slavonian municipality in which Serbs formed a relative majority. It also occupied a strategic position in the middle of Slavonia on the main railway line from Zagreb to Belgrade, just to the north of the Zagreb–Belgrade motorway. In the elections of 1990 Pakrac had voted for Račan's reformed Communists. But, since then, many of the Serb local councillors had trickled away to join Babić's militants, following a trend throughout the Serb municipalities in Croatia after the elections.

On 2 March 1991 a group of Serb policemen from Pakrac, acting in concert with allies among the Serb town councillors, burst into the police station, disarmed the police on duty (many of whom were also Serbs) and declared the district of Pakrac a part of Babić's Krajina fiefdom. The coup failed. Ten months into office, Tudjman had now built up a police force bolstered by paramilitary 'special' units that were wholly Croat and wholly loyal to the new government. The Serbs were surprised. The 'specials' from Zagreb descended on the town in hours, took back the police station and the town hall and hoisted the Croat flag over both buildings. The rebel police, the Bishop and most of the councillors fled into the Papuk hills to the north.

The Pakrac revolt ended without anyone being killed, but its failure triggered an outburst of fury in official circles in Serbia. The media in Belgrade insisted that Ustashe shock troops had carried out a massacre, and that many Serb civilians were lying dead in the street. General Kadijević ordered army tanks into the town centre. They were too late to dislodge the Croat police from the town square and the police station, from where the Croat flag obstinately fluttered. Ostensibly the army was sent in to keep the peace between the two communities; it was noticeable, however, that the army tanks' barrels were trained at the Croat police. The two groups of young men stared at each other in silence in the now eerily deserted main square.

The Pakrac crisis marked the beginning of a dramatic month for Yugoslavia, in which the eye of the storm shifted back and forth between Croatia and Serbia. A week after the affray, on 9 March, it was the turn of Belgrade to experience trouble. The fuse was lit by Drašković, the disappointed loser in the Serbian presidential elections held the previous winter. Quite persuaded that he had lost the poll partly through ballot-box fraud and partly on account of the hostile propaganda of the 'bastille', as he nicknamed Belgrade TV, he summoned his supporters to a rally in the centre of the capital, outside the Opera House. The government forbade the meeting. Drašković, revelling in the chance to engage in a game of brinkmanship, ordered his supporters to turn up. The result was a riot and by nightfall Yugoslav army tanks were rumbling through the centre of Belgrade past smashed shopfronts and upturned trams and buses. The Belgrade riot was an isolated blip on Serbia's passive political landscape which had no long-term repercussions on the republic's internal affairs. Yet the speed with which General Kadijević had sent his tanks on to the streets to defend Milošević's government against a harmless unarmed crowd demonstrated the degree to which the army in fact identified its interests with the Serbian regime.

The events of 9 March in Belgrade also brought about a face-to-face meeting between a momentarily unnerved Milošević and Tudjman, which then failed to avert the prospect of war. The Tudjman–Milošević summit took place at the old Serbian royal hunting lodge of Karadjordjevo, site of the débâcle of the Maspok leaders in 1971. Tudjman's then adviser, Slaven Letica, recalled the event in 1993, when the West was pondering a plan to break up Bosnia into three, ethnic-based republics. 'There were several maps on the table. The idea was close to the recent ideas on Bosnia–Herzegovina, either to divide Bosnia into 10 or 15 units, or three semi-independent states.'[2] Neither Tudjman nor Milošević saw any need to include any Muslims in this intimate discussion. Tudjman did not take Bosnia very seriously. 'Bosnia was a creation of the Ottoman invasion of Europe,' he informed a Western television crew. 'Until then it was part of Croatia, or it was a kingdom of Bosnia, but a Catholic kingdom, linked to Croatia.'[3]

The immediate significance of Karadjordjevo, however, was not a deal about Bosnia but the lack of a deal about Croatia. In a speech to local council leaders, one week after the riots in Belgrade, Milošević made it clear that he intended to incorporate a large slice of Croatia into the new mini-Yugoslavia. 'We have to secure unity in Serbia if we want, as the biggest and most numerous republic, to dictate events,' he said. 'These are questions of frontiers, essential questions of state. And frontiers, as you know, are dictated by the strong, not the weak.' Milošević went on to say that he had decided to mobilise Serbs into the army, and had been in touch with 'our people' in Knin and in Bosnia. But secrecy, he insisted, was essential. 'Are we going to tell everyone what we are going to do on the radio? We can't do that. But if we need to fight, we'll really fight. We may be no good at working or trading but at least we know well how to fight.'4

The Belgrade newspapers and magazines, led by *Politika*, started printing a variety of smudgy maps of the ethnic composition of Yugoslavia, of dubious accuracy and quality. Disturbingly, most of them suggested that between a third and a half of Croatia formed part of what these papers referred to as the Serbs' *etnički prostor*, or ethnic space.

The failure at Karadjordjevo was followed by another army ultimatum on 12 March, sponsored by Jović, President of Yugoslavia's collective state presidency. Again aimed at Croatia and Slovenia, it called on the presidency to endorse the proclamation of 'emergency measures' akin to martial law throughout the country. The proposal split the presidency down the middle. Jović, Serbia's representative, was naturally enthusiastic. So were Milošević's appointee in Vojvodina, Jugoslav Kostić, and Branko Kostić, the representative of Montenegro. The Serbs were certain they had the vote in the bag. The plan backfired when Bosnia's representative voted against the measure. Bogić Bogićević was a Serb, but he brushed aside the appeals to Serb solidarity. Thus, against all expectations, the army was denied an excuse to assume dictatorial powers. This fiasco sent Milošević into a rare public rage. Visibly livid, he took to the airwaves of Belgrade Television and announced dramatically that 'Yugoslavia has entered the final phase of its agony.' Serbia 'would no longer obey the presidency', he added. It would 'arm the Serbian people so they are not left defenceless against the Croatians'.5 Jović obediently resigned as president. Kadijević showed his solidarity with Milošević and Jović by refusing to communicate with the presidency's non-Serb rump.6

The Krajina army was far from defenceless. On 31 March it ambushed a bus carrying Croat police into the Plitvice National Park in the Kordun region, north of the Serb-majority town of Titova Korenica. The Serbs chose the park – as they had chosen Pakrac – for strategic reasons, rather than from any special fears concerning the safety of

Plitvice's local Serbs. While Croats remained in Kordun, Serbs in Lika and Banija were cut off from each other. Slunj was the main town in Kordun, straddling the winding mountain road between Lika and Banija. But Slunj was solidly Croat. Thus the Plitvice campaign marked a new phase in the Serb campaign. This time the Serbs were trying, not to expel Croat police from majority-Serb towns and villages, but to over-run districts where most people were Croat. In these districts, resistance to the Serb paramilitaries was much stronger, and the struggle corre-spondingly more violent, and it was this that forced the army to take a higher profile in supporting Babić's designs.

As in Pakrac, the Croat paramilitary police proved capable of seeing off the Serb insurgents in Plitvice. Hundreds moved into the park, drove out the Serbs and set up a new wooden police station in the middle of the woods. A group of terrified Italian tourists caught in the crossfire was escorted to safety. Babić's counterstroke was to call an assembly of councillors from the Serb districts in Titova Korenica. The meeting demanded help from Belgrade in expelling 'Croatian terrorists' and voted for the Serb Autonomous Region of Krajina to become 'an inte-gral part of the united territories of Serbia'.[7]

In Belgrade, the battle for Plitvice was treated as a *casus belli*. The Serbian parliament met in emergency session. The deputies sidestepped the proposed union with Krajina; Milošević insisted then as later that Serbia was not involved directly in the war in Croatia. But the parlia-ment offered Krajina 'all necessary help', with all that that implied in terms of arms and money. General Kadijević sent tanks and troops to Plitvice, and this time there was little pretence that they were there to keep the peace. As soon as they arrived, Kadijević sent an ultimatum to Zagreb to get out of the park, or be driven out. 'They have told us quite literally that if we do not evacuate Plitvice they will liquidate our police,' Tudjman's aide, Mario Nobilo, reported.[8] Tudjman replied on Radio Croatia; he warned that if the army escalated activity in Croatia, he would declare it an army of occupation.

Eastern Slavonia had until then remained fairly quiet, thanks partly to the efforts of the young police chief of Osijek, Josip Reihl-Kir. But by the spring tension was rising rapidly around Vukovar, an industrial town with an old baroque core lying on the border with Serbia. The town had never been a centre of Croat nationalism, partly because it was so multi-national, with big Ruthene, Ukrainian, Slovak and Hungarian communities, as well as Serbs and Croats. In the 1990 elections the town had kept faith with Račan's reformed Communists. The local Serbs did not like the HDZ government; the troublemakers, however, were not the *starosjedioci* (old settlers) but the more militant Serb and Montenegrin immigrants who had moved into the surrounding villages to replace the expelled ethnic Germans after the Second World War.

It was in the villages of Vera, Bobota and Bijelo Brdo, dotted on the road between Osijek and Vukovar, that groups of paramilitaries based in Serbia found a secure foothold. These paramilitaries operated under the umbrella of the Serbian Interior Ministry. It was the ministry that readily distributed weapons, made available premises for training and provided an enormous amount of favourable publicity on Belgrade Television. In the field the groups acted fairly autonomously, and in different areas. 'Captain Dragan', a mercurial dandy who was reported to have been a pimp in the Sydney underworld, lent the services of his militia to Knin, where his militiamen were dubbed 'Knindjas', after the American TV comic-strip anti-heroes. Željko Ražnjatović, *nom de guerre* Arkan, was more sinister. His scrubbed-looking pink cheeks, baby face, sky-blue eyes and jolly smile concealed a psychopathic nationalist fanatic whose bloodlust would find fullest expression in the wretched Muslim towns of eastern Bosnia in 1992. A robber of banks throughout Europe in the 1970s, he was reportedly recruited into the Yugoslav secret police by Stane Dolanc. His superbly athletic killers, the 'Tigers', were also active in eastern Slavonia in the summer of 1991, where they made a base in the village of Erdut.

More ramshackle than the Tigers were the Beli Orlovi (White Eagles) of Vojislav Šešelj, parliamentary leader of the extreme-right Radical Party, which was then closely allied to Milošević's Socialists. Whereas the Tigers were Arnie Schwarzenegger lookalikes, recruited from gyms and the world of pumping iron, the White Eagles were tatty, gap-toothed folk, mainly working-class city-dwellers for whom Šešelj's doctrine of Serb racial superiority was a compensation for all life's petty setbacks.

The White Eagles more consciously based themselves on the old Chetnik movement of the 1940s, and sported black, cone-shaped furry hats with metal Serbian eagle badges pinned to the front, and black flags with the skull-and-crossbones. Šešelj was a Bosnian Serb from Sarajevo, born in 1954, who had been imprisoned as a Serb nationalist in 1984. He emerged from Zenica jail an impassioned believer in a Greater Serbia. In the late 1980s he teamed up with Drašković, but, finding his brand of nationalism too watery for his taste, joined the more extreme Radical Party. He was proud of having been appointed a Chetnik *vojvode* – duke – by Momčilo Djujić, the old Chetnik boss of Knin in the Second World War who lived in California. If Šešelj's appearance in a cone-shaped furry hat with a double-headed eagle pinned on top was almost comic, his views were not. During his election campaign in 1991 in the Belgrade suburb of Rakovica he had promised publicly to 'butcher the Croats, not with knives, but with rusty spoons'.

Šešelj was quite open about his view that Croatia ought to be reduced to a tiny rump of territory around Zagreb. 'We have nothing in principle against the new Ustashe leader – Tito's general – Franjo Tudjman, planning an independent Croatian state', he wrote. 'But we warn him unceasingly that we will never allow him, at any price, to include within the frontiers of that state, that criminal creation, even a fraction of land on which Serbian villages, destroyed churches or mass graves are to be found. If we would do that, we would dishonour our ancestors and shame our descendants. We have nothing against an eventual Croatian state, but only on condition that it lies west of the line running from Karlobag to Ogulin, Karlovac and Virovitica.'

He went on to suggest that if Croatia did not accept being cut down to one-third of its former size, he would call on Italy to annex the territory west of the Karlobag–Virovitica line for itself.[9]

The Chetniks' main field of activity was Borovo Selo, an industrial suburb of Vukovar with a large tyre factory, which had drawn large numbers of immigrant Serb and Montenegrin workers during the boom years of the late 1960s and 1970s. The neighbouring suburb of Borovo Naselje was mostly Croat. The brewing tension in the triangle of land between Vukovar, Borovo Selo and Borovo Naselje was a constant source of anxiety to Reihl-Kir, who kept a lid on the situation by trying to act as an honest broker between the communities. He would regularly appear unarmed and alone at the barricades put up by the Serbs in the villages around Vukovar to appeal to all sides to keep the peace. But by April 1991 the local Croat militants, as well as the Serbs, were growing a bit tired of Reihl-Kir. In Osijek the police chief had a powerful enemy in Branimir Glavaš, a squat urban warrior who had practically taken over local government from Osijek's liberal Mayor, Zlatko Kramarić. The police chief knew he was in mortal danger and pleaded with the Interior Ministry in Zagreb to transfer him to the capital. Just before he was due to leave Osijek at the end of April, Reihl-Kir went to Tenja, a suburb of Osijek, for another tense meeting on the barricades with one of the local Serb leaders. He was sitting in a car with the Serb when one of his own young policemen, Antun Gudelj, walked up to the car and shot him. Gudelj's family had just been driven out of their home in one of the villages that had been taken over by the Serbs, and he had just learned that several members of his family had been killed. He murdered his commander with the gun that Reihl-Kir himself had presented to him only days before.

Within days of Reihl-Kir's death, the fragile peace he had struggled so hard to maintain between the villages of eastern Slavonia collapsed. On 1 May two policemen were kidnapped in Borovo Selo while on a routine patrol. The following day the Osijek police force sent a busload of reinforcements to rescue the kidnapped police. Many of them were teenage recruits who scarcely knew how to handle a gun. The result was a ghastly massacre. The Serbs ambushed the bus and fifteen police were killed. 'We went to Borovo with a white flag but they opened fire from all sides and massacred our boys,' was the anguished recollection of a survivor at Vukovar hospital.[10] The rumours that several bodies had been mutilated spread all over Croatia, adding to the panic. Mesić, now Croatia's representative on the federal presidency, said the policemen's heads had been cut off.[11] The carnage in Borovo Selo gave the army a chance to interpose itself in yet another part of Croatia 'to keep the peace'. As a result, the town of Vukovar found itself almost cut off from Osijek and the rest of Croatia.

As the Krajina spread its tentacles over more and more of Croatia, the dilemma in the ranks of the HDZ about Croatia's position in Yugoslavia became more acute. At heart Tudjman was a separatist, although his government officially sought the remodelling of Yugoslavia as a confederation, or a 'league of sovereign republics'. He did not wish to be forced into secession. Rather he hoped to use the system of rotation between the republics for posts in the federal institutions, a system known as the 'key', in order to promote Croatia's agenda through political channels.

Stipe Mesić had been Croatia's first non-Communist prime minister until August 1990, when Tudjman appointed him as Croatia's representative on the federal presidency to replace Stipe Šuvar. On 15 May Mesić believed he would take over as president of the presidency from Jović. Since Tito's death in 1980 the principle and the fixed order of the 'key' in the presidency had been scrupulously observed, so much so that, when it was Serbia's turn for the 'key' in May 1990, no vote was even taken. By tradition, the outgoing president simply presented the new candidate and champagne was produced. At midday on 15 May 1991 the eight presidency members, representing the six republics and two autonomous provinces, gathered for the ceremony along with the federal Prime Minister, General Adžić (Kadijević was ill) and the presidents of the republics, Tudjman and Milošević among them, on the first floor of the Palace of the Federation in Belgrade. Jović sat in the middle, Mesić to his right. Until then, nothing untoward had occurred. The first sign that the Serbs were planning something came when Jović broke with tradition and called for a show of hands over Mesić's candidacy. Janez Drnovšek of Slovenia put up his hand, as did Vasil Tupurkovski of Macedonia, Bogićević of Bosnia and Mesić himself. That made four. The hands of Jović, Kostić and the two representatives of the autonomous provinces stayed where they were. That also made four. The non-Serb members were astonished, as was Tudjman, who stormed out of the building. But Jović was confident of where he stood. He would not vote for Mesić and insisted he had a right not to do so. If that meant Yugoslavia had no president, that was too bad.

The Serb decision to block the election of the new president stunned the Croats. They were banking on Mesić being able to use his position to rein in the army. The impasse also shocked the European Community, which was watching Yugoslavia's downward spiral into civil war with growing alarm. On 29 May Brussels despatched a duo to Belgrade, comprising Jacques Santer, the Prime Minister of Luxembourg, and Jacques Delors, the President of the Council of Europe, to knock heads together and talk to the main actors in the drama. The result in the first week in June was an official statement from Brussels of the EC's position. The document declared the community's support for the unity of Yugoslavia (which pleased the Serbs), but called for the principle of rotation in the presidency to be respected (which pleased the Croats). But the West was not really united over Yugoslavia. The French and Spanish placed the greatest emphasis on Yugoslavia's unity. So did the American Secretary of State, James Baker, who was strongly opposed to secession by any of the republics. A different tone was struck by the German Foreign Minister, Hans-Dietrich Genscher. He insisted on the need to respect Yugoslavia's *internal* frontiers as well as its external ones. His standpoint was echoed, even more forcefully, by the Austrian Chancellor Franz Vranitzky.

The worsening crisis in eastern Slavonia heightened pressure on Tudjman to give up the policy of non-confrontation with the Yugoslav army and to drop all the talk about restructuring Yugoslavia as a 'league of sovereign republics'. On 18 May Croatia went ahead with a snap referendum on independence, although the wording was so imprecise that it left open the possibility of a sovereign Croatia remaining in a Yugoslav confederation.[12] Needless to say the vote did not take place at all in Serb-held territory, while in government-held territory the result was a predictable near-100 per cent vote in favour of the government's position.

The other republics were also becoming increasingly alarmed. The Bosnian President, Alija Izetbegović, was particularly worried by the flames of Croatia's civil war licking at the corners of his rickety domain. Izetbegović blamed the army, accusing it of siding with Serb paramilitaries against Croatia's elected government, and of using his own republic as a launch pad for operations in Croatia.

On 6 June Presidents Izetbegović of Bosnia and Gligorov of Macedonia put forward their own initiative to solve the crisis. The two leaders called their proposal the 'Four-plus-two' plan. Welding together federal and confederal concepts, they proposed a weak 'confederal' link between Croatia, Slovenia and a 'federation' comprising the other four republics. However, the four republics in the federation would also have their 'sovereignty' confirmed. At a meeting of the six presidents in Sarajevo the Serbs vetoed the Gligorov–Izetbegović initiative, although Milošević's relaxed manner and his agreement to continue talking raised entirely false hopes at home and abroad that the worst was over. Kučan and Tudjman both supported the 'Four-plus-two' proposal in Sarajevo, but from different standpoints. The Slovenes had been making monetary and military preparations for full independence for several months. Unlike Croatia, Slovenia had successfully hidden most of the republic's territorial defence weaponry when the army tried to disarm Croatia and Slovenia in March 1990. Unlike Croatia, the Slovenes had no Serb minority. Their support for the 'Four-plus-two' proposal was half-hearted and dependent on its being rapidly fleshed out. As nothing happened at all after the Sarajevo summit, the Slovenes soon reverted to their earlier plan. On 15 June a Slovene delegation under Kučan invited Tudjman to Ljubljana for a four-hour summit. There they announced Slovenia's plan to declare independence from Yugoslavia at the end of the month.

Tudjman was determined not to fall out of step with the Slovenes, although Croatia's prospects were much less favourable than those of Slovenia. Prime Minister Marković hurried to both capitals to dissuade them; he warned that independence was 'a bomb that will blow us all up'. The two assemblies heard his plea with stony faces. On 25 June, the Slovene parliament met in Ljubljana to proclaim its 'dissociation' from Yugoslavia. Hours earlier the Sabor in Zagreb had adopted a much briefer five-point act proclaiming Croatia a 'sovereign and independent state'.

For the Croats, the declaration was another bargaining point. They had no intention of expelling the army, taking over the frontier crossings or withdrawing Mesić from the Yugoslav presidency. The Slovenes were more literal in their understanding of the word independence. That night, while the Slovenes drank specially marketed bottles of Independence wine in the restaurants of Ljubljana, Slovene forces seized control of some thirty-seven frontier crossings with Austria, Italy and Hungary, expelled Yugoslav officials from the customs houses, took down Yugoslav signs on the border and hoisted the Slovene flag. The following day in Belgrade Marković announced he had ordered the 'relevant organs', meaning the police and army, to 'secure the execution of federal laws on frontier crossings' and take down Slovene frontier signs. At 2am on 27 June units of the Fifth Army moved out of their bases in the republic and in Croatia and headed towards Ljubljana airport, in the village of Brnik. They met greater resistance than they had anticipated. At dawn there was fighting on the Austro-Yugoslav border crossing at Šentilj between the Slovene forces and federal troops. The Slovenes flung up a wall of lorries and trucks round Ljubljana to block anyone getting in or out.

The fighting in Slovenia divided Tudjman's cabinet. General Špegelj, who had led a semi-clandestine existence since the army had demanded his arrest over the affair of the video, demanded that Tudjman give the order to sabotage the army's progress towards Slovenia through Croatia. Špegelj was convinced it was necessary to go on the offensive before the army had had time to reorganise itself as a purely Serb force. He believed its strength in the Fifth Army region at the time was not more than 27,000 men, most of them raw recruits with little experience or willingness to fight. Against them the Croats had about 60,000 armed men, most of them organised in police units, but battle-ready nevertheless. The prize was potentially of enormous value – about 1,000 tanks, 2,500 pieces of heavy artillery and 800 armoured personnel carriers and enough ammunition, in his estimation, to fight a war for two years.[13] Tudjman would have none of it. The line up of forces was as in December 1990, when Tudjman, Manolić and Boljkovac had combined to block his plans for an attack on Knin.

Šušak also withheld his support. He was a hardline nationalist and a virulent enemy of the Serbs; in the spring of 1991, just before Reihl-Kir's death, he was reported to have accompanied a group that crept up to the outskirts of one of the Serbian villages in eastern Slavonia and fired shoulder-launched missiles at the nearest houses and farms.[14] If anyone should have backed a tough stance towards Serbia and the army it ought to have been Šušak. However, as Špegelj discovered to his shock and distress, Šušak hated old Partisan Croats almost as much as he hated the Serbs. 'This is not 1945', he sneered at Špegelj on one occasion. The son of the Herzegovinian diaspora could never forgive the likes of Špegelj for siding with Tito, for creating the hated 'second Yugoslavia', for destroying the NDH.

At the cabinet meeting, Tudjman proceeded to tear Špegelj's plan apart. 'What Špegelj proposes is very dangerous,' he began. 'It is an adventure with unforseeable consequences. What does it mean? The end of political dialogue! Who dares to bring an end to political talks? I myself am convinced that Kadijević will not attack Croatia.'

He turned then to the military's capabilities. 'Do you know just how strong the Yugoslav army is?' he asked Špegelj sarcastically. 'There are many people in the world who count it as the third or fourth military power in Europe. The army has thousands of tanks, several thousand cannons and three hundred war planes. Besides that, don't you realise this so-called war was practically agreed between the army and the Slovenes?'

Tudjman then ridiculed Špegelj's calculations about the potential death toll, were Croatia to attack the army. 'Are you aware that if we followed your plan, our towns would be destroyed and that we would have thirty thousand or a hundred and thirty thousand dead, and not three thousand, as you claim?' He concluded with a crushing insult: 'With all of these plans, from the one in December 1990 to this latest one, you, Špegelj, would have drawn us into an unimaginable catastrophe and complete international isolation. It seems that is your main aim!'[15]

Špegelj was humiliated. He resigned as Defence Minister and was advised by Manolić that it would be better if he was to leave the country. Manolić told him to go to Canada, though in the end he went to stay with friends in Germany. It was a significant commentary on the state of Tudjman's democracy that a minister who had fallen from favour felt obliged to flee into exile. As the fighting in Croatia grew worse, and Tudjman's faith in Kadijević's good will was shattered, pressure mounted on the President to rescue Špegelj from disgrace. For a few months after his return from Germany he served as Chief Inspector of the Croatian army. He soon discovered it was a post without any substance and he resigned. In retirement he continued to reproach Tudjman bitterly for refusing to listen to his advice.

The fighting in Slovenia flew on to the front pages of every newspaper in Europe. As the border crossing at Šentilj went up in flames before the astonished gaze of the Austrians on the other side, there were rumours that Slovenia's nuclear power station, at Krško, might also be hit, causing an ecological catastrophe. The Europeans hurried back to stop the fighting, despatching a foreign ministerial troika of Jacques de Poos of Luxembourg, Gianni de Michaelis of Italy and Hans Van den Broek of the Netherlands. The three reached Belgrade on 28 June with a three-point plan: to arrange a ceasefire; to persuade the Croats and Slovenes to 'freeze' their independence declarations for three months; and to get the headless Yugoslav presidency back into operation. In Belgrade they found Milošević suave but evasive. Marković was most upset. The Slovenes accused him of attempting to use the army to overthrow their government. In fact he had done nothing of the kind, and his orders had related strictly to securing international border crossings and customs posts. The troika believed they had secured both a ceasefire and Milošević's agreement for Mesić to assume the presidency. Then they departed, returning on the 30th to make sure Mesić was not voted down once again.

After the troika mission, Mesić was indeed installed as president. But he soon discovered that his position as commander-in-chief made absolutely no difference to Kadijević. No sooner had the troika returned to Brussels than the Slovenes and army started fighting again; the Slovenes accused the army of reneging on an agreement for troops to return to bases; the army accused the Slovenes of not releasing kidnapped army officials and their families.

The fighting in Slovenia not only split the Croats; it also split the army. Some generals were 'in the loop', party to Milošević's plan to create a Greater Serbia without Slovenia. Others appeared ignorant of any such design and still believed in a unified, Communist Yugoslavia. Kadijević belonged to the first group and, like Milošević, Jović and Kostić, remained silent throughout the entire Slovene conflict. This group was content with Slovenia's action, as it gave them a legal figleaf to redraw the borders of Yugoslavia. General Adžić, the acting commander-in-chief, was as much 'out of the loop' as Marković. Unable to understand why the army campaign in Slovenia was going so badly and why nothing was being done to rescue the besieged army bases, he rushed on to Belgrade TV on 4 July to declare a war to the bitter end against the Slovene traitors. But there was no war to the bitter end, not even an attempt at a struggle. The tiny force of 2,000 Yugoslav army troops in Slovenia was abandoned to the 40,000-strong Slovene militia. By the time the EC troika flew back on 6 July to shore up their provisional peace plan, the Slovenes had already secured their republic. In the meantime, Brussels passed a ban on the export of weapons to Yugoslavia and suspended financial help.

After the return of the EC troika, the six presidents, the army chiefs and the three foreign ministers met on the Adriatic island of Brioni on 7 July. There the degree to which Adžić, Mesić and Marković had been deceived was revealed. Milošević, Kostić and General Kadijević accepted with alacrity the EC proposal for the army to return to bases in Slovenia, and for the EC to send monitors to oversee the army's withdrawal. They also accepted the three-month moratorium on Slovene independence. But when Marković insisted on the restoration of federal control over the Slovene frontier, the Serbs pooh-poohed the idea as unrealistic. And when the presidency convened on 12 July formally to adopt the EC package, the Serb strategy became even clearer. Jović and Kostić now demanded total withdrawal from Slovenia and the drawing of a new Yugoslav frontier. The Serbs insisted that Slovenia's secession was a *fait accompli*. Mesić discovered that the Serbs and Slovenes had sewn it all up, and when he protested against such a partial solution Kostić told him: 'I have talked about it with Drnovšek. He says such a decision would go down well in Slovenia.' Jović added: 'The decision must be taken immediately.' Kadijević said: 'Most of the army wants to leave Slovenia immediately.'[16] Mesić tried desperately to get the Serbs to agree to the army withdrawing to barracks throughout Yugoslavia, and not just Slovenia, but the Serbs were having none of that. The army would leave Slovenia but there would be no withdrawal to barracks in Croatia.

The outcome was a disaster for Croatia. Milošević had successfully driven a wedge between the two north-western republics, leaving Croatia isolated. Although under the terms of the Brioni package the Slovenes were obliged to continue to attend presidency meetings, they made it clear they were no longer vitally interested in Croatia's unfolding crisis. In the meantime, the troops and military equipment formerly based in Slovenia were rapidly transferred to Croatia and Bosnia. The effects were soon felt in a dramatic upsurge in the level of violence in Croatia. The town of Glina, fifty miles south of Zagreb, was surrounded by Babić's Krajina militia. By the middle of July even Petrinja, only thirty miles south of Zagreb, was under attack. The worst defeats for the Croats, however, were taking place in eastern Slavonia. East of Osijek, the village of Čelija was burned to the ground by the Serbs and the population driven out. Then a large force of Croat police was surrounded in the village of Dalj, on the Danube river border with Serbia, and at least seventy were killed when the village was overrun. Now that they were in control of a sizeable wedge of territory around Vukovar, the local Serb militants proclaimed the second mini-state in Croatia, the Serbian Autonomous Region of Slavonia, Baranja and Western Srem. But it was not the end of the fighting. On 22 July, when the presidency met in Ohrid, in Macedonia, Tudjman left the meeting in a panic after hearing that at least fourteen people had been killed by shelling in Vinkovci. Three days later the border village of Erdut came under attack and another nine people were killed. The following day Egon Scotland, a journalist from the *Suddeutsche Zeitung*, was killed near Glina as the town finally fell to the Krajina militia.

The bloodshed in eastern Slavonia sent shockwaves throughout Croatia and Europe. At home, Tudjman formed a cabinet of national unity at the beginning of August which brought in members of most of the minor parties in the Sabor, including Račan's reformed Communists. Out went the old Maspok veterans such as Šime Djodan, the recently appointed Defence Minister. The post of prime minister went to Franjo Gregurić, Špegelj's old partner in the first weapons purchases. The appointment of Gregurić helped stabilise Croatia's finances. A new currency, the Croatian dinar, was soon introduced and, in spite of the enormous expense of the war, turned out to be less inflationary than the old Yugoslav dinar. On 11 August the Sabor recognised the inevitable drift towards all-out war by elevating certain police units into the Zbor Narodne Garde, the National Guard, in effect an independent army. The Sabor also outlawed the mobilisation of Croats into the Yugoslav army.

In Brussels, the EC decided it was high time the ministerial troika headed back to Yugoslavia. They arrived on 3 August and spent two unhappy days in Belgrade. There was still a strong feeling in Europe and in the Bush administration in Washington that the Croats were as much to blame for the situation in Yugoslavia as the Serbs. But this picture was starting to alter as images of torched Croatian villages and columns of refugees appeared night after night on the world's television screens. Milošević contributed to this change of view by his behaviour.

The troika found him evasive and contradictory; he claimed the Serbs were defending themselves against Fascism in Croatia but would not agree to the EC sending monitors to Croatia to see for themselves. After the troika returned to Brussels, Belgium and Great Britain called for a meeting of the UN Security Council on Yugoslavia.

The troika's visit was a step towards the internationalisation of the crisis, a development Serbia resisted and Croatia supported. But Europe's painfully slow steps, and the refusal to name an aggressor in the conflict, exposed a rift in the Europeans' ranks. In Austria and Germany, public opinion sympathised with the Croats. The Germans had become increasingly vocal in support of the self-determination of nations after the fall of the Berlin Wall and the reunification of East and West Germany. The new reunited Germany was also less inclined to follow docilely the foreign policy of France and Britain.

The German and Austrian Catholic bishops had close ties to their Croat counterparts. Croat *Gastarbeiters* formed a numerous and influential community in Munich and Vienna. Pro-Croat feeling was strongest on the right, but it embraced the entire political spectrum except the extreme left, and was reflected in Hans-Dietrich Genscher, a centrist Free Democrat. On 24 August the German Foreign Ministry issued a landmark statement, that if the bloodshed continued unabated Bonn would 'seriously re-examine' the question of extending recognition to Slovenia and Croatia within their existing frontiers.

Genscher's challenge – which was directed as much to his fellow foreign ministers in the EC as to the Serbs – followed the outbreak of more violence in Croatia in western and eastern Slavonia. In mid-August the Croats had attempted without success to blow up the bridges across the River Sava between Bosnia and Croatia, in order to stop General Nikola Uzelac, commander of the Yugoslav army base in Banja Luka, northern Bosnia, from sending tanks and troops across the river to help the Krajina forces round Pakrac. The Krajina Serbs and the Banja Luka corps struck back, attacking the Zagreb–Belgrade motorway at the town of Okučani. The motorway was the principal means of communication between Zagreb and the embattled eastern city of Osijek, and its loss added to the impression that Milošević and the army were intent on cutting up Croatia into a series of enclaves, which could be then picked off at will.

A week later, over the weekend of the 24th–25th, there was another disaster in the east, when the Yugoslav army without warning overran the fertile region of Baranja, north of Osijek, on the north-east border with Serbia. The offensive in Baranja was the clearest case yet of the army and the Serb paramilitaries acting together to extend the frontiers of a putative Greater Serbia. Firstly, there had been almost no ethnic conflict in Baranja to warrant army intervention. Secondly, the local council was controlled by Račan's reformed Communists, not by Tudjman's HDZ. Thirdly, the Serbs made up only 25 per cent of Baranja's population, compared to the Croats' 44 per cent. In spite of this, the army moved in, handed the region over to the government of the Serbian Autonomous Province of Slavonia, Baranja and Western Srem, and drove out the entire Croat and Hungarian population except for a few old people. After the fall of Baranja, the Croats fell back on another natural landmark, the River Drava. But the new frontline was now directly opposite the Hotel Pannonia in the middle of Osijek, and the city was to pay dearly in terms of shelling in the following three months.

Milošević insisted that Serbia was not involved in the war. Serbia supported the spontaneous uprising of the Serbs against the revived Ustashe government, but was not involved, or at war with anyone. That was the line Milošević gave the troika, Tudjman and Mesić. Yet the fall of every chunk of Croat territory to the Krajina forces was celebrated in almost ecstatic terms in the Belgrade media, to the point where the main evening news programme in Serbia at 7.30pm contained little except victorious battle reports. The Serbian media invented a euphemism for the brutal expulsion of non-Serb civilians from 'liberated' territory. It was called čišćenje terena (cleansing the terrain). It gave rise to a new expression among foreign journalists covering the war: 'ethnic cleansing'.

There was another brutal example of 'ethnic cleansing' the day after Baranja fell. The village of Kijevo, near Knin, perched up in the mountains on the Croat–Bosnian border, was the only solidly Croat community in the entire district. Its 1,000 or so inhabitants were all Croats. Many were elderly, a typical factor in villages in the Dalmatian interior since the Second World War. It had been surrounded for weeks, as the road from Kijevo to the coast passed through Serb villages. It offered no threat to the Krajina authorities. In spite of that, the Knin police and the local army base razed the village to its foundations on 26 August. The inhabitants were expelled to the coast, to eke out a wretched existence alongside the other refugees piling up in Croatia's deserted hotels.

The ominous news from Croatia and Germany's veiled threat to recognise the breakaway republics triggered another flurry of diplomatic activity in Brussels, where the EC decided to put into operation an idea mooted since August for a peace conference on Yugoslavia, to be held in The Hague. The invitation was forwarded to the Yugoslav presidency in Belgrade on 28 August with the news that the former British Foreign Secretary, Lord Carrington, had agreed to serve as president. There was little pretence that the federal government under Ante Marković had anything more to contribute, although Marković himself was invited to attend. The main players were to be the presidents of the six republics and General Kadijević. If Tudjman had hoped for a diplomatic breakthrough in The Hague on 7 September, he was disappointed. The only agreement struck at the talks was an agreement to hold more talks. As soon as Milošević flew back to Belgrade, the lull which invariably coincided with his international engagements gave way once more to renewed fighting.

The liberal Serbian weekly *Vreme* threw an interesting light on why this might have been so at the end of September, when the magazine published a stenograph of a telephone conversation between Milošević and the Bosnian Serb leader Karadžić in the middle of that month. Much of the conversation revolved around General Nikola Uzelac in Banja Luka who, according to the Serbian President, was ready to supply Karadžić with all the arms he needed. 'You will get everything,' Milošević told his Bosnian minion. 'Don't worry, we are the strongest. While we have the army they can do nothing to us.' Karadžić then switched tack to the Yugoslav air force bombing raids over Croatia. 'That's good, but what's going on with the bombing?' he asked. Milošević answered with devastating cynicism: 'Today's no good for aviation, there's a meeting of the European Community.'[17] In public, Milošević continued to claim he was not involved in the war.

The 'aviation' to which Milošević referred was becoming increasingly active. Between 15 and 20 September there were ten air raids in the Zagreb area alone, as the air force tried to cripple the Croat war effort by bombing the city's industrial zone. On 22 September Pleso airport, outside Zagreb, was hit. By far the most intense bombing took place in Vukovar, where a group of about 1,000 Croat fighters led by Mile Dedaković were obstinately blocking the army's advance into Slavonia. In mid-September, when journalists were still able to slip in and out of the town, Vukovar was badly damaged but still standing. By the end of October, it had been shelled from land and bombed from the air to such a degree that scarcely a building was intact. Vukovar assumed enormous symbolic importance to both sides. Without it, Serbia's territorial gains in eastern Slavonia were threatened. To the Croats, the unexpectedly fierce defence of the town against overwhelming odds inspired hopeful, if unrealistic, talk of a 'Croatian Stalingrad'.

Encountering bitter recrimination from the Croatian public for failing to hit back, Tudjman finally gave up his policy of avoiding direct confrontation with the army and ordered the National Guard to surround the army bases. 'Talk of a ceasefire while towns are being destroyed in Croatia is ridiculous,' explained Luka Bebić, who had replaced Špegelj as Croatian Defence Minister. 'Bit by bit we are losing control over our territory, waiting for the results of the EC peace initiative. Now we have no more illusions about getting help and are undertaking an offensive.'[18] It was no longer possible to surround all of the bases. Those in Knin, Vukovar and Petrinja could all be supplied from Belgrade whatever Tudjman chose to do. Vinkovci and Osijek had been emptied of most of their equipment by the army months back. But many lay in government-held territory and, a day after the offensive began on 15 September, Zagreb was already claiming to have taken twenty garrisons and to have captured 400 soldiers. Koprivnica capitulated without a fight. General Vladmir Trifunović surrendered the large base at Varaždin on 22 September, in order to save the lives of his 300 soldiers – a 'crime' for which he was sentenced to fifteen years' imprisonment in Belgrade in the spring of 1992. 'You shouldn't have come back from Varaždin alive,' a colleague told him. 'I was told I did not know Serbian history, because Serbia needs dead heroes it can take pride in,' he recalled, after he was released from jail and pardoned in January 1996.[19] In Bjelovar, one of the largest bases, the local commander went out fighting in a twelve-hour battle, and blew up the ammunition dump; the blast tore the roofs off neighbouring houses.

The siege of the army bases was a risky move and brought down accusations from Brussels of wrecking the EC 'peace initiative'. Van den Broek charged Tudjman with 'deliberately escalating the conflict'.[20] The siege also invited a furious retaliation by the army, which promptly attacked the tourist resort of Dubrovnik, on the exposed southernmost tip of the Dalmatian coastline. By 3 October Mesić was sufficiently anguished about the threat to Dubrovnik to write letters of appeal to the UN Secretary General, Perez de Cuellar, President Bush, Queen Beatrix of the Netherlands, King Baudouin of Belgium, Queen Margarethe of Denmark and the heads of state of Ireland and Czechoslovakia. But the army's assault on Dubrovnik was only the beginning. On the same day Mesić sent his letter to the UN about Dubrovnik, the Yugoslav navy blockaded all the Adriatic ports south of Pula. As rail and most road connections between Zagreb and Dalmatia had been cut already by the Krajina militia, the naval blockade added to Dalmatia's feeling of isolation. The Adriatic islanders were worst off. They were unable even to fish.

In Belgrade, the Serb members of the presidency decided the time was now ripe to stage a putsch to get rid of their unwanted president. While Mesić was in Zagreb on 4 October, Kostić of Montenegro demanded that a meeting be held and gave Mesić a few hours to reach the Yugoslav capital. The air raids on many towns in Croatia that day and the furious fighting round Vukovar made it impossible for Mesić to get to Belgrade in time, as they knew very well. But, claiming that Mesić was neglecting his constitutional obligations, Kostić and the three Serbs pronounced Mesić deposed *in absentia* and declared themselves the sole members of the presidency. The legality of this decision was tested by a summons that arrived from Brussels that day to attend a second session of the peace conference on Yugoslavia in The Hague the following week. Since the first meeting, Lord Carrington and the five-member arbitration commission he had set up had concluded a set of proposals to end the conflict, which they intended to put to Milošević, Tudjman and the other four presidents. Carrington wished to defuse the growing calls for the recognition of Slovenia and Croatia (the Holy See on 4 October for the first time publicly appealed for recognition) by conceding the essence of sovereignty to all six republics within the loosest of possible confederations. There was to be no change in Yugoslavia's internal frontiers. In return, Croatia was to lift the blockade on remaining army bases to enable the army to withdraw from Croatia *in toto*.

The day before the Hague meeting the three Croats – Tudjman, Mesić and Marković – sipped coffee gloomily in the Ban's Palace before the long journey ahead. The Serbs on the presidency were flying direct from Belgrade to Holland. The army refused to open the airspace over Croatia even for the day to let their nominal commander-in-chief get on a plane. As a result, the three Croats faced the prospect of driving to Austria and then catching a plane from there. Just before they were due to set off, they were shaken in their seats by an enormous explosion that blew off part of the palace roof. Tudjman insisted it was an air force jet on a mission to kill him. The patience of the long-suffering Yugoslav Prime Minister finally snapped. Insisting that Kadijević was personally responsible for the outrage, he faxed Belgrade with a demand that either Kadijević resign or he would not return to Belgrade.

The Croats got to Strasbourg, where the European Parliament was in session, with the aura of martyrs after the outrage in the Ban's Palace. At home the Sabor was meeting in the depressing surroundings of the cellars of the Ina gas company. The deputies declared that the three-month moratorium after Brioni had expired without a constitutional settlement and demanded immediate international recognition. The last ties with Belgrade were cut, although Mesić and Marković had no intention of returning to Belgrade anyway. After echoing the Sabor's plea to the European Parliament, Mesić hurried on to The Hague with Tudjman. There, Kadijević and Milošević were told that the army must leave Croatia within thirty days. The Serbs were by now furious with the Europeans. In their eyes, Carrington's plan buried Yugoslavia as an international subject and conceded everything to the Croats and Slovenes. They were particularly annoyed by the order to remove the army from Croatia, and insisted that, while they were ready to quit certain parts of the republic, it would remain to protect districts in which Serbs formed a substantial part of the population.

Kadijević was as good as his word. After the Serbs left The Hague for Belgrade and the Croats returned to Zagreb, the army rapidly pulled out of Istria and Rijeka, only to build up in east Slavonia and around Dubrovnik. In east Slavonia the peaceful community in Ilok was deported westwards in another example of 'ethnic cleansing'. The motive behind the attack on Ilok was pure expansionism. The 5,000 inhabitants of this old castle town surrounded by vineyards were mostly Croat. The Serbs, as in Vukovar, made up about a quarter of the population. There was a sizeable community also of Protestant Slovaks. There was no history of conflict between any of the three groups. In spite of that, the army summoned the townspeople to a public meeting where the Croats were ordered to leave. A handful, including one of the priests and a few women, insisted on remaining. The rest trudged west with their belongings in their hands to a very insecure refuge in Vinkovci.

The worsening fighting in eastern Slavonia, the rumbles south of Dubrovnik and the Serbs' refusal to accept the peace conference's proposals led Carrington to give serious consideration to introducing selective sanctions on Yugoslavia – that is, on Serbia and Montenegro. As a result, the next plenary session of the conference on 18 October opened in an acrimonious mood, with the Serbs increasingly embittered by what they claimed was the Europeans' overt support for the Croat 'separatists'. Even the Americans, the firmest supporters of Yugoslav unity back in June, had changed tack. Still insisting that the US would not recognise any of the new republics, Washington was now blaming Serbia as the chief disturber of the peace, and accusing Milošević of using the army to carve out a Greater Serbia.

Carrington tried to get the six presidents to agree on three points – a ceasefire, deblocking army bases in Croatia and their evacuation from Croatia. He then read out the final constitutional proposals for reforming Yugoslavia as a league of sovereign republics. To Milošević's annoyance, Montenegro accepted them, causing an embarrassing split in the Serb ranks. The Serbs were further nettled when Carrington took the microphone away from Kostić as he tried to speak in the name of the presidency.

Back in Belgrade, Kostić fired off a resolution containing the Serb conditions for accepting the Carrington package. Yugoslavia, he said, would accept the proposed confederation, but only if the Serb regions of Croatia were accorded special status (and not in Croatia but in Yugoslavia) and if the Prevlaka peninsula, south of Dubrovnik, was handed over to Montenegro, assuring Yugoslav control of the bay of Kotor, the only suitable harbour for the Yugoslav navy. Between 18 and 25 October, when the third plenary session was due to take place, the peace conference studied Serbia's objections. But they also studied those of the Kosovo Albanians, the Hungarians from Vojvodina and the Muslims of Serbia's Sandžak region. The result was a compromise:

Serbs in Croatia would be eligible for an ill-defined special status but so would the Kosovo Albanians in Serbia. Milošević was outraged by the attempt to trade off the Krajina against Kosovo and at the end of October mobilisation was stepped up in Serbia and Montenegro. Kadijević obediently accused Croatia of using 'worse methods of genocide than those in the Second World War', and charged Germany with 'attacking our country for the third time this century'. After failing to get the Europeans to condemn 'separatism', the Serbs resolved to finish the war on their own terms, with the capture of Vukovar and Dubrovnik.

17

'Danke Deutschland'

I am deeply worried that any early selective recognition could widen the present conflict and fuel an explosive situation, especially in Bosnia. ...
UN Secretary General to the Dutch Foreign Minister,
10 December 1991[1]

The Serbs tightened their grip round the two hostage cities of Vukovar and Dubrovnik. Of the two, Vukovar was in incomparably the worse position. Bombed by air and land almost day and night, it had no priceless architectural treasures to engage the world's fickle attention.

Dubrovnik was different. Since the first week in October the city had been surrounded by Montenegrin troops of the Yugoslav army on the landward side. Electricity was cut off and so was water. To the east, Božidar Vučurević, the burly Mayor of the Bosnian Serb stronghold of Trebinje (his nickname was *kamijondžija*, meaning lorrydriver), was loudly claiming Dubrovnik as the future seaport of the Bosnian Serb state. But Dubrovnik's ancient churches and monuments were its salvation. Newspaper photographs showing black smoke belching above the medieval walls provoked a collective wail from the world's art lovers, although in fact the black smoke was caused by a bomb hitting the marina. The Serbs and Montenegrins did indeed shell the old city, including the famous street running through the middle, the Stradun. But the damage was trifling compared to the punishment meted out to Zadar, Osijek, Sisak and Karlovac, and was utterly insignificant compared to what was happening in and around Vukovar. The Yugoslav army wanted Dubrovnik whole, not in fragments, and did their best to persuade the Croat troops crouching in the turrets of the city walls to evacuate the civilian population.

By the end of October the situation inside the city was becoming acute, as 50,000 civilians eked out an increasingly precarious existence on diminishing supplies of water and food. However, if the situation inside the city was dire, the Serbs were also suffering – from an unprecedented wave of international criticism. The bombardment of a Unesco-designated historic monument generated enormous ill will among people who had never heard of, and did not care about, the humbler towns and villages of eastern Slavonia. Throughout the siege several highly educated and articulate foreigners remained in the city, such as Kathleen Wilkes, a philosophy lecturer from Oxford University, whose eloquent accounts of the suffering of the inhabitants were published regularly in many Western newspapers. The city was a well-known tourist resort. The fact that Dubrovnik's Serbian population was minute laid bare the ugly nature of Serb 'ethnic cleansing'. The army was embarrassed by the storm of criticism yet too proud to withdraw. They had no clear idea what to do next.

Spying this weak chink in the Serbs' armour, a group of Dubrovnik refugees decided to brazen their way back into the city by sea under the floodlight of international publicity. Their plan was to sail on a ferry through the naval blockade on a purely humanitarian mission, and challenge the Yugoslav navy chief, Admiral Stane Brovet, to stop them in their tracks. After the failure of the third plenary session of The Hague peace conference to achieve any progress, Mesić decided to join the trip himself. He was the lawful President of the presidency, which was the collective commander-in-chief of the army and navy. Let the Yugoslav navy fire on its own supreme chief!

The returning refugees named themselves the St Blaise Foundation, after the city's patron saint. They arranged to depart from Rijeka on 28 October, in the ferry *Slavija*. Mesić jumped on board at Split, where he found himself in the company of a gaggle of human rights activists (most of whom were bitter enemies of the HDZ), one of Croatia's most popular folk singers (whose house near Dubrovnik had been burned down) and about twenty foreign correspondents. As the *Slavija* set out from Split, dozens of smaller boats with other Croats joined the convoy.

The little armada caused a tremendous stir at home and abroad. At the first port of call, on the Adriatic island of Korčula, thousands of local villagers lined the harbour to greet the *Slavija* as it sailed in. But in the Dubrovnik channel, about twelve miles from land, the nerves of the crew and passengers of the *Slavija* were tested when the ferry was stopped by four naval patrol-boats. However, Mesić was one step ahead of the navy. Knowing that the attention of the world's media was concentrated on his ferry, he told the crew to connect the *Slavija*'s loud hailers to the captain's radio, so that everyone on board (and Radio Bar, in nearby Montenegro) would be able to listen in to his conversation with the naval chiefs. The results were sometimes hilarious, as an unidentified colonel from the Yugoslav navy bawled out without any introduction: 'Listen, Mesić!', to which Mesić retorted: 'To you, Colonel, I am a member of the presidency and this year's President of the presidency!'[2]

Admiral Brovet, whether or not he suspected that his words were being recorded, was more polite than the anonymous Colonel. 'I have received reliable information that you are carrying heavy weapons and well-equipped "specials" [paramilitaries],' he said. He insisted that the convoy would be able to proceed only if it docked for inspection in the port of Zelenik, in Montenegro.

Mesić, by now enjoying his public exchange with the disconcerted Admiral, agreed to the inspection, but only on condition that it took place on the high seas. He insisted also that the *Slavija* would not sail alone to Dubrovnik. It was the whole convoy or nothing. 'No one is going back,' he announced. 'Imprison us, fire on us, you're the strongest, you have the force, but we are agreeing to an inspection and then we are all off. You can shoot if you want to shoot, but remember Europe is listening.'[3]

A few of the vessels were sent back after an inspection, because their papers were not in order. The *Slavija* made no complaint about that, and so the diminished flotilla sailed on at a slow pace, arriving at 7am the following morning to a rather bemused welcome from the exhausted and frightened inhabitants of Dubrovnik. Did the flotilla 'save' Dubrovnik? Probably not. The Montenegrin government was already embarrassed by the failure of the siege and had decided to withdraw its troops from the campaign. In one sense it was Dubrovnik which had saved Croatia. The assault on the city, which had not been besieged since the Napoleonic wars, contributed greatly to a climate abroad in favour of granting Croatia diplomatic recognition. More than at any stage in the war hitherto, Milošević was pinpointed as an expansionist bully. The Belgrade media's attempt to portray the conflict as a Yugoslav crusade against revived Croatian Fascism had never been that successful. Now it was shown up as a sham.

But there was a drawback to the Dubrovnik campaign, as far as Croatia was concerned. It diverted what little international attention on Croatia there was from the agony of Vukovar. While foreign journalists and European diplomats complained about the damage to the tiles of the red roofs of the Old Town, and about a few shells which fell into the ancient high street, the Stradun, the Yugoslav army and the Serb paramilitaries had a free hand in Vukovar to wreak a savage revenge on the Croats who had defied them for so long.

The army was hurrying along the assault on Vukovar, as the peace conference dragged on. On 5 November at a session of the conference in The Hague, Lord Carrington produced a document amending the previous proposal for a union of sovereign republics, taking on board some of the Serbs' objections. This time the document recommended a two-tier association of sovereign republics on the one hand, and a state of equal republics 'comprising those republics that wish to remain in it' on the other. In essence, it was a return to the Gligorov–Izetbegović 'Four-plus-two' package. It partly met the Serbs' demand that an internationally recognised Yugoslav state must remain in existence. However, it made no significant concession to the Serbs over the surrender of Croatian territory, and for that reason there was no agreement.

But Milošević could not carry on saying neither yes nor no for ever. The military campaigning season was drawing to a close as winter snows descended on northern Yugoslavia, making the prospect of substantial further territorial gains less likely. Secondly, the EC was trailing the prospect of trade sanctions on Belgrade. With an eye on both factors, Milošević on 9 November told Brussels that he would agree to an international force under UN auspices being deployed in crisis areas of Croatia. Just under two weeks later, the UN Secretary General, Perez de Cuellar, accepted the proposal, on condition that the European Community agreed. By that time Vukovar had fallen.

The last glimpse most outsiders caught of Vukovar before the net closed round it was in late September. By then, the only way in or out of the town was a farmer's track that ran from the village of Bogdanovci through fields of corn. The track was dangerous and no one ever knew whether the Croats still held every stretch of this perilously thin line of communication. The town already was a shocking and disfigured parody of the attractive old town that had existed before the war. The winding high street with its steeply pitched roofs and rustic baroque façades was pitted with craters, fallen masonry and broken glass. The streets were virtually deserted. In a bomb-shelter, one of hundreds built throughout Yugoslavia during the Tito era in the event of a Russian attack, it became clear where the people had all gone – underground. They were all women, faces pale and strained from weeks spent without sunlight, who jumped when any man entered their sanctuary. Children swung from the metal rods of the bunk beds they had rigged up in the darkness, silently and without joy.

Over the next few weeks Vukovar's link to the world through the cornfield became increasingly tenuous as the Yugoslav army concentrated more and more of its manpower and formidable armoury around the city. Most of the younger civilians fled along that dangerous track, usually at night, leaving only soldiers, the wounded, the old and the Serbs behind. Several thousand Serbs, mostly old people, endured the same existence in bunkers as the remaining Croats, keeping their thoughts about the rights and wrongs of the war to themselves. The hospital filled up with wounded soldiers, but the chief doctor, Vesna Bosanac, had less and less space and medicine with which to tend them in the basement, where the hospital had moved to escape bombardment. Two international medical convoys from the organisation Médecins sans Frontières made it into the town, but the Croats accused the Yugoslav army of using the aid convoys as a shield to advance their frontlines. There was talk of sending an aid convoy down the Danube, but it came to nothing; the Serbs did not want any aid reaching the town and prolonging the Croats' resistance.

In Zagreb the success of a few thousand Croat fighters in holding up the might of the Yugoslav People's Army for several months gave rise to optimistic talk of a David and Goliath struggle. Croatian Radio and the television gave themselves over entirely to the war effort. The programmes were now all news reports from the frontlines, uplifting feature stories about patriotic couples, mothers of soldiers and activities of various brigades in the field or during training. Sandwiched between these were slots of patriotic entertainment, pop, rock or folk songs about the war sung by well-known stars of the music world. An enormous amount of Croatia's war art was devoted to Vukovar, not only on radio and television but in the posters reading 'VukoWAR' that appeared on the streets of Zagreb that autumn. It easily eclipsed the slogans devoted to raising public consciousness about other endangered towns, such as 'Osijek will never be Osek' (the Serb version of the word) and 'Vinkovci – gateway to Croatia'.

As October turned into November this huge emotional investment began to look counter-productive, as it became increasingly probable that 'Croatia's Stalingrad' would succumb. On Croatian Radio less time was given to the crackling reports from the sole reporter who had stayed in his home town to record its destruction. There was another problem the government had with Vukovar. There were few paramilitary organisations in Croatia – in contrast to Serbia – but one of them had ambitions to rival, if not supplant, the government army.

Dobroslav Paraga had thickened out since his arrest and imprisonment in 1980 at the age of twenty for collecting signatures for a petition demanding the release of political criminals. With the advent of political freedom, Paraga had embraced the extreme right and revived the old Party of Rights. Like its Ustashe predecessor, the revamped Party of Rights was a more or less Fascist organisation with a large paramilitary wing that attracted the same kind of youths as those drawn into Arkan's Tigers in Serbia. Hos, short for Hrvatske Obrambene Snage (Croat Defence Forces), set up its headquarters opposite the grand old Hotel Esplanade, complete with crewcut paramilitaries in black camouflage strutting around outside the door. Paraga despatched his units to various frontlines to plug gaps left by the National Guard, but they homed in on Vukovar, and by October formed a substantial presence in the town. Tudjman did not like Hos, or the kind of hostile criticism in the foreign press that the organisation provoked. He did not like the way Paraga used every opportunity at his regular press conferences to assail the government for 'betraying' Vukovar and to claim that HDZ was riddled with Kos spies. Nor did he like the commander of the Croat forces in Vukovar, Mile Dedaković, who sided with Hos and used the media to broadcast complaints that the government was deliberately starving the fighters in Vukovar of weapons.

Paraga's tirades and Dedaković's accusations from within the besieged town spawned a host of rumours in early November about deals, betrayals and double-agents. It was said that Vukovar was being abandoned in order to get rid of Hos, and that the town's agony was being stretched out on purpose, in order to force the West to recognise Croatia out of sympathy. Tudjman did want to get rid of Hos, and in mid-November he banned it and had Paraga arrested on trumped-up charges. But the idea that the Croatian government actually *wanted* Vukovar to fall was nonsense. At the most, there was a tacit acceptance of the fact that Serbia would not agree to a genuine ceasefire until Vukovar was in Serb hands.

Four days before the town fell I interviewed General Anton Tus, Croatia's commander-in-chief, who convincingly explained that it was impossible for the government to divert any more arms to Vukovar without leaving the country's other frontlines horribly exposed. Vukovar's fall formed no part of a strategy aimed at recognition; on the contrary, General Tus believed the fall of Vukovar would lead to a massive assault on the rest of Slavonia which could be countered only by years of sustained guerrilla warfare. 'Militarily it would have been better to bypass Vukovar, where they have lost 200 tanks and thousands of troops in fruitless infantry attacks,' he said. 'This is a political matter. The Serbs have proclaimed Vukovar the capital of a new Serb province in eastern Croatia and all military considerations have been subordinated to this.'[4]

On 17 November the half-starved and exhausted defenders of Vukovar surrendered. Dedaković had already slipped out of the town a fortnight previously with some of the fighters, leaving his subordinate, Branko Borković, *mali jastreb* (little falcon), to hold the fort. Through the winding, ruined streets past the blasted 1960s-era hotel, the Dunav, marched victorious columns of Yugoslav army troops and Serb volunteers in Chetnik hats, many of the latter keeping up a chilling chorus of 'Slobo, daj salate, biće mesa biće mesa klaćemo Hrvate' – Slobo, bring the salad, there will be meat, we're slaughtering the Croats. The song was a grimly accurate prediction of the course of events following Vukovar's 'liberation'.

The mostly elderly civilians, who had spent weeks underground in freezing cellars living on food from tin cans, were allowed to trudge out of the town towards Vinkovci in a long, forlorn column, carrying whatever possessions they could hold in their hands. Dr Bosanac's patients in Vukovar hospital, most of whom were soldiers, were not so lucky. A group of observers from the Red Cross had insisted on accompanying the Serbs into the hospital, and on 18 October 106 patients were evacuated to Croatia. But, the following day at 11am, the Red Cross were expelled on the orders of a Yugoslav army colonel, Veselin Šljivančanin. All but 60 of the 420 remaining patients were removed from the hospital, killed and the bodies dumped in a mass grave in a sheep farm outside the town, later to become the subject of a UN war crimes investigation. There were fears that Dr Bosanac might be killed as well, because the media in Serbia quickly started up a strong campaign against 'Vukovar's Dr Mengele', which appeared to pave the way for her execution. Vigorous protests from international medical associations resulted in her release after a few days. Less fortunate was Siniša Glavašević, the young correspondent of Radio Croatia in the besieged town. He 'disappeared' and was almost certainly killed.

The fall of Vukovar was an agonising psychological and military blow to most Croats, so much so that Croatian television delayed broadcasting the news for several hours. However, the collapse could not be concealed for ever and it unleashed a new wave of recrimination against Tudjman's leadership, and even fears of a mini-civil war inside Croatia between the government army and members of Hos. Three days after the fall of Vukovar, Paraga and Dedaković were arrested under a new law enabling the police to hold detainees for up to six days without pressing charges. Tudjman went on to the airwaves to defend the arrests and the decision forcibly to shut down Hos headquarters opposite the Hotel Esplanade. He virtually accused Dedaković of being a double-agent and insisted he had 'proof of direct ties between Kos [the Yugoslav intelligence service] and Hos, with the aim of bringing down Croatia's democratic government'.[5] In a sideswipe at Paraga, he railed at the revival of 'Fascist symbols' – in particular the U sign of the old Ustashe – for which he held Hos responsible. The arrests were signs of Tudjman's grave political weakness, not of his resolve to defend Croatia against the threat of political extremism.

The Yugoslav army and the Krajina Serbs gained an enormous psychological boost from the fall of Vukovar, and pressed forward within hours towards panic-stricken Osijek. 'The moment Vukovar fell, Croatia lost the war, because we could have marched to Zagreb without any problem,' recalled General Života Panić, the commander in charge of the final assault on Vukovar.[6] General Panić claimed that the Yugoslav army in fact entered the outskirts of Osijek. The capital of eastern Slavonia by then was half deserted. Heavy bombardment from Serb-held Baranja, only a mile away on the other side of the River Sava, had done enormous damage to the stately old city, destroying the power supply and forcing most civilians to take up residence in freezing cellars, just as they had done in Vukovar. Several hundred people found an uncertain resting place in the city's deserted underground shopping centre. Priests even held Masses in one of the shops, the city's churches having become too unsafe for services. The news of the fall of Vukovar fell particularly hard on Osijek and the taking of two strategic villages to the south of the city, at Ernestinovo and Laslovo, convinced many people that the dreaded figure of Arkan and his Tigers would soon be strolling down their cobbled streets. As I left the city, one of the few men I saw in civilian dress on the deserted streets ran up to my car and begged me to smuggle him past the police checkpoint in the boot of the car – the authorities having slapped a ban on anyone leaving, in order to stem an exodus. 'The Serbs have hundreds of tanks and we have a couple of rocket-propelled grenades,' one young soldier in the shopping centre-cum-sanctuary said. 'Osijek is finished, we are dead meat already.'[7]

The soldier was wrong. In Dalmatia the Serbs launched a short, bloody offensive, killing twenty-five mainly elderly people in the village of Skradin and destroying the strategically vital bridge at Maslenica, which provided the only land link between Dalmatia and continental Croatia. Dalmatia was as good as cut off. But the knock-out blow that General Tus had predicted never took place. Milošević had already committed Yugoslavia in theory to accepting a UN peace-keeping force and was only stalling until the operation in Vukovar had been wound up. As soon as it was over, he dropped all obstacles to the peace plan, and switched over into a firm supporter of international involvement.

The Serbs accepted the peace plan because their goals had more or less been achieved. According to General Kadijević, the army high command and the Serb leadership had two plans for the creation of a modified Yugoslav state, really a Greater Serbia, which had been formulated shortly before the multi-party elections in Slovenia and Croatia in the spring of 1989.

The first plan was for Slovenia to leave Yugoslavia in peace, enabling the Yugoslav army to withdraw its equipment unhindered into Croatia and Bosnia. Croatia was then to be provoked into an unwinnable conflict, which would be followed by a knock-out military blow. According to Kadijević, the army intended to cut Croatia into four segments, by driving a wedge from Gradiška to Virovitica, another from Bihać to Karlovac and then to Zagreb, and a third from Mostar to Split.[8] With the destruction of Croatia's capacity to resist, Kadijević continued, the new Yugoslav state could then dictate its western frontiers and let whatever fragments of Croatia it did not wish to absorb go free.

Kadijević said that what he called the pro-Yugoslav members of the presidency were party to this plan early on; he himself said the claim that the Yugoslav army was keeping the peace between the warring factions was simply a smokescreen, intended to muddle the non-Serb members of the federal presidency.

The Yugoslav army chief blamed several factors for the failure of this first plan, especially Slovenia's (unnecessary) violence when it broke away from Yugoslavia, German meddling and Milošević's failure effectively to mobilise enough recruits for the front. Thus, although the Croatian army was crippled and drained by the loss of Vukovar, the front in western Slavonia collapsed through lack of manpower.

According to Kadijević, the army in the autumn of 1991 was forced to switch to a modified version of the plan. The attempt to cut Croatia into four enclaves had to be abandoned, as was the assault on Zagreb and the complete annihilation of the Croatian army. 'The lack of success in mobilisation and the desertion rate made it necessary to modify the tasks ... of the JNA in Croatia,' he recalled.[9]

After the fall of Vukovar, Kadijević considered that the balance sheet was as follows:

The main tasks of the modified plan of operation were carried out
- all Serb regions in Croatia, with the exception of part of western Slavonia, in close co-operation with the Serb rebels, had been liberated. That comprised about a third of the territory of the former Republic of Croatia
- in the course of the battle the future army of the Serbian Krajina was built up, and had been equipped by the JNA with the necessary arms and equipment
- the JNA was able to withdraw most of its equipment from Croatia and redeploy it for its future tasks
- severe losses had been inflicted on the Croatian army, so it was no longer capable of any kind of serious activity, even of a defensive nature ... .

The only thing not achieved in the operation in Croatia, and which could have been achieved were it not for the failed mobilisation and desertion, was the complete destruction of the Croatian army. ...[10]

Milošević's view of the war almost certainly coincided with that of Kadijević, although he can scarcely have appreciated the General's complaints about the feeble mobilisation supposedly carried out by the civilian leadership in Belgrade. He had certainly not had his hand forced by the international community, which proved singularly reluctant to take sides or name an aggressor in the conflict. The EC declaration of 12 November came closest to accusing the Serbs when it 'condemned the further escalation of attacks on Vukovar, Dubrovnik and other towns in Croatia'.[11] Other than that, the long list of EC and UN declarations on Yugoslavia consisted of little more than platitudes, oozing 'concern' and expressing a resolute determination 'to remain seized of the situation'.

Nor was Milošević moved by principled opposition to the war at home. The main opposition politicians in Serbia – Vuk Drašković of the Serbian Renewal Movement, Zoran Djindjić of the Democratic Party, and Šešelj, the leader of the Radicals, attacked him for failing, as they saw it, to win the war; some challenged the methods used in the war; they did not challenge the goals of the war itself.

Šešelj remained true to his conviction that Croatia proper consisted of the land that could be seen from the tower of Zagreb cathedral. Any agreement that left the Serbian frontier east of the Karlobag–Karlovac–Virovitica line was a scandal. Drašković and Djindjić were less extreme than that. They hankered after an enlarged Serbia including Bosnia and much of Croatia, but had deluded themselves into thinking this could be achieved without bloodshed. Genuine anti-war groups in Serbia, the 'Women in Black' and the Civic Alliance party, had a minute following.

Milošević faced the same problem as Kadijević – not principled opposition to the Greater Serbian ideology but unprincipled desertions. In several towns in the prosperous Šumadija region of central Serbia there were virtual mutinies as mobilised conscripts refused to go to the front. One soldier in September even drove his armoured personnel carrier back from the frontline at Šid and parked it outside the federal parliament in protest. The liberal journalists of *Vreme* tittered about such antics, comparing him to Mathias Rust, the young German who landed his plane in Red Square. They also published soldiers' accounts of chaotic scenes at the front, of being driven leaderless and goalless into the cornfields of Slavonia. Time and time again the complaint was raised that Serbia's goal in the war had never been stated. No one knew for what frontier the Serbs were fighting.

The muddle in the ranks was compounded by a struggle for power between Milošević and the old generals, headed by Adžić and Kadijević. Although they shared a broad set of aims the generals – many of them Croatian Serbs – were more determined to carry on to Zagreb than Milošević was. The Serbian leader was less interested in a crusade through solidly Croat territory, and he distrusted all the older generals in any case.[12]

The war had already homogenised Serbs behind his government and obliterated the opposition as a serious force. As a politician he had to balance the Serbs' contradictory wish to help the Croatian Serbs win and at the same time keep Serbia out of the war. On 23 November he accepted an invitation from the UN Secretary General's recently appointed mediator for Yugoslavia, the former US Secretary of State Cyrus Vance, to go to Geneva. There, alongside Tudjman and General

Kadijević, he signed a four-point declaration. The terms comprised a pledge by Croatia to lift the blockade on Yugoslav army bases immediately and a pledge by General Kadijević to withdraw the army from Croatia as soon as it was free to move. Both sides agreed to a ceasefire and to allow the unhindered movement of international aid agencies. It was the fourteenth ceasefire so far. But this time, although mutual shelling continued for weeks, it more or less lasted. Three days later Yugoslavia's permanent representative to the UN forwarded a formal request to the Security Council to establish a peace-keeping operation in Yugoslavia.[13] The war was almost over.

The Secretary General gave a favourable response the following day, although the Security Council remained far from convinced. In the meantime Vance and Marrack Goulding, the UN Under-Secretary General for political affairs, drew up a draft plan for the deployment of a peace-keeping force in Croatia. The plan centred on proposals to create three demilitarised 'UN Protected Areas' in Croatia, known as Unpas, covering areas with a pre-war Serb majority, or with a substantial Serb minority, in eastern Slavonia, western Slavonia and Krajina. These Unpas were to be entirely demilitarised and all Yugoslav army, Croatian army or paramilitary organisations would be disbanded inside them. The Unpas were to be patrolled by lightly armed infantry and UN civilian police, operating in concert with local police. Point No. 19 of the plan said that the local police were to reflect 'the national composition of the population before the recent hostilities'.[14] Point No. 20 said the UN would 'facilitate' the return to their homes of all those displaced by the conflict who wished to go back. The plan's authors stressed that the creation of the Unpas would in no way prejudice or otherwise affect the outcome of a political settlement in Yugoslavia, and would not address, therefore, the question of sovereignty over the Unpas. For that reason, the plan made no reference to the form of local civilian government inside the Unpas.

Lord Carrington, chairman of the virtually moribund Peace Conference, certainly did not want the question of Croatia's sovereignty addressed outside the context of an overall package for Yugoslavia, which dealt with all the republics. Nor did the new UN Secretary General, Boutros Boutros-Ghali. He made public his fear about the selective recognition of individual republics in a letter to the Dutch Foreign Minister on 10 December, in which he homed in on worries that recognition could 'fuel an explosive situation, especially in Bosnia'.

Within the Security Council such views won strong support from the British, the French and the Russians. But outside the Security Council they were not supported by Germany, Austria or most of the new, right-of-centre governments in the former Warsaw Pact bloc and the former Soviet Union. A few of them, including the three Baltic states and

Ukraine, had already recognised Croatia and Slovenia, not that their recognition was of great importance. Of the rest, Albania, Slovakia, the Czech Republic and Bulgaria were the most sympathetic. But it was Germany's support for Zagreb that most worried Carrington and the British and French governments. They were used to Germany remaining content with the status of economic giant and political dwarf, and were angered by Genscher's refusal to toe the line. And Genscher's patience with the Serbs had snapped. Since August the Foreign Ministry in Bonn had been warning that, if the Serbs continued to overrun Croatian territory, Germany would be forced to reconsider Croat and Slovene demands for recognition. After 23 November, Carrington, the British and the French thought they finally had a ceasefire. But Genscher's mind had been made up by the butchery in Vukovar, and he resolved on using the European foreign ministers' discussions on the forthcoming Maastricht Treaty to exact a *quid pro quo*: German co-operation with Britain over amendments to the treaty in return for Britain agreeing to Croatian recognition.

Germany's behaviour provoked a spasm of chauvinistic hysteria in Britain in particular, which vented itself in articles in the newspapers suggesting that Genscher had gone mad or resembled Hitler. In parliament there were mutterings on both sides of the political divide about 'the overmighty Hun' rearing his head once again. But even in the anti-recognition camp there was considerable division of opinion.

The former Prime Minister Margaret Thatcher had made plain her opposition to German reunification in 1990 and might have been expected to join the bandwagon against German 'aggression' in the Balkans. Instead, on 22 November, she gave a widely publicised television interview in which she not only pleaded for recognition of the new republics but roundly supported supplying them with arms as well.

In Britain, Thatcher was almost a lone voice. The former Labour Party leader Michael Foot and a few other left-wingers opposed Serbian aggression. But they were most unusual. The Serbs were in the fortunate position of having allies at both ends of Britain's political spectrum. They ranged from Sir Alfred Sherman, Thatcher's former speechwriter, on the right, to Labour MPs such as Tony Benn and Dennis Skinner. Among the country's more influential columnists were strong supporters of the Serb cause. They included Ed Pearce, of the *Guardian*, Richard West, author and frequent contributor to the *Spectator* and the *Daily Telegraph*, and the author and former *Observer* journalist Nora Beloff. A typical British commentary on the nature of the war in Yugoslavia was that of Basil Davidson in the prestigious *London Review of Books* in May 1996 – all the more significant as it came well *after* the horrors experienced by the Muslims of Srebrenica and other towns in eastern Bosnia were revealed to the world. To Davidson, the essential difference between the the Serbs and Croats was that 'between Croat Catholicism, admittedly aggressive and proselytising, and the gentle Serbian Orthodoxy of Byzantium ...'[15] – an extraordinary evaluation of the respective conducts of the Serbian Church hierarchy and its Croat counterpart.

The bitter hostility of so many British writers and politicians to Croatia and the mawkish, sentimental tone so often adopted to 'much misunderstood Serbia' bound many threats together: the average Englishman's almost instinctive Protestant fear of Catholicism, an ever-growing paranoia about Germany which became such a feature of British political discourse in the 1990s, a vague feeling that there was a certain analogy between the Krajina Serbs and the Croats, and between the Ulster Loyalists and Sinn Fein, perhaps even an uneasy feeling that the dissolution of one multi-national state in Europe – Yugoslavia – could not but encourage a similar process in the United Kingdom.

A second factor shaping British perceptions of the Yugoslav conflict were the respective strengths of the Serb and Croat communities in Britain. The Serbs formed a far bigger and better-organised community in Britain than the Croats, linked together through a network of Serb Orthodox parishes and Chetnik associations that dated back to the late 1940s. The exiled Serb royal house was also based in Britain, and maintained strong ties to the British royal family. The Yugoslav Embassy in Britain, as in so many other countries, was manned almost entirely by Serbs.

Finally, there was the Yugoslav leaders' ability to speak English – an important factor in a country where most people believed that all foreigners who wanted to be taken seriously ought to speak English. Again the Croats lagged behind. Milošević spoke English with a kind of folksy, American saloon-bar twang, which sounded good on television, while his foreign minister, Vladislav Jovanović, cultivated a mincing, upper-class brand of English. Tudjman's essays into English were either inaudible or incomprehensible. The Serb leaders were always careful to appear smiling. Tudjman usually looked either nervous or furious.

Although Thatcher's speech was dismissed by the Foreign Office, Britain's Foreign Secretary, Douglas Hurd, believed the façade of EC unity ought not to be broken over Yugoslavia. As a result, at an extraordinary ministerial meeting on 16 December, the EC declared that it intended 'to recognise the independence of all the Yugoslav republics'. It went on: 'The implementation of this decision will take place on 15 January 1992. They are therefore inviting all the Yugoslav republics to state by 23 December whether they wish to be recognised.'[16]

Germany would not wait much longer. On 23 December, the day before Christmas Eve, Bonn announced it was recognising Croatia and Slovenia, although in a concession to its EC partners, the decision would not take effect until the EC foreign ministers' meeting on 15 January. At the end of a very bleak year it was the only thing most Croats had to celebrate, and they came out on to the streets in thousands that night to let off fireworks and shoot guns into the air.

The 'Christmas recognition', as it was called in Croatia, pre-empted a discussion between the EC states on 15 January. But to maintain the pretence that the recognition of Croatia and Slovenia was an open question, the Community went through the motion of passing requests for recognition from Croatia, Slovenia, Macedonia and Bosnia to a commission of arbitration under Robert Badinter of France (Serbia and Montenegro insisted that the rump Yugoslavia did not need recognition), which replied on 11 January.[17] The Badinter commission turned down Bosnia's request, claiming that 'the will of the peoples of Bosnia–Herzegovina to constitute the Socialist Republic of Bosnia–Herzegovina as a sovereign and independent state cannot be held to have been established'.[18] As far as Croatia was concerned, the commission ruled that, subject to constitutional changes on minority rights, 'the republic of Croatia meets the conditions for its recognition'.[19] Macedonia and Slovenia were approved unconditionally. At the January 1992 meeting, the EC foreign ministers gingerly saluted the birth of two more states in Europe.[20] Only Germany opened an embassy in Zagreb immediately. The pretence of European unity had been maintained, but no one was fooled, least of all the Croats, who knew that they owed recognition almost exclusively to Genscher's efforts. In the battered town of Vinkovci, a café was renamed after Genscher, the first of several memorials to the German Foreign Minister's efforts on Croatia's behalf. For a few days afterwards the piping voice of a young singer could be heard on radio and television, singing a new song. Appropriately enough, it was called 'Danke Deutschland'.[21]

18

Thousand-Year-Old Dream

The victors in the Yugoslav wars of 1991–5 have been the Croats and President Tudjman. The losers have been the Croatian Serbs and their useless leader, Martić.

Lord Owen, 1995[1]

In January 1992 I took the road from Belgrade to the hilltop town of Ilok, on the easternmost tip of Croatia, which was then under Serb control. United Nations peace-keepers had not yet been deployed in 'Sector East', as the Serb-held portion of Slavonia and Baranja would be called, and what used to be the Croatian border was marked by a perfunctory booth manned by a couple of bored-looking Yugoslav army troopers.

The approach to Ilok was depressing, the villages on the way disfigured with bent steeples, and burned and half-demolished houses, the vineyards decayed and desolate. Ilok had been famous for its fine white wine, but the vintage of 1991 had not been harvested. From a distance the town itself looked as quaint and peaceful as ever, the spires and battlements of the baroque monastery and castle piercing the winter sky from a thicket of trees. Ilok had not been bombed; on 17 October the previous year the Yugoslav army had simply ordered the town's 3,000 or so Croats to leave without delay. A handful remained, alongside about 1,500 Slovaks, descendants of the grand colonisation programmes of Maria Theresa.

Ilok looked the same, but was not. Inside the town, all authority had passed into the hands of the Republic of Serbian Krajina. The few Croats who had chosen to remain, mostly elderly women, were tearful and afraid for their safety. Their lives were closely supervised. Even telephoning their relatives outside the town was almost forbidden. One woman told me she had waited three months to get permission to phone her son in Switzerland. It was as if they were trapped in prison. 'Only the Serbs are allowed to move in and out of the town. We "Croatian Fascists" have no rights,' she said. 'The authorities are angry we have not left. People phone me at night and say they will kill me if I don't hand over the keys. We cling to the church. It's all we have left.' One

Federal Yugoslavia, 1945–91

Catholic priest had been allowed to stay at his post to minister to the remnant of his former congregation. But Brother Marko said many of the Croats who had remained avoided him. 'People are afraid to have the priest visit them. It might mark them out to the police,' he said.

The winding streets beneath the hilltop castle were full of cars with Croatian numberplates. But the drivers were not Croats but Serbs – refugees who had fled the Croat offensive in western Slavonia in the autumn of 1991 and who had been living ever since in refugee centres in Serbia. Now they were in search of new homes. The cars rumbled along the narrow cobbled streets at a snail's pace, stopping and starting to let the passengers get out and peer through the windows of the houses to see if they were empty. 'If we like the look of one, we just kick the door down and walk in,' one of the Serbs said cheerfully. In one house I encountered two families from Grubišno Polje, in western Slavonia. They were defensive about their decision to take over some-one else's property. 'We haven't changed a thing,' the woman in charge

The wars in Croatia and Bosnia, 1991–2

insisted. 'Look, we've even left their photographs on the mantelpiece.' The invasion of Ilok appeared to have been partly organised and partly spontaneous. For several months the Serb refugees had been camping in sports centres and hotels in the nearby town of Bačka Palanka, a mile away in Vojvodina. Then the word got round that there were houses for those who wanted them in deserted Ilok. The Yugoslav army helped. A local commander told me the army had made a list of all the empty properties and had handed it over to the new Serb authorities of eastern Slavonia.[2]

The Serbs' new statelet covered 15,000 sq. km, 26.5 per cent of Croatia's territory. In parts of it the Serbs had been a majority before the war, in others not. In Banija, Kordun and eastern Lika, Serbs made up 69 per cent of the pre-war population; in western Slavonia 57 per cent, in northern Dalmatia 55 per cent and in eastern Slavonia only 35 per cent.

Croatia had paid by far the highest price for independence of any of the newly recognised states in Europe or the former Soviet Union. Thousands of people had been killed. Officially, 6,651 deaths were accounted for. But another 13,700 were 'missing', the majority of whom were rotting corpses in the rubble of frontline or Serb-held towns. Vukovar accounted for 2,642 of them. Some thirty-five settlements had been razed to the ground. Hundreds had been badly damaged by shellfire. About 210,000 houses had been destroyed, some 12 per cent of the entire housing stock in Croatia. The government calculated that 30 per cent of the republic's industrial infrastructure had been destroyed or lost. The war had severed vital communications routes. The loss of the Maslenica bridge cut off the last land route between Zagreb and Dalmatia, and left the region dependent for communication on a single ferry route to the island of Pag. Slavonia was better off, though the Bratstvo i Jedinstvo (Brotherhood and Unity) motorway and the Belgrade–Zagreb railway line were both severed by the Serb-held chunk of western Slavonia. Altogether 37 per cent of Croatia's railway lines were out of action or in Serb hands; the Serbs had also made off with 92 railway engines and 475 coaches. The loss of potential earnings in the tourist industry, the main source of livelihood in Dalmatia, was incalculable.[3]

The cost to culture from the war was enormous. During the fighting, the Serbs had rarely resorted to infantry attacks to advance their frontlines, preferring to inch forward after saturation shelling of Croat positions. The worst casualty was Vukovar, where the heart of the town was destroyed beyond recognition, including the imposing eighteenth-century château of the Eltz family.[4] Churches were targeted in a deliberate campaign to erase the physical records of the Croats' presence. Altogether 479 ecclestiastical buildings were badly damaged or totally destroyed. Many were not irreplaceable from an artistic point of view. But the late-gothic church of Voćin, in central Slavonia, which had been extensively restored in the 1970s, was a sad loss. In Drniš, in northern Dalmatia, the mausoleum of the great sculptor Ivan Meštrović had been broken into and damaged.

The Croatian government was burdened by 330,000 refugees from eastern Slavonia, Banija, Lika, Kordun and northern Dalmatia. In the spring of 1992 their ranks were swelled by a trickle, and then a flood of Croat refugees fleeing Vojvodina, where the community, almost 100,000 strong, was soon reduced to a fraction of its former size.

A typical story was that of the village of Hrtkovci, in the province of Vojvodina. Before the war it had been a prosperous community of several thousand farmers, most of them Croats.[5] In March and April 1992 a few hundred Serb refugees from Croatia descended on the village, after discovering that it was easy to intimidate Croats into surrendering their homes. But the real trouble only began on 6 May when the Radical Party leader, Šešelj, and his rowdies held a rally in the village to celebrate the formation of a Radical Party branch in the area. In the middle of the main square Šešelj read out the names of seventeen well-known local Croat families, whom he declared were traitors. The named families duly obliged by clearing out in days. Between May and August about 450 Croat families followed them into exile, leaving the village almost entirely 'cleansed'. In many cases Serb refugees from western Slavonia had simply invaded homes and ordered the owners out. Some offered the keys of their empty homes in Croatia to the locals in exchange. Others pinned advertisements on a noticeboard in the main street, giving details of their old addresses and offering an exchange. The new Yugoslav Prime Minister, Milan Panić, protested against this outrageous bullying when the clamour from Hrtkovci reached his office in July, but by then it was too late; and Milošević said nothing, which was interpreted as a sign of support for Šešelj's tactics. In July the new Serb settlers renamed the village Srbislavci – place of Serbs.[6] The pattern established at Hrtkovci was repeated in Novi Slankamen, Peterovaradin, near Novi Sad, and in the other Croat settlements in Vojvodina. In Croatia the arrival of Croatian refugees from Vojvodina was scarcely noticed. They were few in number compared to the tidal wave of a quarter of a million refugees from Bosnia. Nevertheless, it was the end of a historic community.

The deployment of peace-keepers proceeded in a relatively straightforward fashion after the ceasefire was signed on 3 January 1992. The UN had already entrusted Vance with the task of drawing up an agenda for UN intervention. The 'Vance plan' as it was called was completed just before Croatia's diplomatic recognition. It called for the creation of 'UN Protected Areas' covering one-quarter of Croatia's territory, overlapping with the areas in which Serbs had formed a majority or a substantial minority before the war. Serb-held territory outside the Protected Areas was designated a 'pink zone' and earmarked for eventual return to the control of the Croatian authorities. The Yugoslav army was to withdraw from Croatia and armed factions inside the UN Protected Areas were to be disarmed. Conditions were to be created for the return of the 250,000 or so refugees in government-held territory to the UN zones. The three parties – the Croatian government, the Serbian government and the Krajina authorities – were given little time to discuss the Vance plan, which was adopted by the UN at the end of January and presented as the only choice available.

Serbia and Croatia both accepted the plan. Tudjman hoped the presence of a peace-keeping force would consolidate Croatia's international frontiers, aid the government's efforts to recover control over the third of Croatia in Serb hands and give the other two-thirds a breathing space. The biggest drawbacks for Croatia were, firstly, that ultimate sovereignty over the UN zones was not discussed, which left open the possibility that the Krajina might join Serbia; and secondly, the UN was not to administer the area but only to monitor the administration. This meant that the local Serb authorities remained in control of towns where they had seized power, even where they had driven out the elected Croat councils.

The Serbs had seized as much territory as they felt able to absorb, and Milošević was more disposed to accept the presence of a UN force than one controlled by Nato. With the precedent of Cyprus (to which the Krajina Serbs referred often, and with hope) the Serbs calculated that a UN force would freeze the situation on the ground rather than reverse it. An important factor in the Serb leaders' calculations was the worsening situation in Bosnia, where Izetbegović had decided to hold a referendum on independence in December 1991. As Bosnia's crisis deepened, it became imperative for Serbia to disengage from Croatia as fast as possible in order to concentrate its forces on its other neighbour.

Thus Belgrade and Zagreb accepted the Vance plan with opposing agendas in mind. The authorities in Knin did not accept it at all. Babić was convinced that the withdrawal of the Yugoslav army, the disarmament of local armed forces and the introduction of UN troops would lead to the eventual restoration of Croat control. Milošević was ruthless in overcoming his opposition. After he had been summoned to Belgrade on 3 February, Babić and his aides were locked into a room for a forty-hour meeting with Milošević, Jović and General Adžić, who browbeat the leader of the Knin Serbs in shifts. Babić complained afterwards that the Serbian Prime Minister had physically attacked one of his aides and that he himself had been threatened with physical liquidation. 'They said if I did not accept the plan, "We know what to do with you. You are not leaving until you sign this plan".' Babić admitted he had signed the plan but claimed that his signature had been extracted when he fell asleep out of sheer exhaustion.[7]

After failing to 'persuade' Babić of the virtues of the Vance plan, the Serbian President resorted to other tactics. Rašković and Opačić were politically exhumed and put in charge of a revamped anti-Babić SDS. Opačić dutifully accused Babić of heading 'a diabolical plot' to start a civil war inside the Serbian 'motherland'.[8] The Knin police chief, Martić, abandoned Babić. So did Goran Hadžić, the local Serb chief in eastern Slavonia. Finally, on 9 February Milošević convoked his own pet assembly of Croatian Serbs at Glina, which was much nearer to Belgrade than Knin. This 'parliament' obediently voted to accept the peace plan on behalf of Krajina.

With all three sides now nominally in agreement, the Security Council on 21 February passed a resolution authorising the deployment of 14,000 peace-keepers in the four designated sectors under a command centre located in the Bosnian capital. Although fighting had already broken out in Sarajevo after the Bosnian referendum on independence, the commander of the UN Protection Force (Unprofor), General Satish Nambiar of India, raised the UN flag in the city at the end of the month. As the situation in Bosnia worsened, Unprofor was forced to transfer its command centre on 17 May to Belgrade and Zagreb, alternating between one city and the other.

The optimism in Croatia attending the arrival of the UN troops turned to disenchantment when it became clear that their deployment would not disturb the *status quo* after the January ceasefire. For Zagreb's restaurateurs and those with apartments and houses to let, the arrival of the UN peace-keepers was a boon. Most other Croats forgot the desperate, almost hopeless, conditions they had endured at the height of the conflict in Zadar and Osijek. What they recalled was that the UN had appeared to promise the return home of refugees and had failed to act. To make things worse, the Russians and Ukrainians in Sector East fraternised openly with Vukovar's Serb conquerors and provided no protection to the region's remaining Croats.[9] The banner that had hung for several months in the centre of Zagreb in Jelačić Square, reading 'UN come to Croatia', soon disappeared. The relatives of Croats who were missing and presumed dead in the UN zones built a 'wall of remembrance' outside the UN's Zagreb headquarters in which each brick was inscribed with a family name. There the refugees held regular candle-lit protests.

The Croats' anger increased as the UN failed to make any headway on the issue of returning refugees in the 'Serbian Republic of Krajina'. In Baranja, which I visited in September, the new Serb Mayor, Borivoj Živanović, appeared to be presiding over a reign of terror directed against the remaining Croats and Hungarians. The Belgian peace-keepers were in anguish but could do nothing to stop it. 'It ranges from throwing stones to cutting throats,' Colonel Jean-Marie Jockin said. 'You try to get a Croat out of his house and if he won't go you kill him.' was the description of another Belgian peace-keeper. 'To stop it we would need two guards on every Croat house.' Živanović was unrepentant, predicted that Serb rule over Baranja would last 'a thousand years' and said the Belgians were 'worse than the Ustashe. Only the swastika is missing.'[10] The new order had been forced on Baranja with much more ferocity than in Ilok. Every Catholic church had been blown up or thoroughly desecrated. Again, the roads in the villages were full of people on the move, this time Bosnian Serbs from Bugojno, in central Bosnia, many of whom had been bussed into Baranja by the Belgrade authorities.

If Baranja was bleak, the presence of the Belgians at least ensured it was better than Vukovar, where the local Russian garrison had the cosiest of relationships with the Serb militants. A year after 'liberation' Vukovar remained a desolate, windswept ruin through whose blackened and burned-out streets prowled gap-toothed Chetnik crazies still hunting for Ustashe spies and their papal agents. The anniversary party in November 1992 was a gruesome get-together of ne'er-do-wells and fanatics. Colonel Veselin Šljivančanin, the Yugoslav army commander responsible for the slaughter of several hundred patients of Vukovar hospital, strutted around the cemetery, where the Orthodox clergy were holding a service of remembrance. There were sinister volunteer fighters who swapped jokes about which towns they had helped to 'cleanse' in Bosnia. I asked one fighter what had brought him back to the town. 'I fought in the Vukovar front last year,' he said cheerfully. But on being asked what connection he had had with Vukovar before the fighting, he answered, 'None. I never knew anything about it. But I came to fight as soon as I heard the Croats had built catacombs under the town where they tortured Serb children.'[11] Even the suave diplomats of the UN were unable to pretend the situation in the 'Protected Areas' was not disastrous. Cedric Thornberry, the head of the civilian side of the UN mission, admitted it was one of 'anarchy'.[12]

The Serbs who had remained in government-held territory had paid a stiff price for the violent policies of the Serbian Republic of Krajina. During the war there were few racially motivated murders in the main cities of government-held Croatia. In the bitter fight for western Slavonia dozens of villages had been burned to the ground. In Šibenik and Zadar compulsory 'loyalty oaths' had been forced on Serb workers, echoing the Serb practice in enterprises in Kosovo after 1989. The town of Gospić, in Lika, experienced a genuine pogrom, in which about eighty local Serbs were killed under the auspices of Tomislav Merčep, a Herzegovinian who had lived in Vukovar.

But the Gospić murders were not typical. What destroyed the Serbs of Croatia was more the general animosity they experienced after the war – an almost universal conviction that they were collectively guilty for the war and had no right to remain in Croatia.

Milorad Pupovac, the leader of a moderate Serb political group in Zagreb, described the pressures facing the Croatian Serbs in an article in 1992. 'Over the past two years Croatia's Serbs have been wedged between the anti-Serb policies of Zagreb and the anti-Croat policies of Belgrade,' he wrote.

> Serb identity [in government-held Croatia] is being constantly undermined. In the press Serbs are seen as collectively guilty for the war. In schools religious instruction emphasises Catholicism. ... more than 400 people have been killed either as individuals, or in groups, in towns like Zagreb, Sisak, Osijek, Split, Zadar and Gospić. Almost 200,000 have fled

through fear of violent reprisal. Between 2,000 and 3,000 Serb homes have been destroyed. Regulations have been imposed which make the return of refugees impossible. ...[13]

Many Serbs had left their homes during the war to fight for the Yugoslav army or for the Serb militias, expecting to return to their old homes as conquerors. When the frontline froze in January 1992, they found themselves stranded. Others left because they would not fight for anyone's army, like one young former teacher I met in Belgrade. Born in Vukovar to an army family, he had worked as a sports instructor in a secondary school in Borovo. He would not fight for the Croatian army, but would not take up arms against them either. He had returned once to Vukovar after 'liberation', but only to visit the grave of a dead Croat friend. When I encountered him in Belgrade he was selling his gold signet ring – his only possession – to buy a ticket to Cologne. He wished never to return.

Many flats and houses belonging to retired officers of the Yugoslav army were taken over, especially if their owners were not in them. So were thousands of holiday homes on the coast owned by the wealthy middle classes of Belgrade.

The Serbian Orthodox Church practically ceased to exist outside the Krajina. The seats of the bishops of Zagreb, Pakrac, Karlovac and Šibenik all lay in government territory. Metropolitan Jovan of Zagreb–Ljubljana and Bishop Lukijan of Pakrac had noisily supported the Serb war effort, and their return from exile in Serbia was out of the question; on the walls of Pakrac there were posters of Lukijan denouncing him as a war criminal. Orthodox churches were blown up, though much less comprehensively than their Catholic counterparts in Krajina. The baroque Orthodox cathedral and cemetery in Šibenik fortunately were spared, as was the nineteenth-century cathedral in Zagreb.

Inside the Krajina the Serb population also declined, paradoxically enough. This was not the case in eastern Slavonia, where new Serb settlers were bussed into the lush flat farmland from western Slavonia and Bosnia. But there were no settlers in the barren and windswept heartland of the Krajina. Instead there was an exodus. By September 1992 the Belgrade daily *Politika* was complaining that that Serb emigration from Krajina was reaching 'drastic proportions'. The newspaper laid part of the blame on the endemic corruption of the Krajina officials, many of whom used their new positions of authority to buy homes in Belgrade or Novi Sad.[14]

Cut off from Croatia's towns, and almost cut off from Serbia after the fighting started in Bosnia in 1992, Krajina's local economy shrank. There was little to do in Knin, once the railway, which had supported a large number of employees, ceased to run. The Krajina authorities had hopes of reaping a fortune from tourism in the Plitvice national park, but the war in Bosnia put paid to that. Grandiose plans to open a university in Knin and rebuild Vukovar in Byzantine style had to be dropped when the hoped-for funds obstinately failed to appear. What might have saved the Krajina was the reopening of economic ties with government-held territory, but neither Zagreb or Knin could agree on the terms. Croatia suffered also as a result: Dalmatia, in particular, endured constant electricity shortages, as the hydro-electric dam at Peruča, north of Sinj, was in Serbian hands. But the Krajina Serbs suffered most.

While Krajina withered, Croatia slowly recovered. Wages remained at a fraction of what they had been before the war, industrial production was about 40 per cent of the pre-war level and inflation rose. The Dalmatian tourist industry remained in a coma. But there was no mass unemployment, and economic activity in the Zagreb region, which contained about half Croatia's pre-war industrial plant, picked up steadily. The influx of refugees and the trauma resulting from the loss of territory did not lead to the rise of Fascism or a hunger for authoritarian rule, as many domestic and foreign observers had predicted. The Tudjman government made concessions to the extreme right of a symbolic nature: the Square of the Victims of Fascism was renamed Trg Velikana – the Square of Croatian Great Ones, infuriating the country's tiny Jewish community. The Croatian dinar became the kuna: although the word dated back to the Middle Ages, it was better known as the name of the currency under the NDH. Pressure increased on independent voices in the media, such as the Zagreb-based magazine *Danas* and the Split-based satirical paper *Feral Tribune*. The HDZ tightened its grip around the country's economic, political and cultural life by ensuring that HDZ supporters took the lion's share of the important jobs. Nevertheless, there was no return to the totalitarianism of the Communist or Ustashe eras.

As the economy spluttered into life and UN-brokered negotiations between Zagreb and Knin got nowhere, the Defence Minister, Gojko Šušak, busily amassed weapons in preparation for a military solution. The whole of Yugoslavia had been under a UN arms embargo since 25 September 1991, but it was feebly enforced. The authoritative Belgrade daily *Borba* reported that Croatia was 'high on the list' of buyers of parts from the former East German arsenal. The Croats did not deny it, though they insisted they were now capable of producing most of the arms they needed at home. 'We produce our own cannons, mortars, machine guns and even tanks,' Ivan Milas, the deputy Defence Minister, boasted. As the Belgrade magazine *Vreme* noted, Croatia was scarcely unusual in buying arms in the summer of 1992. 'Everyone is buying,' it noted.[15] But the arms spree evidently lent Tudjman greater self-confidence in his dealings with Belgrade and Knin in the autumn of 1992.

By then the war in Bosnia had accelerated and was consuming more and more of Belgrade's attention. After the referendum in March Bosnia declared independence on 6 April. As in Croatia, the local Serbian party, the SDS, was able to draw on the services of the Yugoslav army to carve out its own territory. But in Bosnia the results were more striking. Within a few weeks the Bosnian Serbs held almost 70 per cent of the republic's territory. In spite of an enormous quantity of heavy weaponry, however, the Bosnian Serbs failed to gain control of the Bosnian capital. In the meantime the steadily accumulating reports of atrocities committed against Muslim civilians in eastern Bosnia, and the pictures of civilian casualties from the Serb shelling of Sarajevo carried on CNN, led to demands for economic sanctions against Serbia and Montenegro along the lines of those introduced against Iraq after the invasion of Kuwait. On 26 May the European Community approved a package of sanctions, including an embargo on the sale of oil, and a similar package was then adopted – in spite of Milošević's shrill protests – by the UN Security Council on 30 May, significantly with the support of Serbia's traditional ally, Russia.

At first the wave of international anger over Bosnia was directed entirely against the Serbs. But, although Croatia recognised Bosnia immediately, the relationship between the two victims of Serb aggression was less smooth than it first appeared. One problem was the deep split within the 750,000-strong Croat community in Bosnia–Herzegovina. The majority were scattered in pockets throughout central and northern Bosnia and in Sarajevo itself, where they made up only 7 per cent of the population. They tended to support a unified Bosnian state and a strong alliance with the Muslims as the best guarantee for their communities' survival. Their spokesmen were the leader of the Croat Party in Bosnia, Stjepan Kljuić, and the Archbishop of Sarajevo, Vinko Puljić.

But conditions in Herzegovina, in the south of the republic, differed from those in Bosnia proper. There the Muslims were fewer in number, confined mainly to the region's capital, Mostar, and to a few towns in the Neretva Valley, which bisected the region. The 200,000 Croats in Herzegovina disagreed with the agenda of the half-million Croats of Bosnia. To the west of the River Neretva they lived in compact, wholly Croat, communities. For example, of the town of Grude's 16,000 inhabitants in 1991, some 15,990 were ethnic Croats and the ratio was similar in the neighbouring districts of Posušje, Ljubuški, Neum, Čitluk, Široki Brijeg, Tomislavgrad and Livno. These districts adjoined Croatia proper and were economically and geographically closer to Dalmatia than to the rest of Bosnia. The Croats of western Herzegovina were rural folk. The clan system was still very strong among them; as was the Catholic Church. In their culture and habits they resembled the rural Bosnian Serbs more than the urban Muslims and Croats of Bosnia. From the start of the conflict they were more interested in unification with Croatia than with becoming part of an independent, Muslim-dominated Bosnia.

Many Herzegovinian Croats had fought in the war in Croatia in 1991, especially in the Dubrovnik campaign. After the January 1992 ceasefire they returned to their home villages as seasoned fighters, to prepare for the second round with the Serbs in Bosnia. They were far better prepared for the fighting that broke out in Bosnia in the spring of 1992 than the Muslims, both psychologically and in terms of organisation and supplies. On 8 April 1992 they set up their own militia, the Hrvatsko Vijeće Obrane (Croat Defence Council) or HVO, as the military arm of the HDZ. After the fighting started, President Izetbegović concentrated all his forces on retaining control of Sarajevo. In the rest of Bosnia, the government had to rely on the HVO to stop the Serb advance.

But Tudjman could not make up his mind whether to support the integrity of the Bosnian state or to go for a partition, as many of the Herzegovinians wanted. The opposition parties in Croatia, on the left, centre and extreme right, agitated for a united Bosnia;[16] but Tudjman's heart was not with them. He belonged to a generation that had grown up before the creation of a separate Bosnia in 1945, and long before the recognition of Muslims as a distinct nationality in 1968. Both during and after the 1990 election he had returned to the theme that Bosnia and Croatia formed a historic and geographic unit. Then there had been the secretive meeting with Milošević in Karadjordjevo in March 1991, where he was reported to have discussed Bosnia's partition.

A sign of Tudjman's intentions was the removal of Stjepan Kljuić, the first leader of the Bosnian HDZ, and his replacement with Mate Boban, a Herzegovinian. The changeover in the leadership of the Bosnian HDZ took place at a party congress in winter 1992 in Široki Brijeg, in western Herzegovina. Although Tudjman was not present, he was widely seen as the sponsor of this change of direction. With his portly profile and old-fashioned bowties, Kljuić was every inch a representative of Sarajevo's old middle class. Alone of the three Bosnian leaders, he was a born *Sarajlija*.[17] His agenda was to ensure the survival of the Croats in Sarajevo and central Bosnia, which meant cultivating close ties with the Muslims. Boban, a former supermarket manager, was from Herzegovina and hankered for union with Croatia.

The HVO was only nominally linked to the Bosnian government army. In fact it operated independently and looked on the Muslim-led army with contempt. As one of the Herzegovinian leaders put it: 'They don't have an army in Sarajevo, so how can they expect us to place our forces under their control?'[18] On 15 June the HVO achieved a great victory in the Bosnian war with the recapture of the eastern bank of the city of Mostar, which for two months had been under Serb control. But the victory in Mostar was the start of a real crisis. Once the Serbs had been driven out, thousands of Muslim civilians began to pour back into the town. They were followed by many Muslim refugees from other towns in Bosnia which had been overrun by the Serbs.

The Croats did not like this change in the ethnic balance, and tried to ban Muslims from moving into the city. Nor did they like the fact that in the winter of 1992 Muslim men began drifting out of the HVO and joining units of the Muslim-led Bosnian army, which was beginning to acquire supplies of its own from Croatia.

On 5 July, the new hardline Bosnian Croat leadership under Boban proclaimed a Croat state within a state, the Croat Union of Herceg–Bosna.[19] Like the Serb Krajina in its early stages, the new statelet officially was only 'autonomous'. In practice, it claimed authority over its own police, army, currency and education and insisted on the right to rule several districts with Muslim majorities. The only permitted flag was a modified version of the Croat flag; the only currency was the Croat kuna; the official language was Croat and the Croat curriculum was imposed on the schools. It also declared that its capital was in Mostar, a city where Muslims had (narrowly) outnumbered Croats in the 1991 census. Boban's government was not democratic. He ruled by fiat from his base in the Croat bastion of Grude in the heart of west Herzegovina, not far from the shrine town of Medjugorje.

The formation of Herceg–Bosna sowed great dissent between the Muslims and Croats of the HVO. Muslims resented the fact that in the districts under HVO control, the Bosnian fleur-de-lys was nowhere visible and that Croats held the key offices. They objected to the way that the HVO often took a large percentage of the weapons passing through their checkpoints on their way to the Bosnian government and which the Bosnians had paid for. In Travnik and Zenica, bearded Afghan *mujahedin* volunteers began to make their unfortunate appearance, alongside homegrown 'Islamic legions' with green flags and medallions bearing inscriptions from the Koran. The tension between the Croats and the Muslims was made worse by the string of successes of the Bosnian Serb army under Ratko Mladić, the former Yugoslav army commander in Knin and Sarajevo.[20] As Mladić blasted a trail through northern Bosnia to secure an open road between Belgrade, Banja Luka and Knin, a drive known as Operation Koridor, Muslims streamed south in ever increasing numbers towards the HVO-ruled regions of central Bosnia. In Bugojno and Travnik, Croats found themselves reduced practically overnight from just under half the local population to a small minority.

Throughout the autumn of 1992, Croat–Muslim tension was largely ignored by the international community. Izetbegović derided attempts to equate the HVO's activities with the carnage committed by the Serbs in eastern Bosnia. Western governments and aid agencies were also aware that Croatia was shouldering the burden of some 279,000 refugees from Bosnia, many of whom were Muslim. They were afraid that imposing sanctions against Croatia might mean the expulsion of the Muslims into the rest of Europe.

Tudjman used the almost universal condemnation of the Serbs' war in Bosnia to test the defences of the Krajina. Without warning on 22 January 1993, about 6,000 Croat troops overran the UN demarcation lines around Zadar. It was a three-pronged operation, aiming to recapture Zadar airport, a hydro-electric dam further inland at Peruča and the vital Maslenica bridge linking Dalmatia with northern Croatia. Two French peace-keepers were killed in the attack. Although the Security Council condemned the operation and ordered the Croats to withdraw on 25 May, the Croat army took all three strategic objects without incurring sanctions or more than a squawk of protest from Belgrade. To the Serb authorities in Knin, the loss of the Zadar hinterland proved that their objections to the Vance plan had been well founded. As a reprisal, the Krajina Serbs took back the heavy weaponry that had been handed over under the plan to UN supervision.

The recovery of the Maslenica bridge boosted the morale of the Croatian army, and enabled Tudjman to counter domestic accusations that he was weak in his dealings with the Krajina Serbs and the UN. For all that, the offensive was of limited practical use. The Serbs were still close enough to the destroyed Maslenica bridge to stop the Croats building a new bridge; as a result, the Croats could only build a pontoon bridge, which few car drivers were willing to cross. The same went for Zadar airport, which remained far too close to the Serb frontline to be reopened to regular traffic. The assault frightened the Krajina Serbs but not enough to prod them into opening negotiations on the return of refugees, let alone on Krajina's reintegration into Croatia.

As the Croats rolled over UN lines around Zadar, the Muslim–Croat tension in Bosnia boiled over into firefights between the HVO and the Bosnian army around Busovača, the HVO's military headquarters in central Bosnia.

The fighting followed the publication of a new peace plan for Bosnia[21] drafted by the UN mediator Cyrus Vance and by Lord Owen, the recently appointed mediator for the EU. The Vance–Owen plan proposed to divide Bosnia into ten ethnically based provinces or cantons, two of which would be Croat and one mixed Croat–Muslim.[22] Izetbegović complained that the plan legitimised 'ethnic cleansing' and compared his position to that of Eduard Benes, the Czechoslovak

President in 1938.[23] Sympathetic Western journalists hastily concluded that the peace plan had encouraged the ethnic communities to fight for control over the proposed cantons. It was a simplistic judgment, as there were already plenty of reasons for a full-scale Muslim–Croat conflict.

The clashes around Busovača spread like a bushfire down the Lašva valley of central Bosnia. But the fighting did not go the Croats' way. Instead, the Muslim government troops in the region, boosted by the influx of refugees, surrounded the Croat towns of central Bosnia one by one. The Croat commander in central Bosnia, Dario Kordić, decided to blast his own mini-*koridor* along the Lašva valley, to link up the five besieged towns of Kreševo, Kiseljak, Vitez, Busovača and Novi Travnik. The *casus belli* came on 15 April, when the Muslims kidnapped and almost certainly killed the HVO commander in Zenica. Shortly after, the HVO attempted without success to blast the Muslims out of the Old Town area of Vitez, by detonating an enormous bomb in a van. The explosion ripped the centre out of the town, killed dozens of people and left many others to die a lingering death under the rubble. But it failed to achieve its aim; a couple of hundred Muslim fighters remained ensconced in the rubble-filled centre of Vitez.

The British commander of UN forces in central Bosnia, Colonel Bob Stewart, arranged a ceasefire between the Muslims and Croats to enable the UN's food and medical convoys to get on the road again. But while he was on patrol on the evening of 22 April he encountered a group of Muslim fighters who said they would never adhere to the ceasefire because of 'the massacre of the babies' in the village of Ahmići, a few miles south of Vitez. Stewart hurried to the scene the following morning with the television cameras in tow. The sight was shocking. Dogs lay shot in driveways. The doors of hastily evacuated houses flapped in the wind. In the schoolroom there was a half-completed sentence from an interrupted geography class on the blackboard. The massive minaret of the newly built mosque had been blown off its foundations and lay at right-angles in a field. But the most gruesome sights were in the houses themselves. Stewart recalled: 'On the steps inside the front entrance were two blackened corpses. One was obviously the remains of a man but the other looked like a teenage boy. Both were naked, their clothes having been completely burned off. The boy's arm was pointing in the air but the hand was a balled claw.' The cellar of the same house was 'a black and sometimes reddened mess. Here and there the outline of a body was recognisable.'[24] Stewart later concluded that the village had been attacked by about seventy Croat fighters at 5am on 22 April, that 'each house was systematically taken out by squads of soldiers who killed anyone they found. ... after that the bodies were thrown into the houses as they were destroyed by fire'.[25]

Stewart's forces uncovered 104 bodies in Ahmići and were convinced they averted another massacre when a UN patrol chanced on a column of 150 Muslim civilians being led out of the village by armed Croats. Several hundred other civilians fled to the British UN army base in Vitez – frightened, but angry with the Croats as well. Stewart stormed around in an attempt to uncover responsibility, although Kordić absurdly blamed the Serbs.

This was not the end of the bloodshed in central Bosnia. On 10 May Croat civilians in Novi Travnik stopped an aid convoy named the 'Convoy of Joy', organised by international Muslim organisations for the relief of Tuzla, and murdered eight of the drivers. The atrocity at Ahmići and the bloody assault on the Convoy of Joy were widely reported in the West and caused the HVO immense bad publicity. They did nothing to shore up the Croat position in central Bosnia. Some of the Muslims had already reached the conclusion that, if they could not regain territory from the Serbs, it would be more profitable to turn on the Croats instead. The Ahmići atrocity strengthened their hand and over the following six months most of the fighting in Bosnia was between Muslims and Croats, with the Croats losing heavily. A week after the clash at Novi Travnik the HVO was driven out of Kakanj, Travnik and Kraljeva Sutjeska, forcing about 60,000 Bosnian Croats to flee towards the already overcrowded Adriatic cities. At the end of July, the HVO lost control of Bugojno, triggering the flight of another 15,000 Croats.

The worst of the Croat-on-Muslim fighting was in Mostar, the city that the two communities had successfully recaptured under the HVO's banner in June 1992. The Muslims staged an uprising on the east bank, but were unable repeat the pattern of Travnik and Bugojno and drive the Croats out entirely. On the west bank the Croats remained in control. They then expelled the Muslim population from their sector. Women and children were simply ordered out of their homes and herded at gunpoint over the bridge into the east. Thousands of men were taken away to improvised camps, of which the most notorious was a former heliport near the village of Dretelj. Both sides then settled down to shell and snipe at each other, although the Croats' heavy weaponry enabled them to reduce east Mostar to a ruin over the next year, while the Muslims were able to wreak only superficial damage. The culmination of the campaign was the demolition by Croat artillery of Mostar's famous medieval bridge on 9 November 1993, an act of cultural vandalism which inevitably flew on to the front pages of most Western newspapers.

By the autumn, the Croat presence in central Bosnia had been reduced to a few beleaguered pockets, and about half the region's Croats had fled. Several of Bosnia's most famous monasteries, which had survived centuries of persecution under the Ottomans, stood empty and vandalised. Western liberals who sympathised with the Muslims were outraged. Western conservatives, who had never wanted an independent Bosnia or Croatia in the first place, derived grim satisfaction from the fact that their warnings about 'tribal warfare' had been confirmed. Croat ministers pleaded that they deserved sympathy for taking in hundreds of thousands of Muslim refugees, but international opinion homed in on Mostar's ruined bridge, the blackened corpses in Ahmići and the grim secrets of Dretelj. Tudjman was castigated as a hypocrite, and a willing accomplice in Milošević's partition plans. In Croatia, public opinion was bewildered by the attempt to target the Muslims as the Croats' real enemy. 'From being victims in 1991 and 1992 we have turned into small and unsuccessful aggressors in Bosnia and lost support around the world,' grumbled Zlatko Kramarić, Osijek's liberal mayor.[26]

To quell the surge of discontent at home, Tudjman launched another assault on the Krajina Serbs in September, in the 'Medak pocket' south of Gospić. But this offensive was a failure. The Croats captured a few villages, and then caused an uproar by executing at least eighty villagers who had not fled in time, many of them elderly women. The Krajina Serbs fired long-range missiles from sites in Banija at Zagreb, which caused considerable damage in the southern suburbs. The UN ordered the Croats to withdraw from Medak, which they did, after blowing up many houses.

Covered in obloquy, the President's prestige hit an all-time low. In October a group of Croat intellectuals, including Ivo Banac, Krsto Cviić, Slavko Goldstein and Vlado Gotovac, wrote an open letter to Tudjman calling on him to resign: 'In the name of an alleged national reconciliation you have permitted an invasion of Ustashe symbols and songs, the renaming of streets and institutions, the revision of history, chauvinistic manifestations and acts ... your occasional anti-Fascist declarations are looked on as an unconvincing screen. They fail to allay serious suspicions on many sides of a possibly Fascist development of the Croatian state.' They added: 'Only new policies and new men can return to Croatia her lost credibility in the eyes of the world and at home.'[27] The letter was followed by another public remonstrance on 29 October from leaders of Croatia's small Jewish community, calling on the President to reverse the decision to rename the Croatian dinar after the kuna, not to transfer the remains of those killed at Bleiburg to Jasenovac and to stop municipalities from renaming streets and schools after Ustashe leaders, such as Budak. 'We are worried by the repeated attempts ... to rehabilitate the Ustashe Independent State of Croatia,' they said.[28]

If Croatia's disastrous intervention in Bosnia caused a certain grim satisfaction among pro-Serb circles in France and Britain, the reaction was pure dismay in Bonn and Washington. Public opinion in the US had been powerfully affected by the Serb massacres in eastern Bosnia and the day-by-day, mindless shelling of Sarajevo. US policy towards Yugoslavia had done a 180-degree turn from the days when Baker had toured the Yugoslav capitals in the spring of 1991, lecturing the Croats and Slovenes on the perils of independence. In April 1992 Washington had recognised Croatia, Slovenia and Bosnia simultaneously, and since then the new Clinton administration had lobbied consistently for a hard line against Milošević, a stance that irritated the French and the British, as the US had refused to commit troops to the UN force in Bosnia or Croatia.

The Americans were appalled by the way the Croat–Muslim conflict played into the hands of the Serbs, and applied a great deal of pressure on Tudjman to get him to change his Bosnia policy. They tried to bring the two sides together in September 1993, but the attempt at reconciliation was sunk by continued fighting in central Bosnia and Mostar and by the fact that the Muslims were then not really interested in peace. In the summer of 1993 Milošević and Tudjman took advantage of the collapse of the Vance–Owen plan[29] to put forward their own peace proposal for a loose union of three republics. Izetbegović leaped at the idea of a purely Muslim statelet, on condition that it comprised at least 30 per cent of the territory of Bosnia and enjoyed access to the Sava and the Adriatic. Serb intransigence wrecked this plan, as it had the previous scheme; the Muslims wanted 30 per cent, while the Serbs were not willing to concede much more than 24 per cent. While the three-republics plan was on the table, Croats and Muslims had a strong incentive to fight for the borders of their future mini-states.

But by the spring of 1994 both Croats and Muslims were ready to talk seriously about peace. The plan for a 'three-republic' Bosnia was dead, while the threat of UN sanctions now hung over Croatia. On 1 February that year the Secretary General reported that between 3,000 and 5,000 regular Croatian troops were in Bosnia. Two days later the Security Council condemned Croatia's involvement and threatened 'serious measures' if it failed to end 'all forms of interference' in the republic.[30] At the end of the month the Bosnian Prime Minister, Haris Silajdžić, his Croatian counterpart, Mate Granić, and a leader of the moderate faction among the Bosnian Croats, Krešimir Žubak, met in Washington. Under strong American pressure, they agreed to form a Croat–Muslim federation in Bosnia. Boban and the HVO hardliners were forced to resign and Herceg–Bosna was put in mothballs, although the Croat regions of Bosnia continued to run themselves and Mostar remained a divided city. With a tenuous ceasefire on the ground, UN aid convoys once again were able to trek into central Bosnia from Croatia.

Tudjman's partial rehabilitation by the international community was symbolised that autumn by the visit of the Pope. John Paul II had been harshly criticised by the opponents of Croatia's independence for stoking the fires of confessional rivalry in the Balkans with his strong support for granting diplomatic recognition in 1991. Since then the Vatican had adopted a low profile, beyond uttering unobjectionable pleas for an end to ethnic strife in Bosnia. In fact the Church in Croatia had become critical of Tudjman as Croat–Muslim fighting escalated in Bosnia in the autumn of 1992 and the spring of 1993. The Pope's visit, therefore, was bound to be seen as a form of blessing on the government's change of policy in Bosnia, however much Church officials in Rome and Zagreb insisted on the visit's purely pastoral nature.

Tudjman could not resist the chance to turn the occasion into a state visit, and devoted his welcoming speech to the Pope to a long account of various papal communiqués to Croat kings, starting with John VIII's letter to Prince Branimir in 879, the coronation of Tomislav, and Leo X's famous message in 1519, in which he had declared: 'Let everyone know the head of the Church will not let Croatia founder for it is the sturdiest of shields and the ramparts of Christendom.'[31]

At the height of the Muslim–Croat conflict, the West European papers depicted Tudjman as a bungler who shared Milošević's ambitions without the skill to realise them. The recreation of the Muslim–Croat alliance proved that he was a cannier operator than his detractors made out. That was certainly the opinion of the EU negotiator, Lord Owen. 'In 1991 he held out against the Serbs and, with one-third of his country as he saw it occupied, accepted the Vance ceasefire agreement in January 1992 only as a way of gaining a pause to build up Croatia's military strength and to hit back against the Serbs,' he wrote.

He goes through the rituals of diplomacy, pays lip service to the value of negotiations but would strike militarily as and when he thought he could get away with it. ... unlike Milošević, who is a total pragmatist, Tudjman is an opportunist in the cause of Croatia. He is in many senses a Partisan general, waiting, acting, deceiving, harrying, feinting and kicking whenever there is an opening. He has one purpose in life, to control all the territory that he thinks historically belongs to Croatia, and to that end he will use any means. He will do it with a smile, a quizzical look, or a fit of rage. ... he is a very skilled operator and I often admired his military and diplomatic interventions for their timing even when they ruined or set back our own plans.[32]

The Krajina Serbs failed to take account of the change in the balance of regional power brought about by the American-sponsored Muslim–Croat federation. Babić and Martić cut themselves off from Belgrade and ignored Serbia's hints to negotiate an arrangement with Croatia that would preserve the substance of their struggle. They drew closer to the Serbian Orthodox Church, which was disappointed with Milošević's new-found moderation. And they drew closer to Karadžić and the Bosnian Serbs, who had lost favour with Milošević following their refusal to agree to the latest international peace plan.[33] The Bosnian and Krajina Serbs made a great deal of noise about a proposed union, holding referendums in the Krajina and issuing important-sounding proclamations about welding together the two military command structures. In practice nothing happened at all. The emptiness of the agreement was displayed in May 1995, when the Croatian army launched its third operation against the Krajina since the January 1992 ceasefire.

The Croat attack on UN Sector West, in western Slavonia, came out of the blue. The UN had just reopened the old Bratstvo i Jedinstvo motorway, including the thirty-five-kilometre stretch running through Serb-held territory around Okučani. But on the night of 29–30 April 1995 a Croat refugee from the village of Smrtić in west Slavonia shot dead a Serb from the same village, Tihomir Glagojević, after meeting him at a petrol station outside the Motel Slaven, inside the Serb-held zone.[34] The Serbs closed the road, but agreed to reopen it the following day. The following night, however, some Serbs opened fire at Croat vehicles passing through the UN sector, killing a couple of drivers. Only hours after these killings, at 2.30am, Croatia told UN troops to withdraw from exposed positions. Three hours after that, 3,500 troops backed by about twenty tanks attacked the triangular-shaped zone from the north, east and west. Within hours the only town in the region, Okučani, was in Croat hands and thousands of Serbs were pouring across the bridge at Stara Gradiška into northern Bosnia.

In spite of frantic appeals for help to Pale and Belgrade, the Bosnian Serbs did nothing to defend the Serbs in western Slavonia; nor was there more than a mumbled complaint from Serbia. The Krajina Serbs fired several rockets at Zagreb on Tuesday and Wednesday, destroying a large number of parked cars and killing eleven people. But the rockets only infuriated the international community. They made no difference to the military outcome. Within thirty-six hours the Croats had overrun the pocket.

The fall of west Slavonia showed that the fanfare about union between the Serbs in Bosnia and Croatia was a hollow boast. But the Knin authorities ignored the lesson. After four years of rejecting any compromise, and expunging all traces of Croat history in their domain, they would not alter course. The Europeans, the US and Russia did not ignore the lesson. Keen to forestall another Croat incursion, they drew up a special peace plan for Croatia, which was intended to rectify the loopholes in the Vance plan. The 'Z4 plan', as it was known, attempted to reconcile Croatia's insistence on preserving the integrity of its frontiers with Serb insistence on self-determination. Krajina was to keep its flag and have its own president, parliament and police – even, perhaps, a separate currency. Tudjman agreed to it gingerly, though only as a starting point for discussions. Milošević supported the agreement. But Martić and Babić rejected it outright.

The Republic of Serbian Krajina was wrecked by the folly of the Krajina authorities and their Bosnian Serb allies. After the startling success of the Croat army in May, it was clear that the Croatian Serbs would stand alone if, or rather when, the Croats attacked a second time. It was a moment for Milan Martić and the Knin leadership to be cautious. Instead they plunged into another military campaign, against the Muslims in Bihać.

The fuse was lit in the first week of July, when the Bosnian Serbs attacked and overran two of the three UN-proclaimed 'safe areas' in eastern Bosnia, Srebrenica and Žepa. The offensive encountered no resistance. On 6 July the bombardment of Srebrenica began. On 8 July the Serbs were in possession of the town. About 48,000 civilians were expelled from the enclaves. Between 4,000 and 8,000 were never accounted for, but were almost certainly killed on the orders of General Mladić. In spite of the arsenal of weapons at the disposal of Nato, which, theoretically, the UN might have called on to defend the enclaves, nothing was done to stop the Serbs after two 'pinprick' bombings failed to dissuade them.

The fall of the enclaves marked the high tide of the Serb campaign in Bosnia, and, as soon as they were dealt with, Mladić despatched several thousand fighters to attack Bihać from the east, while the Croatian Serbs pounded away from the west. Once again, the West dithered over its response, even though Bihać was also a 'safe area'. But this time Croatia acted with determination. 'Following the fall of Srebrenica and Žepa, we could no longer afford to wait and see something similar happening in Bihać,' Šušak said. 'We spent several days in preparation; we submitted a report to the supreme commander [Tudjman] which said we were capable of doing it, and he made the decision and signed the order.'[35]

Croatia's diplomatic position was now much stronger than it had been at the time of the offensive around Zadar. Disgust in the US over the Europeans' conciliatory stance towards the Serbs helped Croatia. American sympathies lay most of all with the Muslims. But the Bosnian government's failure, or inability, to build an effective fighting force against the Serbs left Croatia as Washington's only alternative partner. The Secretary of State, Warren Christopher, feared a Croatian offensive might create many more refugees. On the other hand, he felt it might make a new balance of power in the former Yugoslavia, which might pave the way to a peace settlement. 'It always had the possibility of simplifying matters,' he admitted.[36]

US policy towards former Yugoslavia was complicated by the tussle between the Republican-led Congress, which favoured lifting the arms embargo on Bosnia, and President Clinton's desire to maintain at least an appearance of a common position on Bosnia between Washington, Russia and Europe – which meant keeping the arms embargo in place. As the assault on Bihać escalated at the end of July, the Croats decided on an all-out attack against Krajina. The nominal goal would be the relief of Bihać. Tudjman was certain he would not meet an armed response from the demoralised UN, or condemnation in Washington, where a quick Croat victory would solve the row between Clinton and Congress over the arms embargo. Tudjman's guess was correct. The US ambassador to Zagreb, Peter Gailbraith, merely handed Tudjman a message expressing Washington's 'concern' at the build-up of Croatian troops. Tudjman took that as a green light. He roared with laughter when he recalled the American note in an interview. 'I gave it serious thought but I didn't stop,' he said. 'I was confident we would win.'[37]

The Bosnian army's inability to hold the Serbs back on the Bihać front made a quick decision vital; within a week, a quarter of the Bihać pocket fell to the Serbs, who were close to capturing the only working airfield through which the Muslims received weapons from Croatia.

On 22 July, Tudjman and Izetbegović signed a declaration in Split binding both sides to common defence against Serb aggression. Tudjman soon put his words into action. After a lightning attack, Bosnian Croat and Croat forces overran the towns of Glamoč and Bosansko Grahovo in western Bosnia, virtually closing the roads from Knin to Serb-held Bosnia. Even Martić and Babić were shaken by the ease with which the Croats stormed these traditional Serb bastions. So was the UN, which hastily convened new talks between Knin and Zagreb in Geneva on 3 August. Tudjman agreed that Croatia would take part, but the delegation of low-level MPs and translators he sent made it clear that the Zagreb government was no longer interested in the results of talks. The conditions he set amounted to a diktat. The Krajina had to be reincorporated in Croatia within twenty-four hours, the test being the immediate reopening of the Zagreb–Split rail link and the oil pipeline running through northern Krajina. Faced with probable annihilation, Babić caved in, and agreed to a deal proposed by Gailbraith, to reunite Croatia and Krajina in a peaceful fashion.

The outcome of the Geneva talks did not please Tudjman, who suspected that the Serbs were merely playing for time. His army was now mobilised and poised for an offensive. Some 200,000 men were ready to go into the attack, spearheaded by elite units and backed up by reservists and police. In a statement released at 5am on Friday 4 August the President publicly authorised the attack, codenamed Operation Oluja (Storm). He called on the Serb army to lay down its weapons and for the Serb leadership in Knin to surrender. At the same time he told ordinary Serbs to remain in their homes and trust that their property and rights would be guaranteed.

From its new vantage points in Grahovo, and from inside Croatia, the Croatian army attacked the Krajina at some thirty points, concentrating on a pincer movement aimed at Knin, which was shelled heavily in the early hours of the morning.

The Krajina army consisted of about 40,000 men with about 400 tanks. In the north of the Krajina, General Mile Mrkšić, an officer supplied by the Yugoslav army, had reorganised the Krajina frontlines in Lika after the débâcle of western Slavonia. But he had not started work on the south, where the Croats concentrated their firepower. The Croats' decision to head straight for the Krajina's nerve centre in Knin paid off and by 10am on 5 August, the second day of the operation, they had entered Knin and hoisted the chequerboard flag on Knin castle. By 5pm that afternoon Croatian Radio Knin was on the air. Casualties were minimal. As soon as the bombardment started the Serb troops fled the frontlines, provoking a panicked flight into Bosnia by thousands of civilians, who left their houses with washing on the lines and meals half eaten on kitchen tables.

The fall of Knin was the signal for the collapse of the Krajina Serb army. At 3pm that afternoon the Bosnian and Croat armies linked up west of Bihać, splitting the Krajina into two. Benkovac fell at 6pm. That evening tens of thousands of Serbs began to pour out of Croatia in a mass exodus through two gateways left open deliberately by the Croat army, at Srb in Lika and Dvor in Banija. In Zagreb, Tudjman and Šušak joined the celebrations on the streets. By the following morning the whole of northern Dalmatia was in Croat hands and Tudjman was heading for Knin castle, to kiss the chequerboard flag flying from the battlements.

Martić fled to Bosnia after a brief stop in Srb, where on the following Tuesday he issued a futile call for a guerrilla war. Once out of the country, his appeal lacked seriousness. There was no attempt to withdraw to a defensible redoubt in the north, in the dense forests and mountains of Banija or Lika. There, the fighting went on for another two days. But as the Serb population fled *en masse* into Bosnia with their erstwhile leaders, it was clear that the fighting around Petrinja and Glina was only a holding operation, to enable as many civilians as possible to escape to Bosnia before the roads were closed. By about 6am on the morning of 8 August, Oluja was effectively over, and at 9pm General Zvonimir Červenko, Chief of the Croatian General Staff, gave a press conference, at which he announced: 'The territory of the Republic of Croatia occupied by the so-called Republic of Serb Krajina has been completely liberated. There are only two areas, that is the area of Vojnić–Vrginmost, and this area to the right, where there are still encircled formations of the former army and the population who have fled these territories.'[38]

Within the space of eighty-four hours the Serbian Republic of Krajina had dissolved, the only exception being the strip of land surrounding Vukovar in eastern Slavonia, which bordered on Serbia proper. Thousands of Croatian Serbs who had failed to escape in time were huddled in a vast open-air camp at Topusko, awaiting evacuation under UN auspices to Bosnia and Serbia.

The government in Zagreb insisted that Croatian Serbs who were not involved in 'war crimes' would be able to stay, or even return to their home once they had fled. In fact the departure of the Serbs from the Krajina was as final as the flight of the Greeks from Asia Minor in 1921, the Germans from Bohemia and Poland after the Second World War or the *pieds noirs* from Algeria in 1961. After demanding all, they had lost all. Within days of their departure, the returning Krajina Croats and Croat soldiers made a mockery of the government's public promises by burning down dozens of Serb villages and looting the Serbs' empty homes. For the Croat refugees, almost 200,000 in number, it was the day that they had hardly dared to hope for – a chance to return to what was left of the homes that they had been driven from so abruptly four years previously. For Tudjman, the sight of the Croat flag over Knin castle was a moment to savour, the apex of a career that had seen spectacular peaks and troughs. The 'thousand-year-old dream' of which he had spoken so often was a reality at last.

The world was impressed by Croatia's growth into a significant military power. Predictably, Britain, France and Russia condemned the entire operation. But Germany and the US did not. President Bill Clinton significantly said he was 'hopeful that Croatia's offensive will turn out to be something that will give us an avenue to a quick diplomatic solution'.[39]

19

'Freedom Train'

The big heart of Franjo Tudjman has stopped beating.
Vlatko Pavletić, 11 December 1999

On 26 August 1995 Tudjman boarded the first train to travel from Zagreb to Split since that hot August night five years before, when the *balvan* revolutionaries had blocked the line. The train was called the *Vlak Slobode* – 'Freedom Train' – and its most distinguished passenger was in an expansive mood as he talked to the accompanying group of journalists. 'They disappeared ignominiously, as if they had never populated this land,' he said of the recently departed Serbs. 'We urged them to stay but they did not listen to us. Well then, *bon voyage.*'

At Karlovac and Gospić, the Freedom Train stopped on its journey to Dalmatia, and Tudjman got off to acknowledge the cheers of the crowds on the station platforms, the salutes of the soldiers and the addresses of the civic dignitaries.

At Knin, the atmosphere was somewhat different, as there were few people left in the town. Here the Freedom Train was a strange spectacle, winding along the tracks and sounding its horn mournfully as it passed silent and empty blocks of flats before gliding into the station, where the sign reading 'Knin' in Cyrillic letters had been taken down and replaced by one in Latin letters. From there it was on to Split, more delighted crowds and another victorious speech under the palm fronds of the city's elegant corniche.

In the speeches he delivered along the route of the Freedom Train, Tudjman harked back to the theme of the brief addresses he made on kissing the red and white flag fluttering from the battlements of Knin castle, the day after the Croatian army retook the town: the work of creating an independent Croatian state had now been completed and foundations laid that would endure for centuries to come.

The scale of his achievement could not be denied. In 1990 he had won the first genuinely free multi-party election in Croatia since the Second World War. That had been a victory, not only over the

Communists who had ruled Yugoslavia for half a century, but over far better known Croat dissidents, such as Savka Dabčević-Kučar. And this was a man whose political career only took off when he was almost sixty years old, the age at which most people contemplate retirement.

But the triumph of 1990, sweet as it was, was a paltry thing compared to that of 1995. In 1990 the election results had scarcely been counted before the first threatening storm clouds had rumbled over Knin. Tudjman had then been a president of a portion of Yugoslavia, and a president in name only, as his humiliating treatment at the hands of the Knin rebels and the Yugoslav army was so soon to demonstrate.

In 1995 Tudjman's victory had an air of permanence and finality. Historic questions had been settled: whether Croatia's fortunes would be decided in Belgrade, or in Zagreb alone; whether Croatia was a region of a larger state, or a country in its own right; whether Croatia was a land belonging to two nations – Serbs and Croats – or Croats alone. The proof was the sight of those empty tower blocks in Knin, and it is hard to believe Tudjman did not feel an enormous sense of relief when he saw those ghostly buildings for himself from the windows of the Freedom Train.

After a year of hoarse arguments, political deadlock and dreadful uncertainty in 1990, half a year of warfare in 1991, an unworkable ceasefire in 1992 and then more fighting in 1995, Croatia was a state with all the proper accoutrements, both big and small, from an army to stamps, airlines and embassies. The red and white flag, the so-called Ustashe flag that the Serbs had tried to trample into the dust, now flapped outside the headquarters of the United Nations. Zagreb at last had confirmation of that truly metropolitan status for which it had hankered for so long. And there was money, in some people's pockets at least. Although much of Croatia had been laid waste by the war, the capital appeared far less tatty, ground down and embittered than Belgrade. There were plenty of limousines belonging to the newly rich in the streets. A splendid new Sheraton hotel had been built to cope with the growing number of foreign businessmen and diplomats. The shelves of the bookshops were lined with lavish, showy volumes celebrating Croatia's past and present, no longer written in a kind of code, as before, to avoid the charge of nationalism. Just north of the city, in the foothills of Zagorje, the old fortress at Medvedgrad had been restored and refurbished as an 'Altar of the Homeland' – a fitting setting for those heavy, theatrical ceremonies Tudjman delighted in conducting.

It was extraordinary to think that only a few years previously, the very notion of an independent Croatia had been the dream of a few befuddled right-wing émigrés, who spent their lives peering over their shoulders in case their activities should attract the attention of the Yugoslav secret police. Now it was a reality, the true believers had carried the day, and it was the turn of a fast-diminishing band of Yugoslav sympathisers, dubbed 'Yugo-nostalgics', to experience the uncomfortable sensation of being members of a small, minority sect.

But the price of the thousand-year-old dream had been enormous. Apart from Bosnia, no state in Eastern Europe had suffered such material destruction and loss of life to win its independence. From Karlovac in the north to Split in the south, the interior of Croatia was a charred wasteland – mile upon mile of burned-out houses and ruined churches. What had not been burned down by the Serbs in 1991 because it was Croatian had been burned down in 1995 because it was Serbian. Some of the larger towns had escaped this pointless destruction of property, but few of the villages had, for it was in villages rather than in towns that neighbour came back to punish neighbour, repeating the cycle of vengeance that had continued after the Second World War. From time to time on the road to Split one passed a house that had been left intact. Many had the words 'Hrvatska kuća – ne diraj' (Croatian house – don't touch) daubed in large letters on the wall. But in hundreds of villages there were scarcely any usable houses. From the windows of the bus tearing through the hills of Lika from Zagreb to Split one could catch glimpses now and then of old women dressed in widow's black, standing like sentinels in this dark and brooding landscape – Serbs who had been too old to join the frantic exodus of August 1995 and who had been abandoned by their relatives.

South of Zagreb, in the fertile orchards of Banija, the air of desolation was much the same. In the border town of Kostajnica, on the banks of the River Una that divides Croatia from Bosnia, a handful of people hurried through the streets past the ruined façades of what had once been one of the most attractive old country towns in Croatia. There the damage was the work of the Serbs, partly carried out in 1991, the rest shortly before the exodus of August 1995. Of the baroque parish church and the eighteenth-century Franciscan monastery almost nothing remained. Even the late medieval apothecary had been torched in a destructive act of spite. Of Kostajnica's considerable artistic heritage there remained only the medieval castle on the Bosnian side of the river, built by the Frankopans as a fortress against the Turks. Down by the river bank a small group of Croat police stared at their Serb counterparts on the other side of the Una through binoculars. Sometimes these Serbs and Croats would shout at each other across the water. The bridge between the two sides had been blown up. The few Croats who had returned to Kostajnica evinced an air of defiance and gloom. 'We've destroyed the myth of the invincible Serbian army,' one old man remarked. He said he had returned to the town after four years as a refugee 'on the second day after Kostajnica's liberation,' in August 1995. 'My home was all right but as for the others ... they come each day in buses and try and clear up the mess, but without money and jobs, they won't be able to come back and live here for a long time.'

It was much the same situation in a dozen other towns of the fallen Republic of Serbian Krajina. Those lying nearest the big cities, which had had a sizeable Croatian population before the war of 1991, had the best chance of reviving, such as Petrinja, which is near Zagreb, or Benkovac, which is just outside Zadar. But the future looked uncertain for Dvor, Vojnić, Vrginmost, Korenica and other Serb-majority towns which lay far from the big population centres.

The euphoria generated by Operation Oluja encouraged Tudjman to go to the country in October, in the hope that the prestige he undoubtedly enjoyed would induce the voters to give his far less popular HDZ party the absolute majority it sought in the Sabor. The electorate, however, proved able to distinguish between the president and the increasingly unpopular clique that surrounded him and in spite of a blatant attempt to massage the poll by including Bosnian Croats on the electoral roll, the HDZ failed to win convincingly. There was further evidence of resistance to the growing cult of the president in Zagreb, where voters in the local elections reacted against the corruption in the ranks of the ruling HDZ by rebuffing Tudjman and giving a loose coalition of opposition parties a narrow majority in the council chamber. Tudjman's retort to this unexpected show of insolence was characteristic. Instead of examining which of his party's actions might have alienated the voters, he used his prerogative to block the nomination of an opposition mayor in the capital.

Operation Oluja marked the apotheosis of Tudjman's presidency. It was as if all his energy and concentration had been fixed on the goal of securing Croatia's independence over all the territory it had been accorded by the post-Second World War arrangement in Yugoslavia. Once that was achieved, decline set in. Tudjman himself was ill. The year after Oluja, commentators began noting the infrequency of his public appearances, his sudden loss of hair and haggard face. Shielding him from the public gaze, his spokesmen and women insisted there was nothing wrong, but rumours of inoperable cancer continued to spread. They were true, though it would be years before he succumbed.

Tudjman's illness changed the character of his administration. He retreated into his inner sanctum, rarely saw his ministers and let power slip into the hands of his immediate entourage, including his chief adviser, Ivic Pasalić, and to a lesser extent, to members of his family. The needs of post-war Croatia demanded imaginative and dynamic leadership to cope with the challenges posed by a ruined economy, continuing international isolation and the complex question of future relationships with Slovenia, Bosnia, Montenegro and Serbia. Instead, there was a disastrous programme of privatisation and a continuation of the old policy of meddling in the affairs of Bosnia.

That the state economy needed an injection of private and foreign capital was incontrovertible. But the way privatisation was handled in Croatia mirrored Russia's dismal experience more than that of the successful 'transition' economies of Poland and the Czech Republic. Enterprises were parcelled out to cliques of political supporters, many of them Bosnian Croats, creating a network of a few hundred wealthy families.

This strategy of politically driven privatisation need not have spelled disaster if the favoured cronies had possessed economic know-how and the determination to make their assets work. There were some cases of state firms in Zagreb privatised in this way, which continued to function and even grow. But most were handed over to men who simply enriched themselves by stripping the assets, storing the money abroad, and then closing the enterprises down. Miroslav Kutle, Bosnian Croat owner of the Globus media group centred on the Tisak newspaper distribution company, was the most notorious of the new breed of 'tycoons', as they were known. Using his close contacts with the Herzegovinian clique surrounding Tudjman, Kutle got hold of at least 150 state enterprises in this way. 'He would buy a company, take out its cash to buy another company and repeat the process. Tisak was a hugely profitable company when he got control. But he was never able to invest in his acquisitions or put in new management,' Andrew Krapotkin, head of the Zagreb office of the European Bank for Reconstruction and Development, recalled.

The knock-on effects of this development were two-fold. Firstly, unemployment increased as companies were closed, sometimes completely unnecessarily, swelling the ranks of demobilised soldiers who flooded onto the jobs market in autumn 1995. Secondly foreign investors shied away from Croatia, as they did from Russia, out of a well-founded suspicion that it was not a functioning legal state in which investors could operate without encountering mafia-style pressure from politically connected tycoons such as Kutle.[1] Croneyism was an established part of the HDZ political culture, inherited from the old Communist regime. But it took on an increasingly uncontrolled and malevolent aspect after Operation Oluja and Tudjman's sickness.

The abuse of the economy to create a ring of powerful families linked by naked self-interest to the regime's survival worsened an economic downturn fuelled by the government's diplomatic isolation. After the conclusion of the Dayton agreement, Tudjman's American patrons dropped him. Washington had no need of Zagreb's co-operation once the Croatian army had done its job of rolling back the Serb army in Bosnia and forcing Milošević to the negotiating table. The Serb regime remained the number one pariah of the Balkans in US eyes, but Croatia was seen in only a marginally more favourable light. As for the Europeans, they continued to hold Tudjman at arm's length. As usual, Croatia and the Europeans looked at the same situation from entirely different perspectives. Croats of almost all political persuasions saw Oluja as an entirely legitimate operation to recover the national territory, which required no apology. The Western powers were more legalistic, factoring in the point that Croatia had overrun UN Protected Areas – the famous UNPAS – which had been set up by a Security Council resolution. No one for a minute seriously thought the Croats might be persuaded to disgorge any of their gains but the manner with which the Croat army had reoccupied the Krajina still rankled, especially the burning down of several thousand houses. The alienation extended even to Croatia's traditional supporters. In the early 1990s Germany and Austria had championed Croatia against the more pro-Serbian foreign offices of the British and the French, not to mention the Russians. After 1995 those voices fell silent, and the replacement of the Christian Democrat-led government in Germany in September 1998 by a Social Democrat–Green coalition under Gerhard Schröeder ended the era when Zagreb could expect any special treatment from Berlin.

The growing perception of Croatia as an international irritant was boosted by Tudjman's incurable taste for meddling in Bosnian Croat affairs, which reflected the strength of the Bosnian Croat caucus in his immediate circle. The Bosnian state that had emerged from the Dayton agreement in 1995 was, admittedly, a sickly child and the Western powers hovered nervously round the cradle, throwing accusing glances at Zagreb every time they detected a downturn in the child's health. The fact was that while war had impoverished Croatia, it had destroyed Bosnia. The economy of Bosnia, even more than that of Croatia, was geared to supplying the needs of the 23 million inhabitants in former Yugoslavia. Now it served a tiny land-locked state of about 4 million, which had been cut into two. Ruled effectively as a protectorate by Western powers – an unfortunate development which infantilised the political culture – Bosnia failed to revive economically and educated professionals streamed out of the country. In the Muslim Croat federation that covered just over half the republic, the Croats formed a restive and dissatisfied element, envious of the Serbs for gaining a self-governing entity and resentful of the dominant role assumed by the Muslim majority in their own half. The ferment posed a political challenge to any government in Zagreb, which called for great delicacy. Instead, the ailing Tudjman kept Croatia on collision course with Sarajevo and its external sponsors by openly supporting the calls of hard-line Bosnian Croats in western Hercegovina for a revision of Dayton, which neither the US nor the Europeans were willing to even contemplate. In Croatia itself, Tudjman did the Bosnian Croats no favours in the long term. He ensured the politicisation of their cause, which became linked in the public mind with the fortunes of a single political party – his own. After his death and the HDZ's loss of power, the Bosnian Croats suffered an almost total loss of influence.

The year 1998 brought Tudjman one last hurrah: the restoration of full control over Serb-held land in East Slavonia and Baranja, the last remnant of that brief meteor on the European political stage, the Republic of Serbian Krajina. The return of Vukovar had been foreseen at Dayton. After the fall of Knin, Belgrade resigned its interest in Eastern Slavonia, leaving the local Serb authorities no option but to sign a UN-mediated 'Basic Agreement' with Croatia in the border village of Erdut in December 1995. The agreement envisaged a slow transition to Zagreb rule through the auspices of a new UN mission known as UNTAES, the United Nations Transitional Administration for East Slavonia. By mid-1996, UNTAES was in place and had reported the demilitarisation of the region, and over the next 18 months the nervous local population was acclimatised to the inevitable resumption of Croatian rule, which recommenced on 15 January 1998.

After the propaganda debacle in the West that followed Operation Oluja, Tudjman was determined that the re-absorption of Vukovar and its surroundings would not be accompanied by reports of revenge killings and house burning. He gave the job of overseeing the transition to Vesna Škare-Ožbolt, a rising star in the HDZ who spoke several foreign languages, came from Slavonia and belonged to the moderate fraction within the party that orbited foreign minister Granić. 'I need a success,' he told Ožbolt,[2] who managed a remarkably peaceful and painless change of authority in a town that more than any other in Croatia had come to symbolise the horror and brutality of war.

Only a minority of the town's Croatian population returned to Vukovar over the next two years, much to the disappointment of the authorities. For many of them, the business of rebuilding homes from rubble was financially insupportable and the prospect of living side by side with their former Serbian neighbours was unattractive. There were no jobs to go back to, in any case. The huge Borovo rubber complex, which once employed thousands of workers, was a rusting ruin that had next to no chance of being rebuilt. Of all the returnees, the farmers were best off. The cultivators of the famous vineyards of the charming village of Ilok were soon back tending their vines. But after the initial euphoria over the recovery of Vukovar had dissipated, it dawned on people that the industrial town was destined to become nothing more than an outsized, rustic village. The promises that Tudjman extracted from the various local authorities to undertake rebuilding projects in Vukovar were soon forgotten. The towns and cities of Croatia had been obliged to rebuild 29 pieces of infrastructure, but by 2001 only seven were complete, such as the imposing, baroque Franciscan monastery in Vukovar itself and a sports centre in nearby Borovo, the latter a gift of the people of Cakovec on the Hungarian border. But the heart of Vukovar was still a ghoulish ruin where only cafes did good business, helping unemployed men to while away their time. The sole reason why so many people remained in Vukovar was because many Serbs wanting to sell up could not find buyers, in spite of the fact that house prices were a tenth of the value of similar structures in Zagreb.

Tudjman's illness worsened. The president's first examination in the Walter Reed US military hospital in Washington on 26 November 1996 had left him despondent. After the doctors told him his advanced stomach cancer was inoperable and might leave him only weeks to live, he hurried back for a miserable New Year in Zagreb. Hope returned the following spring after a visit by a surgeon from the Gustave-Roussy cancer institute in Paris. The French ditched surgery in favour of less invasive forms of chemotherapy, and at first their course of treatment appeared to achieve remarkable results, immediately halting the erosion of the president's stomach.

The return of all the symptoms in February 1998 came as a terrible blow, particularly as tumours had spread to the brain. Although the French doctors tried treating his brain with radiation, Tudjman no longer entertained serious hopes of long-term survival. 'The last two years were impossible,' Ožbolt recalled. With the president sick and withdrawn – his ministers scarcely saw him at all in the last year – the infighting between Pasalić, Šeks and the moderates around Granić became increasingly frantic in an atmosphere of virtual political paralysis and a continually worsening economic crisis. According to the newspaper *Nacional*, Tudjman lost his ability to concentrate and was only interested in chatting about football.[1]

Symptomatic of the rising concern about the economy was the collapse of much of the banking system, led by the country's fifth largest bank, Dubrovačka Banka, which experienced a disastrous run on its savings in February 1998. The panic at the Dubrovnik bank triggered the collapse of several small and medium sized banks, wiping out about 20 per cent of the savings of Croat investors and presenting a huge compensation bill for the government in the 1999 budget. As the country's foreign debt lurched steadily higher towards the $10bn mark, all hopes were concentrated on a dramatic revival of tourism in Dalmatia. But once again, as so often in its history, Croatia was the victim of events over which it had no control.

This time the proverbial Balkan powder keg was Kosovo. The overwhelmingly Albanian province in southern Serbia slid into a state of growing lawlessness in 1998, as the Serbian police attempted vainly to counter the threat of insurgency from a shadowy new force called the Kosovo Liberation Army (KLA) by burning down the villages of alleged 'terrorists' often with the members of their families inside. The first of these bloody reprisals, at Prekaz, left about 50 dead and only ignited a cycle of violence that rapidly spiralled out of control. If Milošević calculated that it might be smart to let the KLA uprising gather strength precisely in order to crush it more thoroughly, the strategy backfired horribly. A series of atrocities perpetuated against Albanian villagers sparked the exodus of about 800,000 terrified Albanians into neighbouring Macedonia and Albania, placing an enormous strain on both those rickety states and posing an immediate dilemma for the Western powers. Determined not to play the role of the helpless spectator, as it had in Bosnia in 1992, Nato brushed aside Russian opposition and began rocketing the Yugoslav army from the skies. The air war that raged over Yugoslav skies in the summer of 1999 culminated in the Serbs' withdrawal from Kosovo. It did not affect Croatia in the slightest, beyond the fact that Zagreb obligingly lent Nato the use of its air space. But as far as potential holidaymakers in Western Europe and America were concerned, Croatia was part of the Balkans and the Balkans, as usual, was in the middle of some horrible war. As a result, a tentative recovery in tourist results in the summer of 1998 was followed by another disastrous dip in visitor numbers.

While Nato warplanes rocketed Serbia and Milošević skulked in his Belgrade bunker, Tudjman's constitution began to surrender to the ferocious impact on his body of prolonged chemotherapy. The first sign that the end was near came in February 1999, when his immune system collapsed on a visit to Turkey. He struggled through the summer before the final crisis came in October, when he was forced to cut short a trip to Rome and was rushed to hospital in Zagreb on 1 November. He never emerged. Slowly poisoned by sepsis caused by the disintegration of the intestine, he fell into a coma on

22 November. On 26 November, the president's advisers gave up the pretence that he was suffering from a minor illness and authorised parliament to suspend his powers and vest them in the president of the Sabor, Vlatko Pavletic. He died just before midnight on 10 December 1999. His minister of science, Milena Žic-Fuchs, recalled being woken just before the announcement on air by a woman who simply said the president had gone.[4] At 3am, Pavletić addressed the nation on television. 'The big heart of Franjo Tudjman has stopped beating,' he said.[5] The ministers gathered for a cabinet meeting the following day in a mood of despondency. They had all been prepared for his death but it still came as a shock. In spite of his illness and prolonged absence in the last months, he had remained the ultimate arbitrator between the quarrelling factions of the HDZ, which had ruled Croatia since the historic election of 1990. The decade of Tudjman's rule had been one of tumultuous events. Croatia had declared independence, risked total military defeat at the hands of the Yugoslav army and had snatched victory at the last minute. Tudjman's era had been marked by an increasing trend towards authoritarianism, xenophobia and economic and diplomatic incompetence, but to many people he remained a revered father figure. His funeral, held on 13 December in the bitter cold at Mirogoj, was virtually boycotted by the international community. Only Turkey despatched its head of state, Suleyman Demirel. The Bosnians, Slovenes and Macedonians contented themselves with prime ministers, while the Western states sent only ambassadors. But the people turned up in their tens of thousands to line the funeral route.

No sooner was Tudjman laid to rest in a vast, unlovely, black marble tomb in Mirogoj, not far from the resting place of his close ally Gojko Šušak who died from cancer in May 1998, than his political legacy began to unravel. The Croats paid their respects at his funeral, but almost immediately signalled their desire for a complete change of style in the presidential and parliamentary elections that followed on 3 January and 24 January.

The first sign of a new era was the opposition victory in the first of those polls. For years, Tudjman – like Milošević – had confronted a myriad of unstable opposition coalitions that failed to impress the voters with any sense of permanence or resolution. But now it was the HDZ that looked divided and confused, while the two biggest parties of the left and centre, the SDP under Ivica Račan and the HNLS under Dražen Budiša, formed a solid coalition. Moreover, these two large parties had drawn four other smaller parties under their umbrella, the Istrian Democratic Congress, the Peasants Party, the Liberals and the Croatian People's Party. The verdict of the electorate was decisive. The SDP and HNLS together won 71 of the 151 seats in the Sabor, while the additional support of their smaller allies gained them a two-thirds majority. The HDZ was humiliated with only 46 seats.

In one sense, the parliamentary result was not much of a shock, given the obvious unpopularity of the HDZ in the last years of Tudjman's life. The election that followed to the presidency was a bigger upset. 'The Croats want their leader to be someone they are afraid of, or someone they can have a drink with,' Croatian journalist Mirjan Buljan recalled. 'Tudjman was the former and Mesić was the latter.'

The last president of the old Yugoslav federation did not at first appear a very likely victor. The party he had led after leaving the HDZ, the Croatian People's Party, had mouldered away on the fringes of the republic's public life, attracting little attention. The other parties supporting his presidential bid, the Istrian Democrats and the Liberals, were also small fry. One confined its activities entirely to a small region in the far west. The other had little support outside the far east and was little more than a platform for Zlatko Kramarić, the boyish-looking mayor of Osijek. As late as November 1999 public opinion polls suggested Granić was by far the most popular politician in the country.

Many observers at first predictably put their bets on Granić as a safe pair of hands who could be relied upon to preside over Croatia's transition to a more accountable style of government. But it soon became clear that the public revulsion against the HDZ, so clearly expressed in the parliamentary elections at the beginning of the month, was about to be reinforced in the second poll. Granić's campaign was not helped by what Ožbolt called a deliberate campaign of sabotage waged from within the party by the hard-line nationalists around Pasalić and Vladimir Šeks, who seemed to prefer no HDZ candidate to win if the only choice was a man of Granić's convictions. A quiet, rather modest man with the demeanour of a Catholic bishop, Granić proved no match for the effervescent Mesić, who was clearly relishing his return to the centre of the stage after the years of obscurity. An HDZ win, even by Granić, also threatened to lead to confrontation between the presidency and the new constellation of forces running parliament.

The presidential candidates did not only differ over Bosnia, Europe, Serb refugees and indicted war criminals. Mesić's campaign platform involved concrete pledges to oversee the drastic reduction of the presidential prerogatives Tudjman had piled up, and the return of almost all executive decision to the parliament and the prime minister.

The public warmed to the fact that Mesić was as different from his old mentor as could be imagined. Where Tudjman had been stiff, patriarchal and reluctant to display his dry sense of humour. Mesić was an avuncular club man, never happier than when he was holding court with his friends in the Café Charlie, just off Zagreb's Jelačić square. In fact it was his humour that increasingly grabbed the public's attention as he campaigned for the nation's votes.

In spite of the obvious decline of the HDZ since Tudjman's death, the results on 24 January still came as a surprise. Mesić won convincingly, taking 41 per cent of the votes, compared to 28 per cent for Budiša and only 22 for Granić. The HDZ had been buried and Granić was so disappointed with his party, as well as the result, that within a few weeks he left the HDZ with Škare-Ožbolt to set up a new forum for the centre-right called the Democratic Centre. Budiša and Mesić went on to a second round on 7 February, but there were no further upsets. Mesić won as was expected, and assumed Tudjman's vacant seat.

The West greeted Mesić's victory with almost indecent enthusiasm. While only one foreign head of state had attended Tudjman's funeral, 12 showed up in Zagreb for Mesić's inauguration, alongside the US secretary of state, Madeleine Albright. It was not his folksy charm that drew them to Zagreb, but two specific foreign policy pledges. One was to terminate Zagreb's involvement in Bosnia's convoluted domestic arrangements by cutting financial and military aid to the Bosnian Croats. The other was to co-operate fully with the International War Crimes Tribunal, not only over Bosnian Croat suspects, but over the much more sensitive subject of regular Croatian army figures suspected of war crimes in Operation Oluja. Both marked a radical break with HDZ policy which was to support the Bosnian Croats, however covertly, and to deny the Hague Tribunal any authority to investigate the 'Homeland War'.

These promises were not popular, and drew furious opposition from war veteran organisations and more muted criticism from the Catholic Church, not a negligible force in a country where about 30 per cent of the population regularly attended mass. Yet Mesić and Račan were able to deliver to their new Western allies on both counts without encountering a serious threat to public order. A few dangerous moments followed the announcement in early February 2001 of a judicial investigation into Mirko Norac, a former general, over a pogrom of several dozen Serbian civilians in Gospić in mid-October 1991. A youthful 33, Norac was a hero to nationalists far beyond the ranks of the HDZ and the court's announcement sent about 100,000 protesters onto the streets of Split the following weekend, as well as sparking smaller protests in other cities. The size of the Split rally, which included a number of clergy, rattled the authorities but they did not back down, and after the Hague Tribunal helpfully declared it was not intending to seek Norac's extradition, the suspect handed himself in at the end of the month and was charged in March with crimes against humanity. The demonstrations continued but the fact that Norac was going to be tried in Croatia and not the Netherlands defused the issue. The Norac case caused a lot of noise but showed no sign of igniting a campaign of civil disobedience. More importantly, it did not revive the HDZ even though it had positioned itself as the war veterans' champion.

It was the same with the Bosnian Croats. Heavy sentences passed down by the Hague judges in March 2000 and February 2001 on two key figures in the Croat–Muslim conflict in central Bosnia in 1993 aroused a lot of anger in Croatia,[6] but there was no widespread opposition to the government's policy of distancing itself from the Bosnian Croats. Politically, Mesić owed them nothing and it was differences over Bosnia policy that had led to Mesić's resignation from the HDZ in 1994 in the first place. Many of Tudjman's closest advisers came from western Herzegovina. None of Mesić's did. Only weeks after his inauguration on 18 February, Mesić paid a symbolically loaded visit to Sarajevo at the end of March, where the mainly Muslim Bosniak population gave him a warm welcome, and he repeated his message that the Bosnian Croats must turn to Sarajevo for the solution to their problems and abandon hopes of political union with Croatia.

The new team were most successful in their foreign policy objectives. They wanted to dispel international disapproval of Croatia, banish its image as something of a rogue state and start the process of integration into the European Union and other Western financial and defence structures. Mostly they succeeded. The endless international carping and grumbling about Croatia stopped dead. EU delegations came and went and murmured pleasant things. Within a year of taking office, the Croatian government had signed up to Nato's Partnership for Peace programme, joined the World Trade Organisation and had started negotiations on a Stability Pact with the EU, the first step to joining the organisation. The new leaders talked vaguely of being in a position to join by 2005.

The coalition enjoyed other political successes. The inclusion of the main Istrian party partly defused a potentially tricky confrontation with separatism in a geo-politically sensitive region that remained a focus of irredentist agitation for the Italian extreme right.[7] The government lifted the heavy-handed control of the state television and radio, and reporters relaxed in the new, less pressurised, atmosphere. There was an end to the constant, dispiriting xenophobia that marked the Tudjman era and the endless preoccupation with convoluted Western 'plots' against Croatia's independence. The new president lived up to his pledge to preside over the reduction of his own powers, saving his right to command the armed forces. A by-product of the new atmosphere was the decline of the far right. Only a few years previously, the ultra-nationalist far right appeared a disturbing phenomenon that threatened to destabilise the country's infant democracy and deepen its isolation from the Western mainstream. By 2001, the neo-fascists had evaporated as a serious force and their main exponents, the Party of Rights, had toned down its language and largely dumped the cult of the Ustashe.

Croatia was developing into a normal democracy. And yet the country still did not quite feel liberated. Partly, this was because the relaxation in the political atmosphere was not accompanied by an obvious improvement in the economy. Journalists and human rights activists praised the new freedom in Mesić's Croatia.[8] Consumers and wage earners felt less happy. The government's excuse was that it inherited a poor situation, including a balance of payments crisis, a foreign debt of $10bn, zero economic growth, a slight fall in industrial production and an unemployment rate of 23 per cent. In fact, the unemployment statistics obscured a more serious situation. Other EU states, including Spain, lived with high unemployment rates. Croatia's problem was that those nominally in work included many who were rarely or never paid and an even larger number who were paid but could not live on their wages. The average monthly wage of about 3,000 kune, less than $400, was far lower than the Western European average, yet the price of many foodstuffs was almost the same and the cost of rented accommodation was high.

The pattern of unemployment was also geographically uneven, creating pockets of extreme poverty. In some Dalmatian cities, such as Šibenik, it was 50 per cent. The picture was even worse in the old Krajina. Bosnian Croat refugees from central Bosnia had been siphoned into Knin by the Tudjman government to change the area's ethnic composition. But no jobs followed these refugees, few of whom brought any capital with them. Pre-war Knin had lived off the railways, a subsidised nuts and bolts factory and army pensions. The new townspeople were not old army officers, the factory was closed and Knin's days as a Balkan railway junction were over. By 2001 some of the inhabitants were on the edge of starvation.

Like Serbs and Bosnians, Croats were skilled at surviving on small salaries and supplementing their wages through the unofficial 'grey' economy. For all that, life was visibly a disappointment to a great many people. The waving of once-forbidden flags and the singing of once-forbidden songs no longer lifted people's spirits. The Croats had long cherished the notion that it was Belgrade and Serbia that had stopped them from becoming as rich as the Austrians or even the

Swiss. They thought that once they were out of 'the Balkans' and into the dreamland of Central Europe, they would start to enjoy the 'Dolce Vita'. Ten years into independence, Croatia was a more sober, sadder society. The Freedom Train had ground, if not to a halt, to a snail's pace. The Croatian nationalists under Franjo Tudjman had failed to deliver the Promised Land, and so too, to a great extent, had the coalition that had replaced the HDZ. The future appeared to offer young people infinitely more political freedom than their parents had known, more choice in terms of lifestyle and career, and that most elusive of commodities, peace. But there was also a feeling that the nation had been stripped of its comforting illusions, and of the dreams that had kept so many hopes alive.

20

La Dolce Vita

A better life, unburdened of the national disputes and wrangles of the past.
Prime Minister Ivo Sanader's pledge to Croatia, 2005[1]

Behind the ivy-clad walls of Mirogoj cemetery, the ex-president slept under his vast black tomb in the company of the great and the good. A few lamps flickered around the grave. Ten years after his death, the smooth sheen of the marble edifice spoke of permanence.

But if Franjo Tudjman's tomb looked as if it might last for centuries without suffering so much as a hairline crack, the same could not be said of his political legacy. 'It's as if he never existed,' the retired politician Ivo Škrabalo remarked approvingly. 'There are probably more people in Croatia who revere Tito than him, to judge by the coach loads that still visit Tito's birthplace in Kumrovec.' A liberal rather than left-wing critic of the ex-president, Škrabalo never had much time for the self-proclaimed father of Croatian independence. Now in his seventies, he reminisced over past encounters with the general dating back to the 1960s, none of them favourable. 'Tudjman was an elementary disaster,' he said. 'He led Croatia through the war and to victory, but then led us to defeat in Bosnia and wasted our moral capital in doing so.' Croatia's moral standing had been at its peak in 1991, he went on. 'That was then thrown away. He let the spirit out of the bottle over the Ustashe. There had been a consensus that no one should talk positively about the Ustashe, not even relatively. Tudjman destroyed that taboo.' The damning indictment rolled on. There had been a corrupt privatisation process, the 'feudal-style' division of political and economic power between a few hundred families, the alienation of Europe, the pandering to extreme elements among the diaspora.

Ivica Račan, Tudjman's left-wing successor, did not receive a markedly better verdict. 'A ditherer', maintained Škrabalo, who failed to take meaningful advantage of the HDZ's election débâcle in 2000, when he might have delivered a *coup de grace* to the HDZ by calling local elections to accompany the parliamentary and presidential elections. By failing to do so, he allowed the HDZ to retain its power base in local government from which it soon re-launched itself. Škrabalo shook his head, recalling Račan's 'chaotic' cabinet sessions and the plaintive voice of the prime minister struggling to be heard over the cacophony. No wonder that after only three years in opposition the HDZ had returned to office under a new leader, Ivo Sanader, after the latter had cleansed the party of its more embarrassing right-wing elements.

Whether Škrabalo's description of Tudjman as a forgotten figure was entirely accurate is a moot point. Croatia's liberals have always been discontented and frustrated. The country's difficult geopolitical position never favoured them. Liberalism in twentieth-century Croatia had a doomed quality to it. According to the historian and rights activist Andrea Feldman, 'The steady line of suppression of individual rights and national freedoms; dictatorships, ranging from the royal dictatorship of King Aleksandar to the Fascist-sponsored Ustasha dictatorship during World War II to the Communist one in its aftermath, the abolition of democratic procedures by monarchists, Ustasha and Communists alike – all prevented the development of liberalism in any form.'[2]

Tudjman's most important legacy was surely unassailable: the Croatian state, the fulfilment of the 'thousand-year-old dream', as he put it. This was Tudjman's solid creation, achieved in opposition to the will of almost every significant world power apart from Germany. That had lasted, and prospered, to a degree. At the same time, Tudjman had left behind him no personal following. There was no dynasty to perpetuate his memory like that of the Ghandis in India,[3] no personality cult to match that of Ataturk or De Gaulle. Even his own political creation, the HDZ, made no attempt to capitalise on his memory. His name was rarely invoked in speeches and his picture rarely displayed. A trickle of people journeyed to his birthplace in Veliko Trgovišće, only a few miles from Tito's childhood home in Kumrovec. But the modest house in which Tudjman grew up, though now a museum, has never developed into a popular shrine.[4]

For some on the left, naturally, Tudjman remains a hate figure – the destroyer of Yugoslavia. The Amsterdam-based writer Dubravka Ugrešić has described Tudjman and his allies simply as 'criminals out for money who manipulated people with that ethno-nationalist stuff'.[5] But these are hardly mainstream opinions. For most Croats the reason for his falling away into oblivion is less to do with active dislike; they just want to forget the apocalyptic 1990s. The public warmed to the tall Dalmatian Sanader, to his talk of rebranding Croatia as a modern democracy and to his repetition of bland, easily digestible buzzwords about peace, cooperation and prosperity. It was a pleasant change from all those appeals to memory and sacrifice. Most Croats also liked Tudjman's folksy-looking successor as president, Stipe Mesić. As head of state for two terms until 2010, he dispensed with Tudjman's regal style and with most of the president's former prerogatives. Looking more like the convivial landlord of a country inn than a president, Mesić engaged voters in a way that the remote, regal Tudjman had never done. As one journalist, Trpimir Čokolić, not a fan, put it, 'He's a populist with a sense of humour. He talks in a way people like to hear.'[6]

There was, however, a downside to this folksiness. Initially feted abroad merely for not being Tudjman, Mesić was soon equally forgotten in foreign capitals. Whereas Tudjman had made Croatia notorious, Mesić had the contrary effect – of making it look inconsequential. His diplomatic impact outside the old Yugoslav zone was almost nil, his occasional trips to western capitals arousing little interest. If he had anything to say on the great international issues of the day, no one cared to find out what his opinions were. By the end of his second mandate, these slightly underwhelming escapades abroad had more or less ceased. His last official visits, paid to Kosovo and Slovenia, had a pointless air to them. A visit by a Croatian leader meant little to the Albanians of Kosovo, whose new state depended for its existence on the goodwill of America, not Croatia. At the same time, the visit infuriated Serbia.

Relations with Serbia had indeed deteriorated during Mesić's second term. By the time he retired, two moderate, centrist pro-EU governments, in Belgrade and Zagreb, were busy lobbing unwinnable international lawsuits for genocide at one another,[7] while Mesić had further riled the Serbs by threatening military intervention against the Bosnian Serbs should they secede from Bosnia and Herzegovina.[8] It was to be hoped that Mesić's successor, Ivo Josipović, the Social Democrat elected in January 2010,[9] would handle foreign relations – one of the few areas in which Croatian presidents can take the initiative – with a surer touch.

Meanwhile, the determination of Croats to move on and put the dark, dismal 1990s behind them was evident in the transformation of Zagreb. To anyone who had not lived there since the 1990s, it was a different city a decade after Tudjman's death. The bedraggled metropolis of the late twentieth century, with its bone-shaking trams, grime-encrusted facades, dreary shops and weary-looking populace, had more or less vanished. The Upper Town had been scrubbed and repainted, the cobbled lane linking it to the nineteenth-century Lower Town no longer a wasteland but home to craft shops and designer boutiques. Throughout the city a retail revolution was visibly in progress as a new generation of small-scale entrepreneurs rediscovered the value of their country's traditional produce. Upmarket stores no longer proclaimed their elite pretensions by displaying cheap foreign liqueurs in their windows, as if something could only be any good if it were foreign. The new stores, selling wines from Dalmatia, foodstuffs from Slavonia and other old-fashioned peasant products, repackaged and remarketed for a new, urban clientele, were testament to the existence of a new entrepreneurial spirit. Whether all these businesses would survive the recession sweeping Europe was uncertain, but it was clear that Croatia was shedding its old instinct to culturally cringe before everything from abroad.

The most obvious change to overtake Croatia in the decade since Tudjman's death was not the capital's shiny new shops but the astonishing rise in the purchasing power of the average citizen. The battered-looking population of the 1990s looked sleeker and better clad. Youngsters had always paraded the latest fashions in the former Yugoslavia, but that was because their parents and grandparents went without so that their spoiled offspring might shine. What was novel was the sight of so many well-turned-out older women sporting imitation designer watches and handbags. The absence of visible poverty, let alone homeless beggars, was striking. Yet, this wealth was not evenly spread. Parts of the country had fallen behind, relatively and absolutely. Eastern Slavonia, that fought-over border zone between Serbia and Croatia, had not recovered as a centre of industry and agriculture. The martyred town of Vukovar received the clunky appellation of 'hero city' in the 1990s. But this Soviet-style label had not done much to help revive a moribund and still divided community. On Croatian television, I watched the town's desperate-looking mayor alternately pleading with and criticising a panel of fellow mayors from around the country for having failed to honour pledges to rebuild the ruined town. The mighty Borovo industrial complex had once employed some 23,000 people, he said, and 'now it is more like 450!'[10] While the mayor looked overwrought, his brother mayors, seated around a table in the television studio, fidgeted and stared at their watches. They looked smooth and manicured by comparison, worthy human emblems of their prosperous towns. In protesting they murmured the names of various projects they had undertaken in Vukovar.

The hero city had gone the way of countless so-called 'mono-towns' in Europe, Russia and America that had once lived off a single employer and which, following that employer's demise, had lost all sense of purpose. They were effectively orphans. Vukovar's case, for a host of war-related reasons, was among the most extreme. But the whole of Slavonia, including the regional capital of Osijek, had suffered relative economic decline, losing out as the tectonic plates shifted in a general fashion from east to west, from the continent to the Mediterranean. As the national capital and as the centre of approximately half the country's economy, Zagreb was a great exception to this westwards shift. Young people from Split, the biggest city on the coast, continued to gravitate northeast to Zagreb to seek work after completing their studies. And some other continental, Pannonian towns were also doing well, such as the businesslike Čakovec on the border with Hungary or picturesque baroque Varaždin, now reinventing itself as a university city – a miniature Bologna. Nor was the whole of Dalmatia prospering. The war-devastated interior around Knin and Drniš remained stuck in remorseless decline. The government had rebuilt thousands of houses there since 1995 but homes alone had not kickstarted an economic revival. There was, quite simply, nothing to do in these barren uplands. Many of the newer inhabitants, refugees from Bosnia, had no connection to the area and brought little capital with them. Transferred to houses vacated by Serbs and to a landscape markedly different to the one from which they had come, many had drifted into a state of permanent dependency on welfare. According to one study of Knin, about 50 per cent of the population were jobless.[11] The tatty appearance of this long-ago royal capital told its own sorry tale of the town's downward trajectory. As for the outlying towns and villages in the country, the same study had concluded that their prospects were even bleaker. Home to ageing, impoverished and shrinking populations, these smaller rural communities, it said, were 'threatened with extinction'.[12]

Important though they were, these exceptions did not counteract an overall impression that the centre of gravity in Croatia was shifting from the interior towards the Adriatic. Coastal Zadar had been one of the worst hit cities in the 1990s, a traumatised, desperate place, its hotels full of refugees, their washing flapping from the hotel windows. Since then, the town had undergone a renaissance. Tourism boomed following the arrival of low-cost airlines, prompting some to dub Zadar 'a phoenix rising from the ashes'.[13] As for the necklace of offshore islands, these had become the haunts of the rich and famous. The azure waters surrounding Hvar and Korčula had always attracted a sprinkling of wealthy foreigners. Edward VIII and his American mistress Wallis Simpson holidayed in Dalmatia back in 1936. But now the pleasure craft of the super-rich, some resembling small liners in size, jostled for space in the harbour of Hvar's old town – a tourist attraction in their own right in all their vulgar ostentation.

The region of Istria, close to Italy, had also prospered and become one of the country's richest, thriving on a combination of tourism, small industries such as the production of high-quality wine, and popular festivals like the annual film festival in the formerly deserted hilltop town of Motovun. Istria and eastern Slavonia were studies in contrast. Both border regions, one had flourished as a direct consequence of this fact while the other had declined.

Government policy assisted this shift from east to west. Strengthening the bonds between the lands of Slavonia and Dalmatia has been the aim of every Croatian patriot since the revolutionary decade of the 1840s when Ban Jelačić tried and failed to unite Dalmatia and '*banska Hrvatska*' into one polity. Now Jelačić's goal was much more of a reality. Construction of the A1 motorway from Zagreb to the coast, which would one day reach Dubrovnik, had begun under the Communist regime but languished, a casualty of the endless tussles between Zagreb and Belgrade over their respective infrastructural projects. When the Zagreb–Split section of this highly significant transport link was completed in 2005, the journey time by car fell by half from about six hours to three. The installation of a high-speed, 'tilting' train between Zagreb and Split had a similar effect, helping to bring the two cities closer to one another.

Some *grands projets*, predictably, had proved too ambitious for a country on limited resources. Plans to build a vast and expensive bridge linking the Pelješac peninsula near Dubrovnik to the rest of Dalmatia had to be shelved in 2009.[14] Like the A1, this was a project whose purpose was as much symbolic as practical. The bridge was not only intended to cut the journey time from Zagreb to Dubrovnik but also to save travellers from the need to cross Bosnian coastal territory around Neum when they did so. Like the A1, the bridge was really about knitting the Croats' fragmented lands into a seamless whole. But as the cost of the bridge soared, as scandals emerged over profiteers buying the surrounding land and as the economy deteriorated, the bridge began to appear an unaffordable luxury.

The loser in all this frantic infrastructural activity was Slavonia. No longer sitting at the busy crossroads of northern Yugoslavia, the region was now more of a cul-de-sac at Croatia's forgotten east end. Once a breadbasket for the whole of Yugoslavia, it remained the agricultural heartland of Croatia. But this obviously was a much smaller market, containing fewer than 5 million people as opposed to

23 million.[15] By the start of the twenty-first century, Slavonia's farmers were struggling. Their chief political advocates, the Croatian Peasants Party, the old party of Radić and Maček, had succeeded in extracting significant state subsidies for farmers as the price of their support for various coalition governments. But even with subsidies Croatian farming was in deep trouble, unable to compete against cheaper imported foodstuffs from Hungary or Ukraine. Slavonia's farmers would have to diversify and specialise. Some were doing so, moving into the production of organic foods and high-end delicacies like salamis and better wine varieties, or raising newer crops like lavender. But diversification requires start-up capital, professional know-how and oodles of confidence. Most Slavonian farmers had little, if any, of these.

Osijek was becoming the Cinderella of Croatian cities, having been left out of the ambitious infrastructural plans of the previous decade. Though closer to Zagreb than Split – 130 miles away as opposed to 160 – the country's fourth city had a marooned feel to it. It took a ridiculous eight hours to reach by train from Zagreb, far longer than it takes to go from London to Marseilles. It was equally ill served by bus. While the low-cost airlines had helped open up Dubrovnik and Zadar, as well as Split, Osijek remained in the middle of an airline black hole. As a result the city's elegant Secessionist facades were totally unknown to the kind of international travellers who had long since discovered other Eastern European 'second cities' like Timişoara and Gdańsk. The nearby Kopački Rit marshes, potentially one of Europe's best bird-watching centres, was another unexploited asset. Fifteen years on from the signing of the Dayton Peace Accords, parts of the marsh were still mined.

In politics, there was a changing of the guard at the end of the decade. Mesić, a longstanding president, departed and so did Ivo Sanader, a longstanding prime minister. Sanader resigned early in July 2009, without warning or much in the way of subsequent explanation. Some saw it as a Houdini-like escape from a rapidly worsening economic situation, others as the denouement of an internal party coup staged by disaffected HDZ right-wingers. His disappearance caught the public completely by surprise. The great showman of politics vanished on 1 July, handing the reins to a little-known understudy, a former minister for family and war veterans, Jadranka Kosor. While the public was mystified and felt vaguely insulted by the secretive and abrupt manner of Sanader's leave-taking, it was not difficult to list some of the factors that might have led him to throw in the towel.

In his six years as prime minister, following the ejection of Račan's centre-left coalition in 2003, Sanader had staked his reputation on two pledges. One was to raise the living standards of ordinary Croats; give them a taste of *la dolce vita* – 'a better life, unburdened of the national disputes and wrangles of the past', as he put it.[16] The other was to deliver membership of the European Union – proof that the Croatian state had finally arrived. For most of those six years Sanader appeared to succeed in his pursuit of both ambitions. Wages and pensions rose and EU talks proceeded, plus or minus a few hiccups. After the arrest in Spain in 2005 of the last major war crimes suspect, General Ante Gotovina, and his subsequent transfer to The Hague,[17] the government in Zagreb felt the dead weight of the unpopular tribunal slipping from its shoulders. Now it would be full steam ahead to Brussels. But in the summer of 2009 the Dalmatian wizard lost his touch. As the chill wind of global economic downturn blew over Croatia, it became clear that the public finances were in a far deeper state of disarray than people had realised, largely as a consequence of Sanader's headlong dash for instant prosperity. As for the EU, the eruption like a painful boil of a simmering dispute with Slovenia, and its careless and overconfident management by Sanader, dashed Croatia's immediate hopes of joining the club. It could no longer even be taken for granted that Croatia would become the 28th member, now a stricken Iceland had expressed an interest in joining.

The conflict with Slovenia was almost inexplicable, both to outsiders and to most of the inhabitants of the countries concerned. The Slovene demands concerned minor adjustments of the land border on the Istrian peninsula and, more importantly, of the maritime border in the Piran Bay, so as to grant Slovenia access to international waters in the Adriatic. Precisely what the Slovenes wanted, why they wanted it and what the Croats had in principle conceded or might concede in future was far harder to work out. Thus had a small ghost of the terrible Yugoslav wars of the 1990s returned in farcical form. Unlike the conflict with Serbia in the early 1990s, no great principle about freedom or self-determination was at stake. This was the original 'senseless Balkan quarrel' of media legend. The struggle for access to the Adriatic Sea was almost devoid of significance because the Italians' appetite for seafood had already emptied it of most of its fish. Slovenia had joined Italy in torpedoing a Croatian plan to protect what remained of the fish in 2008; the two countries united to compel Zagreb to abandon its plans to set up a maritime protection zone, invoking the usual threats about blocking Croatia's EU accession plans.[18] At least Italy's interest in the dispute was real, for the Italians caught about ten times more fish in Croatian waters each year than did the Croats. Slovenia, on the other hand, had no identifiable interest in hastening the environmental destruction of the Adriatic, but had merely found the temptation to humiliate its neighbour irresistible.

If the Slovenes were guilty of abusing their insider position in the EU to blackmail their neighbour, Sanader had also been at fault, having failed to spot that the Slovenes were not bluffing. Unwisely, he had encouraged the Croats to believe that in this poker game he held an ace up his sleeve; he had only a joker. He would have been better off coming clean and confessing he had no secret weapon to deploy against Slovenia. Perhaps he assumed Germany would dig him out of this hole. If so, not for the first time, Croatia fell victim to its exaggerated faith in German intentions. Neither Germany nor any other big state in the EU had applied any pressure against Greece to stop it from blackmailing its Macedonian neighbour over the use of its name. It was foolish of Croatia to imagine that Brussels would be more pro-active against Slovenia. Brussels did nothing, washed its hands of the row and declared, as with the Greece–Macedonia conflict, that this was a purely bilateral dispute. Having led Croatian public opinion up the hill on the question of the dispute with Slovenia, Sanader now faced the disagreeable task of leading it back down again – or would have done had he remained in office. His successor, Jadranka Kosor, was left to pick up the pieces. In the event, she did better in attempting to defuse the dispute, as a result of which Slovenia seemed willing to lift its blockade on the closure of the remaining chapters of Croatia's EU accession negotiations. In its interim report in October 2009, the European Commission suggested that if Croatia made more progress in reforming the judiciary and in tackling organised crime, it might yet join the EU by 2010 or 2011. Weary of the endless wrangling over Europe and the constant demands to reform their country, most Croats were no longer listening.[19] Still, in her handling of the border dispute, Kosor had showed a degree of form. She would show form again in January 2010, when Sanader suddenly re-emerged from nowhere, demanded his old job back and dramatically accused Kosor of presiding over a sell-out to Slovenia. His reward for this crazed-looking attempted putsch was his immediate expulsion from the HDZ. A political career that had once promised much appeared to have ended on a forlorn note.

Apart from the Slovenes, the economy had also risen up to stab Sanader in the back. During his years at the helm he had presided over the steady rise in living standards that had given Croatia its sudden, glossy patina. Hence the fast cars that almost everyone seemed to own, the smartened up population, the new shops catering for clients who could afford fripperies as well as essentials, the advertisements for holidays in Cuba, Vietnam and Cambodia rather than good old Opatija. To outward appearances, Croatia had undergone a German-style *Wirtshaftswunder*, an economic miracle. The trouble was that it had done no such thing. By the time Sanader left the stage it was clear the Croatian wizard had presided not over a miracle but an elaborate conjuring trick. Economists had been warning for years that Croatia was purchasing prosperity on the cheap by running up eye-watering amounts of foreign debt whose repayment was only possible while yet more foreign credit remained obtainable at low-interest rates. Croats had often complained about the voodoo economics of the old Yugoslavia, which had ratcheted up living standards by borrowing more and more money. As an independent state, Croatia pursued a very similar approach, borrowing money to pay wages and social security bills and increase pensions rather than to invest in the future.

When the credit crisis struck, Croatia's position looked difficult as the budget deficit yawned, prompting speculation over whether Croatia could retain its international credit rating. According to one leading economist, the decade since Tudjman's death had been largely wasted. While Croatia's neighbours had in some cases doubled their export share to the European Union, Croatia's share had remained almost static. The public sector was overstaffed and unreformed. The private sector had failed to diversify and become more competitive. 'Croatia spent half the previous decade in war and we're still facing the consequences,' Hrvoje Stojić said. 'War veterans' pensions alone consume about 2.5 per cent of our GDP, which is a huge amount of money taken out of the economy every year.'[20] Croats had failed to realise, Stojić continued, that their former modest prosperity had been anchored to the existence of a captive Yugoslav market. It had relied on the export of finished food products and other consumer items to less developed Yugoslav republics, which were foreign states and often less reliant on Croatian imports than before. Meanwhile, there had been insufficient effort to compensate for this loss by increasing exports to the EU.

Throughout almost two decades of independence, with only one interval, the HDZ, a nominally right-wing party, had been running the economy. But neither Tudjman nor Sanader had pursued a particularly conservative, free market agenda. On the contrary, the HDZ had thrown a Scandinavian-style safety net under the least productive sectors of society without bothering to find out whether the country had the means to pay for it. The beneficiaries included not only pensioners and the unemployed but a huge number of war veterans. Other sectors of society, such as farmers, received constant injections of public funds through subsidies. The ratio of wealth-producers to subsidy-consumers and pensioners was unsatisfactory. Croatia had become a country with proportionally one of the largest, and youngest, categories of pensioners in Europe, a country in which about one-quarter of the adult population paid for the other three-quarters. 'By constantly raising taxes they're penalising the workforce and distributing the proceeds to those requiring state support,' said Stojić, who insisted that the government had to start cutting public spending. 'We're one of the highest taxed states in the EU already,' he went on. The question was whether the political will to reform matters existed. This economist was doubtful. 'The ruling party has wasted the good years and failed to reform the economy during all that time. They just used cheap money raised on external markets to increase spending.'[21]

As with the tangled dispute with Slovenia, Sanader had not bequeathed a favourable situation to his successor. Kosor would have to preside over the inevitable painful public spending cuts that he had avoided, and address the question of whether a relatively poor country could afford to keep hundreds of thousands of war veterans on pensions for life when some of those 'pensioners' were still in their forties. As veterans minister, she had defended their interests. Meanwhile, the veterans' associations remained a powerful political force. They were unofficially affiliated to the HDZ, and their leaders could deliver a sizeable bloc vote on polling day. It was hard to imagine any HDZ-led government, let alone one led by Kosor,[22] risking a clash with them by subjecting their long membership rolls to close examination.

Another obstacle preventing reform of the country's finances was the electoral system.[23] In some ways, the system of proportional representation had become a curse, inflicting unstable and unprincipled coalitions on the country and saddling the ruling party with a clutch of allies whose support in parliament came at a high price. The system put small regional or special interest parties in a peculiarly strong position, effectively able to dictate marriage terms with the HDZ or the Social Democrats even when they held no more than a couple of seats. Hungry for those extra votes in parliament, the big parties had no option but to sign up to these arrangements, for, as in the dispute with Slovenia, only one side held a loaded weapon. The HDZ was not even entirely free to select with which minor parties it wished to work because for political and historical reasons no government could be seen to turn to the extreme right for support. That left a clutch of regional and ethnic minority parties, the party representing the pensioners[24] and the Peasants

Party, the latter two of which set tough terms in demanding money for farmers and above-inflation deals for the elderly. According to some gloomy economists, Croatia had become caught in the coils of economic populism and the only hope was that some external force, like the IMF, would literally force the government to change its spendthrift ways.

The authorities still hoped that the annual summer influx of foreign tourists would continue to rescue Croatia's finances from meltdown and so postpone the day of reckoning. In fact, the tourism industry held up remarkably well. Regular predictions that foreign visitors would grow bored of Croatia and go elsewhere, put off by rising prices and often sullen service, proved unfounded. The high exchange rate of the national currency, the kuna, had pushed up prices. But prices in holiday resorts in other countries had risen even faster, especially in Greece and Turkey, the two most direct competitors, as a result of which Croatia never lost its competitive advantage. In spite of the credit crunch, Italian, German, British and Czech families continued to spend their summers on Croatian beaches, whatever their financial troubles at home. Accounting for about 20 per cent of the country's economy, tourism, therefore, looked set to remain an important pillar of the country's prosperity. But tourism alone could not support everything. The high season was relatively brief at no more than two months, and the beaches were already very full, which suggested that future expansion in the hospitality industry would have to involve greater diversification into luxury, off-season and winter tourism. The country needed more foreigners to visit Zagreb and the continental spa towns. It needed more ecological and wildlife tourism.

Not everything to do with the Croatian economy was doom and gloom. Academics complained of falling standards at universities and of an exodus of graduates, but the brain drain from Croatia was as nothing compared to what was going on in Serbia, let alone Bosnia and Herzegovina. An agreeable climate, a relaxed lifestyle and all those beaches kept many people at home. In spite of high VAT rates and the depressive effect this had on trade and consumption, plenty of young businessmen and women were still willing to make a go of things in Croatia. The country remained more favourably positioned economically than several others in Eastern Europe, such as hugely indebted Latvia and most of its Balkan neighbours. The national bank was respected. But as Darko Markušić, editor of the business daily *Poslovni dnevnik*, explained: 'We're now having to confront the issues we failed to resolve in the 1990s.' Governments would pay a price for the fact that 'after the war the people wanted everything – and now!'[25]

On 24 July 2009, the recently inaugurated high-speed tilting train from Split to Zagreb came off the tracks killing six passengers. Some careless workers, tasked with spraying the sleepers underneath the line with a solution to prevent fires, had not left sufficient time for the greasy fluid to dry before the next train passed through. On a flat track it might not have mattered, but the railway from Zagreb to Split resembled a fairground dipper, rising up and plunging down a series of steep valleys in Lika and Dalmatia. Not far from Split the wheels on the train began to skid and the driver lost control. It was an unfortunate accident, perhaps, which could have happened anywhere. But the arrest only days earlier of a former director of the railway company and two of his colleagues, on suspicion of embezzling about €3 million, added to suspicions that the railway's ills were deep-seated and that both the train crash and this exposure of corruption symbolised what had gone wrong with the public sector in Croatia. A flurry of investigative articles in the media painted an unflattering portrait of an overstaffed and unreformed corporation whose finances were far from transparent, which had used up large sums of public money with scant results and which was riddled with corruption. They cited a 2005 World Bank study, which showed that the level of productivity per staff member was only 50 per cent of the EU average.[26] The Bank had said it was urgent to reduce state subsidies, close unprofitable lines and shed at least 30 per cent of the staff over a three-year period. But a separate World Bank report,[27] following up a bank loan of $100 million granted in 2001, revealed that those recommendations had not been acted on, with the exception of the axing of a number of jobs.[28] The story of the railway loan was, it seemed, a familiar one. Officials had made various pledges to secure the cash only to abandon those pledges, one by one, under the pressure of domestic vested interests. The unions had demanded and obtained thumping pay increases of about 40 per cent for most staff. The company had sacked some personnel, but, fearing union trouble, achieved this by offering costly severance packages. As a result, a loan taken out to 'modernise' the railway had largely been diverted into wage increases. Meanwhile, the company managers were busy sucking out funds and stashing the loot in offshore accounts. 'What is clear', fumed the *Nedeljni Jutarnji*, 'is that there will be no change in the circumstances of Croatian Railways while petty theft from the company remains an everyday phenomenon.'[29]

Scandals never dominated the headlines for long in Croatia, however, simply because a new one always came along. True enough, a bigger scandal, concerning the Virovitica-based food giant

Podravka soon grabbed the public by the ears. Was Croatia a more corrupt society than it had been in the 1990s or 1980s, or did the difference lie chiefly in the fact that the people now talked openly about it? It was certainly becoming the number one issue in public. The fact that Ivo Josipović had not been tainted by corruption allegations was an important factor behind his successful bid to secure the presidency in 2010. A few startling events had pushed matters out into the open in the preceding years. One was the assassination in 2008 of Ivo Pukanić, publisher of the magazine *Nacional* and a personal friend of president Mesić. A bomb placed in his car killed him and his marketing manager in front of the publication's office on 23 October that year. Pukanić had become a notorious figure thanks to his reported ties to the secret services and tragic personal life. The twilight world of gangsters clearly fascinated him, prompting accusations that he had become part of a phenomenon he claimed to be investigating. More recently, his public profile had been raised by the release on the Internet of a video that showed police dragging his distressed wife out of her apartment in handcuffs and taking her off to a psychiatric hospital. Pukanić's murder a few months later was not linked to his dysfunctional marriage. The most likely explanation was that his media investigations into the subterranean world of cigarette-smugglers had annoyed some of the mafia dons. Normally, such feuds were resolved far from the public gaze. This one was not. To the inhabitants of sedate, early-to-bed Zagreb, a Chicago-style assassination in the middle of the street was shocking, still more so as it followed only days after the gunning down of the daughter of a prominent lawyer.[30]

Sanader's reaction to these events had been inept, an early sign that he was losing his touch. Pledging in panicky fashion not to allow Zagreb to become a new Beirut, his choice of words suggested that law and order in Croatia had broken down completely. In reality, Zagreb bore no resemblance to the war-torn Lebanese capital, which, incidentally, now boasted one of the lowest homicide rates in the world. Zagreb was not even in danger of becoming the new Sofia, a city that really had fallen into the maw of conflicting mafias.[31] Far from becoming Europe's crime central, Zagreb remained the sleepy capital of a country with a remarkably low annual murder rate of about 1.62 per 100,000. Croatia was, in fact, less murderous than New Zealand. The average American was more than four times likely to be a victim of homicide than was a citizen of Croatia, and the average Russian ten times.[32] Nevertheless, while Sanader's reaction to the Pukanić murder was overblown, the event itself could not be brushed aside as a complete aberration. It was a watershed of sorts, a reminder that under the placid surface Zagreb was not the 'Little

Vienna' of many Croats fond imagination. The dreaded 'Balkans' was nearer than they knew.

To some, the blame for this loss of innocence lay with the wars of the 1990s, when many things were permitted and when people who might have remained in obscurity had obtained great wealth and power. Others blamed the blanket of silence thrown over Croatia's Communist past, one result of which was that society had never started afresh. 'It's not possible for Croatia to be more corrupt now than it was in the 1990s,' the Dalmatian-born journalist Barbara Matejcic told me. She believed that in Croatia a culture of 'shared secrets' welded together a political class that was heavily dominated by ex-Communists and former party apparatchiks, from President Mesić downwards. This culture of silence had provided a cover under which criminal and secret societies had flourished. 'This country has never addressed the communist past. The changes have all been folkoric; street-names, statues and language,' Matejcic said. 'But nothing really changed.' Mate Meštrović, the last surviving son of the great sculptor Ivan Meštrović and a former parliamentarian and diplomat,[33] made a similar point. 'The Communists in Croatia gave up power so they could retain power,' he told me.[34] This position is not only held by former exiles from the Communist regime. The rights activist Andrea Feldman made a similar diagnosis of the root ills of Croatian society. 'No dissidents ever took over here,' she said. 'The only dissident party was the Social Liberals and even they became penetrated by the police. As for the HDZ, they collected up all the old [secret] police apparatus, so there wasn't the same rupture with the past that you had in other countries.'[35] Feldman has angered elements of the Croatian left by questioning their favourite dogma, which is that corruption and organised crime only began in the 1990s, arriving in Tudjman's wake. She disagrees: 'Socialism was a corrupt system that the new system inherited.'[36]

It is arguable that the smoothness of the transition from Communist republic to capitalist independent state was advantageous to Croatia in the 1990s, providing a needed period of internal stability. Comparisons with Spain after the death of General Franco can be evoked, justifiably. Tudjman had clearly wanted an historic reconciliation between former Communists and Fascists, having concluded that without it independence would remain a dream. His own life had illustrated the way in which many Croats had tacked back and forth across the great ideological divides of twentieth-century Europe. His father had been a stalwart of the Peasants Party. Tudjman junior had crossed over to Communism but in late middle age staged a return journey. The cross on the marble surface of his tomb bore witness to where this particular ideological pilgrimage had ended.

It was also arguable that the smooth quality of Croatia's transition in the early 1990s had entailed less benign consequences, at least in the longer term. It created a world of smoke and mirrors in which no one was quite what they seemed; a world of conversations whispered in corridors and of things that went unsaid, and in which subterfuge and deception thrived. Other critics of the way that society had developed pointed a finger in the direction of Herzegovina, blaming the influx of ethnic Croats from over the border for some of the less agreeable changes to the country's character. One of my interlocutors said the Herzegovinians were 'just like Sicilians'; clannish and pushy, showing scant regard for the law. Their influx had been a 'disastrous feature of the Tudjman era', the same man added, and was one of the factors behind what he called 'the militant mediocrity of modern Croatia'.

Whatever the causes of corruption in Croatia, no one seriously doubted that it existed and now touched the lives of almost everyone. One woman, who asked not to be named, told me of her shock on discovering that a widely admired university professor had been found to be selling pass grades to students. A man told me of a disturbing visit to a doctor who made it clear he wanted a backhander. The man's elderly mother needed treatment, and the doctor had suggested they all adjourn to another room to 'discuss terms', to make sure the woman went to the head of the queue. According to this source, 'organised crime is both increasing *and* is being more talked about. Public tenders are corrupt. Exam results are for sale and doctors want bribes before undertaking surgery.' Whether this was a new thing, he couldn't tell. 'In the old Yugoslavia you could also buy the right exam results,' he said.

To some, the failure of the powerful Catholic Church to spearhead a fight-back against these corrosive trends in society was disappointing. Superficially, the Church in Croatia had never been in ruder health. For the first time in a thousand years it was truly free to pursue its mission, unimpeded by meddling interference on the part of foreign Hungarian, Habsburg, Venetian or Serbian rulers, not to mention Communists. Its careworn buildings had mostly been refurbished. New churches were still being built and on a much greater scale than in Western Europe. No churches in Croatia were being sold for conversion into apartment blocks, or mosques. The clerical body and religious orders were younger on average than their counterparts in France, Spain or Italy. This was not a Church that was going to have to rely for the foreseeable future on priests and nuns imported from Latin America and Africa. Yet, all was not well with the Church in Croatia and the decline in its influence and prestige, especially among the young, was palpable. I encountered few people who would admit to having any connection to the Church, and even fewer under 40. Most people in their twenties seem puzzled when questioned about it, its irrelevance to their lives being seen as obvious. Some become annoyed by the question, seeing it as symptomatic of an erroneous foreign assumption that all Croats are 'big Catholics'. Even among the hard core of churchgoers, enthusiasm seems at a low ebb. Cardinal Bozanić, archbishop of Zagreb and Primate since the death of Franjo Kuharić in 2002, is not generally seen as the latter's equal.

One possible reason for the Church's apparent failure to connect with the young is its continuing obsession with its past sufferings in the 1940s and 1950s. It was not willing to relinquish the memory of the tragic, last years of Cardinal Stepinac, the Croats' Thomas a Becket. I found the bookshop inside the offices of the Catholic newspaper, *Glas Koncila*, full of hagiographical accounts of the cardinal whose life-size image stood in the window. The newspaper routinely carries reports of new church buildings, bishops' pastoral addresses and pilgrimages. But there is little in it these days to suggest that *Glas Koncila* once played a significant role in Croatia's cultural and intellectual life, as it did in the 1960s, when Vlado Pavlinić was editor. Still vigorous in his eighties, Pavlinić expressed dismay over what had happened to his former newspaper – 'It's just a church bulletin these days' – and by what has happened to the Church in which he once served as a priest. It was ironic, he noted, that financial and political security had proved so lethal to the Church's spiritual health. Jailed for three years in the 1950s for anti-state activities, Pavlinić looked back on that hard, slate-grey era with a surprising degree of nostalgia. 'At one point, there were forty of us priests in the same prison,' he recalled. 'But it was a time of great spirit, a truly evangelical time. No one went into the Church those days in search of a new car or an easy life!'[37]

The Croatian Church has no shortage of people to staff its houses of worship. At the same time, a self-consciously Catholic intelligentsia seems to have died out, along with a long and illustrious tradition of oddball intellectual bishops. The episcopal hierarchy contains no heirs to the likes of Strossmayer and Vrhovac, or, reaching back into history, of Antun Vrančić,[38] Ivan Vitez and Ivan Česmički, alias Janus Pannonius, the great fifteenth-century Latinist and humanist.[39]

Over the road from the office of *Glas Koncila*, outside the cathedral, I visited the Stepinac museum. Wandering around the exhibits under the fitful gaze of a bored-looking nun – I was the sole visitor that afternoon – I stared at the archbishop's vestments, gloves and photographs. There was Stepinac, handsome in white chinos in the blazing sunshine, leading a national pilgrimage to Palestine in the 1930s. There he was again, older, tenser, perspiring under a harsh light at his trial. There was Stepinac's mother, the incredibly pious Barbara, enveloped in her voluminous peasant headscarf. Near the museum exit lay a selection of souvenirs for sale – portraits, mostly, but cartoonlike, the famous face infantilised and exaggerated, the luminous eyes and the mouth absurdly magnified so as to resemble a kind of faun. There is nothing inappropriate about the Church in Croatia honouring Stepinac's memory. Along with Mindszenty of Hungary and Wyszyński of Poland, he was one of a trio of Catholic primates carved out of granite and who gave the Communist regimes after 1945 a run for their money – at immense personal cost. Yet, one could not help wondering whether the younger generation in Croatia, none of whom had any personal memories of the Cold War and few of whom remembered much about Yugoslavia, identified with this backward-glancing cult.

Chris Cviić, who experienced the very real difficulties of being a young churchgoer in the Zagreb of the late 1940s, said he feared the Church in Croatia had 'missed its opportunity' after the fall of Communism and Yugoslavia. 'It's become a wealthy corporation and is out of touch. The Church became too close to the HDZ and was flattered by the attention of the authorities who gave them a good financial deal.'[40] The Church in Croatia is not the only one in the region to lose its hold on the young. In Slovenia, where the Catholic clergy were politically influential before the Second World War, the decline is even more startling and obvious. The number of Slovenes professing even nominal Catholicism has fallen steadily since independence. According to a European Commission poll of social values in the EU in 2005, only 37 per cent of Slovenes believe in God at all – roughly the same percentage as in highly secular Britain. In Malta, at the other end of the spectrum, the figure was 95 per cent.[41]

The poll did not include Croatia because it was limited to EU member states, but other surveys have suggested that about twice as many Croats as Slovenes retain some kind of belief in God. Catholicism, if only of a nominal, nebulous form, has a more secure future in Croatia because the Church is more closely bound up with the national identity than is the case in Slovenia. The Croatian Church can count on receiving a certain amount of deference in public, at least from the parties on the centre-right, simply for its historic services as keeper of the national flame. However, if it is not careful it could end up like the Church in Spain, a kind of historical relic allowed out for ceremonial occasions but at the same time isolated from the broader currents of national life and essentially talking to itself, while catering to the needs of ageing and diminishing rural, conservative congregations.

One area of public life in Croatia in which the situation had incontrovertibly improved in the early twenty-first century was the treatment of minorities. In the mid-1990s, when Serb militants were in physical possession of almost one-third of the country and when so many Croats lived wretched lives as refugees in hotels, rational discussion of the 'Serbian question' was almost impossible. Then, in the summer of 1995, came Operations Flash and Storm, and almost 200,000 Serbs were swept out of the country, an exodus that left much of the old military border and northern Dalmatia deserted.

While only a minority of that number has returned to Croatia, life has regained a greater semblance of normality for the Serbs who remained in Zagreb, Osijek, Split and the other towns. 'The situation for the Serbs in Croatia is increasingly less bad!' was the semi-humorous formula employed by Croatia's ebullient, and very Serbian, deputy prime minister Slobodan Uzelac. 'The position is not good for sure, but don't forget that for many Croats life is also bad,' he told me. 'The economic transition process has hit everyone.'[42]

Of the 200,000 or so Serbs who either left or were forced out, Uzelac believed about 130,000 had returned at some point or other. 'But that only means they took up Croatian papers,' he cautioned. 'It doesn't mean they actually live here today, and most do not.' These were the Serbs one used to see queuing outside the Croatian consulate in Belgrade, seeking Croatian passports to travel to Europe. Whether the Croatian Serbs living in Serbia would continue to feel much interest in taking up Croatian citizenship in future remained to be seen, because in 2009 Brussels abolished visa requirements for citizens of Serbia.[43] In other words, the main incentive for Croatian Serbs to become Croatian passport-holders disappeared. As for the Serbs who have remained in government-held Croatia following independence, their numbers have also fallen as a result of emigration, Uzelac added. Whether or not the war had directly touched the areas where they lived, they had been affected by the closure of factories and the deliberate 'Croatisation' of such major employers as the police and army. The traditional lifesaver of so many Croatian Serbs, a career in the Yugoslav National Army, evaporated as an option in the 1990s. 'When Serbs were left without jobs, they tended to leave and sell their houses to Croatian refugees from Bosnia and from the Posavina in particular,' Uzelac explained, referring to the region of northern Bosnia 'below the Sava' that now formed part of the Republika Srpska. Those Serbs who had remained in Croatia Uzelac described as 'the most competent members of the community – and the least'. They were well-placed lawyers and professors, people with a stake in their community who didn't want to leave Croatia, or the old, sick and hopeless who couldn't really leave, whether or not they wanted to, and had nowhere to go. According to Uzelac, there was no point in pretending that the average Croat felt anything other than relief at the decline in the size and strength of the Serbian community. 'You won't find many people today who regret the exodus of the Serbs,' he said. 'It's the dominant mind-set; an ethno-centric concept that has not yet disappeared.' He, for one, felt no nostalgia for the Tudjman era when 'the then leadership linked itself to extremist émigrés who were anti-Serbian, and when we were not welcome'.

The tide had started to turn under Račan's left-wing coalition from 2000 to 2003 and this improvement in community relations had continued, against the expectations of most Serbs, when the HDZ under Sanader regained power in 2003. In January 2004, the prime minister had appeared at a Serbian Orthodox Christmas celebration and notably employed the Serbian Orthodox greeting '*Hristos se rodi*' (Christ is risen), a small but symbolically significant gesture. Uzelac claimed that 'Sanader got more out of that than we did', meaning that the gesture cost the prime minister little, while drawing admiring comments from Brussels. 'This is a region of big clashes – religious, political and ideological but we are starting to learn to live with our differences,' he said. 'It's going slowly, but at least it is going in the right direction.'

The Serbs, reduced force that they are, remain *the* minority in Croatia, and their ability to retain their own schools and churches, obtain jobs, be represented in parliament and other state structures – in short, to remain a coherent and visible community – is still seen as a test of Croatia's suitability to join a Europe that no longer defines itself purely in Gaullist terms as a '*Europe des patries*'. But the treatment of the Serbs is not the only test of Croatia's willingness to 'live with minorities', to borrow Uzelac's phrase. Other, smaller communities are also struggling to avoid assimilation and are taking advantage of a reaction, however slight, against the older and more monolithic conception of Croatian society.

In Split, I met the Jewish community activist Ana Lebl. Archaeological discoveries, she explained, proved the existence of a Jewish community in the city at least as far back as the seventh century when the first Latin refugees from the Roman city of Salona made their homes in Diocletian's deserted mausoleum. The Jews had found Split a tolerant and easy-going environment. They were never expelled in the Middle Ages, or subjected to pogroms, as they were in so many cities in England and Germany. Although the area surrounding the present synagogue in Split is still known as 'the ghetto', Lebl said she did not believe this had ever been an isolated ghetto, in the sense of a gated community. Although the laws of Dalmatia's Venetian rulers had applied to Split, as Lebl noted with a laugh, 'Dalmatians are not particularly law-abiding.' Never large in size – Lebl believes it never numbered more than about 500 persons – the Jewish community in Split had been rejuvenated over the centuries by fresh waves of immigrants. The original Roman Jewish community was joined in the early sixteenth century by Sephardic Ladino-speakers, refugees from the intolerant Spain of Ferdinand and Isabella. Ashkenazi settlers from the Habsburg lands came later. These two strands fused in Split, creating the rich variety of names still found in the city – Papos, Finzis, Alkalajs and Altarases on one hand, and Ginsbergs, Schwarzes, Handlers and Morpurgos on the other.

Lebl drew pride from the long and unbroken history of the Jewish community in Split, pointing out ancient niches carved in stone doorways in the old ghetto area to hold *mezuzoth*, tiny prayer scrolls. The name of the street in which I had stayed, Rodrigino Street, honoured Daniel Rodrigo, the sixteenth-century Portuguese immigrant who had designed a new harbour for Split that helped make the city a more important trading destination. It was Rodrigo who, in 1573, had persuaded the city authorities to permit the Jews to open their own cemetery, which remains on the pine-clad hills just above the city.

Disaster struck this ancient, well-integrated community in the Second World War as two plaques on the walls of the synagogue show. The larger of the two commemorates 115 Jewish citizens murdered by the Germans and their Croatian allies, 14 Papos, 12 Finzis and seven Morpurgos among them. The smaller plaque names another 24 who died fighting in the ranks of Tito's Partisan army; four more Papos and three more Finzis. The creation of the State of Israel in 1948 and the imposition of Communist rule confirmed the decline of a wounded community. Youngsters moved to Israel while others married out and assimilated. The synagogue fell silent and about thirteen centuries of history seemed about to come to an end.

Initially, the end of Communist rule did not help matters because Jewish–Croatian relations in the Tudjman era had evolved in a highly depressing fashion. The crimes that the local Fascists had committed against the Jews in the 1940s, which Milošević's Serbia enthusiastically revisited in order to throw a smokescreen over its own atrocities in the 1990s, cried out for some form of intervention. A gesture, or word, was called for, to put to rest any lingering suspicions that the new independent Croatia regarded itself as the heir to Pavelić's creation. Instead, the Croatian leader had waded into a dispute over the number of Jews killed in the Second World War, predictably resulting in obloquy and instantly alienating Jewish opinion worldwide, above all in the United States. Tudjman's naïve and egotistical outburst helped cement a suspicion that all Croats were anti-Semites and Holocaust deniers. Yet, historically, most Croats had never been markedly anti-Jewish. There had been attacks on Jews in towns like Osijek in 1848. In her study of nineteenth-century Croatian liberalism, Feldman cited the letters of the contemporary merchant Ignjat Brlić to his son in which he complained that the 'people of Osijek expel Jews and fool around in different ways'.[44] Overall, however, the Croats had been a lot less prone to anti-Semitism than the Germans, the French, the Balts, or, closer to home, the Hungarians or Romanians. The Croatian peasants entertained no burning grudges against Jews as a group. Writing of Lithuania, Anatol Lieven notes that folkloric renditions of the devil in that part of the world were clearly based on caricatures of Jewish features. 'When a Lithuanian traditional artist wanted a model for the devil, he selected a Jew,' he writes.[45] A fixed idea of Jews as Christ-killers who 'trap Christian children, to sacrifice them and use their blood'[46] was embedded in the national consciousness. None of this applied to Croatia. On the contrary, when the sculptor Meštrović took the daughter of a Varaždin Jewish family, Ruža Klein, as his first wife in the 1900s, his rural relatives in Drniš embraced her without reserve. Meštrović's daughter Maria preserves a charming vignette of her father taking Klein to the family homestead in Otavice, where she gallantly threw herself into carving branches into staves, scything meadows for livestock in winter and joining the Meštrović women 'at the stream to wash clothes that they would spread out to dry on the lawn',[47] tasks probably unfamiliar to a hat-maker in Vienna whose preferred hobby was translating Dante.

Tudjman had missed an historic opportunity to apologise for what had been done to Jews in the name of a warped version of nationalism and at the same time open up a discussion on the generally fruitful relations between Jews and Croats before the Ustashe appeared. Yet, against an otherwise unpromising background, Croatia's small Jewish remnant became more assertive. As Lebl recalled, the community in Split had even expanded briefly in the early 1990s, as Jews fleeing besieged Sarajevo made their way to Dalmatia and, in some cases, remained. The challenge now was to make use of a more pluralistic atmosphere to bring coherence to a small fragmented group many of whom had not gone near a synagogue in years. Lebl had lit upon reviving the Friday night Sabbath meal as a communal act of prayer, culture, conversation and eating. 'We do the basic prayers and then chat,' she said. 'We light the Sabbath candles and for ten minutes or so read the Torah. We have Sephardic cooking and kosher food. Now people know much more about their religion.' Lebl was philosophical about the long-term survival chances of her ageing community but not without hope: 'More and more foreigners are buying homes in Dalmatia, including Americans; maybe some will be Jewish and they will join us.'

In Zagreb, in a small bar near Zrinski park, I met another activist, representing a much larger minority than the Jews. Marko Jurčić is that newest of phenomena in Croatia, a gay rights activist. Only 18 in 2002 when he attended the first Gay Pride march held in Zagreb, he was part of a new generation that barely remembered the wars of the 1990s. 'There can't have been more than 300 of us at the time,' he recalled of that small parade in 1992. 'There were cordons of police around us and the whole square was full of people shouting "Zieg Heil!" and throwing vegetables. Some threw ashtrays.'[48]

Seventeen years on, it is premature to talk of a revolution in social attitudes in Croatia. The 2009 march was another precarious affair in which a thick police cordon separated a slender column of about 600 marchers from a whistling mob of beefy right-wing protesters waving flags and shouting 'Faggots!' Just as Zagreb is not a new Beirut, it's no new Sydney or Madrid either. Like the Spanish, the Croats have declined to revisit the old, destructive left–right ideological disputes. The difference is that whereas Spain shed its reputation for social conservatism almost overnight after Franco's death, Croatia is in some ways more socially conservative than it was in the late 1980s. There is no sign of mainstream Croatia even grudgingly accepting outsiders such as gays and lesbians as part of the national mosaic. In 2007, the Pride march saw violence, with marchers being picked off and attacked as they headed home. Worryingly, most of these assailants were teenagers, which suggests that the phenomenon of aggressive homophobia is growing, not declining. Yet my interlocutor was upbeat, convinced that gays and lesbians were raising their profile in Croatia and would nudge their way into the mainstream in the end. Laws against discrimination and hate speech now formed part of the legal code and even if there was little sign of these laws being applied, their existence had set a standard.

In terms of the social acceptance of gays and lesbians, Jurčić said: 'I wouldn't exclude the possibility that Croatia will be like Britain in ten years' time.'

The Croats are still experimenting with their identity in the same sort of way that people try out new hats. They are not yet certain they have found one with which they can feel comfortable. More than most peoples, they have assumed identities only to complain, sometimes with justification, that they were not suitable. In their time, they have been junior partners in Hungary, a dominion of the Habsburgs, played second fiddle to the Serbs in royal Yugoslavia and then been one of six theoretically equal republics in Communist Yugoslavia. Each arrangement has been angrily discarded.

A small but strategically positioned country on the crossroads of Europe, their lands have always been the object of predatory interest on the part of stronger neighbours. Divided and passed from one power to another, Croats weathered all these changes by adapting. A pragmatic survival instinct has served them well. But it has not come without cost. Too often, the Croats have settled for the role of passive onlookers in their own historical pageant, waiting for others to give directions.

Ivan Rupnik, a young architect, explained the impact of the dramatic changes in Croatia's political landscape on the physical appearance of the capital. The striking-looking pavilion built by Meštrović, he noted, was originally conceived as a monument to King Peter I of Serbia, 'Peter the Liberator' (of the Habsburg Slavs), as he was known. By the time the building actually opened in 1938, however, Serbian kings were no longer seen in Croatia as liberators and Maček's Croatian *Banovina* was about to become a reality, so the pavilion opened as an exhibition centre for Croatian art. When the Fascist Ustashe took power only a few years later the building was transformed into a mosque, complete with freestanding minarets, symbolising Zagreb's new role as the capital of Bosnia as well as Croatia. After the Partisan victory, and Bosnia's separation from Croatia, the minarets came down and the building was rededicated to the 'Victims of Fascism'. In 1955, it became a 'Museum of the People's Liberation' and in 1962, in a vague nod to growing national sentiment, a 'Museum of the Revolution of the Peoples of Croatia'. After Croatia declared independence in 1991, museums commemorating the Communist Partisans went out of fashion and the pavilion again became an art gallery.

'The Meštrović Pavilion is a register of the successive political shifts that marked Zagreb's twentieth-century history,' said Rupnik.[49] The effects of such repeated regime changes had been multiple, he added:

Croats quickly acclimatised themselves to constant rebranding, to 'cultural recycling – the continuous reworking and editing of what is there', as he put it.[50] They instinctively suppressed the more controversial and contradictory episodes of their history to create an appearance of continuity. There was a tendency to airbrush out previous, discarded, identities. Another tendency was to treat all authority as ultimately foreign and hostile, but to subtly evade and subvert rather than confront it. 'It's in the DNA to treat the government as a foreign government,' Rupnik asserted. Zagreb's own history, he continued, was one of opportunistic manoeuvring, the characteristic response of an urban polity positioned 'at the centre of the edge' of a sequence of great empires and multinational states.[51]

This opportunistic attitude has helped Zagreb to flourish. An ancient but somewhat marginal and rustic town of about 15,000 inhabitants in the mid-nineteenth century had become home to almost a million people by the end of the twentieth.[52] But the challenge of the twenty-first century is to move beyond opportunist manoeuvring and accept the responsibilities that came with independence. Croats have to stop looking at governments, including their own, as alien entities and accept ownership of their destiny. For many Croats this will be hard because the long centuries of foreign rule have implanted a deep inferiority complex; foreigners know best, and when they don't they still need to be appeased. At the same time, they are to blame for everything. Even Croatia's own governments sometimes give the impression of not quite comprehending that independence is now a fact, not an aspiration. Their enthusiasm to shelter under the umbrella of Brussels, logical for a host of reasons, sometimes has an almost abject quality to it, suggesting the existence of a desire for some more adult authority to take charge of the big decisions.

Another hangover from the past is the continuing obsession with conspiracies. The common belief that Croatia is a plaything of cruel gods is both frustrating yet also a source of psychological satisfaction, absolving the Croats of ultimate responsibility for their own situation. To many Croats, perhaps especially those who lived abroad and who had a foot in two camps, the survival of this attitude is puzzling. Croatia is not as powerless and uninfluential as many Croats appear to believe. It is, as Chris Cviić pointed out, a member of both the UN and of NATO and still the only southeastern European state likely to join the EU in the near future. 'Croatia's position as a player on the international stage is undoubtedly a reality, yet many Croats, great patriots as they are, continue to be pessimists about their country and find this hard to believe,' he said. 'They've got too used to worrying about conspiracies emanating from various international centres of power where decisions affecting Croatia are allegedly still being made and plots against it are still being hatched.'[53] One can only hope that those obsessions will fade as the prospect of a more secure future within the European Union helps to reshape a national consciousness that has been moulded by too many centuries spent living precariously, 'at the centre of the edge'.[54]

Notes

Chapter 1: 'The Unfaithful Croats'

1. See Z. Črnja, *Cultural History of Croatia*, Zagreb, 1962, p. 134, citing the *Chronicle of the Priest of Dioclea*.
2. See R. Ivančević, *Art Treasures of Croatia*, Zagreb, 1993, pp. 50–66.
3. Črnja, p. 72.
4. H. Evans, *The Early Medieval Archaeology of Croatia 600–900*, Oxford, 1989, p. 242.
5. Emperor 945–59. He is the principal source of information about the early Croats thanks to his book *De Administrando Imperio*, dedicated to his son, later Rhomanos II, giving him advice on the nations surrounding the empire. Chapters 26–31 deal with the southern Slavs, and 29–31 with the Croats in particular. For more on the book's contents, usefulness and errors, see Evans, pp. 64–70.
6. Diocletian was probably born in Dalmatia, hence his decision to build his retirement palace there.
7. V. Klaić, *Povijest Hrvata*, Zagreb, 1980, vol. I, p. 62.
8. Vjekoslav Klaić, 1849–1928, one of the most eminent Croat historians. *Povijest Hrvata*, published 1899–1911, though intended as a complete history of Croatia, did not advance beyond 1608.
9. Klaić, vol. I, pp. 50–1.
10. Some scholars believe the word *ban* is derived from a Mongol–Turkish word *bajan*, meaning rich or powerful one.
11. Klaić, vol. I, p. 62.
12. S. Guldescu, *History of Medieval Croatia*, The Hague, 1964, p. 99.
13. Ibid., p. 116.
14. B. Franolić, *Historical Survey of Literary Croatian*, Paris, 1984, pp. 16–18.
15. Črnja, pp. 149, 151.
16. The first hilltop settlement was called Gradec, which became the ecclesiastical centre. In the valley below grew up the town of Zagreb. Although the two remained under separate jurisdictions for centuries, for the sake of convenience the term Zagreb has been used throughout.
17. Unfortunately no copies of the *Pacta Conventa* survive.
18. Črnja, p. 160.

Chapter 2: Croatia Under the Hungarians

1. E. M. Despalatovic, *Ljudevit Gaj and the Illyrian Movement*, New York and London, 1975, p. 10.
2. Z. Sabol, ed., *Croatian Parliament*, Zagreb, 1994, p. 14–15.
3. 'The good old days of Ban Kulin' has endured as a phrase describing any time of great wealth, peace and prosperity.
4. T. Jones and A. Eirera, *Crusades*, London, 1994, p. 201.
5. 400 silver marks as compared to 500 in both Zadar and Zagreb. See V. Klaić, *Povijest Hrvata*, Zagreb, 1980, vol I, p. 326.

6. Ibid., vol I, p. 249.
7. I. Babić, *Trogir's Cultural Treasures*, Zagreb, 1990, p, 13.
8. Z. Črnja, *Cultural History of Croatia*, Zagreb, 1962, pp. 189–91.
9. See M. Brandt, *Wyclifova hereza i socialni pokret u Splitu u krajem 14 stoljeća*, Zagreb, 1955.
10. S. Guldescu, *History of Medieval Croatia*, The Hague, 1964, p. 217.
11. The other Latin-based dialect which survived until the beginning of the nineteenth century was on the island of Krk.
12. See B. Krekić, *Dubrovnik, Italy and the Balkans in the Later Middle Ages*, London, 1986.
13. The event is commemorated in a large wall painting in the Church of the Holy Cross by the artist Oton Iveković.

Chapter 3: The Ramparts of Christendom

1 Z. Sabol, ed., *Croatian parliament*, Zagreb, 1994, p. 27.
2. I. Omrčanin, *Military History of Croatia*, Bryn Mawr, 1984, p. 77.
3. L. Dobronić *Zagrebacka Biskupska Trvdja*, Zagreb, 1978, p. 18.
4. C. Bracewell, *The Uskoks of Senj: Piracy, Banditry and Holy War in the Sixteenth-century Adriatic*, New York, 1992, p. 22.
5. Sabol, ed., pp. 27–8.
6. E. Rothenberg, *The Austrian Military Border in Croatia 1522–1747*, Champaign, 1960, p. 50.

Chapter 4: 'The Remains of the Remains'

1. P Tvrtković, *Bosnia–Hercegovina*, London, 1993, p. 18.
2. The Orthodox *millet*: the system by which the Ottomans grouped the monotheistic peoples in the empire into religious communities. Thus, alongside the privileged Muslim *millet* they recognised an Armenian, Orthodox and Jewish *millet*, each of which was accorded a degree of self-government under its religious leaders. The head of the Orthodox *millet*, the *millet bashi*, was the patriarch of Constantinople, under whom were the (Serb) archbishop of Peć and the (Bulgarian) archbishop of Ohrid. See B. Jelavich, *History of the Balkans*, vol. 1: *Eighteenth and Nineteenth Centuries*, Cambridge, 1983, pp. 48–52.
3. Ivo Andrić, 1892–1975, author and diplomat. He was born in Travnik, central Bosnia, and baptised a Catholic. Interned by the Austrians during the First World War for strong Yugoslav sympathies, he entered the diplomatic service, serving in Berlin when the Second World War broke out in 1939. Awarded the Nobel Prize for literature in 1961 for his chief works, *Bridge over the Drina* and *Travnik Chronicles*.
4. See N. Malcolm, *Bosnia: a Short History*, London, 1994, pp. 51–81, and R. Donia and J. Fine, *Bosnia and Hercegovina: a Tradition Betrayed*, London, 1994, pp. 35–70.
5. The monastery at Orahovica in eastern Slavonia, for example, was most probably built on the ruins of a Catholic foundation.
6. In 1634 ten Catholic villages in Srijem were reported to have embraced Orthodoxy: Suljan, Velike Remete, Male Remete, Dobrinci, Kraljevci, Golubinci, Ruma, Vodinci, Mandeloš and Mitrovica. See 'Migracije u Sjeveroistočnoj Hrvatskoj', in S. Sršan, ed., *Hrvatska – Povijest Sjeveroistocnog Područja*, Osijek, 1994, p. 119.
7. C. Bracewell, *The Uskoks of Senj*, Cornell University, 1992, p 31.
8. Ibid., p. 74. The author cites a Venetian unimpressed by one of these Albanian Muslim converts, who knew neither the 'Our Father'

nor even how to cross himself.

9. 'The Catholic Church and the Croatian National Identity', *East European Quarterly*, XIII, 1979, p. 330.

10. T. Eekman and A. Kadić, eds., *Juraj Križanić: Russophile and Ecumenic Visionary*, The Hague and Paris, 1976, p. 161.

11. Ibid., p. 185.

12. Ibid., p. 162.

13. *A declaration of reasons which moved Marcus Antonius de Dominis, Archbishop of Spalato or Salonas, Primate of Dalmatia and Croatia, to depart from the Romish religion*, Edinburgh, 1617.

14. Ibid., p. 18.

15. H. Blount, *Brief Relation of a Journey ... by way of Venice into Dalmatia, Sclavonia, Bosnah, Hungary, Macedonia*, London, 1636.

16. Ibid., p. 7.

17. Ibid., p. 8.

18. Ibid., p. 109.

19. Tvrtković, p. 20, citing the Italian historian Montalbano.

20. Ibid., citing Bishop Baličević's memorial on the position of the Church in Bosnia in 1600.

21. G. E. Rothenberg, *The Austrian Military Border in Croatia 1522–1747*, Champaign, p. 71.

22. Ibid., p. 71.

23. Ibid., p. 73.

Chapter 5: From Liberation to the French Revolution

1. Zlatar, Z., *The Slavic Epic: Gundulic's Osman*, New York, 1995, p. 141.

2. 'Migracije u Sjeveroistočnoj Hrvatskoj', in S. Srsan, ed., *Hrvatska – Povijest Sjeveroistočnog Podrucja*, Osijek, 1994, p. 119.

3. Further back in time these villages were Catholic. They were most probably settled by Orthodox immigrants in the sixteenth century under the Turks.

4. The village gained notoriety in 1992 when it was 'ethnically cleansed' of its Catholic population by Serb nationalists led by the Radical Party leader, Vojislav Šešelj. By then the local population spoke Serbo-Croat and considered themselves Croats.

5. Until 1735, after which the care of Bosnian Catholics was entrusted to Vicars Apostolic.

6. Whether Baranja should be included in a history of Croatia at this time is disputable. The majority of the population from the mid-eighteenth century until the end of the Second World War was either Hungarian (about 33 per cent) or German (about 32 per cent) followed by smaller communities of Croats (about 20 per cent) and Serbs (about 13 per cent). After the expulsion of the Germans and many Hungarians in 1945, Baranja was awarded to Croatia by the Communist border commission, under Milovan Djilas, because its economy gravitated towards the nearby Croatian city of Osijek.

7. See 'German nobleman reclaims his castle', *Times*, 3 August 1992.

8. G. E. Rothenberg, *The Austrian Military Border in Croatia 1522–1747*, Champaign, p. 104.

9. G. Stanojević, *Dalmatinska Krajina u 18 Veku*, Belgrade, 1987, p. 88.

10. Ibid.

11. H. Bjelovučić, *The Ragusan Republic*, Leiden, 1970, pp. 11–12.

12. Stanojević, p. 91.

13. A. Fortis, *Travels into Dalmatia*, London, 1778, p. 46.

14. Ibid., p. 50.

15. Ibid., p. 61.

16. Ibid., p. 57.

Chapter 6: 'Still Croatia Has Not Fallen'

1. V. Bogdanov, *Historija političkih stranaka u Hrvatskoj*, Zagreb, 1958, p. 126.
2. E. Laxa and W. Read, 'The Drašković Observance: Eighteenth Century Freemasonry in Croatia', *Transactions of Quatuor Coronati Lodge*, XC, 1977.
3. For the whole poem, see Bogdanov, pp. 46–8.
4. Martinović's family were Serbs who fled from Serbia during the great emigration into Hungary in the 1690s. His parents had him baptised a Catholic. He wrote in French 'Le Testament politique de l'empereur Joseph II' and a philosophical treatise, 'Mémoires philosophiques de la Nature devoilée'. See B Franolić, *L'Influence de la langue française en Croatie*, Paris, 1975, pp. 70–1.
5. The Jacobins planned to recruit some 200,000 members into a secret society, the Society for Equality and Freedom, launch an uprising in Hungary and proclaim a republic. Martinović wanted Hungary broken up into self-governing units, Hungarian, Illyrian, Slovak and so forth.
6. 'The Catholic Church and Croatia's National Identity', *East European Quarterly*, XIII, 1979, pp. 334–5.
7. Bartol Kašić, a Jesuit from Pag, in his landmark Croatian grammar in 1604 drew on *štokavian* rather than *čakavian* sources in an attempt to find a language comprehensible to all southern Slavs. Juraj Ratkaj, canon of Zagreb, presented in his *Memoria Regium et banorum regnorum Dalmatiae Croatiae et Sclavoniae* of 1652 the history of Croatia from an Illyrian angle.
8. G. Prpić, 'French Rule in Croatia 1806–1813', *Balkan Studies*, vol. 5, no. 2, Thessaloniki, 1964, p. 231.
9. Franolić, pp. 75–6.

10. E. Murray-Despalatovic, *Ljudevit Gaj and the Illyrian Movement*, New York and London, 1975, p. 41.
11. I. Banac, 'The Place of Dubrovnik in Modern Croat National Ideology', in *Nation and Ideology*, ed. I. Banac, G. Ackerman and R. Szporluk, New York, 1981, pp. 149–75.
12. They numbered just under 7,000 in the 1840s, enjoyed freedom from taxation and were represented in the *županije* (district) elections and in the Sabor.
13. See Bogdanov, pp. 97–124. Bogdanov draws on the number of letters written to Gaj from frontier officers and the subscriptions to his newspaper to back up his claim.
14. The Illyrians supported equality between the confessions and an end to Catholic privilege. However, they were interested in promoting Zagreb to an archdiocese in order to release the Croatian Church from its subordination to Hungarian metropolitans.
15. M. Murko, *Početak Gajevih Novina*, Matica Hrvatska, Zagreb, 1900, pp. 567–81, in Bogdanov, p. 252.
16. Bogdanov, p. 253.

Chapter 7: 1848

1. I. Sivric, *Bishop Strossmayer*, London, 1975, p. 14.
2. (Anon), *Scenes of the Civil War in Hungary in 1848 and 1849, with the personal adventures of an Austrian officer in the army of the ban of Croatia*, London, 1850, p. 8.
3. Ibid., p. 11.
4. Ibid., p. 17.
5. Ibid., pp. 23–6.
6. M. Hartley, *The Man Who Saved Austria*, London, 1912, p. 134.
7. Ibid., p. 171.
8. J. Krnjevic, 'Croats in 1848', printed in *Slavonic Review*, vol. XXVII, 1948, p. 107.
9. Hartley, p. 198.
10. Ibid., p. 261.

11. See I. Roberts, *Nicholas I and the Russian Intervention in Hungary*, London, 1991.
12. Krnjević, p. 114.
13. Hartley, p. 353.
14. A. Fernkorn: born 1813 near Leipzig, died 1878 in Graz. One of the most famous of nineteenth-century Austrian sculptors. He went mad shortly before the statue of Jelačić was unveiled.
15. Z. Milčec, *Povratak Bana*, Zagreb, 1990, p. 23.
16. For a description of the ceremony, see ibid., pp. 37–8.
17. E. Crankshaw, *Fall of the House of Habsburg*, London, 1963, p. 58.
18. V. Bogdanov, *Historija političkih stranaka u Hrvatskoj*, Zagreb, 1958, p. 307.

Chapter 8: 'Neither with Vienna Nor with Budapest'

1. F. Šišić, *Korespondencija Rački-Strossmeyer*, Zagreb, 1930, vol. III, p. 199.
2. R. W. Seton-Watson, *The Southern Slav Question and the Habsburg Monarchy*, New York, 1969, p. 118.
3. Ibid., p. 128.
4. I. Sivric, *Bishop Strossmayer*, London, 1975, p. 14.
5. Ibid., p. 37.
6. Seton-Watson, p. 435. The two men were linked by Lord Acton, who admired the Bishop's stand against the Vatican in 1871. They corresponded regularly, especially during the crisis in Bosnia, when Strossmayer hoped to win over Gladstone to the idea that Bosnia should be placed under Serbian rule or made an autonomous protectorate of the great powers. They never met. In appendix XVII, pp. 416–44, Seton-Watson reproduces Strossmayer's letters to Gladstone, and some of Gladstone's replies, from the period 1876–86.

7. Ibid., p. 444.
8. V. Koščak, ed., *J. J. Strossmayer F. Rački, Politički spisi*, Zagreb, 1971, 'Jugoslavenstvo', p. 278.
9. Seton-Watson, p. 121.
10. In 1868 the Academy began publishing *Monumenta spectantia historiam Slavorum meridionalium* and in 1869 the first volume of *Starine* (Antiquities) dealing with historical documents. The next important phase in publishing activity was the multi-volume dictionary of Croatian in 1880. See D. Skok, ed., *Croatian Academy of Sciences and Arts*, Zagreb, 1994.
11. Sivric, p. 225.
12. Seton-Watson, p. 435.
13. In Montenegro the position of Catholics was rather better and the ancient archbishopric of Bar functioned without harassment.
14. Šišić, vol. III, p. 199.
15. M. Spalatin, 'The Croatian Nationalism of Ante Starcevic', *Journal of Croatian Studies*, XV, 1975, p. 65.
16. V. Karadžić, 'Serbs All and Everywhere', reprinted in *Roots of Serbian Aggression*, ed. B. Čović, Zagreb, 1993, p. 89.
17. Spalatin, p. 86.
18. B. Raditsa, 'The Risorgimento and the Croatian Question', *Journal of Croatian Studies*, V–VI, 1964–5, p. 20.
19. See B. Franolić, *L'Influence de la langue française en Croatie*, Paris, 1975.
20. Šišić, vol. IV, p. 378.
21. 'Najjača Stranka u Hrvatskoj' in *Radić, Politički Spisi*, ed. Z. Kulundžić, Zagreb, 1971, p. 203.

Chapter 9: 'Our President'

1. *Radić Politički Spisi*, ed. Z. Kulundžić, Zagreb, 1971, p. 327.
2. The offending article, 'Rat do Istrage' (war to destruction), by Nikola Stojanović, was a reprint

from the Belgrade magazine. *Srpski Književni Glasnik.* It violently denounced the idea that Croats were a nation and insisted they would all become Serbs sooner or later.

3. *Radić,* ed. Z. Kulundžić. Zagreb. 1971. p. 55.

4. S. Gaži. 'Stjepan Radic. his Life and Political Activities (1870–1928)'. *Journal of Croatian Studies,* vol. XIV–XV. 1973–4. p. 33.

5. As they had little capital of their own. Croat railways were built with German and Hungarian finance and with Hungary's interests in mind. The lines radiated out from Budapest towards Zemun, Slavonski Brod and Zagreb rather than connecting Croat towns with each other.

6. One of the participants was Ante Dabčević, father of Savka Dabčević-Kučar, the popular Communist leader of Croatia during the time of the 'Croatian Spring' of 1971.

7. See Chapter 8, note 17.

8. B. Jelavić, *History of the Balkans,* vol. 2: *Twentieth Century,* Cambridge, 1983, p. 69.

9. I. Meštrović, *Uspomene na ljude i dogadjaje,* Zagreb, 1993. p. 10. Meštrović was born in Dalmatia in 1883. At seventeen he moved to Vienna and joined the Secessionist movement. He quickly achieved success after his *Well of life* was exhibited in the Secession building in 1905. In 1904–11 he worked on an unrealised project for a temple to the heroes of the Battle of Kosovo. After the First World War he became the most important artist of the Yugoslav state and close friend of King Aleksandar. Among his most famous works were the monument to France in Belgrade, 1930; *Croatian History,* 1932; the Tomb of the Unknown Soldier at Avala, near Belgrade, 1935–8; the monument to Petar Petrović Njegoš in Montenegro, 1958; and *Stepinac Meeting Christ,* 1961. He died in South Bend, Indiana, in 1962.

10. Gazi, p. 41.

11. R. W. Seton-Watson. Born 1879. Historian. Educated at Oxford, Berlin and the Sorbonne. Published numerous books on the future of Austria–Hungary. In 1922 appointed professor of Central European history at King's College, London. Died 1951.

12. G. Grlica, 'Trombic's Policy and Croatian National Interests from 1914 to the beginning of 1918'. *Journal of Croatian Studies,* vol. XIV–XV. 1973–4. p. 79.

13. Collapse of Serbia in 1915: after repelling the Austrians in 1914 Serbia succumbed to a German–Austrian–Bulgarian offensive in the autumn of 1915, after which the Serbian army, King and government withdrew through Albania to Corfu.

14. H. and C. Seton-Watson, *The Making of a New Europe: R. W. Seton-Watson and the Last Years of Austria–Hungary,* London, 1981, pp. 131–2.

15. Meštrović, p. 66.

16. H. and C. Seton-Watson, p. 156.

17. Ibid., p. 211.

18. G. Brook-Shepherd, *The Last Habsburg,* London, 1968, p. 176.

19. I. Banac, 'Emperor Karl has become a Comitadji', *Slavonic and East European Review,* LXX/1, 1992, p. 289.

20. Ibid., p. 290.

21. Gazi, p. 50.

22. 'Leroy King's Reports from Croatia from March to May 1919', *Journal of Croatian Studies,* I, 1960, p. 134.

23. Ibid., p. 154.

24. I. Banac, *The National Question in Yugoslavia,* London, 1984, p. 390.

25. R Horvat, *Hrvatska na Mucilistu,* Zagreb, 1992 (reprint of 1942 edition), p. 375.

26. Ibid., p. 386.

27. Ibid., p. 388.

28. Ibid., p. 411.

29. A. Vojinović, *Ante Pavelić,* Zagreb, 1988, p. 33.

30. Horvat, p. 432.

31. In Croatia's poisoned atmosphere, Pavelić's sentence contrasted markedly with that of Račić, who

was sentenced to only twenty years, in spite of killing three deputies in the parliament.

Chapter 10: The *Sporazum*

1. H. Pozzi, *Black Hand over Europe*, Zagreb, 1994 (reprint of 1935 edition), pp. 15–20.
2. H. Tiltman, *Peasant Europe*, London, 1934, p. 59.
3. Pozzi, pp. 15–20.
4. See R. W. Seton-Watson, 'Jugoslavia and the Croat problem', *Slavonic and East European Review*, XVI, 1937–8, p. 103. He wrote: 'Even among those who a year ago opposed concessions to the Croats, many now urge a rapid settlement as the only way of ending the internal deadlock and presenting a united front towards friend and foe in Europe.'
5. N. Balfour and S. Mackay, *Paul of Yugoslavia: Britain's Maligned Friend*, London, 1980, p. 58.
6. Ibid., p. 59.
7. Ibid., p. 119.
8. Count Galeazzo Ciano, 1903–43. Educated at Rome university, his marriage to Mussolini's daughter Edda assured his rise through the diplomatic service. In 1936, aged thirty-three, he became foreign minister. An opponent of the war, he was killed on Mussolini's orders for supporting the royal coup in 1943.
9. J. Hoptner, *Yugoslavia in Crisis 1934–1941*, New York and London, 1962, p. 66.
10. Ibid., p. 112.
11. Ibid., p. 119.
12. Ibid., p. 88.
13. Ibid., p. 95.
14. I. Meštrović, *Uspomene na ljude i dogadjaje*, Zagreb, 1993, p. 204.
15. V. Maček, *Memoari*, Zagreb, 1992, p. 130.
16. Balfour and Mackay, p. 188.
17. *The Ciano Diaries 1939–1943*, ed. H.

Gibson, New York, 1947, p. 46.
18. Ibid., p. 84.
19. Ibid., p. 85. Maček later insisted he had never promised to prepare a rebellion and never took any money.
20. Ibid., pp. 87–8.
21. Ibid., p. 342.
22. Maček, p. 147.
23. Speech by General Mirković to the Ex-Serviceman Club on 26 March 1951, reprinted in *Peasant Yugoslavia*, No. 108, 26 March 1951.
24. *A King's Heritage: The Memoirs of King Peter II of Yugoslavia*, London, 1955, p. 68.
25. Maček, p. 150.
26. E. Barker, *Državni Udar u Beogradu i Britanci, Časopis za suvremenu povijest*, Zagreb, 1981, p. 11.
27. Maček, p. 153.

Chapter 11: The Ustashe

1. S. Alexander, *Church and State in Yugoslavia since 1945*, Cambridge, 1979, p. 32.
2. B. Jelavić, *History of the Balkans*, Cambridge, 1983, p. 264.
3. E. Kvaternik, *Sjećanja i zapažanja 1925–45*, Zagreb, 1995, p. 27.
4. Ibid., pp. 31–2.
5. Ibid., p. 45.
6. D. Sagrek, *Zagreb 1941–1945*, Zagreb, 1995, p. 62.
7. Alexander, citing *Katolički List*, 29 April 1941.
8. Sagrek, p. 72.
9. Meštrović, *Uspomene na ljude i dogadjaje*, Zagreb, 1993, p. 321.
10. Known as the uncle of Europe on account of the highly successful marriages of his daughters. Two married Russian archdukes, one married Petar Karadjordjević, while Elena married Victor Emmanuel III of Italy. He was deposed by his son-in-law, Petar, King of Serbia from 1903, in 1918, when Montenegro was incorporated into Yugoslavia, and died in exile in Italy.

11. *The Ciano Diaries, 1939–43*, ed. H. Gibson, New York, 1947, p. 342.
12. Ibid.
13. Ibid., p. 364.
14. B. Krizman, *Pavelić, između Hitlera i Mussolinija*, Zagreb, 1980, p. 39.
15. Kvaternik, p. 54.
16. Ciano, p. 348.
17. Ibid., p. 408.
18. V. Novak, *Magnum Crimen*, Zagreb, 1948, p. 604, citing a report of a speech by M. Budak, in *Katolički Tjednik*, 20 July 1941.
19. *Jews in Yugoslavia*, Zagreb, 1989, pp. 80–2.
20. H Arendt, *Eichmann in Jerusalem*, Harmondsworth, 1979, p. 184.
21. *Jews in Yugoslavia*, p. 112.
22. Letter from Mihael Montiljo to Petar Grisogono, 7 May 1995. Copy lent by B. Franolić.
23. Alexander, p. 22, citing *Hrvatski Narod*, 26 June 1941, says that Budak made a speech at Gospić on 22 June announcing that one-third of Serbs would be expelled, one-third converted and one-third killed. However, there are doubts whether this speech was ever made, or at any rate whether it was made by Budak.
24. Novak, p 606, citing speech by M. Žanić reported in *Novi List*, 3 June 1941.
25. Alexander, p. 24.
26. I. Banac, 'The Main Trends in Croatian History', in *Documenta Croatica*, ed. Z. Separovic, Zagreb, 1992.
27. B. Čović, ed., *Croatia between War and Independence*, Zagreb, 1991, p. 35.
28. Krizman, p. 71.
29. A. Vojinović, *Ante Pavelić*, Zagreb, 1988, p 297. According to the author, the Poglavnik's wife was wont to say that, although she was born in Croatia, she was Italian in spirit.
30. Alexander, p. 32.
31. The letter is reproduced in *South Slav Journal*, V/1, Spring–Summer 1982, p. 46.
32. Alexander, p. 37.
33. Meštrović, p. 326.
34. Interview with A. Shomrony, *Glas*

Concila, 21 April 1996, p. 4.
35. Conversation with the author, May 1996.
36. Meštrović, p. 322.
37. *The Goebbels Diaries*, ed. L. P. Luckner, London, 1948, p. 261.
38. V. Ćurić, *Ustashe i pravoslavlje – Hrvatska Pravoslavna Crkva*, Belgrade, 1989, p. 207.
39. Goebbels, p. 343.
40. Fitzroy Maclean, *Eastern Approaches*, London, 1949, p. 281.
41. Ibid., p. 390.
42. Ibid., p. 403.
43. The Sandžak liberation council was subsequently abolished under Serbian pressure and Sandžak was incorporated into the new Republic of Serbia, without autonomous status, much to the disappointment of the local Muslims who made up a narrow majority in the region.
44. V. Dedijer, *War Diaries of Vladimir Dedijer*, Michigan, 1990, vol. II, pp. 403–6.
45. Ibid., p. 431.
46. J. Irvine, *The Croat Question: Partisan Politics in the Formation of the Yugoslav Socialist State*, Boulder, CO, 1993, p. 151, citing *Zavnoh, Zbornik Documenata*, 1943, vol. I, Zagreb, 1964, p. 397.
47. Irvine, p. 164, citing *Zavnoh, Zbornik Documenta*, 1944, vol. II, Zagreb, 1970, p. 604.
48. Irvine, p. 197.
49. J. Korbel, *Tito's Communism*, Denver, 1951, p. 348.
50. This message was the principal theme in the posters for the first postwar elections in Croatia in 1946.
51. *Journal of Croatian Studies*, XIV–XV, 1973–4, p. 178.

Chapter 12: 'My Conscience Is Clear'

1. M. Djilas, *Tito*, London, 1981, p. 176.
2. V. Dedijer, *The Beloved Land*, London,

1961, p. 306.

3. V. Dedijer, *Novi prilozi za Biografiju Josipa Broza Tita*, Rijeka and Zagreb, 1981, vol. II, p. 1146.

4. Djilas, p. 78.

5. V. Maček, *Memoari*, Zagreb, 1992, p. 173. Maček was living in Zagreb at the time, although his movements were still supervised by the NDH's police.

6. V. Dedijer, *Tito Speaks*, London, 1953, p. 10. Tito particularly disliked the clergy, and not just Vjekoslav Homoštarić, the parish priest in Kumrovec. In his account they are all fat, covetous spies for the authorities. In Bjelovar, he remembers that it was the priest who reported him to the police for organising 'a Communist funeral' for a dead comrade in the cemetery (p. 44).

7. I. Banac, *With Stalin against Tito*, London, 1988, p. 106.

8. F. Trgo, ed., *National Liberation, War and Revolution in Yugoslavia 1941–5: Selected Documents*, Belgrade, 1982, p. 725.

9. Ibid., p. 727.

10. The bay of Kotor had been included in the 1939 Croatian Banovina on ethnic and historical grounds, as Kotor had been a possession of the city-state of Dubrovnik. Before the end of the war the Montenegrin Communists prejudged the territorial issue by changing the name of the local Anti-Fascist Council from that of Montenegro and Kotor to Montenegro alone.

11. R. W. Seton-Watson, 'Jugoslavia and the Croat Problem'. *Slavonic and East European Review*, XVI, 1937–8, p. 104.

12. Maček fled to Austria, where he surrendered to the Americans. He then travelled through Germany to Paris, where a severe illness detained him for weeks. He spent the remainder of his life in the United States. There he conducted the affairs of the Peasants Party in exile, and died in Washington in 1964. None of his

writings was published in post-war Yugoslavia, even at the height of the Croatian Spring in 1971, as it was felt his strongly anti-Communist tone was too controversial. His body was returned to Croatia and reburied in 1996.

13. I. Jukic, *The Fall of Yugoslavia*, New York and London, 1974, p. 287.

14. Djilas, p. 176.

15. M. Djilas, *Wartime*, London, 1977, p. 317.

16. For a short essay on Nazor, see A. Kandic, 'Vladimir Nazor', *Journal of Croatian Studies*, XVII, 1976.

17. The definition of collaborators was made as broad as possible, to include, for example, most businessmen whose factories had remained open under German occupation. The entire ethnic German community in Vojvodina, numbering some 400,000, was judged guilty and expelled. There were plans to expel all the Vojvodina Hungarians as well, but for no clear reason a proposal to this effect from Jovan Veselinov, the Party leader of Vojvodina, was neither adopted nor followed through.

18. E. Waugh, 'Catholic Croatia under Tito's Heel', reprinted in the *Salisbury Review*, September 1992, along with the British Ambassador Stevenson's letter to Eden. pp. 10–18.

19. S. Alexander, *The Triple Myth*, New York, 1987, p. 117. Djilas and Kardelj were horrified by Tito's slip of the tongue and his reference to himself as a Catholic deleted from the official account of the meeting.

20. Bishop Varnava Nastić was the first Serb Orthodox bishop subjected to a show trial in 1948, although his crime was not Serb nationalism but his pacifism and his open admiration for the United States. He was sentenced to eleven years' imprisonment and released after three, on condition that he resign his diocese.

21. M. Djilas, *Rise and Fall*, New York,

1983, p. 40.
22. Ibid., p. 39.
23. Copy of the reply of Dr Politeo on behalf of the accused. T. Dragun, *Le Dossier du Cardinal Stepinac*, Paris, 1958, p. 128.
24. Ibid., p. 134.
25. Djilas, *Rise and Fall*, p. 99.
26. Banac, p. 110.
27. Ibid., p. 113, citing Dragoljub Jovanović's *Ljudi, Ljudi*, Belgrade, 1975, vol. II, p. 240.
28. Djilas, *Tito*, p. 124. Djilas recalled that this remark was met with an embarrassed silence from the rest of the group.
29. Banac's *With Tito against Stalin* is a detailed analysis of the strength of Cominformism in the various republics, especially chapters 4 to 6. His study suggests that Cominformism was weakest in Croatia and Slovenia and strongest in Serbia and, especially, in traditionally Russophile Montenegro.
30. D. Russinow, *The Yugoslav Experiment*, London, 1977, p. 36.
31. The Archbishop's international fame ensured that he was treated with kid gloves. He was fed decently, granted a regular allowance of wine and šljivovica, and permitted to receive books (though not newspapers) and to say Mass. He was also allowed visits from his mother, his sister, the bishops and occasionally from foreign correspondents.

Chapter 13: Croatian Spring

1. M. Djilas, *Rise and Fall*, New York, 1983, p. 268.
2. In 1954 he was expelled from the Party. From 1956 to 1961 he was imprisoned, and again from 1962 to 1966.
3. Većeslav Holjevac, 1917–70, a pre-war Communist and commissar of the First Zagreb Corpus during the war. Attacked for Croat nationalism while he was mayor of Zagreb, for which he was forced out of office. Expelled from the Party for his role in the *Declaration*. A leading force in the Croatian Spring until his death.
4. Djilas, p. 346.
5. Other leading members of the reformist group included Pero Pirker, mayor of Zagreb from 1963 to 1967 and head of the Party in Zagreb from 1967 to 1969, Dragutin Haramija, who became prime minister of Croatia in the late 1960s, and Srećko Bijelić, a Serb in the Zagreb Party hierarchy.
6. S. Alexander, *The Triple Myth*, New York, 1987, p. 192.
7. T. Sommelius, *The Iron Gates of Illyria*, London, 1955, p. 59.
8. In spite of its inconspicuous nature, Stepinac's tomb rapidly developed into a pilgrimage site for Catholics and nationalists alike.
9. J. Ridley, *Tito*, London, 1994, p. 377.
10. M. Tripalo, *Hrvatsko Proljeće*, Zagreb, 1989, pp. 69–70.
11. Over 100,000 people attended Ranković's funeral in Belgrade in 1986, which turned into a Serbian nationalist demonstration, with people shouting 'Serbia has awoken'.
12. I Omrčanin, *Croatian Spring*, Philadelphia, 1976, p. 58.
13. Tripalo, p. 93.
14. Ibid., pp. 97–8.
15. P. Ramet, *Nationalism and Federalism in Yugoslavia 1963–83*, Bloomington, 1984, p. 116.
16. Tripalo, pp. 112–13.
17. Ibid., p. 117.
18. Ramet, p. 117.
19. Tripalo, p. 153.
20. *Hrvatski Književni List*, July 1969.
21. Bušić was assassinated, almost certainly by the Yugoslav secret police, in Paris in 1979.
22. Ramet, p. 32. The Yugoslav economy had grown massively since the war, so Croatia's decline was relative, not absolute.
23. S. Djodan, 'The Evolution of the

Economic System of Yugoslavia and the Economic Position of Croatia', *Journal of Croatian Studies*, 1972, vol. XIII, p. 11.

24. Ibid., p. 81.
25. Ramet, p. 132, citing *Oslobodjenje*, 17 May 1982, p. 5. Although the Croats blamed discrimination, another factor was that the Bosnian Serbs had formed the bulwark of the Partisan movement in the war, and naturally made up a disproportionately large percentage of the Communist movement.
26. Ridley, p. 395.
27. Ibid., p. 396.
28. Tripalo, p. 161.
29. Ibid., p. 169.
30. Ibid., p. 178.
31. *Hrvatska Revija*, December 1971, p. 376, citing *Vjesnik*.
32. Tripalo, p. 194.
33. Ibid., p. 196.
34. *Hrvatska Revija*, p. 374.
35. Tripalo interview with P. Ramet on 8 September 1989, *South Slav Journal*, XII/3–4, Autumn–Winter, 1989, p. 89.

Chapter 14: 'Comrade Tito Is Dead'

1. D. Bilandžić, *Jugoslavija poslije Tita*, Zagreb, 1986, p. 90.
2. A. J. P. Taylor, *The Habsburg Monarchy 1809–1918*, London, 1948, p. 261.
3. G. Sher, *Praxis*, Bloomington, 1977, p. 239.
4. D. Russinow, 'Nationalities Policy and the National Question', in P. Ramet, ed., *Yugoslavia in the 1980s*, Boulder, CO, 1985, p. 141.
5. W. Höpken, 'Party Monopoly and Political Change: The League of Communists since Tito's Death', in Ramet, ed., p. 45.
6. Ibid., p. 46.
7. District Public Prosecutor's indictment against Tudjman, reprinted in

Croatia on Trial: The Case of the Croatian Historian Dr F. Tudjman, Amersham, 1981, p. 3.
8. Ibid., p. 4.
9. Ibid., p. 5.
10. Ibid., p. 7.
11. See *Sjaj Optuženih i Bijeda Režima*, *Sudjenje Vladi Gotovcu i Dobroslavu Paragi*, London, 1981.
12. P. Ramet, 'The Dynamics of Yugoslav Religious Policy', in Ramet, ed., p. 175.
13. P. Ramet, 'The Yugoslav Press in Flux', in Ramet, ed., p. 119.
14. See *Sarajevski Proces. Sudjenje Muslimanskim intelektualcima*, Zurich, 1987.
15. I. Botić and S. Djureković, *Yugoslavia in Crisis*, New York, 1983, p. 13.
16. Bilandžić, p. 50.
17. Botic and Djurekovic, p. 18.
18. Ibid., p. 19.
19. Ibid., p. 17, based on a Radio Free Europe research report of 30 August 1982.
20. Bilandžić, p. 85.
21. Ibid., pp. 90–1.
22. A. Dragnich, 'Upsurge in Serb Nationalism', *East European Quarterly*, 1989, XXIII, p. 193.
23. Drašković's novel *Nož* (Knife), published in 1982, marked a revolutionary step in treating the Chetniks as a largely apolitical, spontaneous and heroic movement of self-defence by the Serb nation, rather than an instrument of the pre-war Great Serbian bourgeoisie. Veselin Djuretić's *The Allies and the Yugoslav War Drama* in 1985 took a similar line, on account of which the author was expelled from the Party.
24. Bilandžić, p. 204.
25. A landmark was Isaković's call for a re-evaluation of Tito's role in history at a Sanu meeting in autumn 1984 and for the Socialist Federal Republic of Yugoslavia to be renamed the Republic of Yugoslavia.
26. See Dragnich, p. 190. According to Drašković, pressures against use of the Cyrillic script and the closure of specifically Serb cultural associa-

tions were tantamount to genocide.
27. 'The Memorandum', cited in B. Čović, ed., *Roots of Serbian Aggression*, Zagreb, 1993, p. 324.
28. B. Čović, ed., *Croatia between War and Independence*, Zagreb, 1991, p. 65.
29. See D. Pejnović, 'Changes in the Ethnic Structure of Eastern Lika', in *Geographical Papers*, ed. A. Bognar, Zagreb, 1991, pp. 221–53.
30. Interview with Stambolić in *Vreme*, 4 September 1995, p. 32.
31. Ibid., p. 35. According to Stambolić, 'he didn't care about the Serbs over the Drina'.
32. Ibid.
33. Ibid., p. 37.
34. None looked as uncomfortable as Janez Drnovšek, the President of Yugoslavia, a Slovene and an avowed pro-Western liberal.
35. S. Milošević's speech at the 600th anniversary of the Battle of Kosovo, cited in *Etničko Čišćenje*, ed. M. Grmek, M. Gjidara and N. Simac, Zagreb, 1993, p. 180.
36. 'Od Govornica do barikada', *Nedeljna Borba*, 20 October 1990.

Chapter 15: God in Heaven and Tudjman in the Homeland

1. J. Rašković, *Luda Zemlja*, Belgrade, 1990, p. 309.
2. S. Mesić, *Kako smo rušili Jugoslaviju*, Zagreb, 1992, p. VII. The other members of the HDZ presidency were professors Dalibor Brozović and Krešimir Balenović, Vladimir Šeks, a lawyer, Josip Manolić, a former high-ranking official in the Yugoslav secret police, and Milivoj Slaviček, a writer.
3. See Chapter 13 note 33.
4. Conversation with the author, April 1996.
5. Friends urged her to go to Canada in spring 1990 but she refused, apparently afraid of encountering a hostile Ustashe audience. She was also unwilling to appear on the BBC.
6. On Tudjman's Canadian trip he was seated in the same room as the son-in-law of Ante Pavelić, husband of the late dictator's daughter Višnja. The error was spotted by one of his aides, who ensured the seating was rearranged.
7. Mesić, p. VII.
8. Ibid.
9. Ibid., pp. 8–9.
10. Rašković, p. 320.
11. Ibid., pp. 157–8.
12. Ibid., p. 321.
13. Ibid., p. 235.
14. Ibid., p. 230.
15. V. Kadijević, *Moje Vidjenje Raspada*, Belgrade, 1993, p. 92.
16. B. Jović, *Last Days of the SFRY*, cited in *VIP*, 16 November 1995, p. 3.
17. I. Crkvenčić, 'Northern Dalmatia, the Croatian Bridge', in *Geographical Papers*, Zagreb, 1991, p. 216.
18. See *Independent*, 18 April 1990.
19. 'Tudjmanove izjave uznemirile Jevreje', *Politika*, 5 May 1990.
20. One of the first to be renamed was Republic Square in the centre of Zagreb, which returned to its former name, Jelačić Square. More controversial was a later decision to rename the Square of the Victims of Fascism as Trg Hrvatskih Velikana or Square of Croatian Great Ones, or rulers.
21. Z. Milčec, *Povratak Bana*, Zagreb, 1990, p. 61.
22. See 'Croatia's Answer to Le Pen', *Independent*, 21 May 1990.
23. M. Thompson, *Forging War: The Media in Serbia, Croatia and Bosnia–Hercegovina*, Bath, 1994, p. 147.
24. Ibid., p. 155.
25. Kadijević was Croat on his mother's side and Serb on his father's. He was from Imotski, the same region as Šuvar. A declared Yugoslav in the census, he became more and more overtly Serbian in his sympathies as

the war unfolded in Croatia in 1991.
26. See note 1 above.
27. Rašković, p. 326. On 24 August Rašković met Boljkovac for a secret dinner on the outskirts of Zagreb. He told the Interior Minister that the decision to publish his conversation with Tudjman was 'Letica's big mistake'.
28. See 'Proglašena autonomija Srba u Hrvatskoj', *Politika*, 26 July 1990.
29. See 'Confused Reports of Violence in Yugoslav City', *Independent*, 18 August 1990.
30. As Dalmatia was ruled by Venice until the Napoleonic wars, it was never part of the Habsburg Vojna Krajina. The term Kninska Krajina was simply a reference to the fact that the town was on the border, as was Imotska Krajina, further south in Dalmatia, the Negotinska Krajina in Serbia, and so forth.
31. Interview with Martin Špegelj in *Globus*, Zagreb, 7 July 1995, p. 62.
32. Ibid.
33. Set up in October 1990 as a vehicle for Marković and his reformist party with Goran Milić, a Croat, as editor in chief and based in Sarajevo. Owing to the hostility of Serbian and Croatian television it was never seen throughout the country, except for a couple of months in 1991. Croatian TV, for example, would only broadcast Yutel at 1am, when most people were asleep. Weakened by the war in Croatia it ceased to broadcast in May 1992 during the siege of Sarajevo. See Thompson, pp. 38–50.
34. The first three SAOs (SAO is short for *Srpska Autonomna Oblast* – Serb Autonomous Region) were set up in Romanija, in east central Bosnia, in eastern Herzegovina and in the Banja Luka region. The last to be set up was centred on Bijeljina, in north-east Bosnia. The SAOs broadly covered the territory claimed by the Bosnian Serb leadership for the new Bosnian Serb republic.
35. See Chapter 14, note 22.

36. See 'Croatian Outburst Fuels Tension', *Independent*, 6 February 1991.

Chapter 16: 'Serbia Is Not Involved'

1. Stenograph of a conversation between the two Serb leaders on 30 September 1991 printed in *Vreme*, September 1991. At first thought to have been supplied by Prime Minister Marković, it later emerged that the recording was the work of the Bosnian police.
2. S. Letica interviewed in 'A Greater Croatia', *Dispatches*, Channel 4, shown on 5 January 1994.
3. F. Tudjman, interviewed in 'A Greater Croatia'.
4. S. Milošević, *Nin*, 8 November 1991, cited in *Etničko Cišćenje*, ed. M. Grmek, M. Gjidara and N. Simac, Zagreb, 1993, p. 181.
5. 'Yugoslavia Has Entered the Final Phase of its Agony', *Independent*, 18 March 1991.
6. 'Yugoslav Army Breaks Contact with Presidency', *Independent*, 19 March 1991.
7. 'Croatian Rebels Declare Unity with Serbia', *Independent*, 2 April 1991.
8. 'Yugoslavia on the Edge of Serb–Croat War', *Independent*, 3 April 1991.
9. V. Šešelj, *Horvatove Ustashke Fantazmagorijc*, Belgrade, 1992, p. 65.
10. Interview with the author: See 'Barricades Up after Serbs Shoot 12 Croats', *Independent*, 4 May 1991.
11. See Ibid.
12. According to official statistics, 85 per cent of the republic's 3.5 million voters turned out to vote, of whom 95 per cent delivered a 'yes' vote to sovereignty. See 'Croats Likely to Vote for Independence', *Independent*, 20 May 1991.
13. Conversation between General

Špegelj and Tim Judah, *The Economist*, 28 October 1995.

14. L. Silber and A. Little, *The Death of Yugoslavia*, London, 1995, p. 140.

15. Interview with General Špegelj in *Globus*, Zagreb, 30 June 1995, p. 58.

16. S. Mesić, *Kako smo rušili Jugoslaviju*, Zagreb, 1992, p. 108.

17. *Vreme*, 30 September 1991. The conversation is reproduced in *Etničko Čišćenje*, ed. M. Grmek, M. Gjidara and N. Simac, Zagreb, 1993, p. 183.

18. 'Europe may use Force in Yugoslavia', *Independent*, 17 September 1991.

19. Interview with General Trifunović, *Vreme*, 27 January 1996.

20. 'Croatia Goes on the Offensive', *Independent*, 16 September 1991.

Chapter 17: 'Danke Deutschland'

1. S. Trifunovska, ed., *Yugoslavia through Documents from its Creation to its Dissolution*, Dordrecht, London and Boston, 1994, p. 428.

2. S. Mesić, *Kako smo rušili Jugoslaviju*, Zagreb, 1992, p. 298.

3. Ibid., p. 299.

4. 'Croatian General Awaits the Real Battle', *Independent*, 13 November 1991.

5. 'Mortar Shells Rain Down on Osijek', *Independent*, 26 November 1991.

6. L. Silber and A. Little, *Death of Yugoslavia*, London, 1995, p. 206.

7. 'Osijek Awaits its Liberation', *Independent*, 25 November 1991.

8. V. Kadijević, *Moje Vidjene Raspada*, Belgrade, 1993, p. 135.

9. Ibid., p. 142.

10. Ibid., pp. 142–3.

11. Trifunovska, p. 382.

12. Kadijević resigned within weeks of the fall of Vukovar.

13. Trifunovska, p. 413.

14. Ibid., p. 423.

15. 'Misunderstanding   Yugoslavia',

London Review of Books, 23 May 1996, p. 20.

16. Trifunovska, p. 431.

17. Born 1928 in Paris, the son of Russian Jewish parents, he became head of the EEC constitutional court 1986–95. In 1991 he was appointed head of the arbitration panel dealing with the legal and constitutional aspects of the break-up of Yugoslavia.

18. Trifunovska, p. 488.

19. Ibid., p. 490.

20. Macedonia's recognition was held up by Greek objections to, among other things, the name Macedonia, the flag and certain articles in the Macedonian constitution which Athens believed hinted at a claim on Greek territory.

21. It has to be added that the song made only a very brief appearance in the Croatian media, and was played rather more often on Serbian radio and television as convincing proof of the Croats' filial attitude to Germany.

Chapter 18: Thousand-Year-Old Dream

1. D. Owen, *Balkan Odyssey*, London, 1995, p. 353.

2. 'Serbs Find Home Is Where Croats Used to Live', *Independent*, 24 January 1992.

3. Figures are from the Croatian government, reproduced in B. Čović, ed., *Croatia between Aggression and Peace*, Zagreb, 1994, pp. 43–5.

4. For information on the Eltz family of Vukovar and the great families of Ilok and Baranja, see Chapter 5, note 1, and *Hrvatska – Povijest Sjeveroistočnog područja*, Osijek, 1994.

5. See p. 55.

6. 'Cleansing Row Prompts Turmoil in Vojvodina', *Independent*, 24 August 1992.

7. 'UN Deal Signed While Babić Was Asleep', *Independent*, 4 February 1992.

8. 'Serbs Launch New Party', *Independent*, 5 February 1992.

9. On 11 April 1995 the Russian commander of Sector East, Alexander Perclyakin, was dismissed for having aided the resupply of Serbian forces in eastern Slavonia with weaponry from over the border in Serbia. See *International Security Review 1976*, Royal United Services Institute for Defence Studies, London, 1976, p. 57.

10. 'Killing That Makes Croatia Fit for Serbs', *Independent*, 27 September 1992.

11. 'Macabre Rite', *Independent*, 19 November 1992.

12. 'Anarchy Rules', *Independent*, 2 October 1992.

13. M. Pupovac, 'A Settlement for the Serbs', in *Yugofax: A Project of War Report and the Helsinki Citizens Assembly*, London, 1992, p. 17.

14. 'Home of Ethnic Cleansing Faces Empty Future', *Independent*, 14 September 1992.

15. 'Croatia Seizes Chance to Buy an Army', *Independent*, 19 February 1992.

16. The former Communists and the centrist Social Liberal and Peasant parties accepted Bosnia's integrity without equivocation. Paraga's Party of Rights, true to its roots in Starčević's writings – and the NDH – supported a united front of Catholics and Muslims and thus championed Bosnia's territorial integrity, albeit as a prelude to union with Croatia.

17. Kljuić came from the traditionally Catholic suburb of Dolac Malta. Izetbegović was born in Bosanski Šamac, in northern Bosnia, while Karadžić was not from Bosnia at all, but from the Mt Durmitor region of Montenegro.

18. 'Croat Road Helps Divide Bosnian Spoils', *Independent*, 13 July 1992.

19. 'Bosnian Fury over Betrayal by Croats', *Independent*, 7 July 1992.

20. Mladić succeeded General Kukanjac in Sarajevo on Milošević's recommendation after the army quit Sarajevo in June 1992.

21. The first plan, proposed by the Portuguese Foreign Minister in April 1992, proposed the division of Bosnia into three big cantons, or provinces, organised on purely ethnic lines.

22. The plan, unveiled on 2 January 1993, allotted provinces 3 (Posavina) and 8 (western Herzegovina) to the Croats, 10 (central Bosnia and Livno) to joint Muslim–Croat rule, 1 (Bihać), 5 (eastern Bosnia) and 9 (north-central Bosnia) to the Muslims and 6 (east Herzegovina), 4 (Bijeljina region) and 2 (north-west Bosnia) to the Serbs. The greater Sarajevo region was to remain undivided, home to all three communities and under international control. The plan was modified on 8 February to give Muslims access to the Sava river at Brčko. The plan failed to win US endorsement and was rejected by the Bosnian Serbs at a special assembly in Pale on 6 May 1992.

23. Owen, p. 94.

24. B Stewart, *Broken Lives*, London, 1993, p. 296.

25. Ibid. p. 298.

26. Report of Kramarić's speech in London in *Hrvatski Glasnik*, 20 March 1996, p. 2.

27. *South Slav Journal*, XIV 3–4, Autumn–Winter 1993, pp. 95–6.

28. *South Slav Journal*, XV/1–2, Spring–Summer 1994, pp. 109–10.

29. The plan was rejected by a special assembly of the Bosnian Serbs held on 6 May 1992. On 21 May the US effectively buried it by announcing an alternative 'Joint Action programme' with Russia which aimed to contain the conflict rather than roll back Serb gains. The fundamental problem for the US was the need, implicit in Vance–Owen, to deploy US troops on the ground in Bosnia as part of a peace force.

30. *UN and the Situation in Former Yugoslavia*, published by the UN, 1995, p. 20.
31. *South Slav Journal*, XV/3–4, Autumn–Winter, 1994, pp. 65–6.
32. Owen, p. 74.
33. This plan, put forward by the so-called Contact Group on former Yugoslavia of the big powers, awarded 51 per cent of Bosnia to the Muslims and Croats and 49 per cent ot the Serbs.
34. *Vreme*, 8 May 1995.
35. Press conference on 8 August 1995 by Šušak carried on Croatian TV.
36. Interview with Christopher in *The Death of Yugoslavia*, Brian Lapping Associates, shown by BBC Television on 6 June 1996.
37. Interview with Tudjman in ibid.
38. Interview on 8 August 1995 with General Červenko on *Slikom na Sliku*, a programme on Croatian TV.
39. *International Security Review* 1996, Royal United Services Institute for Defence Studies, London, 1996, p. 67.

Chapter 19: 'Freedom Train'

1. 'Zasto se Nijemci boje investirati u Hrvatsku', *Vjesnik*, 27 May 1999. German investors were overwhelmingly deterred by the level of criminal involvement in the economy, the article said.
2. Conversation with the author.
3. I. Pukanic, *Nacional*, 22 September 1999.
4. Conversation with the author.
5. Hina, Zagreb, 11 December.
6. The former Bosnian Croat general Tihomir Blaskic was sentenced to 45 years in March 2000, the longest sentence handed down by the court, while the former HDZ leader in Bosnia, Dario Kordić, was sentenced to 25 years in February 2001.
7. In spite of this, the question of whether Italian would be granted equal status with Croatian as the region's official language continued to vex relations between the Istrian Democrats and their coalition partners.
8. T. Judah, 'Croatia Reborn', *New York Review of Books*, 10 August 2000.

Chapter 20: La Dolce Vita

1. I. Sanader, 'Croatia in the New Millennium', *Mediterranean Quarterly*, vol. 16, no.1, Winter 2005.
2. A. Feldman, 'Imbro Ignjatijević Tkalac and Liberalism in Croatia', unpublished PhD dissertation, Yale University, 2009, p. 235.
3. The political career of Tudjman's eldest son, Miroslav, did not get far.
4. http://veliko-trgovisce.hr/udruge-gradjana.htm
5. 'Balkan Warrior', *Guardian*, 23 February 2008, interview with M. Jaggi, http://www.guardian.co.uk/books/2008/feb/23/politics2
6. Conversation with the author, Zagreb, 17 July 2009.
7. In January 2010, Serbia responded to Croatia's lawsuit for genocide by initiating a lawsuit for genocide against Croatia at the International Court of Justice in The Hague.
8. Mesić caused a storm on 21 January 2010 by telling a group of journalists that if the Republika Srpska attempted to secede, the Croatian army might cut the Posavina corridor, separating the RS into two pieces. The Croatian army would be used to 'break Republika Srpska in half,' he said. 'If [Bosnian Serb prime minister] Milorad Dodik scheduled a referendum for the secession of Republika Srpska from Bosnia and if I were the president . . . I would send the army,' he said.

9. Josipović won by a large margin in the second round of the presidential elections on 10 January, taking about 60 per cent of the votes against about 40 per cent cast for his opponent, the mayor of Zagreb, Milan Bandić. Turnout, at just over 50 per cent, was low.

10. Croatian television, HTV, *Otvoreno*, 14 July 2009.

11. M. Glamuzina, Ž. Šiljković, N. Glamuzina, 'Demographic development of the town of Knin in 1991/2001 intercensal period', *Geoadria*, vol. 10, no. 1, Zadar, 2005, p. 87.

12. Ibid., p. 88.

13. C. Metcalf, 'Beautiful Zadar', *The Spectator*, 17 June 2009.

14. At almost 2,400 metres, it would have been the second longest in Europe, with an estimated cost of around €300 million. In July 1999, the expected date of completion was pushed back to 2015.

15. According to the 1991 census, the last held in Yugoslavia, the population totalled 23,229,846.

16. See note 1.

17. Gotovina, then 50, was located in the Canary Islands on 8 December 2005 and transferred to The Hague on 11 December.

18. Under pressure from Slovenia, Croatia and the EU Enlargement Commissioner Olli Rehn, in March 2008 Croatia ceased enforcing protection measures against EU member states inside the Protected Ecological Fishing Zone, or ZERP.

19. One poll published in February 2009 suggested that the percentage of Croats that viewed EU membership as beneficial was only slightly larger than the percentage holding the opposite view – 29 as against 26 per cent, while 38 per cent had no view at all. This was a striking contrast to surveys conducted at the start of the decade, when more than three-quarters of those polled regularly indicated strong support for EU membership.

20. Conversation with the author, 20 July 2009.

21. Ibid.

22. As 'minster of social welfare and veterans' under Sanader, Kosor championed the veterans' interests in what seemed an attempt to build up a political constituency within the country and the party.

23. For a discussion of Croatia's voting system, see I. Škrabalo, 'Croatia, the History of Elections', in A. Nathan, I. Škrabalo, *Total Representation: A New Electoral System for Modern Times*, London, 2009, pp. 179–291.

24. The Croatian Pensioners' Party, Hrvatska Stranka Umirovljenika, won 4 per cent of the votes in the 2003 general election.

25. Conversation with the author, 25 July 2009.

26. The World Bank, 'Railway Reform in the Western Balkans', December 2005, p. 60.

27. The World Bank, 'Implementation Completion Report on a loan in the amount of US 101.0 million equivalent to the Republic of Croatia for a railway modernisation and restructuring project'. December 2005

28. According to one expert study, Croatian railways employed 40,901 staff in 1989 and only 21,055 in 2005. S. Stevicar, K. Mindum, D. Petrovici, 'Reform of Croatian railways in the context of national and regional transport policies, a trade union view', *South-East Europe Review for Labour and Social Affairs*, no. 1, 2006, p. 68.

29. 'Kronicni gubitas na tragicama', *Nedeljni Jutarnji*, 26 July 2009, p. 11.

30. Ivana Hodak, 26, was shot dead in Zagreb on 6 October 2009. Her father, Zvonimir, was a prominent lawyer involved in the high-profile trials of several suspected mobsters.

31. Since it joined the EU in January 2007, the EU has on several occasions said that reducing the number of gangland murders in Bulgaria is a matter of urgency as well as complaining of the courts'

apparent paralysis in bringing any of the perpetrators to justice.

32. In 2006, the homicide rate in Croatia per 100,000 was 1.62, roughly the same as for Scotland, Ireland, Cyprus and France. The rate for Russia was 16.5 in 2008, down from 20 in 2006; that for the US was 6.8 in 2008, up on 5.7 in 2006. See 'List of countries by intentional homicide rate': http://en.wikipedia.org/wiki/List_of_countries_by_intentional_homicide_rate

33. Following his return to Croatia in the early 1990s, after several decades in the US, Meštrović was successively a deputy in parliament and then ambassador to Bulgaria.

34. Conversation with the author, 25 July 2009.

35. Ibid.

36. Ibid.

37. Conversation with the author, 7 October 2009.

38. Antun Vrančić, 1504–73, humanist scholar, poet and diplomat, bishop of Eger and Esztergom in Hungary.

39. Vitez's nephew or kinsman, born 1434, died 1472. Educated in Italy under Guarino of Verona, he returned to the Hungary of Matthias Corvinus as Bishop of Pécs.

40. Conversation with the author, London, 7 September 2009.

41. European Commission, Special Eurobarometer 225, Social values, Science and Technology, 2005, p. 9.

42. Conversation with the author, Zagreb, 15 July 2009.

43. On 30 November 2009, EU interior ministers in Brussels decided that from 19 December citizens of Macedonia, Serbia and Montenegro would be able to travel to most of Europe without visas.

44. Feldman, 'Imbro Ignjatijević Tkalac', p. 77, citing Brlić. *Pisma sinu Andriji Torkvatu 1836–1855*. Zagreb, 1942, p. 8.

45. A. Lieven, *The Baltic Revolution: Estonia, Latvia and Lithuania and the Path to Independence*, London and New Haven 1994 (1st edn, 1993), p. 143.

46. Ibid., p. 144.

47. M. Meštrović, *Ivan Meštrović: The Making of a Master*, London, 2008, p. 43.

48. Conversation with the author, 27 July 2009.

49. E. Blau and I. Rupnik, *Project Zagreb: Transition as Condition, Strategy, Practice*, Zagreb, 2007, p. 158.

50. Ibid., p. 52.

51. Ibid., p. 26.

52. Ibid., pp. 32–3. The population figures are given as 15,000 in 1848, 40,000 in the 1900s, 100,000 by the 1920s, 334,000 in the 1950s and 768,000 in the 1980s.

53. C. Cviić, 'Croatia as a European and Regional Player', talk given to the British-Croatian Society, London, 24 June 2009.

54. Blau and Rupnik, *Project Zagreb*, p. 26.

Selected Bibliography

Alexander, S., *Church and State in Yugoslavia since 1945*, Cambridge, 1979
Alexander, S., *The Triple Myth*, New York, 1987
Babić, I., *Trogir's Cultural Treasures*, Zagreb, 1990
Balfour, N. and Mackay, S., *Paul of Yugoslavia: Britain's Maligned Friend*, London, 1980
Banac, I., 'The Main Trends in Croatian History', *Documenta Croatica*, ed. Z. Separovic, Zagreb, 1992
Banac, I., *The National Question in Yugoslavia: Origins, History, Politics*, London, 1984
Banac, I., 'The Place of Dubrovnik in Modern Croat National Ideology', *Nation and Ideology*, ed. I. Banac, G. Ackerman and R. Szporluk, New York, 1981
Banac, I., 'Emperor Karl has become a Comitadji: the Croatian Disturbances of 1918', *Slavonic and East European Review*, LXX/1, 1992
Banac, I., *With Stalin against Tito*, London 1988
Bennet, C., *Yugoslavia's Bloody Collapse*, London, 1995
Bilandžić, D., *Jugoslavija poslije Tita*, Zagreb, 1986
Bjelovučić, H., *The Ragusan Republic*, Leiden, 1970
Blount, H., *Brief Relation of a Journey ... by way of Venice into Dalmatia, Sclavonia, Bosnah, Hungary, Macedonia*, London, 1636
Boban, L., *Hrvatske Granice 1918–93*, Zagreb, 1993
Bogdanov, V., *Historija političkih stranaka u Hrvatskoj*, Zagreb, 1958
Botić, I. and Djurekovic, S., *Yugoslavia in Crisis*, New York, 1983
Bracewell, C., *The Uskoks of Senj: Piracy, Banditry and Holy War in the Sixteenth-century Adriatic*, New York, 1992
Brook-Shepherd, G., *The Last Habsburg*, London, 1968
Čerovac, I., *Hrvatski Politicki Leksikon*, London 1983
Crankshaw, E., *Fall of the House of Habsburg*, London, 1963
Črnja, Z., *Cultural History of Croatia*, Zagreb, 1962
Ćurić, V., *Ustashe i pravoslavlje – Hrvatska Pravoslavna Crkva*, Belgrade, 1989
Dedijer, V., *Novi prilozi za Biografiju Josipa Broza Tita*, Rijeka and Zagreb, 1981.
Dedijer, V., *The Beloved Land*, London, 1961
Dedijer, V., *Tito Speaks*, London, 1953
Dedijer, V., *War Diaries of Vladimir Dedijer*, Michigan, 1990
Despalatovic, E. M., *Ljudevit Gaj and the Illyrian Movement*, New York and London, 1975
Djilas, M., *Rise and Fall*, New York, 1983
Djilas, M., *Tito: the Story from the Inside*, London, 1981

Dobronić, L., *Zagrebacka Biskupska Trvdja*, Zagreb, 1978
Eekman, T. and Kadić, A. (eds.), *Juraj Križanić. Russophile and Ecumenic Visionary*, The Hague and Paris, 1976
Evans, H., *The Early Medieval Archeology of Croatia 600–900* Oxford, 1989
Dusa, J., *Medieval Dalmatian Cities*, 1991
Fortis, A., *Travels into Dalmatia*, London, 1778
Franolić, B., *Croatian Glagolitic*, London 1994
Franolić, B., *An Historical Survey of Literary Croatian*, Paris, 1984
Franolić, B., *L'Influence de la langue française en Croatie*, Paris, 1975
Guldescu, S., *History of Medieval Croatia*, The Hague, 1964
Grenzebach, W., *Germany's Informal Empire*, 1978
Hartley, M., *The Man Who Saved Austria*, London, 1912
Hoptner, J., *Yugoslavia in Crisis 1934–1941*, New York and London, 1962
Horvat, R., *Hrvatska na Mucilistu*, Zagreb, printed 1942, reprinted 1992
Hrvatski Politicki Plakat, Hrvatski Povijesni Muzej, 1991
Irvine, J., *The Croat Question: Partisan Politics in the Formation of the Yugoslav Socialist State*, Boulder, CO, 1993
Ivančević, R., *Art Treasures of Croatia*, Zagreb, 1993
Jelavić, B., *History of the Balkans*, 2 vols, Cambridge, 1983
Jelavić, B. and C., *The Establishment of the Balkan States 1804–1920*, Lexington, 1986
Jews in Yugoslavia, Zagreb, 1989
Jukic, I., *The Fall of Yugoslavia*, New York and London, 1974
Kadijević, V., *Moje Vidjenje Raspada*, Belgrade 1993
Karadjoredjevic, P., *A King's Heritage: the memoirs of King Peter II of Yugoslavia*, London, 1955
Klaić, V., *Povijest Hrvata*, Zagreb, 1980
Krekić, B., *Dubrovnik, Italy and the Balkans in the Later Middle Ages*, London, 1986
Krizman, B., *Pavelić, izmedu Hitlera i Mussolinija*, Zagreb, 1980
Krizman, B., *Pavelić u Bekstvu*, Zagreb, 1986
Kulundžić, Z. (ed.), *Radic Politicki Spisi*, Zagreb, 1971
Kvaternik, E., *Sjećanja i zapažanja 1925–45*, Zagreb, 1995
Laxa, E. and Read, W., 'The Drašković Observance: Eighteenth-Century Free-masony in Croatia', *Transactions of Quatuor Coronati Lodge*, ed. E. Laxa and W. Read, 1977
Maček, V., *Memoari*, Zagreb, 1992
Maclean, F., *Eastern Approaches*, London, 1949
Mesić, S., *Kako smo rušili Jugoslaviju – politički memoari posljednjeg predsednika SFRJ*, Zagreb, 1992
Meštrović, I., *Uspomene na ljudi i dogadjaje*, Zagreb, 1993
Milatović, M., *Slucaj Andrije Hebranga*, Belgrade, 1952
Milčec, Z., *Povratak Bana*, Zagreb, 1990
Novak, V., *Magnum Crimen*, Zagreb, 1948
Omrčanin, I., *Croatian Spring*, Philadelphia, 1976
Omrčanin, I., *Military History of Croatia*, Bryn Mawr, 1984
Owen, D., *Balkan Odyssey*, London, 1995
Persen, M. and Gruic, M. (ed.), *Vjesnik 1940–1980*, Zagreb, 1986

Pozzi, H., *Black Hand over Europe*, printed 1935, reprinted Zagreb, 1994

Prpić, J., 'French Rule in Croatia 1806–1813', *Balkan Studies*, vol. 5, no. 2, Thessaloniki, 1964

Raditsa, B., 'The Risorgimento and the Croatian Question', *Journal of Croatian Studies*, V–VI, 1964–5

Ramet, P. (ed.), *Yugoslavia in the 1980s*, Colorado, 1985

Ramet, P. (ed.), *Nationalism and Federalism in Yugoslavia 1963–83*, Bloomington, 1984

Rašković, J., *Luda Zemlja*, Belgrade, 1990

Ridley, J., *Tito*, London, 1994

Rothenberg, E., *The Austrian Military Border in Croatia 1522–1747*, Champaign, 1960

Russinow, D., *The Yugoslav Experiment*, London, 1977

Sabol, Z. (ed.), *Croatian Parliament*, Zagreb, 1994

Sagrek, D., *Zagreb 1941–1945*, Zagreb,1995

Seton-Watson, H. and C., *The Making of a New Europe: R. W. Seton-Watson and the Last Years of Austria–Hungary*, London, 1981

Seton-Watson, R. W., *The Southern Slav Question and the Habsburg Monarchy*, New York, 1969

Seton-Watson, R. W., 'Jugoslavia and the Croat Problem', *Slavonic and East European Review*, XVI, 1937–8

Seton-Watson, R. W., *Absolutism in Croatia*, 1912

Silber, L. and Little, A., *The Death of Yugoslavia*, London 1995

Sinković, M. (ed.), *Ilustrirana Povijest Hrvata*, Zagreb, 1971

Šišić, F., *Pregled povijesti Hrvatskog naroda*, Zagreb, 1975

Šišić, F., *Korespondencija Rački-Strossmeyer*, Zagreb, 1930

Sivric, I., *Bishop Strossmayer*, London, 1975

Spalatin, M., 'The Croatian Nationalism of Ante Starcevic', *Journal of Croatian Studies*, XV, 1975

Stanojević, G., *Dalmatinska Krajina u 18 Veku*, Belgrade, 1987

Supek, I., *Povijesne meditacije*, Zagreb, 1996

Szabo, G., *Stari Zagreb*, Zagreb, 1990

Taylor, A. J. P., *The Habsburg Monarchy 1809–1918*, London, 1948

Tiltman, H., *Peasant Europe*, London, 1934

The UN and the Situation in Former Yugoslavia, UN, 1995

Thompson, M., *Forging War, The Media in Serbia, Croatia and Bosnia–Herzegovina*, Bath, 1984

Trifunovska, S. (ed.), *Yugoslavia through Documents from its Creation to its Dissolution*, Dordrecht, London and Boston, 1994

Tripalo, M., *Hrvatsko Proljeće*, Zagreb, 1989

Trgo, F. (ed.), *National Liberation, War and Revolution in Yugoslavia 1941–5: Selected Documents*, Belgrade, 1982

Vojinović, A., *Ante Pavelić*, Zagreb, 1988

Zlatar, Z., *The Slavic Epic, Gundulic's Osman*, New York, 1995

Index